This book is dedicated to
all the players, selectors, supporters, officers and officials
who kept the dream alive for Limerick hurling
in that momentous year of 1973.

May the pages within stand testament to all their exploits and endeavours.

KEEPING THE DREAM ALIVE

1973

THE STORY OF LIMERICK'S HISTORIC
ALL IRELAND SUCCESS 50 YEARS ON

Dec. 2023

James,

we all keep the dream alive in our own way.

Luimneach Abú!

Jaz.

James Lundon
Liam O'Brien Niall Deegan

James Lundon

James was born and bred on the Cappamore side of the bridge over the Mulcair river, near the cross at Dromkeen, in the townland of Pallasbeg, under the shadow of the Oyster Ballroom. He spent eight years in Tineteriffe NS, in the very safe hands of Mary Teresa O'Dea (nee Holmes) and Enda O'Mahoney (nee Ryan). He attended Doon CBS and then graduated from NIHEL/UL with BSc and MSc degrees, both in Applied Mathematics and Computing. He has lived and worked in Galway ever since, over 30 years at this stage, mostly in the greater Athenry area.

He has attended 121 Limerick senior hurling championship games and has seen Limerick in nine All Ireland finals, winning five of them; five more than most ever thought they would see a few years ago. James is not old enough to remember 1973, so the journey travelled in this book is pure history.

James has contributed 'The Lundon Eye' for a dozen years to the continually excellent *'The Green & White*' magazine, a print magazine that has kept the publishing flag flying locally when it was neither profitable nor easy to do so. Much kudos to Joe Lyons and Ciarán Crowe for that. He is in the process of finishing a full statistical history of Limerick inter-county hurling, which builds very substantially on a small publication produced in 2009, with Henry J Martin, called *'From The Great Depression* to NAMA: *Limerick Senior Inter-county Hurling Championship Records, 1929-2009'*.

He compiled a booklet, called 'Making The Welkin Ring', in 2014 for Cappamore's 50th anniversary celebrations of the club's last senior hurling championship success. It is not unlike the current publication in many ways. He has contributed to, and guided, many other GAA publications over the last 15 years, from Sligo down to Kerry, but mostly in and about Limerick.

His playing career was low key, losing a Minor B hurling final for Cappamore in 1986. He was also part of a winning Junior C hurling panel for St. Mary's, Athenry in 1997. He does a bit of hurling and camogie refereeing, mostly in Galway, as well as being a plodding road runner. He collects a few GAA programmes, books, and other memorabilia, mostly Limerick related. He is married to a West Clare lady called Clare, and is father to two Galway girls, Maria and Imy. He remains a lifelong teetotaller.

Preface

I received a WhatsApp message from Liam O'Brien at 18:44 on 9 January 2023, asking whether I had considered doing a book for the upcoming 50th anniversary of Limerick's remarkable 1973 hurling success. I should not have been surprised by his enquiry. After an hour considering my options, I decided to go for it and here we are.

I would like to thank both my co-authors for their constant support and outstanding work herein: Liam O'Brien (agent and editor) and Niall Deegan (research and designer). They have regularly read my mind, or pre-empted my next move, which is always a good thing. They have clarified the project's objectives and direction many times and, on occasion, cajoled me back onto the right path.

This book outlines some of the events leading up to 1973, with a whistle-stop tour of the early 1970s, especially 1971, starting in earnest with the National Hurling League (NHL) campaign of 1972-73, moving on through a series of old-style challenge games, and then on to the four epic games that made up the 1973 championship season – a game a month between June and September. We cover in great detail the All Ireland Hurling Final of 2 September against Kilkenny and the Munster Hurling Final of 29 July versus Tipperary. Certain legends have grown up around these two games in particular, but also regarding various other episodes during that season. The truth is here.

It examines the aftermath of this All Ireland final success, and some of the games played the following season, but is mostly concerned with Limerick's 1972-73 league and 1973 championship seasons. Most of the content of the book is reportage and wonderful images (many expertly colourised) from the ten games that made up the 1972-73 NHL season, the five challenge games, and the four championship matches of the summer of 1973 – nineteen in total. There are also a large number of side stories, all giving some context to the main text and the times they took place in.

The year 1973 holds a special place in every Limerick person's heart and memory, even if those memories are second hand from people who lived through them, or taken from books and other media. There is that wonderful story told by Jimmy Magee the weekend after the All Ireland Final. He recalled "the 50-year-old fan who warmly congratulated Eamonn Cregan with words that freed a million frustrations and spoke a sermon of sincerity". Those words stayed with Magee: 'We'll remember you for the rest of our lives.'" (Sunday World, 9 September 1973). This magnificent accomplishment was the single most important success in the county's GAA history, since it proved that Limerick hurling was still a force to be reckoned with. Their victory also served as an important marker to succeeding teams, underlining that it was possible even if doing so did eventually take another 45 years – to be successful on the biggest day of the hurling year.

The magnificent success of 1973 kept the dream alive for succeeding generations, even during the darkest times that many Limerick teams endured since then. We are eternally grateful to the current generation of Limerick's hurlers for giving us all the necessary energy to produce this book. We hope we have done the subject matter justice and brought this epic era in Limerick hurling back to life. The 1973 success will never be forgotten. The net profits of this book are going to *The Children's Ark* in University Hospital Limerick, as well as the Limerick chapter of *The Society of St. Vincent de Paul* (SVP).

We are no longer on our knees. Luimneach Abú!

James Lundon, Liam O'Brien and Niall Deegan – 2 September 2023.

Email: 1973LimerickBook@gmail.com
Website: https://1973LimerickBook.wordpress.com
Phone: 085 1436727

Foreword

A chairde,

I am delighted to welcome this extensive and detailed publication under the very committed editorial team of James Lundon, Liam O'Brien and Niall Deegan.

I know they have put in tremendous work to bring the book to publication and I thank them for their endeavours.

The team of 1973 bridged a gap for us which sustained Limerick GAA and kept our hopes alive until we finally re-emerged in 2018 again as All Ireland Champions.

They deserve to be recognised and acknowledged and this book does that to a very high standard.

Limerick GAA has delivered a number of initiatives to recognise the team on their 50th anniversary, in particular the function at The Strand Hotel, with the team also introduced to the crowd at the TUS Gaelic Grounds on 28 May.

We later saw the team recognised by the GPA in Croke Park at a function on 21 July.

I wish the team and their families well. I thank them sincerely for the great joy and fantastic memories they have given us down through the years.

Le gach dea ghuí,

Séamus McNamara

Cathaoirleach

1973 KEEPING THE DREAM ALIVE

Contents

Chapter 1 1972 And Before (Prologue)	10
Chapter 2 1972-73 National Hurling League (I) Before Christmas	60
Chapter 2.1 Limerick v Clare	62
Chapter 2.2 Kilkenny v Limerick	66
Chapter 2.3 Limerick v Galway	69
Chapter 2.4 Limerick v Offaly	72
Chapter 3 1972-73 National Hurling League (II) After Christmas	76
Chapter 3.1 Tipperary v Limerick	78
Chapter 3.2 Limerick v Cork	90
Chapter 3.3 Limerick v Wexford	94
Chapter 4 1972-73 National Hurling League (III) Knockout Stages	100
Chapter 4.1 Limerick v Tipperary	102
Chapter 4.2 Limerick v Tipperary (Replay)	107
Chapter 4.3 Limerick v Wexford	120
Chapter 5 1973 Challenge Games	134
Chapter 5.1 Limerick A v Limerick B	138
Chapter 5.2 Limerick v Offaly	139
Chapter 5.3 Limerick v Cork	140
Chapter 5.4 Limerick v Kilkenny	143
Chapter 5.5 Limerick v Cork	144
Chapter 5.6 Limerick v Waterford	149
Chapter 6 1973 Munster Hurling Semi-Final v Clare (24 June - Semple Stadium, Thurles)	156
Chapter 7 1973 Munster Hurling Final v Tipperary (29 July - Semple Stadium, Thurles)	178
Chapter 8 1973 All Ireland Hurling Semi-Final v London (5 August - Cusack Park, Ennis)	232
Chapter 9 1973 All Ireland Hurling Final (I) Pre-Match	246
Chapter 10 1973 All Ireland Hurling Final (II) V Kilkenny (2 September - Croke Park, Dublin)	284
Chapter 11 1973 All Ireland Hurling Final (III) Post-Match	384
Chapter 12 1973 All Ireland Hurling Final (IV) Aftermath	414
Chapter 13 1974 And Beyond (Epilogue)	456
Chapter 14 1972-73 Facts and Figures	512

CHAPTER 1
1972
AND BEFORE

PROLOGUE

By 1973, it was 33 years since the Liam MacCarthy Cup had last been won by Limerick. There had been very few highlights in those wilderness years. A wondrous victory over Clare in 1955 was the only Munster Hurling Championship success. The many near misses of the 1940s were a prelude to the, otherwise, very hungry 1950s and 1960s, with no Munster final appearance from 1957 to 1970. It was not much better in the National Hurling League, with only one final victory from 1938-39 to 1969-70. Limerick beat Kilkenny after a replay in the 1946-47 season, and got to the final of 1957-58, losing a great game to Wexford, one of four league successes for them, the last being in 1972-73.

Limerick had three victories in the Munster Hurling Championship between 1957 and 1969, two of them against Galway, who themselves only had a solitary win in their 11 seasons in Munster between 1959 and 1969. Limerick's only other victory was against Tipperary in 1966, to derail their three-in-a-row All Ireland attempt. A narrow loss to Cork weeks after that was a very sore one for various reasons. A mere 14 championship games were played in the 1960s. The solitary draw was another near miss in 1962 against Tipperary.

Things were little better in the National Hurling League. Limerick spent much of the 1960s in the "second" tier, though these leagues were structured in a manner not dissimilar to the 2020s set-up, with 1A and 1B divisions. Limerick qualified for a league semi-final in 1963-64, losing badly to Tipperary. Limerick reached the same stage in 1966-67, failing to Wexford. Limerick lost to the same opposition in a 1968-69 semi-final by two points, not sixteen like two years before. The league final was reached in 1969-70, for only the second time since 1946-47, but resulted in a heavy loss to Cork, after beating Offaly in the semi-final. Forty-one league games were played in the 1960s with an almost equal number of wins and losses recorded.

The year of 1971 will live long in the memory of Limerick supporters. The National Hurling League was won after an epic battle with Tipperary in the old Athletic Grounds in Cork, 3-12 to 3-11. Clare were beaten in the semi-final. Hopes were justifiably very high for the championship. Those hopes heightened further after beating Cork by two points in Thurles in the Munster semi-final, Limerick's first win against them since 1940. The Munster final was played in Killarney later in July. After a torrid game, dominated by the prevailing wet conditions, Tipperary won by one point in a thriller, 4-16 to 3-18. Many legends have grown up around this game – dry ball(s) etc. Limerick added the Oireachtas Cup later in 1971, only the county's second success in the history of this once venerable competition. The other Oireachtas success was in 1939. Kilkenny were beaten in the semi-final at the Gaelic Grounds, while Wexford were overcome in Croke Park. Both these games are still fondly recalled by players and fans alike.

Hopes were sky high that 1972 would be Limerick's year! Another league final was contested but Cork were victorious again, by three points in Thurles, 3-14 to 2-14. Kilkenny had been beaten in the semi-final. Limerick played Tipperary in Wembley Stadium soon after, the first time the Limerick hurlers were shown live on television, losing a goal-fest on a very small pitch, 8-7 to 4-12. Clare were the opposition at Ennis in the Munster Championship. It was a very bad day for Limerick, beaten by more than the four point full-time margin, 3-11 to 2-10. There was a lot of fallout after that game. Joe McGrath took the brunt of the criticism, losing his position as trainer of the team. There were also interesting selectorial changes made before the start of the new season.

A few pages in the middle of this chapter are dedicated to a prescient report of the *Commission of Inquiry*, produced at the end of 1971, into the performance of Limerick teams over the previous 30 years. Some other significant events of the years before 1973 are also outlined in this chapter, including the election of the five selectors for 1973, plus the underage and colleges' successes of the mid-1960s that were important building blocks towards the ultimate success of 1973.

Cregan the Star as Limerick Rock Tipp
(Limerick Leader, 29 July 1963)
Worthy Minor Hurling Champions

By "Limerick Leader" Staff Reporter

Limerick 4-12
Tipperary 5-4

Limerick, winners in 1940 and again in 1958, have a wonderful chance of carrying off the minor All Ireland hurling championship for the third time. Yesterday, in sweltering heat, at the Ennis Road Grounds, and before close on 40,000 spectators, they pulled off the surprise of the year, beating the holders, Tipperary, by 5 points in the Munster final. The game was way above the senior match (Waterford 0-11 Tipperary 0-8) in quality. Inspired, by the great leadership of Eamonn Cregan, Limerick set about their work in workman-like manner, and inside ten minutes were 2 goals and 2 points in front. By interval time, they had increased the advantage to 9 pts., and in the second half, the gap was 11 pts. at one stage and never below five. It was as clear-cut a victory as one could imagine, but the winning margin should have been greater. When Tipperary were rallying is the final quarter, the homesters missed some good chances through over elaboration. There was not enough ground pulling.

For all that, full marks to players and all connected with the win. When Limerick cleared the first hurdle, they looked anything but a team that would land the Munster title. Many changes were made for the semi-final clash against Waterford, but it was not until the replay with Waterford in Waterford that the right blend was pieced together. Again, yesterday, they struck a purple patch, and now look to have more than a fifty-fifty chance going into the final against Wexford. Tipperary did not measure up to expectations. Their defence was easily rattled into mistakes and the forwards, for much of the hour were well held by a strong and rugged defence.

The foundation for success was laid at midfield, where Eamonn Cregan was in brilliant form. He was coolness personified and covered acres of ground both in defence and attack. Next to young Cregan, I would place goalkeeper Andy Dunworth, who made a couple of wonder saves, at a time when Tipperary were fighting hard for their heads. Others to shine in defence for the winners were full-back, John Egan; Stephen O'Shaughnessy, Pa O'Brien and, of course, Cregan's midfield partner, Tony Roche. In attack, Bernie Savage was on top of his form, receiving very capable support from B. Cobbe, J. Geary and M. Graham. The substitutes who replaced the injured W. Kiely and C. Danagher, G. Barry and E. Grimes, also played their parts.

The covering in the Tipperary defence left a lot to be desired. John Costigan and Michael Flanagan were the pick, but with the side well beaten at the vital midfield sector, they were in trouble from the start. Frank Loughnane took a deal of watching in the losers' attack and A. Ayres and J. Cooke were others who never stopped trying. Limerick opened in promising manner with a first-class point from Eamonn Cregan in the fourth minute. Bernie Savage added a goal, and B. Cobbe, too, sent to the net before Conny Danagher made it 2-2 to 0-0. Back came Tipp. with a goal from J. Cooke, but Eamonn Cregan had his second point.

Then Tipperary goalkeeper M. Mahoney did well to save from J. Cosgrove but had no chance when B Cobbe pointed, and then C. Danagher sent over the bar at the same end. From a '70, J. Moroney cut the lead with a point, but it was Tony Roche's turn then to point. From a free, F. Loughnane had a point for Tipp, but B. Savage and Roche had Limerick sitting pretty at the interval, when the score read: 2-8 to 1-2. Just before the half-time whistle, Dunworth made a spectacular save from Ayres of Tipperary. Tipperary, following their interval pep-talk, looked to be going places when A. Ayres (point) and Frank Loughnane (goal) were on the mark. But in the 7th minute, M. Graham restored Limerick's confidence with a goal, and when J. Geary added a green flag, the homesters' tails were up. F. Loughnane had a further point for Tipp, but B. Savage had Limerick happy with a pair of points. M. Loughnane, a substitute for Tipp signalised his introduction to the game with a goal.

Next Tony Roche had a point for Limerick from a free. It was not all over yet, for Pat O'Neill lashed in a goal for Tipp, and after Roche had pointed from free, J. Quirke goaled for the Premier County but then came the final whistle, with Limerick richly deserving of the honour of Munster champions.

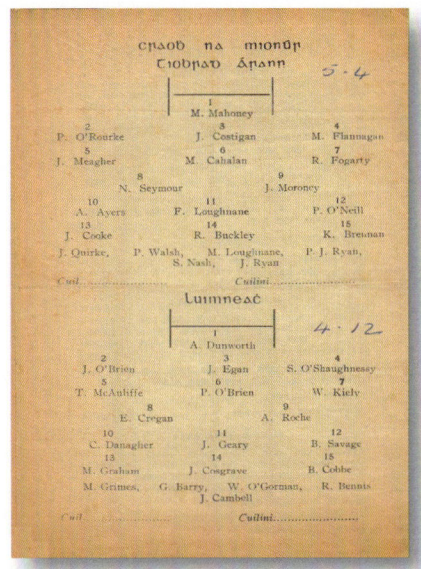

Limerick - A. Dunworth; J. O'Brien, J. Egan, S. O'Shaughnessy; T. McAuliffe, P. O'Brien, W. Kiely; E. Cregan, A. Roche; C. Danagher, J. Geary, B. Savage; M. Graham, J. Cosgrove, B. Cobbe. Subs: G. Barry for C. Danagher, E. Grimes for W. Kiely.

Tipperary - M. Mahoney; P. O'Rourke, J. Costigan, M. Flanagan; J. Meagher, M. Cahalan, R. Fogarty; N. Seymour, J. Moroney; A. Ayres, F. Loughnane, P. O'Neill; J. Cooke, R. Buckley, K. Brennan. Subs: J. Quirke for Cahalan, M. Loughnane for J. Moroney.

Referee - Paddy Cronin (Cork).

The Limerick minor hurling team that defeated Tipperary in the Munster final at the Gaelic Grounds on July 28th 1963

Back Row: (L-R) Peter Fitzpatrick (selector), John Egan, Frank O'Sullivan (selector), Pa O'Brien, Eamonn Cregan, John Frost, unknown supporter, Timmy McAuliffe, Jim O'Brien, Fr G. McNamee, Billy O'Gorman, Billy Kelly, Mr Mackessy (selector) and Richie Bennis. Front Row: (L-R) Gerry Cosgrave, Michael Graham, Andy Dunworth, Stephen O'Shaughnessy, Jim Geary, Bernie Savage, Tony Roche, Brian Cobbe, Con Danagher and Éamon Grimes.

1973 Keeping the Dream Alive

Limerick Minors Best in Tense Decider
(Cork Examiner, 26 July 1965)

Limerick 5-5
Tipperary 3-9

The hurling was fast, and the scores came quickly in the minor hurling final at Limerick yesterday, so quickly in fact that the scoreboard credited Limerick with a point in the first half, they apparently did not get. At the interval, the scores on both scoreboards read Limerick 1-3, Tipperary 0-6. Pressmen in the Hogan Stand were unanimous that Limerick beat Tipperary by two points and not by three as the official scoreboard said. But by either reckoning nobody will deny that Limerick minor hurlers "won" this game apart from final scores. On their dazzling display yesterday, they fully deserved victory over Tipperary, which brought them their second minor title in this grade in three years. After a closely contested first half in which Tipperary led the Limerick lads by a point, the second half blossomed into a tense decider which was fought out to the last whistle. Indeed, for a minute or so, it looked as if Tipperary well going to snatch victory from the grasp of a Limerick team which was leading by two points, with less than two minutes to go. The occasion was a close-in free for Tipperary and right half-forward Jim Flanagan, who had earlier proved himself a more than able marksman, walked up to take it. His low hard shot could have spelt disaster for the homesters had it not been blocked down by one of a wall of Limerick defenders and cleared up field before referee Mick Hayes of Clare sounded the full-time whistle.

High standard

Limerick CBS, who earlier this year were finalists in the All Ireland Colleges Hurling Championship provided five of the winning team and the high standard of hurling in the county was evidenced in full by each of the fifteen players. They matched Tipperary in speed and skill and outshone them in determination. The first half was rather tame, in comparison with the second thirty minutes. Tipperary were first to find their feet and pointed in the third and fifth minutes. However, Limerick with P. Doherty and D. Foley pulling well together in midfield soon settled down and Paddy Doherty pointed from a free in the 6th minute to open their account. Shanahan had a point for Limerick to bring them to equality before Seán Bourke put them in the lead after twelve minutes. Tipperary keeper Paul Kennedy, a member of the St. Flannan's College side, was put to the test with a fine shot from centre forward Hayes. Diving full length, he managed to stop the ball, but Bourke was quickly in from the corner to scoop the ball into the net. It was the first of five goals for Limerick. Tipperary were soon to recover from this setback and assumed control of the game. The backs were displaying a good understanding for the Limerick forwards' tactics, but the forward line never really impressed, though they had good individuals in Flanagan, Loughnane and Cross.

Six minutes after the Limerick goal, Tipperary raised another flag and points in the 20th and 21st minute saw them level. Flanagan, playing from the right half position, put them in the lead for the first time when he sent over the bar shortly before the half-time whistle. Both sides had hurled well in the first half, but the standard was even higher on the turnover. After Éamon Grimes had put Limerick again on level terms, Tipperary shot into prominence with a goal after 44 minutes. One of the backs in endeavouring to clear to a loose ball hit it off centre forward Loughnane's hurley and it ended up in the Limerick net. But this was only an indication of things to come. Both sides were really battling it out for the honour to go forward for the All Ireland semi-final. The result was a display of good, crisp, clean hurling which had the crowd on their feet.

Same again

The second half was barely seven minutes old when Seán Bourke goaled for Limerick. This score was similar to the first half goal with goalie Kennedy blocking down the ball, but Bourke was on hand to tap the ball home. The same player had Limerick supporters really wild when he had his third goal within less than a minute and half. But the Limerick cheers were soon swallowed up in the roar of Tipperary appreciation when first Flanagan pointed and then Willie Cross had a goal to bring them back into the reckoning. But Limerick were not to be denied.

With their forwards really hitting their form they swung play to the other end, and left corner forward Matt Grace had Limerick's fifth and final goal when he received a beautiful pass from Grimes. Tipperary, undaunted, tried hard and Jim Flanagan reduced the arrears with two points from frees to make it 5-4 to 3-9. Limerick again took over, however, and in the remaining minutes Noel Hayes finished off their tally with a point. Limerick supporters breathed a sigh of relief when Jim Flanagan's 21 yards free was blocked down and cleared up field. It was Tipperary's last chance.

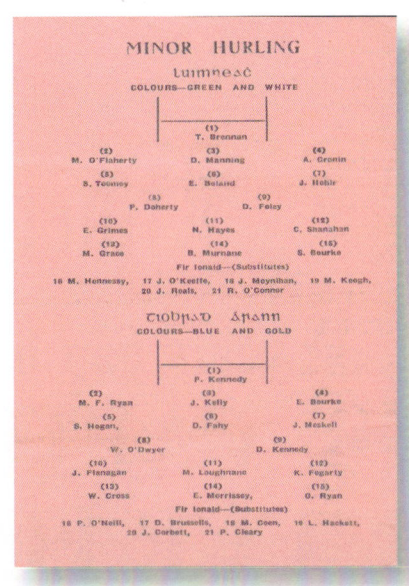

Scorers for the winners were S. Bourke 4-0, M. Grace 1-0, E. Grimes 0-2, N. Hayes and P. Doherty 0-1. Tipperary replied per J. Flanagan 1-5, W. Cross and M. Loughnane 1-2.

Limerick - T. Brennan; M. O'Flaherty, D. Manning, A. Cronin; S. Toomey, E. Boland, J. Hehir; P. Doherty, D. Foley; E. Grimes, N. Hayes, C. Shanahan; M. Grace, B. Murnane, S. Bourke. Subs: M. Hennessy for Hayes and Hayes for Murnane.

Tipperary - P. Kennedy; M.F. Ryan, J. Kelly, E. Bourke; S. Hogan, D. Fahy, J. Meskell; W. O'Dwyer, D. Kennedy; J. Flanagan, M. Loughnane, K. Fogarty; W. Cross, E. Morrissey, O. Ryan. Sub: D. Brussels for Fogarty.

Referee - Mick Hayes (Clare).

The Limerick minor hurling team that defeated Tipperary in the Munster final at the Gaelic Grounds on July 25th 1965

Back Row: (L-R) Br Burke, Jimmy Millea, Éamon Grimes, John Hehir, Richard O'Connor, Pat O'Doherty, Con Shanahan, Matt Grace, Denis Foley, Mike Hennessy, Bertie Murnane, Donal Manning, Selector Murt O'Connor and Peter Fitzgerald.
Front Row: (L-R) Jimmy Moynihan, Mike Keogh, Tony Brennan, John Reale, Ned Boland, Michael O'Flaherty (Capt) Nick Hayes, Seán Burke, Jimmy O'Keeffe, Séamus Twomey, Tony Cronin and Fr McNamee.

32-Year Gap Bridged in Glorious Honour
(Limerick Leader, 16 March 1964)
CBS Capture Dr Harty Cup for the 6th time

By Des Hanrahan

Limerick CBS 6-10
St. Flannan's College 4-7

Limerick Leader
MONDAY, MARCH 16, 1964

32 years gap bridged in glorious hour
C.B.S. CAPTURE DR. HARTY CUP FOR 6th TIME

Telegrams and messages of congratulation have been pouring in all day to Sexton Street, acknowledging yesterday's brilliant win over St. Flannan's College, in as good a Dr Harty Cup final as was ever witnessed. A 3 goals margin at the finish can have left none of the 11,000 attendance in doubt as to the outstanding quality of the fare dished up by Limerick CBS, but with only ten minutes remaining the gallant boys from Ennis had cut a one-time gap of 11 pts to 5, and their supporters must have had visions of what could have been for them win number 9 in the competition.

However with the emphasis on ground striking and first-time pulling, Limerick CBS easily resisted the challenge, and a goal by Brian Cobbe - his third in the hour, fairly clinched the issue. CBS hurling enthusiasts, who had been doing "penance" since 1932, were able to spend the last five minutes speculating on the possibility of yesterday's stars pioneering another "rags-to-riches" trail for the county... a repeat of the golden years that followed the win of 32 years ago.

Captain's part in 3 goals win

This tonic win at the Ennis Road grounds will have given the game a tremendous "face lift" in the county. While all played their parts in turning the tables on the "slayers" of what was reckoned a very powerful CBS side of six years ago, one must single out for particular mention the part played by the captain, Eamonn Cregan. That visit to Croke Park last September when he led the Limerick minors in the All Ireland final against Wexford (winners), even that did not bring the expected results, did him a power of good.

He was coolness personified, positively "lorded" at midfield, and under his leadership one can entertain genuine hopes of the sixth CBS side to win the trophy - previous winners, 1920, '25, '26, '27 and '32-pushing out the boundaries of attainment even further by becoming the first Sexton Street XV to win the colleges' All Ireland Championship. They meet the Connacht champions, St. Mary's, Galway, in the semi-final, at Ennis, on April 12, and if successful will oppose the Leinster champions, St. Peter's of Wexford, who yesterday beat Mount St. Joseph, Roscrea, by 3-5 to 2-4, in the decider, possibly at Thurles.

Cregan's personal tally of 1-7 was quite an achievement equalled only by the 3-1 notched by Brian Cobbe who looks all set to follow in the footsteps of his brothers, Vivian and Paddy, who have worn the county jersey with distinction. The switching of young Cobbe from the half-line to top of the left was a master stroke by the team's trainer, Br Michael Burke, a native of Powerstown, County Tipperary. From his new position, Cobbe cut loose in the devastating manner and made it a nightmare afternoon for cornerback, Jackie Kennedy, and, of course, St Flannan's pocket-sized 'keeper, fifteen years-old, Paul Kennedy. The loser's 'keeper could not be faulted for any of the shots that beat him, and he made a few daring saves to enhance an already established reputation.

CBS elected to play with a rather telling breeze that was blowing from the Clare end. They opened with the emphasis on mobility and in almost the first movement of the hour, give of their players starting with the rock-like right corner back, Tom O'Brien and the wiry and tremendously efficient right half, Donal Russell, doubled on the ball with as fine a series of ground strikes as one could wish to see. Had the sliotar ended in the net it would have been the goal of a lifetime. Instead it flashed inches outside of the left upright.

This was to be the pattern for the remainder of the game but CBS were having difficulty in their full-forward line, and with the 11 Limerick wides the first 20 minutes, and only a goal separating the sides, inside the first 20 minutes and only a goal separating the sides, one could sense the feeling of urgency in the Limerick "camp". Three minutes later, there was further cause for alarm when Flannan's right corner forward, Seán Dwane, levelled the scoring at 1-3.

Turning Point

Then came the turning point, the goal that had the Limerick "tenors?" in the well-filled terraces at full throttle again. A 21 yards free four minutes from the interval left no room for half measures. It was a do-or-bust effort, and with all the power at his command, Eamonn Cregan scooped the ball a mere few inches off the sod, and with a drive that made it almost impossible for the human eye to follow, he had the Flannan's net bulging.

Inside seconds, Cregan had an umpire working overtime with the white flag to widen the gap to five points, and with Jackie Ryan (Flannan's) and Jackie Kennedy (Christians) exchanging points, the locals turned over leading by 2-6 to 1-4. During the interval "pep" talk the wind took a breather and it was soon evident that St. Flannan's had half burned themselves in trying to contain the Limerick standard-bearers in the first half.

Switch paid off

They had a point from Pierce Dooley soon after the resumption, but with Brian Cobbe in the full-forward line the homesters gradually gained the upper-hand. The switch had immediate results with a sparkling goal, and Eamonn Cregan then tacked on a splendid point.

Jackie Ryan, at the other end, balanced his white flag, but Cobbe had the green flag, showing again almost immediately and when Cregan topped the bar again, "Christians" were well on the road to victory we thought.

But St. Flannan's best forward, Ollie Ryan (14) had other ideas. Inside 60 seconds he netted twice but Brian Cobbe quickly silenced their supporters with his third goal and with Eamonn Cregan bringing his total to 1-7 with another white flag, the visitors had a real fight on their hands.

They answered very gamely with 1 goal from Seán Dwane and a point from Pierce Dooley, but Limerick were calling the tune at the "death" and a goal by Pat Nash and a point by Brian Cobbe left them clear-cut winners. While thirteen first half wides were a cause of regret at certain stages of the game, the fact that St. Flannans's never nosed their way to the front is indicative of the team spirit and the ability of the winners.

Stole the show

Midfield supremacy is vital in any game and Limerick could certainly claim that they were masters in this section. Eamonn Cregan stole the show here, but he had a very able seconder in Pat Doherty, who was of great assistance to the attack, particularly in the second half. Flannan's made positional changes in the hope of subduing the pair, but it would have taken players out of the ordinary to win the day against the CBS stars.

Séamus Shinnors was excellent in goal for the winners, his lengthy clearances being of immeasurable value. The strongly built Tom O'Brien was a tower of strength at right corner back. He broke up many threatening movements, cleared his end with minimum delay, and seldom failed to find a maroon and white persey with his deliveries.

The fact that Ollie Ryan scored three goals for St. Flannan's might give the impression that full-back Noel O'Gorman had an off-day, but this was far from being the case. Like JJ Fitzgerald, on his left, he worked very hard. In the midfield "pull" contributed handsomely to success, the play of the half-back line of Donal Russell, Donal Manning and Eddie Power was also a great source of inspiration.

Russell and Power, although lacking the size of their opposites and opposed by inter county players of very high rating, Jackie Ryan (Tipperary) and Pierce Dooley (Laois), turned in heartwarming performances. There was a tremendous "cut" in the work of the wing-halves and Donal Manning in the centre, too, held up his end.

CBS, SEXTON ST.

HARTY AND CROKE CUP WINNERS, 1964

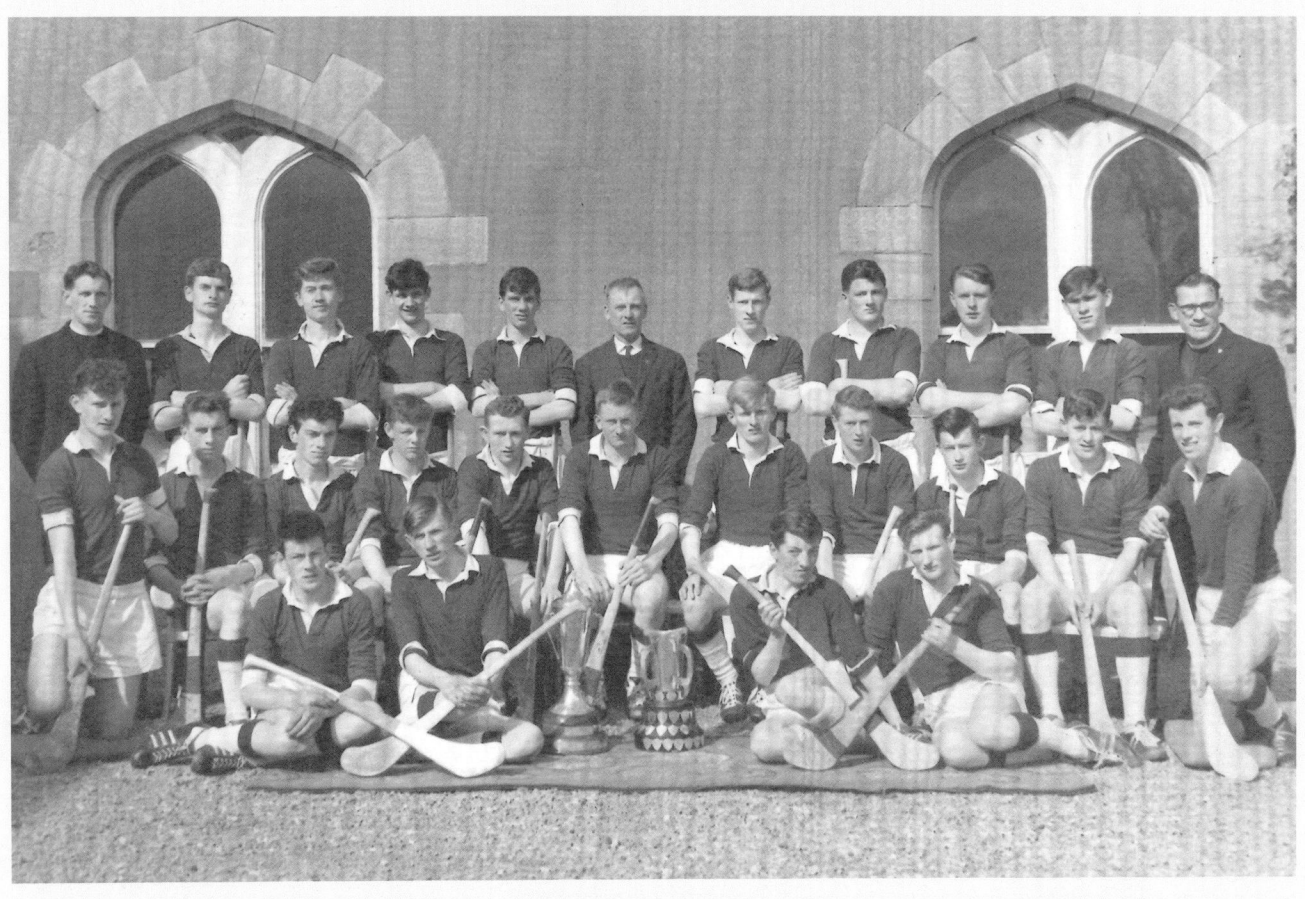

Back Row: (L-R) Rev. Br Hennessey, G. Boland, L. Moloney, J. Finucane, J. Leonard, S. Keogh, E. Power, N. O'Gorman, J. Fitzpatrick, R. Hayes and Rev. Br Burke.
Middle Row: (L-R): D. Manning, P. Nash, J. Kennedy, B. Cobbe, T. O'Brien, E. Cregan (Capt.), E. Grimes, D. Russell, T. Clohessy, S. Shinnors and P. Doherty.
Front Row: (L-R): T. Crowe, M. O'Brien, P. Ahearne and N. O'Carroll

Was sick and played

A flu victim and a very doubtful starter up to the morning of match, Éamon Grimes was, naturally, not at his towering best in the half-forward line. But he warmed to his task and after being switched about somewhat, eventually hit top form and gave the visitors defence a bit of a "roasting." However, the fact that Brian Cobbe scored three great goals must have him heading the forward list. His second half display had class stamped all over it. Add the fiery and polished work by Tom Clohessy, son of Deputy Paddy Clohessy, of All Ireland fame; Pat Nash, Roger Hayes and Jackie Kennedy and you have a team of grand all-round ability a side of tremendous possibilities.

Wind "Died"

St. Flannan's may well claim that the fact that the wind died down when they should have had it at their backs was a big set-back. But they were within striking distance of the champions at the interval and 10 minutes from the end, but could pull out nothing extra that would swing the issue. In the loser's defence Val Arthur, Ted Dwyer, Pat Carey and Gerry Cleary made a great impact on the game, but Ollie Ryan and, to a lesser extent, Jackie Ryan and Seán Dwane were the only forwards to keep the home defence at full stretch.

Scorers for the winners who were led by 2-6 to 1-4 at the interval were B. Cobbe 3-1; E. Cregan 1-7, (1-6 from frees); E. Grimes 1-1; P. Nash 1-0; J. Kennedy 0-1.

Limerick CBS - S. Shinnors; T. O'Brien, N. O'Gorman, T.J. Fitzpatrick; D. Russell, D. Manning, E. Power; E. Cregan, P. Doherty; E. Grimes, B. Cobbe, P. Nash; T. Clohessy, J. Kennedy, R. Hayes.

St. Flannan's - P. Kennedy; J. Kennedy, T. Dwyer, V. Arthur; M. O'Loughlin, P. Carey, G. Cleary; D. Cahalane, P. Tobin; P. Dooley, M. Hurley, J. Ryan; S. Dwane, O. Ryan, D. Dwyer.

Referee - T. McElgun (Tipperary) did an excellent job.

Eamonn Cregan holds the Croke Cup aloft after Limerick CBS's 1964 All Ireland final victory in Croke Park.

80 Minute Games

1970 Congress

The playing time in senior All Ireland semi-finals, finals and provincial finals in hurling and football was extended from 60 to 80 minutes at the 1970 GAA Congress held at Coláiste Mhuire, Galway in late March. It was the first Congress to be held outside Dublin for 34 years, but the spirit of adventure ended there.

This particular rule change was generated by the Rules Revision Committee who worked on proposed changes for the previous 12 months. The duration of all other senior championship games remained at 60 minutes.

1975 Congress

The major changes in the playing rules, introduced on a trial basis in 1974, were formally adopted at Bundoran, County Donegal in late March. Approval was given for the enlarged parallelogram; goalkeepers in both hurling and football were afforded the same protection inside the small square, and the third man tackle continued to be outlawed.

Several new rules were passed, the most significant being the decision to discontinue the 80-minute game, which pertained to provincial finals, All Ireland semi-finals and finals since 1970, and to make all upcoming senior inter-county championship matches 70-minute games.

Limerick Dual Players

Many of the 1973 Limerick hurling team played for the Limerick footballers over the years too, starting out, most famously, with our singular appearance in the Munster Football Final of 1965 against Kerry, having beaten Cork in a famous semi-final upset that year.

It was Limerick's first appearance in the Munster senior football championship since 1952. Both Bernie Hartigan and Eamonn Cregan played in the Cork and Kerry games, with Eamonn scoring 1-1 in the semi-final and 0-4 in the final.

A warrior from an earlier era, Mick Tynan, was also on the team that year. Bernie continued to tog with the footballers through much of the rest of the 1960s, while Eamonn made a few more appearances afterwards. Other county hurlers were in and out of the football team during this time, most especially Michael Graham who played between 1969 and 1972.

Pat Hartigan made his debut for the senior footballers in 1970 and played through to 1974, including the game against Tipperary on Sunday, 3 June 1973, that Limerick lost by 4-13 to 1-7. Bernie played that afternoon with his brother, as they did against Kerry in 1970.

Richie Bennis made one appearance for the senior footballers in championship, in the 1974 loss to Waterford on Sunday, 2 June. Pat Hartigan played full back for Limerick that day too. These were not successful times for the footballers of Limerick: between 1966 and 1979 only one championship success was recorded, Tipperary in 1967, with the aforementioned Mick Tynan scoring 2-5 of Limerick's 4-10 that afternoon. The 1970s consisted of ten championship losses, against Clare (four), Tipperary (three), Waterford (two) and Kerry (one).

The Limerick senior football panel before the 1965 Munster football final.

Back Row (L-R): Mick Cuneen, Pa O'Brien, Eric Ryan, Paddy O'Dwyer, Tom Meaney, Bernie Hartigan, Séamus Cox, Pat Murphy, Joe Maher, David Quirke, John Aherne, Johnny Mullane, Basil Fitzgibbon, Tom Downes and P.J. Ryan.
Front Row (L-R): Paddy O'Connell, Jack Quinlivan, John Meade, Donie Nestor, John Culhane, Liam Moloney, Timmy Woulfe, Tommy Carrig, Tony Fitzgerald, Mick Tynan, Liam O'Shaughnessy, Pat Reidy, Eamonn Cregan, and Fr Dermot McCarthy.

The Limerick team that beat Tipperary in the first round of the Munster hurling championship in Cork on June 5th 1966.

Back Row (L-R): Jim Hogan, Bernie Hartigan, Kevin Long, Mick Savage, J.J. Bresnan, Eamon Rea, Eamonn Cregan and Tom Bluett.
Front Row (L-R): Mick O'Brien, Phil Bennis, Andy Dunworth, John McDonagh, Tony O'Brien (Capt), Séamus Quaid and Éamon Grimes.

1973 Keeping the Dream Alive

"I guarantee you within five years this team will have won every major trophy that the association has to offer" (Joe McGrath speaking to RTÉ in 1970).

The Limerick team tha[t]

Back Row (L-R): Tony O'Brien, Jim Hogan, Pat O'Brien, Jim C

Front Row (L-R): Phil Bennis (Capt), Tom Bluett, Éamo[n]

in the 1970 NHL final.

...artigan, Jim O'Donnell, Eamonn Cregan and John McDonogh.
...er Bennis, Richie Bennis, PJ Keane and Bernie Hartigan.

Thrilling Success as Tipperary are Beaten for Third Time
(Limerick Leader, 24 May 1971)
Limerick Sparkled to Win National League
Back on Top Again

By Cormac Liddy

Limerick 3-12
Tipperary 3-11

Those know-all Dublin Gaelic reporters - with one exception - got a rare kick in the teeth by the Limerick hurling team which rattled, bustled, but most important of all, outhurled a highly-rated Tipperary team to win the National Hurling League title for the first time in 24 years at a crowded Cork Athletic Grounds on Sunday. This was a sparkling display by a Limerick side which, had all their skilful efforts been turned into scores, would have left them several goals, instead of a solitary point, in front at the end of an hour which produced all that is best in hurling. The moaners from Tipperary did their best and even to the extent of calling up Jimmy Doyle to try and prove a match-winner. It was good to see Doyle on the field, but he did not strike one ball, in my opinion. Without doubt this was Limerick's hour of glory and one that all city and county will join in celebrating.

For so long the hurlers and officials had become something of a joke for the cynics, all of whom were answered in recent months, but who were silenced on Sunday. This was as thrilling a game as one could wish to see: stroke for stroke was matched by rival backs and forwards and while at times it looked as if matters might get a little out of hand, any dangerous situation was smoothed over. One decision that must be condemned, though, was that of the taking of Mick Cregan's name in the first half for the substitute was as innocent as could be when struck several times by a justifiably-panicky Tipperary defender.

Longest Serving

While a point in the last minute by Richie Bennis was really the match-winner, every score in this exciting hour was vital, but the moment that will long remain in my mind when all the natural and deserved hullaballoo has died down will be that miraculous save of Jim Hogan's at the end. From nowhere Hogan grabbed a shot from Jack Ryan and had to race thirty yards out of goal under pressure before getting in his clearance which brought the final whistle. For Hogan, longest serving member of the side, it was a great hour and in front of him, Pat Hartigan, I rated slightly the better of the full-back line. He once again mastered Mick "Babs" Keating who was taken away from him subsequently in Tipp's bid to get in front. Keating did a little better in a roving capacity and with his boots discarded but like all the other Tipperary players he did as well as he was allowed to do. Tony O'Brien played a captain's part in the right corner and on the far side Jim O'Brien had perhaps his best ever hour.

Also Shone

Jim O'Donnell once again was the star of the half-back line with Phil Bennis being little behind. Christy Campbell was doing very well too until he had to be taken off with an aggravation of his leg injury. Eddie Prenderville came in and showed that not all the stars were on parade from the beginning by having a terrific game. Jack (Seán) Foley and Michael (Mick) Graham got that fractionally on top in this vital sector and the latter contributed handsomely with a badly needed goal just on half-time.

Forwards Click

Eamonn Cregan, Richie Bennis and Éamon Grimes were the forward stars and the former kicked in a goal that would have done justice to "real" soccer players such as Eusebio and Pele and not the kick and rush commercially-minded merchants that are to be found in these parts! Bennis was a man inspired in this hour. His match-winning point under such tense conditions was a master stroke, and he also clicked over seven others as well as shining in ordinary play. The other three, too, did well and a special word of praise is due to Mick Cregan, who came in as a substitute when the luckless Willie Moore had to withdraw because of a thumb injury.

More Effective

For Tipperary, goalkeeper O'Sullivan, John Kelly and Len Gaynor were best in defence. Mick Jones was more effective than a lethargic Mick Roche at midfield, while opportunist Jack Ryan and Keating, when on the 40, were the only consistently dangerous forwards.

Scorers

Limerick - R. Bennis 0-8; E. Cregan 2-1; M. Graham 1-0, M. Cregan, B. Hartigan and E. Grimes 0-1.
Tipperary - J. Ryan 2-3; M. Keating 0-6; P. Byrne 1-0; M. Roche, and J. Flanagan 0-1.

Teams

Limerick - J. Hogan; T. O'Brien, P. Hartigan, J. O'Brien; C. Campbell, J. O'Donnell, P. Bennis; S. Foley, M. Graham; R. Bennis, B. Hartigan, E. Grimes; D. Flynn, M. Cregan, E. Cregan. Sub: E. Prenderville for Campbell.

Tipperary - P. O'Sullivan; N. Lane, J. Kelly, W. Ryan; J. Fogarty, T. O'Connor, L. Gaynor; M. Roche, M. Jones; F. Loughnane, J. Flanagan. J. Ryan; R. Ryan, M. Keating, P. Byrne. Subs: J. Gleeson for W. Ryan, M. Nolan for Flanagan and J. Doyle for R. Ryan.

Referee - Frank Murphy (Cork).

The Limerick team that beat Tipperary in the 1971 NHL final.

Back Row (L-R): Jim Hogan, Richie Bennis, Eamonn Cregan, Pat Hartigan, Jim O'Brien, Jim O'Donnell, Bernie Hartigan and Mick Cregan.
Front Row (L-R): Christy Campbell, Éamon Grimes, Michael Graham, Tony O'Brien (Capt), Phil Bennis, Jack (Seán) Foley and Donie Flynn.

1973 Keeping the Dream Alive

The Limerick team that beat
Back Row (L-R): Bernie Hartigan, Richie Bennis, Jim O'Do...
Front Row (L-R): Christy Campbell, Phil Bennis, Donie Flynn, To...

1971 Munster Championship.
...nn Cregan, Jim O'Brien, Pat Hartigan and Éamon Grimes.
...apt), Michael Graham, Seán Foley, Mick Cregan and Jim Hogan.

Thriller at Killarney - Tipp Fight Back For Heroic Win
(Limerick Leader, 26 July 1971)
Disallowed Goal a Major Talking Point as Luckless Limerick Lose in Last Minute

Tipperary 4-16
Limerick 3-18

Fighting Spirit Wins A Remarkable Contest

TERRIFIC MUNSTER HURLING FINAL OF '71

Another episode in the Limerick and Tipperary hurling saga was enacted at Fitzgerald Stadium, Killarney, on Sunday. This time it was the Munster Senior Championship final and it ended in yet another sorrowful note for Limerick fans as Tipperary gained revenge for their three league defeats and so finished Limerick's high hopes of a major breakthrough to the pinnacle they once adorned.

Thus the "Killarney Hoodoo" continues for the Shannonsiders as Limerick have yet to win a hurling game at "Heaven's Reflex". And the story of disallowed goals continues. In 1966 it was a heroic effort by Bernie Hartigan which still evokes discussion. On this occasion it was a brilliant move finished to the Tipperary net by substitute Willie Moore in the 34th minute of the second half which sent Limerick supporters wild with delight only to be whistled back to reality by referee Frank Murphy (Cork) which will figure in the post mortems of this pulsating final in the years ahead. But let there be no detracting from the merits of Tipperary's victory. It was a case of the "ould dog for the hard road."

Determination

Limerick hurled with such fluency and determination in the opening moiety, that even neutral followers doubted the wisdom of having a second half! But this was the rock on which Limerick perished. Tipperary appeared a transformed side on resuming. Noel Lane and Jimmy Doyle had been relegated to the reserves bench and in came Liam Ryan and burly Roger Ryan.

Immediately, all the Tipperary "ifs" became a reality! Liam King knitted the defence, Mick Roche began to play his usual proverbial blinder, their mid-fielders, P.J. Ryan and Séamus Ryan ruled the roost in facile fashion and Michael "Babs" Keating struck a real Keating purple patch. Within five minutes, Tipperary's half-time six point deficit was turned into a one point lead. First, Francis Loughnane shot a point from play after three minutes.

Then a minute later, Keating brushed aside a wall of defenders to raise a green flag and 80 seconds later, gave Tipperary the lead for the first time when he blasted a 21 yards free to the roof of the net.

Dominance

A Len Gaynor point from a free and a further Francis Loughnane point from play left Tipperary leading by three points after only eight minutes play. Immediately panic set-in in the Limerick camp. So pronounced was Tipperary's dominance at this stage that one had visions of they annihilating the opposition. They matched brawn with brawn and they ruled with such authority that Limerick appeared to have shot their bolt. The Limerick selectors began to re-shuffle their team in an effort to stem the tide. But to me it was just a game of chess.

You move next! Every player from mid-field to the left corner forward position swopped places with Bernie Hartigan eventually figuring as full forward! The "Big Five" who have earned much praise for their handling of switches in the team's long, run of successes to data made a cardinal error (if they were responsible?) of switching Eamonn Cregan to mid-field.

The tireless Claughaun stalwart hurled himself to a standstill in a herculean attempt to rally his team-mates but our front line was left without a striker when the chips were really down. Why was Con Shanahan not drafted in to bolster our fading midfield partnership earlier? Another factor which militated against Limerick's chances at this crucial first quarter period was their defensive tactics which cut no ice against opposition of calibre of Tipperary. In fact it suited them down to the ground.

Comeback

In spite of all their shortcomings Limerick weathered the storm and displaying great tenacity fought back to be only a point in arrears, 2-14 to 3-10, with 17 minutes remaining. But then disaster struck once more! First Mick Keating weaved his way through for another spectacular goal and John Flanagan tacked on a point. Éamon Grimes and Dinny Ryan exchanged points before Éamon Grimes raced on to a Richie Bennis centre to shoot a goal reminiscent of his historic CBS days.

Then came Moore's disallowed goal and Richie Bennis' point from the resultant free to level matters with 8 minutes remaining. Len Gaynor pointed a Tipperary free but Richie Bennis equalised and a draw seemed inevitable when livewire John Flanagan shot the winning point for Tipperary two minutes from time. So only a puck of the ball remains between the teams, but as I warned in my preview, unfortunately, it went the wrong way on this occasion! It was a galling experience for the huge throng of Limerick supporters who made the trek to Killarney to see that long awaited victory, so near and yet so far!

Never have I seen such an enthusiastic and colour festooned band of Limerick fans.

Rain

True to tradition, heavy rain felt throughout this rip-roaring Munster final, which I viewed from the comfort of a stretcher (courtesy of Killarney Knights of Malta). Limerick opened in hectic fashion with an early point from Bernie Hartigan plus a Richie Bennis white flag from a free and Donie Flynn finished a sideline puck to the net to leave the Shannonsiders five points clear after 6 minutes play. Although Tipperary fought back for a Dinny Ryan goal in the 8th minute, Limerick continued to dictate terms. The defence repulsed attack after attack, while the forwards were picking scores at will. So at the break Limerick led 2-10 to 1-7, and were worthy of even more.

This makes it even more difficult to explain their almost total collapse for that Tipperary spell of terror on resuming. They were outmanoeuvred and out hurled with such ease by a power-packed Tipperary fifteen that the difference between the sides was like chalk and cheese. The root of Limerick's troubles can be diagnosed at mid-field, where a variation of pairings was always playing second fiddle to P.J. Ryan and Séamus Hogan. The half-back line, so often the sheet anchor of the side, also collapsed during those early second half Tipperary onslaughts. The ease with which Dinny Ryan and Francis Loughnane were allowed to career through in menacing runs was heart-breaking and put further pressure on an already over burdened full-back line.

Handful

The latter two could never come to grips with Tipperary's second-half top line of forwards John Flanagan, Roger Ryan and Mick Keating. Pat Hartigan found the burly Ryan a rare handful, while Mick Keating enjoyed much more freedom on the wings for his devastating runs. This will be remembered as Keating's hour as the legendary Babs scored 3-4 of his side's total. After their long and successful innings, and losing Sunday's game to a super strong Tipperary side by only one point, it would be invidious of me to criticise strongly the Limerick team. Suffice to say, they failed in what was considered to be their hallmarks, stamina, and coolness under pressure. They failed to match Tipperary's guts and speed, and strange to relate, they panicked when the Tipperary hurricane struck in the early stages of the second half. The selectors too were a shade slow in introducing reserves to remedy apparent weaknesses. Overall, it was the craft and experience of Tipperary which carried the day.

Cregan Stars

Eamonn Cregan emerged as the shining star of the Limerick team. First at left full forward, later at centre-forward and finally at midfield he played himself into the ground. Even in those last five minutes he was back helping a harassed defence. This was Cregan at his almighty best. He tackled with rare gusto, displayed great positional sense and every move had method in it. Cregan was the only Limerick player to figure prominently throughout the 80 minutes. The remainder all had their moments of glory, especially in the first half when Jim O'Donnell, Christy Campbell, Tony O'Brien, Bernie Hartigan, Richie Bennis, Michael Graham and Mickey Cregan were monarchs of all they surveyed. But what a change on the turnover! Few are blameless, so 'nuff said. Keating was, of course, Tipperary's hero, ably supported by Mick Roche, who had a majestic second half at centre-back; Tadgh O'Connor, Len Gaynor, P.J. Ryan, Noel O'Dwyer, Dinny Ryan, John Flanagan and Séamus Hogan.

Scorers

Tipperary - M. Keating 3-4; J. Flanagan 0-5; F. Loughnane 0-3 and P.J. Ryan 1-0; L. Gaynor 0-2; N. O'Dwyer and J. Doyle 0-1. Limerick - R. Bennis 0-10; E. Cregan 1-2; E. Grimes 1-1; D. Flynn 1-0; M. Graham 0-2; B. Hartigan 0-1.

Teams

Tipperary - P. O'Sullivan; E. Lane, J. Kelly J. Gleeson; T. O'Connor, M. Roche, L. Gaynor; S. Hogan, P.J. Ryan; E. Loughnane, M. O'Dwyer, J. Flanagan; J. Doyle, M. Keating, D. Ryan. Subs: L. King for Lane, M. Ryan for Doyle, P. Byrnes for O'Dwyer.

Limerick - J. Hogan; T. O'Brien, P. Hartigan, J. O'Brien; C. Campbell, J. O'Donnell, P. Bennis; B. Hartigan, S. Foley; R. Bennis, M. Graham, E. Grimes; D. Flynn, M. Cregan, E. Cregan. Subs: W. Moore for Flynn, E. Prenderville for P. Bennis, C. Shanahan for S. Foley.

Referee - Frank Murphy (Cork).

The Limerick team beaten by Tipperary in the 1971 Munster Hurling Final in Killarney.

Back Row (L-R): Jim Hogan, Bernie Hartigan, Seán Foley, Jim O'Donnell, Jim O'Brien, Pat Hartigan, Eamonn Cregan and Richie Bennis.
Front Row (L-R): Phil Bennis, Donie Flynn, Tony O'Brien (Capt.), Michael Graham, Éamon Grimes, Mick Cregan and Christy Campbell.

The Limerick team that beat Wexford in the 1971 Oireachtas final at Croke Park.

Back Row (L-R): Eamonn Cregan, John Frost, Seán Foley, Jim Allis, Richie Bennis, Willie Moore, Jim Hogan and Pat Hartigan.
Front Row (L-R): Phil Bennis, Michael Graham, Bernie Hartigan, Tony O'Brien (Capt.), Jim O'Brien, Éamon Grimes, Andy Dunworth and mascot Richie O'Brien.

1973 Keeping the Dream Alive

The Limerick team that be
Back Row (L-R): Bernie Hartigan, Jim O'Brien, Pat Hartigan, J
Front Row (L-R): Seán Foley, Éamon Grimes, Richie Ben

the 1972 NHL semi-final.
Willie Moore, Eamonn Cregan, Tony O'Brien and Mick Cregan.
...raham, Jim Hogan (Capt), Phil Bennis and Donie Flynn.

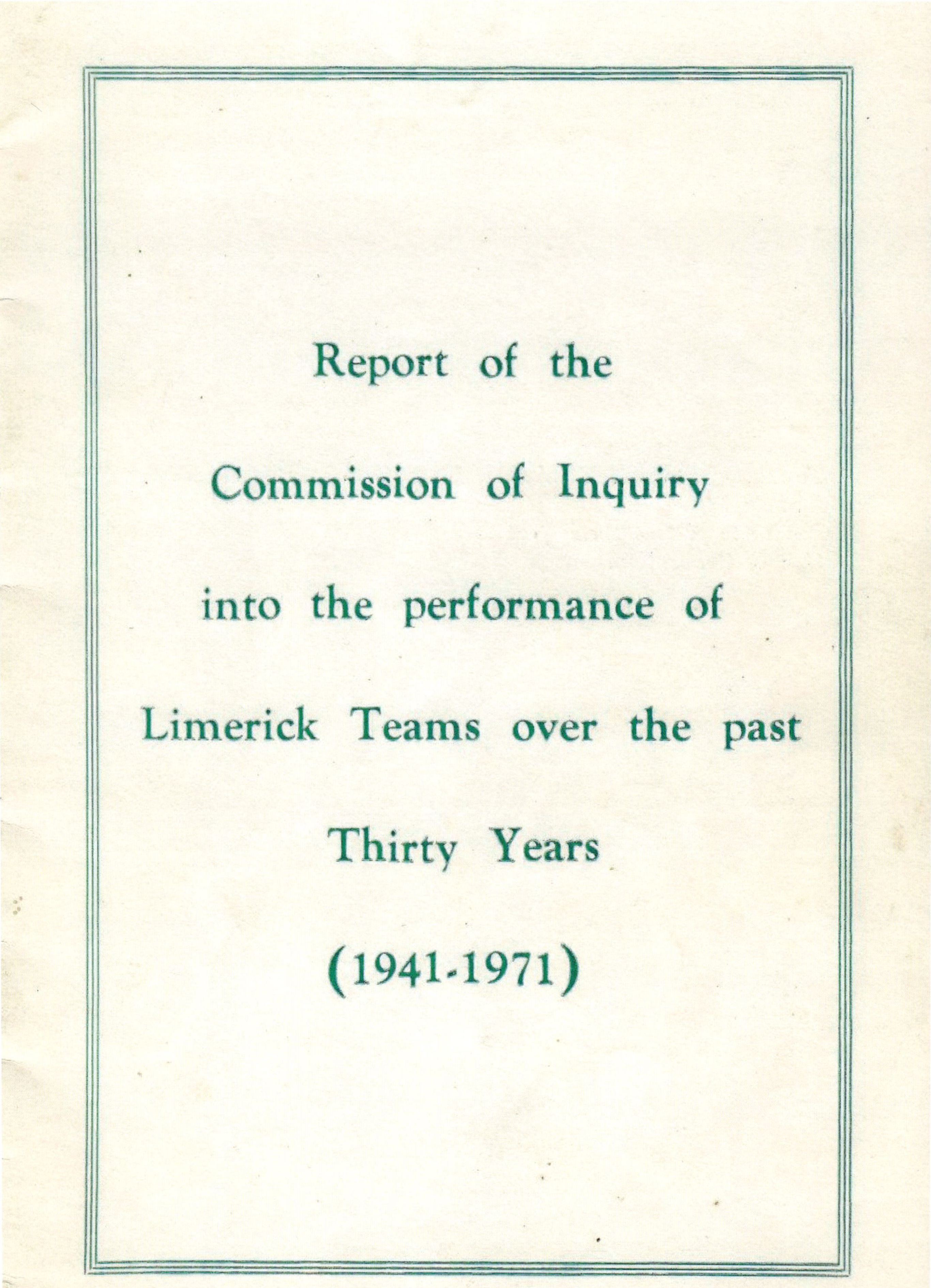

Report of the

Commission of Inquiry

into the performance of

Limerick Teams over the past

Thirty Years

(1941-1971)

Cover of the Commission of Inquiry report.

Report of the Commission of Inquiry into the performance of Limerick Teams over the past Thirty Years (1941-1971)

SECTION III

FACTORS RELATED TO PERFORMANCE

(3.1) The record of Limerick's performance in the period 1941-71 suggests that the lack of success is not due to any single cause. There are a great many factors involved, and a convergence of these, rather than any single factor which can be suddenly put right, is the explanation for defeat. These factors centre around three items all of which are important in achieving victory in the inter-county competitions:

1. The standard of hurling within the county - ensuring that the fifteen players who represent the county are the best available and are well up to the general standard of inter-county play.
2. Ensuring that these fifteen players are moulded into an effective team.
3. Ensuring that these fifteen players whether as individuals or as a team perform to the best of their ability on the day of an important game.

(3.2) It is the opinion of the Commission that these three items have rarely been achieved in Limerick hurling over the past thirty years. Number 1 has to do with the type of competition available within the county, with the general development of players, and with the selection methods in operation at a particular time. We have already indicated that the over emphasis on junior competitions depressed the standard throughout the county and still continues to do so in particular areas. Number 2 has to do with training and coaching and team building, and which because of a constant turn-over of trainers and team personnel was rarely achieved in the past thirty years. Number 3 has to do with team management especially on the day of a match, and here we find that the lack of a single individual who was ultimately responsible for switches and substitutions has been an important factor in Limerick's defeats in the past.

(3.3) Consequently, we feel that it might be helpful to list all the factors which we consider relevant to the standard of hurling within the county and to the performance of our county teams. Each of these factors will be examined under the following headings:

1. The present situation.
2. The aspects of this situation which lead to poor performance.
3. Recommendations for improvement.

1. The Manner of Running the Provincial Championship

(3.4) At present there is not an open draw for the provincial championship. The two finalists of the previous year are "guarded" in the draw, and this inevitably favours the stronger teams. We feel that this has been a factor of considerable importance in explaining Limerick's poor record, since the come-back of a weaker team is made more difficult under this system because it has to beat the two finalists of the previous year to win a championship. Anything less than an open draw in the Munster championship is inequitable.

(3.5) We recommend that the Limerick County Board should press for the ending of the present "guarded system" in hurling and football championships.

The present system has been one of the most important factors in preventing the weaker counties achieving any success in the Munster senior football championship.

2. Senior Inter-County Teams

(a) Manner of Selection

(3.6) At present the Senior Inter-County teams are selected by committee composed of five members nominated by the senior clubs and elected annually by the County Board before the start of the National League campaign.

(3.7) The present system has the disadvantages that (1) the selection committee may not have a representative from each division and (2) the nominations received from the clubs are often motivated by area loyalties rather than the overall interests of the county.

(3.8) However, we consider that these disadvantages are less than would result from any alternative system, and we recommend that the present arrangement be continued.

(3.9) Care should be taken to nominate and elect suitable and dedicated selectors. These should be men who are known to be in position to attend games regularly and be present at all meetings of the selection committee.

(3.10) To develop self-reliance and confidence a player needs to be assured of a permanent place on the panel consistent with reasonable opportunity to prove his worth. This is an important factor in team building and one which may not have been given sufficient attention in the past. Too frequent changes undermine confidence in a player and in a team.
(b) Training and Management of Team

(3.11) We consider that some of the defeats of Limerick in the past have been due to the fact that management of the team on the field was not delegated to a single individual with responsibility for such matters as positional changes and substitutions.

(3.12) To remedy this defect, we recommend the appointment of a Team Manager in addition to the already existing positions of Coach and Trainer. The Manager, Coach and Trainer would have the following specific responsibilities:

Team Manager: He is one of the Selection Committee, is elected by that committee as their chairman, and acts in that capacity at all their meetings. He keeps a record of the attendance of individual selectors at meetings. He has complete responsibility for the management of the team on the field of play, including such matters as switches and substitutions. The Manager reports to the County Board after each inter-county match.

Coach: His main task is that of moulding fifteen individual players into an effective team. He coaches the players and acts as liaison officer between the players and selectors. He supervises the individuals in training and recommends team tactics. He is available to the manager for consultation during a match.

Trainer: He is responsible for the physical fitness and general condition of the players and for the arrangement of their training schedule. A well turned out team can be a great morale booster, and it is the task of the trainer to ensure it. The servicing of the team on the field with hurleys, resin, first-aid, etc., should also be his responsibility.

3. Senior Competitions within the County

(3.13) At the present time there are two competitions at senior level in the county - the championship and county cup. These do not provide a sufficient number of games for the majority of players.

(3.14) In addition, there are not sufficient senior teams in the south and west divisions to provide adequate competition, nor sufficient matches to enable players to attain the standard required of inter-county players.

(3.15) The only real competition is provided by the county championship. The county cup never aroused real interest, was played only intermittently and achieved little towards improving standards. We consider that a second competition to the championship is needed but that the county cup in its present form cannot provide this.

(3.16) To replace the present arrangement, we recommend:
1. A more developed senior championship - to be achieved mainly by increasing the number of senior teams in the south and west.
2. A new league run on a divisional basis with promotion and relegation.

(3.17) The senior championship should continue to be played on a divisional basis as at present. There should be a fixed number of senior teams in each division - possibly eight in the city and six in each of the other divisions, but eventually six in each division. Initially, senior status should be decided by the divisional boards in consultation with the member clubs, and thereafter it shall be decided by promotion and relegation through the new League.

(3.18) The championship should be played on a knock-out basis without losers' group, and the winner and runner-up in each division participate in the final stages of the county championship as at present. We feel that the losers' group system is unsuitable to the championship and delays its progress. Its purpose is to offer teams extra matches, but this can he better achieved through the new League.

(3.19) We recommend that a League for senior teams be played in each division on the results of which senior status for the following year will be determined. The team finishing at the bottom of this league in each division to be relegated to junior status. This permits the promotion of the winner of each divisional junior championship to both senior championship and league in the following year.

(3.20) We suggest that the senior league be played on a home and away basis, two-year cycle, with the home club taking the gate and having full responsibility for field arrangements, etc. We recommend that definite dates be fixed for league matches throughout the county and that all teams in the county participate on the same day.

(3.21) This system will assure each senior team a minimum of six competitive matches per year - five in the league and at least one in the championship.

(3.22) The promotion of teams to senior status in each division each year should provide new incentive to junior teams and generally enhance the value of the junior competition. It is recommended that the junior championship be run on a league system within each division, the winning team in each division to play for the county championship on a knock-out basis as at present.

F. Sheehan, Secretary

Cumann Luthchleas Gael
Coisde Conndae Lonndain

ag tairiscint an

Cluichi Gaelacha

Wembley Stadium

Official Programme 5p

SATURDAY, MAY 27th, 1972

Cover of the 1972 Wembley Games programme.

Limerick Did Well At Times But Defensive Weaknesses Must Be Settled

(Limerick Leader, 29 May 1972)

Tipperary 8-7
Limerick 4-12

Limerick scored more from play yet suffered a tidy beating at Wembley on Saturday last and to apportion blame for this further set-back at the hands of Tipperary is difficult. That eight goals were conceded, though, must give the selectors plenty to ponder about.

Many will fault 35-years-old Jim Hogan with the blame for some of them and this seemed to be the case but his cover left a great deal to be desired on more than a few occasions. Hogan brought of some top-class saves to offset the lapses of which he was culpable.

But his full-back line did not by any means afford the proper type of cover and over the hour. The three Tipperary front men of Mick Keating, Paul Byrne and Roger Ryan had the edge of the various combinations placed against them.

Donal Manning, in his first major test, got through an amount of good work and so, too, did Tony O'Brien, while Jim Allis also hurled well at times. The trio as a unit, though, were outsmarted, while Manning did better when switched with Allis for the second half.

Limerick hurled superbly on occasions and led quite a few times, but having scored seven times (1-6) they still found themselves in arrears for Tipperary had rammed in three goals.

Jim O'Donnell returned to action for the first time since breaking his leg last August, and he was badly in need of the outing. He was taken out prematurely, but seems certain to figure on the July 2nd team to oppose Clare a game which is still fixed for Thurles, though Cusack Park in Ennis has yet to be inspected by Munster Council officials.

Shone

Once again the Limerick defensive star was Pat Hartigan, who operated this time at centre-back, while Christy Campbell was also doing well until he received a nasty injury.

Phil Bennis and Jim O'Brien were brought into the side for the second half after Limerick had been seven points behind at the interval, and this pair both did well and gave notice they must still command strong attention for a permanent inclusion and that neither is in any way finished.

Unlucky

Limerick were most unlucky in that Eamonn Cregan had to retire at the interval, but the ligaments he tore in the concluding stages in the National League final against Cork were giving too much trouble to continue, and, rather than risk further aggravation, he was kept out of the fray. A pity this, for he was hurling well, as was evidenced by the great first half goal he cracked in when he connected first time with a splendidly taken side-line cut by Bernie Hartigan.

Seán Foley hurled well at centre-field and Bernie Hartigan got through a deal of work but failure in the full-forward line was much too obvious. Donie Flynn did nothing of consequence but Frankie Nolan took his goal well though achieving little else.

Éamon Grimes and Richie Bennis did moderately, but generally it was an all-round further poor disappointing display by Limerick.

Challenges

Limerick would now want to set about getting a number of challenge games to try and sort out further problems before July 2nd.

Scorers

Tipperary - M. Keating 2-1, P. Byrnes 2-0 and R. Ryan 2-0; F. Loughnane 0-4, J. Flanagan 1-1, M. Roche 1-0, S. Hogan 0-1.

Limerick - R. Bennis 1-4, E. Cregan 1-3, E. Grimes 1-2, B. Hartigan 1-0, S. Foley 0-2, P. Hartigan 0-1.

Teams

Tipperary - P. O'Sullivan; L. King, J. Gleeson, J. Kelly; T. O'Connor, N. Lane, M. Esmonde; M. Roche, S. Hogan; F. Loughnane, J. Flanagan, N. Dwyer; P. Byrne, R. Ryan and M. Keating. Subs: M. Coen for O'Dwyer and J. O'Donoghue for Hogan.

Limerick - J. Hogan; A. O'Brien, J. Allis, D. Manning; C. Campbell, P. Hartigan, J. O'Donnell; S. Foley, B. Hartigan; R. Bennis, M. Graham, E. Grimes; F. Nolan, D. Flynn, E. Cregan. Subs: J. O'Brien for Campbell (injured), P. Bennis for O'Donnell and S. Bourke for Cregan (injured).

Referee - E. Murray (Wicklow/London).

Telefís Éireann

3.05—GAELIC GAMES FROM LONDON: At 3.15 Tipperary play Limerick — who are making their first appearance at Wembley at 4.45 football champions Offaly meet Cork— whose football team has not played in London before (C).
6.00—THE ANGELUS
6.01—NEWS HEADLINES
6.06—THE BIG TOP
6.15—GETTING TOGETHER
6.45—THE ARTIST AS A REPORTER: Franklin McMahon is the artist in this illustrated discussion of the artist as a reporter, and of the differences between art and photography.
7.15—AN NUACHT
7.20—WEEKEND SPORT
7.30—THE BLASKET ISLANDS: A present-day film portrait of the island group off the Kerry coast immortalised in Muiris O Suilleabhain's "Twenty Years A-Growing". The narration is by the writer's son, Eoin. Traditional music played by Eoin O Suilleabhain and Mike Townsend.
7.45—SATURDAY CINEMA: The Phantom of the Opera. Nelson Eddy and Susanna Foster star in a re-make of the classic silent film horror story of a crazed human who conducts a murderous vendetta against the management of the Paris Opera House.
9.30—NEWS
9.45—THE LATE LATE SHOW
11.15 (approx.)—NEWS HEADLINES

Teilifís Éireann programmes for 27 May 1972.

HURLING 3.15 p.m.

LIMERICK
Green and White

LIMERICK	Goals	Points
1st Half		
2nd Half		
TOTAL		

1. J. HOGAN

2. T. O'BRIEN 3. P. HARTIGAN 4. J. ALLIS

5. P. BARRATT 6. J. O'BRIEN 7. M. GRAHAM

8. J. FOLEY 9. B. HARTIGAN

10. S. HOLAN 11. R. BENNIS 12. E. GRIMES

13. D. FLYNN 14. W. MOORE 15. E. CREGAN

Subs: J. Frost, C. Campbell, J. O'Donnell, S. Burke, M. Cregan.

Versus

TIPPERARY
Blue and Gold

TIPPERARY	Goals	Points
1st Half		
2nd Half		
TOTAL		

1. P. O'SULLIVAN

2. M. LANE 3. J. KELLY 4. J. GLEESON

5. M. ESMOND 6. T. CONNOR 7. L. GAYNOR

8. M. ROCHE 9. P. J. RYAN

10. F. LOUGHNANE 11. J. FLANAGAN 12. M. DWYER

13. P. BYRNE 14. R. RYAN 15. M. KEATING

Subs: J. O. Donoghue, D. Ryan, S. Hogan, J. Ryan, J. Fogarty.

Referee: E. MURRAY

Hurling teams for the 1972 Wembley Games.

1973 Keeping the Dream Alive

Jack Kirby, club president, presents appreciation awards to the Claughaun players on the Limerick team that won the National League in 1971. They are Mick Cregan, Jim Hogan, Michael Graham and Eamonn Cregan watched by Joe Power, the Club Chairman.

1973 Keeping the Dream Alive

Clare Began in a Flurry as ... Limerick Deservedly Trounced and Had No Answer

(Limerick Leader, 3 July 1972)

Clare 3-11
Limerick 2-10

By Cormac Liddy

It's not to win but to take part in . . . the Olympic motto certainly seems to be that adopted by Limerick senior hurlers. This hammering by Clare at their own dearly beloved Cusack Park in Ennis was as thorough a carving up of Limerick championship hopes as one could hate to see and, if anything, the final result is a trifle flattering to the losers. If nothing else, this convincing pounding has set the scene for inquests galore by the saddened thousands who went in anticipation of a hard game but a sweet victory.

Question number one must be directed to team manager, Rory Kiely. If Richie Bennis was not fit enough to play because of a right hand injury at the start, how in the name of goodness was he fit enough to be brought into the game before even ten minutes had elapsed? To have brought him in was to my mind the tactical error of years. It was grossly unfair to the player himself who, naturally, could not achieve anything and then to have thrown him in on top of the superman that was Gus Lohan at that time was even more unjust. By bringing in the injured Bennis I think Limerick showed their hand at that early stage for what could a then rampant Clare but say . . . this crowd haven't even a fit substitute for the forward line.

Why the fit-as-a-fiddle Liam Lawlor or the equally well prepared Seán Bourke were not called into action after Mick Cregan's injury is something I will never understand even the previous week Leonard Enright, substitute goalie for this game had been an outstanding success when a mid-fielder for the under-21s. He, too, could have been introduced or, for that matter, Christy Campbell with his forceful style and tactics might have been the best bet of all. Bennis has my sympathies. To his credit, he tried as hard as he could but I doubt if there was a hurler in the land who could have upset the inspired Lohan during that half-hour of magic for Clare. His display was one of ruthless efficiency as he belted Limerick into subjection any time they got into that area of operation.

Memories

Now all that we are left with are memories of golden days we can only compare the display of Lohan with that given by Michael Graham in his superb first-half League final display against Cork. With Lohan, spiritedly backed up by Jackie O'Gorman and D.J. Meehan in the half-line, curbing and blunting the Limerick half line. Other changes were made which saw the shunting of Bennis into the left-hand corner and Eamonn Cregan coming to centre-forward in an effort to blunt Lohan. He met with equally as little success and then Michael Graham was involved in a brief switch as Cregan began to move backwards to try and get the front line into operation. This again met with little success and while all the time Limerick were trying to get moving, Clare had stormed into top gear from the very start.

Just as Danny McAlinden had done some days previously in his big battle with Jack Bodell so too did Clare . . . hit hard, early, and when I say that, let me hasten to add that they struck very hard, but it was all equally fairly and well within the rules and there was nothing suspect about the ferocity and speed with which they began their carving up process.

Stunned

By two minutes Limerick were stunned. Noel Casey whipped in a goal and before the Limerick defenders could sort out who was responsible Jimmy McNamara had rammed in a second and after four minutes Clare were in the driver's seat in a big way.

Not unnaturally these scores bustled and upset Limerick and proved of tremendous advantage to Clare who, if they harboured any doubts about losing, had them by now dispelled. A side that, no matter what they may try to say, must have gone out more in hope than in confidence had by now the spur they needed to convince them that a big shock could be brought about.

Those of the huge crowd with Limerick hopes who could do so could only cast their minds back to that sickening day in 1953 which I reproduced last week-end. Those who kept their cool cast their minds back to that terrible day as Clare continued to dominate.

Injury

In seven minutes came Mick Cregan's injury and the call-up of the injured Bennis. Gus Lohan pointed a Clare free after nine minutes and then out came Eamonn Cregan in the switch with Bennis.

But all this was to no avail and with the Clare half-back line still clearly masters of proceedings Limerick tottered at the back and all over the field. Jimmy Cullinan hit over another point after ten minutes to leave Clare in front 2-2 to nil.

Then Limerick hearts fluttered ... an actual attack of note occurred and Séamus Durack in the Clare goal had to make the first of his many fine saves as he prevented Willie Moore from opening Limerick's scoring account.

After 14 minutes I saw Graham at top of the left and Bennis at right half-forward but switch as they might there was precious little advancing to be done against the Clare defence.

But the light was, in a very minor way, beginning to break through the darkness for Limerick. Jim O'Donnell was by now in the second quarter - getting a grip on Jimmy Cullinan and Pat Hartigan, too, was coming more into the game while at the back Eamonn (Ned) Rea was settling down and so too was Manning after that terrible start. Jim O'Brien was operating in the right corner but if he was achieving a great deal it was not to any great degree noticeable and every Clare attack in their non-stop wave of assaults was fraught with danger from a Limerick viewpoint.

Limerick had been awarded a free in the sixteenth minute which Grimes took without success. This further convinced me of the state of Bennis. If the regular free taker was not able to take this one - he subsequently took over his usual role - how in the name of all that was holy could he expect to win hard tussles from actual play?

What A Score?

Still the Claremen onward went and Noel Casey made it 2-3 to nil after seventeen minutes but two minutes later Andy Dunworth, in virtually the first chance to come his way, hit over a lovely point for Limerick. This, we thought, would get Limerick going but it was not to be. Four minutes later Timmy Ryan hit over what was to be the first of his six Clare points from frees. Willie Moore had a second Limerick point, and in a lively Limerick attack Durack saved but a free in was awarded and this time Bennis pointed.

But this was negatived just before the interval when Ryan had a similar Clare score from a 21 yard free to leave it Clare. 2-5; Limerick 0-3 at half-time.

During the break the huge Limerick crowd could only ponder and hope that just as Cork had done the previous week so, too, might the League champions of last season do on this occasion.

It had been a first half in which Limerick were well and truly out-hurled, outpaced and out-manoeuvred by a Clare side that had everything going for them. Their supporters were naturally thrilled with such a great thirty minutes, and when referee, Frank Murphy of Cork - having criticised him in the past, let me pay tribute to him for his fine handling of the game this time - called up the mid-fielders to renew hostilities, it was abundantly clear that the first ten minutes of the re-start would be vital.

Hope

Limerick's hopes prospered when Grimes hit a wide . . . at least proceedings were happening at the Clare end, and then after two minutes Dunworth had another Limerick point, and we thought a start was on its way to whittling down the arrears. Tim Ryan pointed a Clare free after six minutes, and sixty seconds later Willie Moore had a point from play for Limerick, but again Tim Ryan had a Clare point, followed by Limerick wides from O'Donnell (a '70) and Grimes.

Bennis pointed a free, after fourteen minutes, but by now time was beginning to tell on Limerick, and at the three-quarter stage it was Clare 2-8 to Limerick's half a dozen points.

By now it was clear that Limerick were for the hammer. Casey pointed for Clare after eighteen minutes but Bernie Hartigan had a grand point for Limerick from a side-line cut.

Changes

During the interval Clare - in another of their wise moves - switched Cullinan and Ryan and then, with about twelve minutes remaining, Mick Kilmartin was brought in for Casey.

It was as good as ended for Limerick eight minutes from the end. Michael Keane slammed in a Clare goal, to leave it 3-10 to a miserable seven points.

Whether it was that Clare eased off or Limerick improved I do not know but in the concluding stages Limerick got in for four well-taken scores. Bernie Hartigan got a point. Dunworth another - his third of the hour. Grimes got a terrific goal from 30 yards when he dispossessed a Clare back, but Limerick had the last score - a typically opportunist goal by Eamonn Cregan.

Equal

It is ironic that Limerick scored 2-5 in the second half, just as Clare had done in the first half, but the home side did appreciably better throughout the hour.

Criticise

It would be no trouble to castigate individually. I won't do so for this was not a day which allows for such. Those on the field tried their hardest. They were well and truly beaten in defence and attack.

Suffice it to say that just as Roberto was whipped, so too were Limerick. Jim O'Donnell and Pat Hartigan did do well deep into the second half when their efforts helped halt Clare from a landslide but could do nothing to get an inept and in-efficient Limerick attack to get the necessary goals.

Jim Hogan did not do badly in goal, but I could not give any other Limerick credits.

Lohan, O'Gorman - over the hour the best player of all - DJ Meehan, Vince Loftus and Séamus Durack were Clare defensive stars, and the other two were little behind.

Pat O'Leary and Mick Moroney had the better of the mid-field clashes with Seán Foley and Bernie Hartigan, and in an attack that were not as brilliant as they might think in their hour of glory, Jimmy Cullinan and Tim Ryan were the pick, with Noel Casey not far behind.

Sad

It was a sad hour for Limerick, who can have no excuses. Granted, playing at Cusack Park did not help them, but I doubt if even at Thurles would Limerick have been able to better of this all-action, full of spirit Clare side.

Now is the time for Limerick's backroom boys, selectors and team manager, etc., to sit down and take stock. Sixteen months ago it was possible to win a League title. Now nothing is left but the future. Get down and draw up a plan of campaign for there is, I believe, sufficient talent in the county to still regain the glories of old.

Scorers

Clare - T. Ryan 0-7, (0-6 from frees); N. Casey 1-2; M. Keane and J. McNamara 1-0; J. Cullinan 0-1 and G. Lohan 0-1 from ('70).

Limerick - A. Dunworth and B. Hartigan 0-3; E. Cregan and E. Grimes 1-0; R. Bennis (0-2 from frees) and W. Moore 0-2.

Teams

Clare - S. Durack; V. Loftus, J. Power, P. Moloney; D.J. Meehan, G. Lohan, J. O'Gorman; P. O'Leary, M. Moroney; J. Cullinan, N. Casey, T. Ryan; J. McNamara, M. Keane, P. McNamara. Sub: M. Kilmartin for Casey (injured, 52nd minute).

Limerick - J. Hogan; J. O'Brien, D Manning, E. Rea; T. O'Brien, P. Hartigan, J O'Donnell; S. Foley, B. Hartigan; M. Graham, M. Cregan, E. Grimes; A. Dunworth, W. Moore. E. Cregan. Sub: R. Bennis for M. Cregan (injured, 10th minute).

Referee - F. Murphy (Cork).

Power Topped Poll
(Limerick Leader, 2 September 1972)
Three new senior hurling selectors

Two of the men who helped Limerick win their last All Ireland senior hurling championship title back in 1940, Jackie Power and Dr Dick Stokes, have been elected to the five-member senior hurling selection committee for the new season.

Jim Quaid is another new member of the five, and Denis Barrett, Bruff, and Seán Cunningham, Doon, are two of the outgoing four who sought re-election to have retained their places.

Last year's team manager and County Board chairmen, Mr Rory Kiely, did not seek re-election.

Team manager, Jackie Power.

Fourteen candidates contested the five selectorial positions. The election was held under the proportional representation system, with Mr Jack Quinlivan as returning officer. The transfer of votes was a most interesting operation. For the past two seasons Jackie Power has been coach to the county team. His efforts were obviously appreciated by clubs throughout the county for he topped the poll and received thirteen votes. Popular Denis Barrett of Bruff got nine votes and was second in the poll and then followed Dr Stokes and Jim Quaid of Feohanagh each of whom obtained seven votes. Then followed Seán Cunningham, Doon (6); Mick McDonnell, Croom (5); and Declan Moylan, Claughaun (5). Eventually it boiled down to Mr Cunningham ousting Mr McDonnell (outgoing) for the final place, with Mr Moylan being eliminated by lot in the previous count.

The following is how the delegates voted:

Jackie Power 13 - Denis Barrett 9 - Dick Stokes 7 - Jim Quaid 7 - Seán Cunningham 6 - Declan Moylan 5 Mick McDonnell (outgoing) 5 - Dan Hickey (outgoing) 5 - Matt O'Connell 3 - Fr J. Neville 3 - Kevin Lynch 3 Paddy Shanahan 2 - J.P. Ryan 1 - Pat Clohessy 1.

1973 Selectors Seán Cunningham, Denis Barrett and Jim Quaid watch the Limerick hurlers in training.

FOOTBALL

Only six contested the five places on the senior football selection committee. Here a selector of long standing, Mr Frank Sullivan of Claughaun was the one to lose his place. The five elected were: Messrs. J. Collins, Fr Casey's, Abbeyfeale; J. Doran, Monaleen; P.J. Cussen, Galbally; Tom Downes, Askeaton; and Tom Fitzgibbon Snr., Oola.

MANAGERS

The five selectors in each grade must now elect a team manager for each side from amongst the five.

Jackie Power team manager
(Limerick Leader, 13 September 1972)

At a meeting of the recently elected Limerick senior hurling selection committee, Mr Jackie Power was appointed team manager for the coming year. A member of the last Limerick team to win the All Ireland back in 1940, Mr Power was coach to the team which won the National League two seasons ago.

The selectors will meet again on Sunday evening next to drew up a panel of players to go into training in preparation for the first National League game which will be at the Gaelic Grounds against Clare on October 8th. This should afford Limerick an ample opportunity of gaining revenge for the shock Munster championship defeat suffered at Cusack Park on July 2nd.

Dr Dick Stokes (selector), Jackie Power (coach), two of the 1940 All Ireland team, and Séamus Horgan pictured at a training session.

Liberties Champions after 82 Years
(Limerick Leader, 11 December 1972)
Grimes and Hartigan were Magnificent

By Seán Murphy

South Liberties 4-8
Patrickswell 1-5

Unprecedented scenes of enthusiasm were witnessed at Gaelic Grounds on Sunday when South Liberties, appearing in their third final in five years, eventually captured that elusive Limerick Senior Hurling Championship when with tidal wave ferocity they crushed the challenge of former king-pins Patrickswell in a rip-roaring game in near Arctic conditions on the scoreline - 4-8 to 1-5. It was Liberties first crown in this grade since 1890 - 82 years ago.

Those advocates of a "closed season" in hurling or at least an earlier finish to the Blue Riband of the domestic scene were certainly given much food for thought in Sunday's encounter. The weather clerk was severe to the extreme! A gale-force breeze blew with rigorous force from the windswept hills of the Windy Gap and the accompanying showers of rain, hail and sleet made it a test of stamina and dedication. The gale was so strong in the opening moiety that even the team names on the scoreboard were blown away in the direction of Greystones.

Amazing

But both sides defied the conditions in amazing fashion and served up hurling the grandeur and honest endeavour of which warmed the hearts of the chilled spectators. Both teams went at it hammer and tongs from the throw-in and the honest tenacity of the many exhilarating hip-to-hip confrontations made this set-to one of the greatest hurling deciders in the history of Limerick's coveted senior championship.

From the outset it became increasingly evident that the result of the game would hinge around a battle of tactics. In the prevailing conditions ground hurling and short-passing were essential. The Liberties dished up these ingredients in abundance and coupled with their wholehearted fire and dash they laid the foundation for their well-merited and astutely-executed victory.

The game was won and lost in the opening half when South Liberties played with the aid of the elements into the city goal. Although Richie Bennis opened the scoring for the 'Well in the first minute, South Liberties were soon on the trail of building up a substantial lead before playing into the teeth of the bowling gale on change-over.

McKenna Goal

They opened their scoring when Offaly inter-county player, Joe McKenna, lobbed a shot from 40 yards to the 'Well net in the 5th minute and two minutes later Éamon Grimes pointed a free. The 'Well enjoyed a period of supremacy at this juncture, but found the tricky breeze a difficult proposition, although with points from Richie Bennis (9th minute free) and another from play by Liam Foley in the 10th minute, they trailed by only a single point - 1-1 to 0-3 - at this stage. However, Liberties began to fire on all cylinders and started to assert their superiority in all sectors with their first-time no-nonsense hurling.

The goal that put them on the high road to victory came in sensational fashion in the 11th minute. Hero of the hour, Éamon Grimes, tore through the 'Well defence, but parted to Mike Shanahan, who planted the sliothar in the net for a great goal.

Great Points

Points from Éamon Grimes (13th minute free) and two longer range beauties from Joe McKenna put Liberties in front 2-4 to 0-3 mid-way through the first half. The 'Well were pegged further into arrears in the 17th minute after another dazzling Liberties forward movement. Denis O'Sullivan weaved his way goalwards, but when his way was blocked, he slickly passed to Wally O'Donoghue, who sent a dazzling shot to the rigging for a picture goal.

The 'Well struggled against all odds, and goalkeeper, Mike Lundon, was forced to make one of his many good saves in the 20th minute, However, Liberties continued to force the pace, but over-anxiousness in the forward line cost them many scores, although the scarred quagmire in the goalmouth did not help matters either. A goal seemed certain in the 23rd minute, when Joe McKenna placed Wally O'Donoghue for a rasper from close range, but Jimmy Shields deflected it for a 70 which was subsequently saved.

Tom Ryan pointed from play for South Liberties in the 24th minute, and although they enjoyed territorial advantage, they failed to transfer their dominance into scores. Their only other flag in the first half was raised in the 29th minute from a 70 by Mickey Butler. And so the scoreboard read: South Liberties, 3-6; Patrickswell, 0-3 at half-time.

Was Lead Big Enough?

As the Limerick Girls Pipe Band, resplendent in their new attire, tried to raise our sagging temperature with martial airs at the break, the size of Liberties lead was also a topic of discussion, and the majority view was that it was "hardly big enough," taking the elements into consideration. Bolstered by the strong wind, the 'Well resumed with high hopes of success. But their aspirations were rudely shattered with severe pressure from the Liberties.

Walter O'Donoghue tore lanes through the 'Well rearguard, but his effort was expertly saved by Jimmy Shields at the expense of a 70 in the opening minute. In the 3rd minute the real life-saver for Liberties was registered in snap fashion.

Walter O'Donoghue gained possession on the right wing, centred to Denis O'Sullivan, whose speculative shot into the square was flashed to the net by Eamonn Dooley, and even at this stage Liberties title was as good as assured. With Seán Foley and Leonard Enright gaining supremacy at mid-field Patrickswell tried valiantly to reduce the deficit but found the all-round composure of Liberties an impregnable barrier.

Spectacular

In the 6th minute Richie Bennis was wide from a free and three minutes later the usually accurate Bennis tried desperately for a goal but Mike Lundon saved and Bennis shot the rebound wide. In the 13th minute Mike Lundon in the 'Liberties goal, drew rounds of applause when with a spectacular dive that would do justice to Gordon Banks he pushed a pile-driver around the upright for a 70 which Tony O'Brien shot wide. In the 14th minute Richie Bennis raised hopes of a 'Well revival when after being fouled he crashed the resultant 40 yds free to net and then grabbed the puck-out and returned it between the posts for a flaming point. Bennis tried once more to goal a free in the 17th minute but a rock-like defence stopped this shot and Bennis hooked the rebound wide.

In the 25th minute Richie Bennis broke a 9 minute spell when he pointed a free but the Liberties finished in a blaze of glory. Éamon Grimes pointed a free in the 28th minute and a minute before the final whistle Tom Ryan closed the scoring and sealed the issue for Liberties who thus bridged an 82 year gap.

Valiant

South Liberties won for themselves many new friends with this valiant display in terrible conditions. It was essentially a team success achieved by an unerring goalie, a rock-like rearguard, a flawless mid-field pairing and an impeccable forward sextet, who tossed the ball about with amazing accuracy and were always capable of notching scores when needed. However a few players stand out in my memory as the heroes of this long overdue success. Number one is undoubtedly Éamon Grimes who really played a captain's part, a performance on a par with his balmiest days with Limerick CBS in their Harty Cup bonanza in the mid-sixties. The blonde-bombshell was here, there and everywhere. The mercurial Grimes covered himself with absolute glory, and his crisp striking, daring thrusts and general leadership.

Pat Hartigan was once again monarch of all he surveyed on the fringe of the square with a flawless display of fielding balls and lengthy clearances. He marshalled the defence, all of whom were undisputed heroes in that crucial second half - with the determination of a general and his all-round play always inspired his colleagues. Joe McKenna of Offaly fame fitted into the 'Liberties regime well and left a decided impact on the game. He was a constant threat to the 'Well and took his scores in masterly fashion. In spotlighting this trio, the deeds of the others cannot be overlooked. Mike Lundon had an unerring hour between the posts. Joe Grimes and Séamus Hartigan were two capable corner men.

Éamon Grimes accepts the John Daly Cup for South Liberties in 1972.

1973 Keeping the Dream Alive

The victorious 1972 South Liberties team (Pat Hartigan is missing as he was already togging out to play the proceeding National Football League game).

Strongest Sector

The half-back trio of Micky Grimes, Walter Shanahan and Mickey Butler were the strongest sector of the team for spirit and ability, with Butler again adding further to his growing reputation as a club hurler. Tom Ryan was a trojan for work, while Larry Grimes and Mike Shanahan were in top form throughout. Wally O'Donoghue was in classical mood in the top line of forwards and his cheeky ball jugglery and jinking runs always upset the opposing defence. Eamonn Dooley took his goal well and Denis O'Sullivan got through an amount of work in regal style. What of the 'Well … ? Very definitely it was not their day. They never displayed the fluent team-work for which they are noted, but to their credit they bowed out in a sporting and gracious manner. Tim Quaid, Phil Bennis, Richie Bennis, Tony O'Brien, Leonard Enright, Frankie Nolan, and Liam Mann strove manfully to stem the tide for the 'Well, but their task was insurmountable.

Scorers

South Liberties - J. McKenna 1-2; M. Shanahan, E. Dooley and W. O'Donoghue 1-0; E. Grimes 0-3; T. Ryan 0-2; M. Butler 0-1.

Patrickswell - R. Bennis 1-4; L. Foley 0-1.

Teams

South Liberties - M. Lundon; J. Grimes, P. Hartigan, S. Hartigan; M. Grimes, W. Shanahan, M. Butler; T. Ryan, E. Grimes; L. Grimes, J. McKenna, M Shanahan; E. Dooley, D. O'Sullivan, W. O'Donoghue.

Patrickswell - J. Shiels; P.J. O'Grady, T. Quaid, B. Nolan; P. Bennis, T. O'Brien, T. Bennis; R. Bennis, L. Enright; F. Nolan, S. Foley, L. Foley; C. Jeffers, L Mann, P. Bennis.

Referee - John Moloney (Tipperary).

Patrickswell Senior hurling team 1972 city champions and beaten county finalists.
Back Row: (L-R) Michael O'Connell, Richie Bennis, Mike Quaid, Noel Darcy, Micheal Sheehan, Seán Foley, Tim Quaid, Liam Mann, Leonard Enright, PJ O'Grady, Tom Bennis, Tony O'Brien, Phil Bennis and Paul Lynch.
Front Row: (L-R) Jimmy Shiels, Benny Nolan, Tony Foley, Liam Foley, Matthew Murray, Peter Bennis, Frankie Nolan, Christy Jeffers and Joe Lynch.

Tribute to Joe McGrath 1936-2012

Joe was renowned throughout Ireland as a legendary GAA man and strategist *par excellence* as well as an accomplished coach in hurling, camogie and gaelic football.

He held many coaching positions within the GAA including chairman of the National Coaching Committee. Former Cork secretary and chairman, Tom O'Sullivan described him as an extremely professional coach.

He guided his club, Blackrock, to County Hurling Championship victories in 1973, 1975, 1978 and 1979, and to All Ireland club successes in 1974 and 1979.

Joe was at the helm when Limerick beat Tipperary at the Cork Athletic Grounds in 1971 to win the National Hurling League title for the first time in 24 years.

In 1983, he coached the Cork senior footballers when they scored a dramatic victory in the Munster final in Pairc Uí Chaoimh, denying Kerry and Mick O'Dwyer a record ninth consecutive provincial title.

Five years later, the Down native coached Cork to the All Ireland U-21 hurling title, defeating Kilkenny 4-11 to 1-5 in the final.

Credited with revolutionising training sessions, he was also involved in setting up coaching structures at national level and was one of the first full-time coaching officers in Cork. This labour of love Joe continued until his health deteriorated last year.

He had a huge impact on GAA and coaching in Munster throughout his lifetime and his legacy lives on in the form of the McGrath Cup which sees the inter-county and Third Level clubs of Munster compete with each other in a bid to promote gaelic football in Munster.

(HoganStand.com, 16 January 2013)

Please bring this Report to Convention

Cumann Luith Chleas Gael

COISDE CO. LUIMNI

Limerick Co. Board
CONVENTION
1973

AT PARKWAY MOTEL

Sunday, 28th Jan., 1973

AT 1.30 O'CLOCK SHARP

Secretary's Report
Statement of Accounts & Balance Sheet
Nominations, Motions, etc.

1973 Limerick GAA Convention Secretary's Report
(28 January 1973)

INTER-COUNTY ACTIVITIES

The year gone by was not a very successful one in the inter-county sphere. Our hurlers, starting the second half of the League with full points, suffered defeats at the hands of Cork and Tipperary but qualified for the decider when defeating Kilkenny in the semi-final. After a very poor first half we stormed back in the second moiety but had to concede victory to old rivals Cork. An indifferent display in the first round of the championship saw our exit at the hands of Clare. Two wins and a draw in the current League from four games leaves us reasonably well placed.

The displays of our Football teams are far from impressive. Granted we had to line out in the current League without some of our key players but our performances in the championship over the past few seasons are not very encouraging. We must face up to it and ask ourselves if we should be regraded. Our Football Committee should give serious thought to the matter.

Kerry were our masters in Intermediate Hurling, Junior Football and Under 21 Football and Waterford ended our hopes in Senior and Minor Football, all first round defeats. Our Under 21 Hurlers proved too good for Kerry in the opening round but lost to Tipperary in the semi-final. In Minor Hurling we qualified for the final with a good win over Clare. A good preparation proved fruitless against a very strong Cork side.

Divisional Boards report a successful year's work and deserve our congratulations. A word of praise also to the various Bord na nÓg and Schools Boards. Following the suspension of a school from competitions in the City Primary Schools Board and subsequent complaint by that school, the Board Officers met Officers of the Schools Board and representatives of the school concerned and are at present examining the working of the Schools Board.

Sincere thanks to our Referees who never failed to answer the call. Our thanks also to the Referees from outside the county who were always willing to assist when requested. It is regrettable, however, that we had to seek outside assistance on so many occasions. A Referees' Association was, with the approval of the Board, formed during the year. A good start was made but support was lacking in some areas and the early promise never materialised. Maybe a fresh start could be made and every support given to those willing to recruit and train the referees of tomorrow. Congratulations to Brother Perkins and his Committee on their wonderful work and successes in the Mini-Olympic Games.

Our congratulations also to the Handball and camogie Boards on their great work and again to the latter on their Munster championship success.

Another link with the great sides of the thirties was broken during the year with the passing of Ned Cregan. Also called to his reward was the long serving Fedamore secretary Tommie Fitzgerald. To their relatives and to all who suffered bereavement we offer our deepest sympathy.

Ar dheis Dé go raibh a h-anama go léir. Holy Mass will be offered for the happy repose of the souls of departed members in St. John's Cathedral at 11:00AM on Convention Day. Mo bhuidheachas le gach duine a cabhruig liom i rith na bliana, an t-Ard-Stiurthoir, Runai Comhairle na Mumhan, Comh-Oifigi, Runaithe Bhuird agus Cumainn, Lucht na paipéir nuachta agus na daoine conghanta uile.

Rath Dé oraibh go léir.

Mise,

TOMÁS Ó BEOLÁIN

CHAPTER 2
1972-73
NATIONAL HURLING LEAGUE (i)

BEFORE CHRISTMAS

1973 Keeping the Dream Alive

Limerick competed in the National Hurling League (NHL) Division 1A for the 1972-73 season with the following teams: Kilkenny, Tipperary, Wexford, Clare, Cork, Galway and Offaly. Division 1B featured Waterford, Kildare, Dublin, Antrim, Laois, Westmeath, Wicklow and Kerry. There are no programmes known for any of these pre-Christmas games, but mock-ups are provided in this chapter. At the time the league was split across two years, as it would be every year up to 1995-96 games would be played before and after Christmas. The first official single year national league was 1997, which Limerick won. All game reports in this chapter are taken from the following Monday evening's Limerick Leader. The "Penny" Leader did actually cost 1p (new) in 1973. These reports were mostly bylined by Charlie Mulqueen. Reports were usually written out in longhand and then either dictated directly to the typesetter, or delivered to the Limerick Leader offices that evening. The newspaper was printed overnight on site and distributed to all local newsagents early the next morning. It was an era before pervasive internet and social media existed.

Limerick's newly elected selectors were Jackie Power (Ahane/Austin Stacks), Dick Stokes (Pallasgreen), Denis Barrett (Bruff), Jim Quaid (Feohanagh) and Séan Cunningham (Doon), with Mick Cregan (Claughaun) as the trainer. Vincent O'Connor was both masseur and medic. Jackie Power was elected as team manager by the other selectors, albeit this term was not much used in subsequent reports and had little additional responsibilities. Jackie Power had served as trainer of the team in previous years. Meals were taken by the team after training in the Shannon Arms on Henry Street. Tommy Casey and a number of others continued to drive the players to game related engagements. The 1973 county board executive comprised of Rory Kiely (chairman), Tom Boland (secretary) and Declan Moylan (treasurer). Declan acted as informal liaison officer for the senior hurling team.

The 1972-73 NHL season started with a draw against Clare in the pre-Mackey Stand Gaelic Grounds. Cars were still scarce enough, and most big grounds were located close to large train stations, with many supporters continuing to travel to games by this convenient mode of transport. On the weekend of the game, a shock announcement was made regarding the proposed closure of Clover Meats in Mulgrave Street, subsequently partially rescinded. There were 300 people employed in that factory at the time. Limerick played Kilkenny in Nowlan Park in round two and went down to a surprising loss against what was described as a "makeshift" local team. It was the only game that Richie Bennis played during this league and championship season where he was held scoreless. There were conflicting lists of Limerick scorers in the newspapers afterwards, something that will never be resolved. Crescent Comprehensive School was officially opened the day after this game.

Galway were next on the schedule and a facile win was secured against a very weak combination. The Tribesmen were missing John Connolly, their talisman, who was away in the US at the time. He would be unavailable for much of 1973 also. Andy Dunworth scored 2-2, while Richie was back on the scoreline with points from play, a '70 (an unusual feat at the time), a free and a sideline (even rarer than a '70). The Irish Independent did not bother with a report from the game, just printing the result. Offaly were next up in early December in the Gaelic Grounds, where all home games were played at the time – Kilmallock was not used for any NHL games between 1966 and 1977. A narrow win resulted. Michael Slattery of Clare refereed this game, not the last time he features hereabouts. Joe McKenna played centre forward for Offaly and was held scoreless before being replaced. Joe made his debut for Offaly in late 1970 and quickly established himself as a regular fixture on an emerging Offaly team, a team that had been slightly unlucky in the 1969 Leinster Hurling Final against Kilkenny. Cork and Tipperary participated in a "disgraceful" game in Thurles on the same day, with no punches pulled in the reports printed in the three national newspapers the following day. A number of players received long suspensions following this game. Limerick had two wins, one draw and one loss from their first four games with three group games to be played after Christmas. The Wexford game was scheduled to be played on 19 November but was postponed due to a request from the Limerick county board related to delays in the running of the county senior championship. Both semi-finals went to second games, one a replay, the other a refixture.

NATIONAL HURLING LEAGUE
SUNDAY 8th OCT. 72
AT 3 P.M.

LUIMNEACH

v

An Clár

Clár Oifigiúil

REITEOIR : F. MURPHY

LUACH   5P

SHANNON PRINTING CO. LTD

*Imagined programme cover in the absence of original archive material

Thrilling Draw At Gaelic Grounds
(Limerick Leader, 9 October 1972)
Late Richie Bennis Goal Saves Limerick
Defensive Slips Could Have Been Fatal

By Charlie Mulqueen

Limerick 3-8
Clare 4-5

BENNIS STEALS A POINT

Stirring stuff, indeed. Limerick and Clare served up a genuinely exciting and entertaining National League tie at the Gaelic Grounds on Sunday on a pitch that was in no way suited to the finer points of hurling. Heavy rain before the start which lasted through the first half, had the ground like a skating rink, but the fervour and courage of the competitors tempted one to overlook the inevitable mistakes and errors, and instead glory in a fast, rip-roaring game in which Limerick eventually snatched a draw when a Clare victory looked all sewn up. Limerick had to rely on a goal from a Richie Bennis 21-yard free with the second last puck of the game to force a draw, but I hope I won't be accused of parochialism when offering the view that Limerick did not deserve to lose on the run of play. However, had defeat been their lot, they would have had only themselves, to blame, and those shrewd judges, Dr Dick Stokes and Jackie Power, must have been appalled at the defensive lapses that allowed Clare in for each of their four goals.

All could indeed, and should have been, prevented, but Jim Hogan was given scant cover by a full-back line that never settled down and rarely got to grips with their opposite numbers. Particularly disappointing was big Pat Hartigan, who was left floundering far too frequently for comfort by Clare's substitute full-forward, Martin Cummane. Cummane was introduced to the game after only eight minutes, when his Killnamona team-mate, Michael Keane, was obliged to leave the field with a nasty head injury, and he emerged as one of the great personalities of the game. There is little doubt that Noel Casey's would have travelled to the net in any case, but Cummane was on the spot to make certain for Clare's first and crucial goal.

Clare Ahead

This score came in the 15th minute and put Clare ahead by 1-0 to 0-2, Limerick's two early points having been scored by Richie Bennis, from a free, and Michael Graham. But Cummane's goal exposed Limerick's defensive limitations, and the home citadel was to come crashing down twice more before the interval. The second goal came in the 20th minute when Casey shot across goal, Pat McNamara's drive was brilliantly saved by Jim Hogan, who was, however, powerless when Cummane flicked home the rebound. Where, one might well ask, was the full-back line? Immediately, Limerick hit back with a class goal by Willie Moore after Éamon Grimes and Eamonn Cregan had made the running, and they also had points from Grimes and Bennis from a free, so the situation at that stage wasn't too bad . . . Clare 2-2, Limerick 1-4, a difference of only one point. But Clare's goal scoring exploits weren't over yet. First Jim McNamara pointed a free and then Pat McNamara flashed the ball to the net. A Cregan point helped, but Clare retired to the dressing rooms quite happy, leading by four points, 3-3 to 1-5.

Disaster

Further disaster struck five minutes into the second half. Jim McNamara shot hard and low from the right wing, but Hogan covered it splendidly. However, as he grabbed the ball, he was left uncovered and a Clare forward crashed into him. Hogan definitely gave ground, but got the ball clear. Then, however, the goal umpire waved the green flag, indicating that the goalkeeper and the ball had crossed the line. Jim himself thought that, while his body was over, the ball wasn't. But the umpire's decision was final, and a goal it was.

This left Limerick 7 points in arrears, and they could have been excused for feeling down-hearted. To their credit, however, they came back in style. Seán Foley towered over everyone in the centre of the field and now the Limerick attackers had plenty of the ball. This was one of Séamus Durack's good games, and he brought off superb saves from Bennis and Frankie Nolan to deny Limerick the goal they so badly needed, Still, they gradually dwindled away the deficit with two points from frees by Bennis and then a goal by the Patrickswell ace from a 30-yard free. Now, there was only a point in it, 4-3 to 2-8, and with fourteen minutes to go, Limerick were smiling again.

Woke Up

Clare's only second half score had been that fortuitous goal. Now they woke up again and sure enough, it was the amazing Cummane who set them on the right road. He banged over two glorious points in quick succession, and now the Banner County had a goal to spare.

The minutes ticked away, and Limerick's cause appeared lost as the match entered the final sixty seconds.

Then came the vital moment of this absorbing contest. Substitute Andy Dunworth weaved his way through. He couldn't find room to swing his stick, so was forced to palm his attempt at goal. This was comfortably saved by Durack, but to Clare's consternation, Dunworth had been needlessly fouled. A 21 yard free it was, and Richie Bennis once more came to Limerick's rescue. Although he appeared to slip as he raised the ball, his fast ground shot skidded into the net, and the final whistle sounded from the puck out.

Stupidly, some Clare followers attempted to get at referee Frank Murphy at the finish, but thankfully the only abuse he received was of the verbal nature, and the incident was of little consequence.

Equitable

So ended an exciting, interesting and entertaining match. I still believe that a draw was a fair and equitable result, though Limerick left things much too close for comfort.

As I have said, the defensive limitations were alarming. Jim Hogan made a number of fine saves, but the cover he was afforded was paper thin and consequently Clare grabbed some soft scores, just as they had done at Cusack Park in the championship. Though he did many fine things, Pat Hartigan had one of his poorer games, and the corner backs, were a disappointment. On the contrary, the half-back line acquitted itself well, with newcomer, Willie Conway, trying very hard and effecting some grand clearances.

Jim O'Donnell looked a polished centre-back, though perhaps he was a little over complacent on occasions, and Christy Campbell showed again what a great little fighter he is.

The star of the show, however, was midfielder, Seán Foley, who more than anyone else was responsible for Limerick's long stretch of supremacy in the second half. This was probably his best game in the Limerick jersey, and he certainly struck up a happy partnership with his Patrickswell club-mate, Leonard Enright.

Big Bennis Contribution

Richie Bennis was again Limerick's marksman, and his contribution of 2 goals and 4 points was a mighty impressive one. But all six scores came from frees and frankly the half-forward line, completed by Frankie Nolan and Éamon Grimes, wasn't very impressive, though they did indulge in some grand and attractive inter-passing that led directly to Willie Moore's goal.

Moore took his score well, but was otherwise relatively subdued. Eamonn Cregan roved out from his top of the left position in an effort to get the team moving, and did so to effect, but his Claughaun clubmate, Michael Graham, was eventually replaced by Andy Dunworth, who, of course, did the spadework for the equalising goal.

Brilliant Durack

In the corresponding game last year, Séamus Durack was a brilliant goalkeeper for Clare, but he couldn't prevent a pretty substantial beating. This time, he very nearly won the game, and two second half saves from Bennis and Nolan had the blue and yellow flags waving high! Jackie O'Gorman was magnificent at left-half, and Jimmy Cullinan and Michael Moroney were always dangerous in the half-forward line.

But with Gus Lohan almost disappearing from the scene in the second half, it was surprising that Moroney wasn't moved to midfield at some stage.

All the full-forward line were a menace but Martin Cummane will have especially fond memories of his first big game in a Clare jersey. His total of 2 goals and 2 points was some effort!

Scorers

Limerick - R. Bennis 2-4 (all frees); W. Moore 1-0; E. Cregan 0-2; E. Grimes and M. Graham 0-1.

Clare - M. Cummane 2-2; J. McNamara 1-3; P. McNamara 1-0.

Teams

Limerick - J. Hogan; P. Bennis, P. Hartigan, J, O'Brien; C. Campbell, J O'Donnell, W Conway, L. Enright, S. Foley; F. Nolan, R. Bennis, E. Grimes; M. Graham, W. Moore, E. Cregan. Sub: A. Dunworth for Graham.

Clare - S. Durack; J. Power, M. Considine. W. Meehan; N. McInerney. M. McKeogh, J. O'Gorman; G. Lohan, P. O'Leary; J. McNamara. M. Moroney, J. Cullinan, N. Casey, M. Keane, P. McNamara. Sub: M. Cummane for Keane.

Referee - Frank Murphy (Cork).

NATIONAL HURLING LEAGUE
SUNDAY 22nd OCT. 72
AT 3 P.M.

CILL CHAINNIGH

v

LUIMNEACH

Clar Oifigiúil

REITEOIR : S. O'REGAN

LUACH   5P

SHANNON PRINTING CO. LTD

Imagined programme cover in the absence of original archive material.

Limerick Eclipsed By Kilkenny
(Limerick Leader, 23 October 1972)

By "Leader" Representative

Limerick 4-2
Kilkenny 1-16

NATIONAL HURLING LEAGUE
LIMERICK ECLIPSED BY KILKENNY

Limerick Senior hurlers, National League specialists of the past three years, received a further jolt in their bid to remain in the top flight when failing to a makeshift Kilkenny team at Nowlan Park on Sunday when the host county had five points to spare on the scoreline 1-16 to 4-2. After their poor performance against Clare in the opening round, this game further emphasised that Limerick have their problems and these will have to be rectified if further defeats are to be avoided.

On paper this appeared to be a cake-walk for Limerick. But what a rude awakening the lethargic Shannonsiders got! Fielding only four of their All Ireland winning side - namely Pa Dillon, Liam O'Brien, Eamonn Morrissey and Kieran Purcell. Kilkenny handed out a hurling lesson to a Limerick side who lacked drive and purpose. Limerick lined out with Michael Graham at left-half back, and played with the advantage of a strong wind in the opening moiety. They dominated the early exchanges, but the forwards could not penetrate a resolute Kilkenny rearguard, and when they did, the resulting shots always went astray. Kilkenny showed a sample of their ability in the 5th minute when Kieran Purcell left the Limerick defence floundering when he shot a pile-driver from close range past reserve 'keeper Séamus Horgan.

Not Upset

However, Horgan was not upset by this reverse, and made a number of good saves to emerge from this clash as one of the few successful Limerick players. With minor captain, Brian Cody, in complete control at centre-back, and Liam O'Brien in rampant mood at midfield, Kilkenny continued to set the pace and led 1-4 to nil after 13 minutes. Limerick tried hard to come to grips with the situation, but poor striking, plus too much picking and poking, hampered their efforts. This was in complete contrast to Kilkenny whose lengthy striking and forceful ground hurling were a treat to watch. To the delight of the local fans, they continued to forge ahead, and after 27 minutes were ahead 1-7 without a reply. Limerick opened their scoring after 28 minutes, when Éamon Grimes pounced on a clearance after goalie Mick Moore had saved and flashed it to the net, and 60 seconds later, Willie Moore raised a white flag to leave the scoreboard reading, Kilkenny 1-7, Limerick 1-1, at the interval.

Hopes for a Limerick revival rose rapidly three minutes after resuming when Michael Graham, now operating at corner forward, lashed home a typical goal, but sad to relate the hopes died a sudden death! The Kilkenny half-forward trio, excellently led by Senan Cooke, were running amok, and with excellent service from Liam O'Brien, who also contributed some beautiful points, the homesters continued to stay in front, although Frankie Nolan, with a spectacular goal in the 8th minute, reduced the deficit to three points.

But the fluent hurling of Kilkenny continued to mesmerise Limerick, and the Black and Amber squad tapped over 4 points to which Limerick's only answer was a white flag from Frankie Nolan in the 20th minute.

Uncertain

Limerick's hitherto uncertain defence took on a new composure with the advent of Eamonn Rea midway through the second half. The Faughs man replaced Mossie Dowling (Killmallock), who had earlier substituted for Matt Grace. Rea took over the No. 2 spot, releasing Phil Bennis for half-back duty, and immediately the full-back line became rock-like. Even Pat Hartigan took on a new lease of life, grabbing high balls and making his usual long clearances. But the shake-up came too late, and the second string Kilkenny team coasted to an unexpected victory, although a goal by Éamon Grimes in the 22nd minute made the Limerick tally more respectable. The message for Limerick from this setback is clear-cut. Many of the stalwarts who spearheaded the revival over the past three years have gone over the top and must be replaced.

Reserve goalkeeper, Séamus Horgan, made a great debut and could not be faulted for the lone shot that beat him. In front of him, only Jim O'Brien redeemed himself. Pat Hartigan improved immensely in the final quarter, but Phil Bennis found Kieran Purcell a rare handful. The half-back line - although Jim O'Donnell got through an amount of good hurling - lacked cohesion and were always in trouble with the daring thrusts of their opponents. Seán Foley, after a tremendous first half, faded badly on resuming, and Leonard Enright ploughed a lone furrow with great success in the midfield sector.

Although Eamonn Cregan, Éamon Grimes and Frankie Nolan tried their hearts out, they achieved little of note, and the remainder of the forward division also played well below par. True enough, the selectors made switches, but all to no avail. Even some of the switches made were puzzling, with Richie Bennis sampling four forward positions, including the full-forward berth! One begins to wonder why Limerick name a substitute panel when reserves are so seldom introduced, and has Andy Dunworth been relegated to the subs. bench for good?

For Kilkenny, Mick Moore in goal, was most competent. Pa Dillon was sound at fullback, with excellent support from Jim Lynch and Eamonn Morrissey, who gave a five-star performance. Minor captain, Brian Cody, showed what an attacking half-back he can be with two wonderful points. Liam O'Brien was in complete command at midfield, while Senan Cooke, Kieran Purcell. Mick O'Dwyer and Brendan Phelan were most prominent in the attack.

Scorers

Limerick - E Grimes 2-0; F. Nolan 1-1; M. Graham 1-0; W. Moore 0-1.

Kilkenny - L. O'Brien 0-5; K. Purcell 1-2; S. Cooke 0-4; M. O'Dwyer and B. Cody 0-2; P. Phelan 0-1.

Teams

Limerick - S. Horgan; P. Bennis. P. Hartigan, J. O'Brien; C. Campbell, J. O'Donnell, M. Graham; S. Foley, L. Enright; F. Nolan, R. Bennis, E. Grimes; M. Grace, W. Moore, E. Cregan. Subs: M. Dowling for M. Grace, E. Rea for M. Dowling.

Kilkenny - M. Moore; W. Murphy, P. Dillon, J. Lynch; E. Morrissey, B. Cody, G. McCormack; L. O'Brien, P. Dowling; S. Cooke, B. Phelan, M. O'Dwyer; J. Dunphy, M. Murphy, K. Purcell. Subs: N. Morrissey for W. Murphy, J. O'Shea for M. Murphy

Referee - John O'Regan (Waterford).

NATIONAL HURLING LEAGUE
SUNDAY 5TH NOV. 72
AT 3 P.M.

LUIMNEACH
v
GAILLIMH

Clar Oifigiúil

REITEOIR : P. CRONIN

LUACH   5P

SHANNON PRINTING CO. LTD

*Imagined programme cover in the absence of original archive material.

Back On The Right Road, But … Limerick Never Extended By Hapless Galway
(Limerick Leader, 6 November 1972)
Still A Lot Of Work To Be Done

By Charlie Mulqueen

Limerick 2-18
Galway 1-1

Limerick never extended by hapless Galway
Still a Lot of Work to be Done

A victory by 24 points to 4 might give the impression that Limerick's much-changed side came up trumps and that recent disappointing displays can be forgotten. Such, however, is far from the case, for while Limerick were the complete masters of this terribly one-sided National League game against Galway at the Gaelic Grounds on Sunday, the opposition was so weak that one must reserve opinion on the new-look team until more worthwhile counties are encountered.

Galway won the All Ireland Under 21 title recently, and included five of that team, but so unskilled and even spiritless were they that they could manage only two flags in the entire hour. Galway had precious little to redeem them, so it is futile to heap praise on a Limerick side that itself plumbed the depths of their opponents on occasion and perpetuated inefficiencies that had their supporters in torment and anguish.

Some of the shooting by the forwards was too bad to be true and it was a common sight to see them bang their hurleys on the ground in disgust after sending yet another sitter wide of the posts. Of the front six, I can only speak well of Andy Dunworth, who scored two fine goals and also two points, although he, too, missed quite a few good chances. Éamon Grimes knocked over two beautiful points from the touchline, but was also guilty of many uncharacteristic errors, and the rest of the line was lifeless and unimaginative.

Bennis Shines

Richie Bennis is one who must be excluded from criticism for marksmanship. Operating from the strange position of midfield, he was not only well on top in the area in general play, but pointed seven shots, one from a '70, another from a 75 yard free and a third from a superb sideline puck. Leonard Enright made a very agile and suitable midfield partner, and in the half-back line, Tom Ryan signalled his return with a splendid fighting performance. Centre-back, Jim O'Donnell was one of the coolest and most polished hurlers on view, and on his left, Seán Foley, completed a very competent half-back line.

All the full-back line were adequate, but they were rarely tested, but goalkeeper, Séamus Horgan, plucky and skilful, looks like he could be the man to bring the reign of the great Jim Hogan to an end. He was confidence personified and didn't allow a heavy looking first-half knock to upset him. After their recent hammering by Cork, Galway came to the Gaelic Grounds full in the knowledge that victory was essential to restore prestige and morale. But this feeling can't have been conveyed to the players, who strolled lackadaisically and almost philosophically, to yet another drubbing. Keeper Seán Kelly, Pádraig Niland, Iggy Clarke, Padraig Fahy and substitute PJ Molloy did very well, but Galway were very, very bad and made the afternoon a disappointment for the many who wished to see Limerick fully extended.

One Way Traffic

Almost from the throw-in it apparent that Galway lacked the guile and class of the Limerickmen who without ever looking great were completely dominant. It took Galway 22 minutes to open their account by which stage Bennis had totalled three point, Grimes two and Foley one. After Fahy's well-taken point, Limerick dispelled any question of Western joy when Bennis, Dunworth and Grimes flashed over points before Dunworth flashed home a goal from a ball sent in by Enright. Bennis put over another point from a free to make it 1-10 to one point for Limerick. The second half continued in the same vein. After a boring scoreless gap of 12 minutes, points were flashed over by Dunworth, Frankie Nolan (2), Grimes (2), and Bennis from his sideline puck. Willie Moore had the ball in the net but was adjudged to be in the square, and the "goal" was disallowed. Galway briefly interrupted the Limerick flow when the ball flashed past Horgan after a clash of sticks between Hartigan and O'Connor, but back came the home side with Dunworth's second goal, a cracking shot from thirty yards, followed by two subsequent points from Eamonn Cregan and Bennis to make the final tally: Limerick, 2-18; Galway, 1-1,

Andy Dunworth sets off for the Galway goal with Willie Moore in support, during Limerick's National Hurling League win on Sunday.

Scorers

Limerick - A. Dunworth 2-2; R. Bennis 0-7 (0-1 free, 0-1 '70, 0-1 sideline); E. Grimes 0-5; F. Nolan 0-2; E. Cregan and S. Foley 0-1 each.

Galway - B. O'Connor 1-0; P. Fahy 0-1.

Teams

Limerick - S. Horgan; P. Hartigan, E. Rea, J. O'Brien; T. Ryan, J. O'Donnell, S. Foley; R. Bennis, L. Enright; F. Nolan, M. Graham, E. Grimes; A. Dunworth, W. Moore, E Cregan.

Galway - S. Kelly; L. Glynn, J. Fawl, L. Bohan; P. Niland, I. Clarke, J. Walsh; F. Burke, G. Glynn; T. Cahalan, T. Murphy, P. Fahy; G. Coone, B. O'Connor, P. Glynn. Subs: P.J. Molloy for Cahalan, D. Furey for Burke.

Referee - Paddy Cronin (Cork).

NATIONAL HURLING LEAGUE

SUNDAY 3rd DEC. 72

AT 3 P.M.

LUIMNEACH

v

UÍBH FHAILÍ

Clar Oifigiúil

REITEOIR : M. SLATTERY

LUACH 5P

SHANNON PRINTING CO. LTD

Imagined programme cover in the absence of original archive material.

No Joy For Limerick After Labouring Display
(Limerick Leader, 4 December 1972)
Two Late Goals Save Home Side

By Charlie Mulqueen

Limerick 3-8
Offaly 3-4

LIMERICK BEST Tough on Offaly

There can be no joy for Limerick after this labouring 3-8-to 3-4 victory over lowly Offaly at the Gaelic Grounds on Sunday. Indeed, Limerick played second fiddle for all too long against a visiting side that took what appeared to be an unbreakable grip on the proceedings midway through the second half. Happily for Limerick, and tragically for luckless Offaly, two late goals won the points for the home team who now enter the winter break in quite a useful league position.

On a heavy pitch, Limerick's more open style of hurling was naturally at a handicap, and their difficulties were added to within six minutes of the start, by which time Barney Moylan had banged in a goal and a point for the visitors. Éamon Grimes raised Limerick's first flag with a glorious left wing point, but further progress was slow, chiefly because of some atrocious shooting by the normally so accurate Richie Bennis, among others.

But it was Bennis, as so often in the past, who was to save this match for Limerick. After Andy Dunworth had sent over a long range point, Bennis put Limerick in front with a goal from a 21 yard free, and then followed points from Dunworth, Bennis and Moore in a period of total Limerick supremacy.

The game appeared to be taking its predictable course at this stage, and even a P.J. Conroy point on the stroke of half time wasn't unduly worrying. After all, Limerick led by 1-5 to 1-2, and a quick Bennis point on the resumption increased the margin to four.

Siesta

This score, however, appeared to signal "siesta-time" for Limerick, and they didn't score again until the 25th minute of the half. In the meantime, fighting Offaly took control, with Conroy and Moylan sandwiching points in between two great goals by left corner forward, Gerry Burke.

As Limerick struggled to get back into the picture, there was a semblance of panic about the side, but eventually, five minutes from time, Bennis came to the rescue once more. His first effort from a 21 yard free was saved, but an Offaly defender picked the ball off the ground and he got another chance.

Again, the defence got a stick to the ball, but it trickled into the left hand corner and Limerick were a point in front. Then tragedy really struck for Offaly; the wily Éamon Grimes floated in a centre from the left wing and goalkeeper Damian Martin; one of the stars of the game up to then, slipped as he went for it. The ball beat him, wound up in the net, and to all intents and purposes, the match was over.

Hartigan Supreme

This was by no means a convincing display by Limerick, and the team as it stands at present is no answer to the problems besetting the county. The game's central figure was Pat Hartigan, yet Limerick play him in the right corner when be is generally acknowledged as one of the game's greatest full-backs.

Against Offaly, he looked a class apart, plucking high balls out of the sky with aplomb and sending raking clearances way down the field. Behind him, Séamus Horgan was again a considerable success, but Eamonn Rea was uncertain in his pulling at full-back and could be faulted for the second Offaly goal. Jim O'Donnell stood out in the half-back line but midfield was a none too successful area and only Éamon Grimes of the six forwards on view impressed me.

The full-forward line, in particular, was a grave disappointment, especially when Limerick were pressing for vital scores in the last quarter of an hour. One's sympathies rest with Offaly who now look certain to be relegated. They look too good and spirited a side for that indignity, and in Damian Martin, a class goalkeeper; Eugene Hannon, Padraig Horan, Joe Hernon, Declan Hanniffy, Barney Moylan and goal poacher supreme Gerry Burke, they have players of much ability.

Scorers

Limerick - R. Bennis 2-2 (1-0 free); E. Grimes 1-2; A. Dunworth 0-2; E. Cregan and W. Moore 0-1.

Offaly - G. Burke 2-0; B. Moylan 1-2; P.J. Conroy 0-2.

Teams

Limerick - S. Horgan; P. Hartigan, E. Rea, J. O'Brien; T. Ryan, J. O'Donnell, S. Foley; L. Enright, R. Bennis; F. Nolan, M. Graham, E. Grimes; A. Dunworth, W. Moore, E. Cregan.

Offaly - D. Martin; J. Dooley, E Hannon, E. Moyles, P. Corcoran; P. Horan, J. Hernon; P. Moloughney, D. Hanniffy; B. Moylan, J. McKenna, M. Cleere; P.J. Whelehan, P.J. Conroy, G. Burke. Subs: W. Gorman for McKenna, S. Moylan for Moyles.

Referee - Michael Slattery (Clare).

Munster Championship and League Medals

Munster championship medals are quite distinctive, as they have been since at least the early 1910s, with two hurleys holding the three crowns on a green/blue enamel background, sitting atop three Gaelic footballs and dual shamrock embroidery. This design has remained pretty much intact for over 100 years. The other three provinces have their own unique design pattern too, some being in place since at least the 1910s, in particular Leinster.

The design of National League medals has not changed much since these competitions were first instituted in the mid-1920s, in both hurling and Gaelic football. There is a constant design with the emblems of the four provinces on the obverse quadrants of all these medals, clockwise from top: Ulster (red hand with vertical and horizontal sashes), Leinster (green harp), Munster (three crowns on green/blue background) and Connacht (half black eagle and half bent arm holding a dagger). These medals are not as well known as All Ireland examples and rarely enough come onto the open market. They are observed much less frequently than equivalent provincial championship medals.

The design of Limerick senior championship medals has been mostly unchanged since the 1950s, and is also quite distinctive in its own way. These medals are usually produced to order by local jeweller, JJ Kenneally. These medals are usually quite chunky and big, relative to other counties who produce similar silver *objects d'art* for their county senior championship winners.

Mind these medals well! They were hard won and must be well minded to be passed onto the next generation as touchstones of a glorious past, be it club, school, county, province or even country.

Top: front and back of 1973 Munster championship winner's medal.
Bottom: front and back of 1971 NHL winner's medal.

CHAPTER 3
1972-73
NATIONAL HURLING LEAGUE (ii)

AFTER CHRISTMAS

The rest of the 1972-73 Division 1A National Hurling League (NHL) fixtures were played off in the months of February and March 1973, with important games against Tipperary, Cork and Wexford. There were programmes issued for all these games, with the Cork one of particular interest as there is no mention of the NHL game on its front cover. It advertised the Sigerson Cup that was hosted by UCC on the same weekend, although the middle pages do contain the Cork and Limerick line-outs.

The game against Tipperary was interesting as the Limerick team named was much changed compared to previous recent combinations. That was because a number of players were not selected as they did not train in the run-up to the game, in sympathy with Joe McGrath. He had been relieved of his duties as trainer the previous autumn, to be replaced by Mick Cregan. The game finished in a draw, which was a very good result in the context of the deep personnel changes made. It could have been an even better result but for a last-gasp '70 from Len Gaynor that saved (some of) the day for the visitors. All the missing players were back for subsequent games and the protest quietly petered out. There is a wonderful team picture from this game reprinted in the following pages. There were other big gatherings in Limerick that weekend, with all three major political parties picking their candidates for the late February General Election.

An exceptional performance away to Cork was recorded in early March at the old Athletic Grounds. It was on the site of the present Páirc Uí Chaoimh, twice rebuilt since 1973. It was the curtain raiser to the Sigerson Cup final, won by UCD. It may have been against an experimental Cork team but the wide margin of victory was still very noteworthy. The Limerick Leader reporter at the game, Sean Murphy ('S.M.'), was very excited about the newcomers and the general performance. This win was enough to ensure progression, at a minimum, to a NHL quarter final. The Mayorstone Garda station was opened the day after this game was played.

Limerick's final game was away to Wexford, at Bellefield, Enniscorthy. It was due to be played on 19 November but got pushed back to 25 February. It was not played that day either, due to an inch of snow on the pitch. The decision to postpone was made very late, with some supporters already having arrived at the ground. It resulted in another "meritorious" win for the away team, thus ensuring that Limerick finished behind Kilkenny in Division 1A. Maynooth College won their first Fitzgibbon Cup that weekend beating UCG, with Paudie Fitzmaurice starring for winners. Fr Dick Browne was goalkeeper for Maynooth, a man well known in East and South Limerick over the many decades since.

Three Division 1A teams (Tipperary and Wexford were the other two) finished on 10 points each after the 7 games, with Limerick qualifying in second place, having a better scoring difference than the other two. Both Kilkenny and Limerick qualified for the semi-finals and would be kept apart at that stage. Tipperary (3rd) and Wexford (4th) won crossover quarter finals against the top two teams in Division 1B, Waterford (1st) and Kildare (2nd). Kildare's appearance in the 1972-73 NHL quarter final was one of four times they qualified for the knockout stages of the top league, all of them in the early 1970s when they were relatively competitive.

Newspaper coverage of Gaelic Games was ultra factual at the time, with little room for the sort of soft coverage that is now commonplace across all media. RTÉ may have had cameras at one or two games each weekend, with a highlights programme being televised on Sunday evenings. There would also be a Sunday afternoon sports programme on the radio, with an outside broadcast unit at the main game of the weekend. Recall, this was a time before local radio stations, where the state strictly controlled both national radio and television channels. It was a time when the GAA ban had only recently been lifted (Rule 27 being rescinded at GAA Congress in Easter 1971). It prevented GAA players from also playing soccer or rugby, something that had a detrimental effect on the GAA in Limerick city over many previous decades.

National Hurling League

Sunday, 11th February, '73

AT 3 P.M.

TIOBRAID ARANN

v

LUIMNEACH

CLAR OIFIGIÚIL

REITEOIR : M. SLATTERY

LUACH — **5p**

Shannon Printing Co. Ltd.

SHEILS

*ALL-IRELAND CHAMPIONS
AND
LEAGUE LEADERS
IN*

NEW AND USED CAR SALES

T. SHEILS & CO. LTD.

FORD MAIN DEALERS

Lansdowne, Limerick

Telephone No. 47933

Des Fitzgerald

VICTUALLER

MEAT TO PLEASE YOU

PLEASE TO MEET YOU

ALL GAELS GET A GOOD CUT AT

39 UPPER WILLIAM ST., LIMERICK

Telephone No. 47716

LUIMNEACH
GREEN & WHITE

1
S. HORGAN

2
W. MOORE
(Doon)

3
E. REA
(Faugh's)

4
J. O'BRIEN
(Bruree)

5
T. RYAN
(Ballybrown)

6
J. O'DONNELL
(Doon)

7
S. FOLEY
(Patrickswell)

8
R. BENNIS
(Patrickswell)

9
J. QUINLAN
(Doon)

10
L. O'DONOGHUE
(Mungret)

11
E. CREGAN
(Claughaun)

12
P. FOGARTY
(Ballybrown)

13
A. DUNWORTH
(Faugh's)

14
M. DOWLING
(Kilmallock)

15
F. NOLAN
(Patrickswell)

(16) P. BENNIS   (17) J. ALLIS   (18) M. GRAHAM
(19) D. CONNOLLY   (20) T. HEHIR

TIOBRAID ARANN
BLUE & GOLD

1
T. MURPHY
(Roscrea)

2
J. FOGARTY
(Moyne-Templetuohy)

3
J. KELLY
(Kilruane)

4
J. GLEESON
(Moneygall)

5
J. CRAMPTON
(Roscrea)

6
T. O'CONNOR
(Roscrea)

7
L. GAYNOR
(Kilruane)

8
S. HOGAN
(Kildangan)

9
P. J. RYAN
(Carrick-Davins)

10
F. LOUGHNANE
(Roscrea)

11
N. O'DWYER
(Borrisoleigh)

12
J. RYAN
(Moneygall)

13
P. BYRNE
(Thurles Sarsfields)

14
M. KEATING
(Ballybacon-Grange)

15
J. FLANAGAN
(Moycarkey)

---

(16) R. RYAN   (17) D. RYAN   (18) M. ESMONDE
(19) J. CUNNINGHAM   (20) J. KEOGH   (21) W. BLAKE
(22) J. KENNEDY

1973 Keeping the Dream Alive

The Limerick team that drew with Tipp
Back Row (L-R): Mossie Dowling, Eamonn Cregan, Willie Moore,
Front Row (L-R): Séamus Horgan, Andy Dunwor

...tional Hurling League in February 1973.
...n Quinlan; Pat Fogarty, Jim O'Donnell, Seán Foley and Eamonn Rea.
...s, Tom Ryan, Liam O'Donoghue and Frankie Nolan.

Gaynor '70 Robs Limerick
(Limerick Leader, 12 February 1973)
Draw A Fair Outcome Of Thrilling Match

By Charlie Mulqueen

Limerick 3-7
Tipperary 2-10

Oh, the pain and the agony! Tipperary dashed the sweet cup of victory from Limerick's lips at the Gaelic Grounds with two of the finest '70 shots ever taken under pressure. It was Len Gaynor, that pillar of the Tipperary team for many years, who lofted two magnificent pucks from placed balls as his side struggled to gain parity with Limerick's magnificently-battling makeshift side. And even though in the end they had to settle for a draw, 3-7 to 2-10, the spirit of the team at the Gaelic Grounds made Limerickmen proud and happy after the controversial and tragic pre-match happenings.

One doesn't suggest for one moment that Limerick's ills are suddenly at an end - there were glaring weaknesses against Tipperary that simply will have to be remedied if the highest prizes are to be won. Yet, let us give the fullest credit to Limerick for the manner in which they courageously took on a Tipperary side that, with one exception, had humbled the mighty All Ireland champions or Kilkenny just a short week previously.

Let us admire them for the way they came back from conceding a freakish goal after only seven minutes that left them trailing by three points after ten minutes and a gale force wind at their backs. They ploughed devotedly through the soft, yielding surface of the Gaelic Grounds, and in a golden four minute spell had their fans enraptured with three golden goals. Backed up by three invaluable points, and offset by only two like scores from the superb Francis Loughnane, Limerick went in at half-time with an eight point lead, 3-4 to 1-2.

We wondered was it enough, and regretted that a try for a goal from a 21-yard free by Richie Bennis just on the interval didn't result in at least a point.

Refreshed

Tipp. came out refreshed in the knowledge that they would have that powerful breeze behind them, and straight away they were on the attack. Loughnane was their inspiration, for, without any great support from his fellow forwards, who, without exception, were a disappointing bunch, he had Limerick in serious trouble. He first banged over two points, and then his rasping 21-yard free was poked over the line by Roger Ryan.

Home hearts were low, with still 22 minutes remaining, but now the spirit, the will-to-win of the Limerick side burst to the surface. Inspired by a brilliant Eamonn Cregan, back they came and the Claughaun man himself sent over a left-handed shot that put four points between them again.

The excitement was now at fever pitch, and though Seán Foley had one of his finest ever games in the green of Limerick he still found the roving Loughnane just too much to hold. The superb Roscrea man pointed another free, but again, to cheers of jubilation, Limerick were back with a beautifully taken point by Liam O'Donoghue. Roger Ryan restored the goal difference for Tipp. and then Limerick lost a good chance when Bennis's 21-yard free was blocked down. Again it was Loughnane with a free narrowing it to two points, and still twelve minutes to go.

But once again Limerick picked themselves off the ground, and hit back with another lovely Cregan point. How the crowd roared Limerick on; how Tipperary battled and fought, strictly, I should point out, in the metaphorical sense of the words, to get on terms.

Like the Limerick team of yesterday, Tipperary were men of stature, and they also had the players for the crisis. The game was in its last five minutes when P.J. Ryan slammed over a great point from way out on the left wing. Now, two between them and only three minutes to go, a Tipp. '70, and the ball is handed to Len Gaynor. Up comes the immaculate left-half, the ash swings, the ball bisects the uprights and now only one solitary score separates them.

Surely, these gallant men are not to be deprived now. The game enters its 60th minute, and dramatically the ball goes out off a defender's stick and it's another Tipp. '70. Again it's Gaynor, the cool man from Kilruane, But wait . . . as he stoops over the ball, the black-clad figure of Clare referee, Michael Slattery, rushes up-field and tells Len . . ."You must score direct, this is the last puck of the match." The tension was almost unbearable, but the admirable Gaynor remained the coolest man in the ground. Once more, his lovely, slow swing and again the perfectly struck and placed shot dashes Limerick's victory hopes.

Just Outcome

A draw it is ... and on reflection it was a good and equitable outcome.

As I said already, Limerick are by no means out of the wood despite this grand performance.

I spoke to selector Jackie Power after the game, and he wasn't too disappointed at the outcome.

"When you're team building, you don't want to get carried away with one good result. This game will keep up our spirit, but we mustn't get carried away by it."

Mr Power, one of the greats of Limerick hurling of the past, is also adamant that he wants the so-called "rebels" back as quickly as possible.

When they turn up for training, we will welcome them with open arms," he told me.

Still, Jackie Power and his fellow-selectors must be very pleased with the way the side played.

First and foremost they had spirit and dedication, and that's why they withheld the Tipperary pressure so well. In defence, none did better than the "Tournafulla Rock," Séamus Horgan. This is a real find and no county can boast a more courageous, talented goalkeeper or one with a bigger puck-out!

The full-back line may have fouled a little too much, but all three were splendid. At centre-back, Jim O'Donnell was a commanding figure, though inclined to "disappear" from time to time. Tom Ryan's forcefulness was never seen to better effect, and on the left flank, Seán Foley's class and style kept the side together when the going was roughest. The midfielders were in trouble against powerful opposition, though Richie Bennis accomplished many useful things. The pity was that he failed to gain a flag off two 21-yard frees, a factor that eventually proved costly.

Willie Moore (facing) and Tom Ryan (no. 5) in action against Tipperary during the NHL clash in February 1973.

1973 Keeping the Dream Alive

Frankie Nolan contesting a high ball with John Gleeson and Tadhg Ó Connor in Birr.

Frankie Nolan in a tussle for possession against Tipperary during the NHL game in February.

The dominant personality up front was Eamonn Cregan, confirming a long-held opinion that centre-forward is his best position. His contribution of three points, all beauties and all from play, were far more than they sound.

I very much liked Mungret's Liam O'Donoghue, who also picked off two vital points. The others compensated for what they lacked in style by 100 per cent effort, a fact typified by Mossie Dowling's jubilation after scoring one of those exciting first-half goals. Frankly, I was very disappointed with Tipperary, and they showed their relief at the finish by embracing Len Gaynor in the manner of English soccer players! Considering the latitude allowed midfielders, Séamus Hogan and P.J. Ryan, the Tipp. attack, with the obvious exception of Francis Loughnane and possibly Roger Ryan, was a flop.

In defence, Tadgh O'Connor had a good game on Cregan, but the pick were left-corner, John Gleeson and match saver, Len Gaynor.

Scorers

Limerick - R. Bennis 1-2 (1-1 frees); M. Dowling and P. Fogarty 1-0 each; E. Cregan 0-3; L. O'Donoghue 0-2.

Tipperary - F. Loughnane 1-6; R. Ryan 1-1; L. Gaynor 0-2; P.J. Ryan 0-1.

Teams

Limerick - S. Horgan; W. Moore, E. Rea, J. O'Brien; T. Ryan, J. O'Donnell, S. Foley; R. Bennis, J. Quinlan; L. O'Donoghue, E. Cregan, P. Fogarty; A. Dunworth, M. Dowling, F. Nolan. Subs: M. Graham for Dunworth, A. Dunworth for Dowling.

Tipperary - T. Murphy; J. Fogarty, J. Kelly, J. Gleeson; J. Crampton, T. O'Connor. L. Gaynor; S. Hogan. P.J. Ryan; F. Loughnane, N. O'Dwyer. J. Ryan; P. Byrne, R. Ryan, J. Flanagan.

Referee - Michael Slattery (Clare).

SIGERSON 73

U.C.C. v **MAYNOOTH**
(Holders)
2.15 p.m.

QUEENS v **U.C.D.**
(League Champions)
3.30 p.m.

MARDYKE, CORK
SATURDAY, 3rd MARCH, 1973

● FINAL ●

CORK ATHLETIC GROUNDS
SUNDAY, 4th MARCH, 1973

Souvenir Booklet · · 10p

COLAISTE NA hOLLSCOILE
CHORCAI

Programme cover for the Limerick v Cork NHL game which was paired up with the Sigerson Cup final on 4 March, 1973

Brilliant Limerick Crush Cork
(Limerick Leader, 5 March 1973)
Grimes, Hartigan Star In Great Team Display

By Seán Murphy

Limerick 3-13
Cork 1-7

Limerick senior hurlers, after many months of internal strife and dissention, travelled to Cork Athletic Grounds on Sunday in complete harmony and celebrated the occasion with a whopping 3-13 to 1-7 defeat of Cork and so qualified for the quarter-finals of the current National League competition at least. They thus maintained the county's rating as the modern day League specialists.

A win over Cork in a major hurling game is always an occasion for celebration, but while the gloss of Sunday's success is somewhat dented when one studies the composition of the Cork fifteen, nevertheless the manner in which it was achieved raises hopes once again for the future of Limerick hurling.

Weakened

Cork, considerably weakened by injuries, were forced to find replacements for a further three of their second-rate team. They put up a brave show but overall, they were sadly outclassed by the superb fitness and confidence of a re-united Limerick side.

It was a comprehensive performance by Limerick who looked a well-balanced combination and played with real purpose, although their relaxing periods could prove fatal against stronger opposition. A full 60 minutes of hurling like that served up in the opening 20 minutes of Sunday's game would mesmerise any team in the land. Yes indeed, Limerick have the talent if only it can be exploited to its full potential.

Played on a slippery surface that made ball control almost impossible, this game provided excellent entertainment for the fair-sized crowd. It was a game of two distinct halves. In the opening thirty minutes Limerick were simply brilliant. With Éamon Grimes playing the proverbial blinder at midfield ably assisted by a fighting fit Bernie Hartigan, the Shannonsiders completely upset Cork with a fantastic display of precision passing and magnificent team-work,

Copy-book Hurling

It was real copy-book hurling that had friend and foe alike gasping in admiration. Limerick tore the Cork defence to shreds and in a purple patch between the 12th and 15th minute of the first half killed off prematurely any hopes of a Cork survival. The first major attack came in the 12th minute when Michael Graham spread eagled the Cork defence before parting to Frankie Nolan who unbelievably shot over the bar from 5 yards range. Then 60 seconds later Éamon Grimes dashed along the left wing before easing to Eamonn Cregan who flashed home a spectacular goal. Straight from the puck out Limerick were on the move once more and Eamonn Cregan placed Michael Graham for a great goal to put Limerick ahead 2-4 to 0-1. Liam O'Donoghue looked like wrapping it for good in the 14th minute but his stinging shot was expertly saved by Paddy Barry.

After this period of complete supremacy, Limerick were lulled into an air of complacency and seemed to rest on their oars. Although they continued to enjoy territorial advantage, their play lacked real urgency and the forward finish was extremely weak. Cork rallied strongly near the close of the half with points from C. McCarthy (2) and Pat Doherty to leave the scoreboard reading at the interval; Limerick 3-7, Cork 0-4.

Treacherous

A slight shower at the break made underfoot conditions treacherous on the resumption but Cork seemed to revel on the muddy surface. Mick Malone raised their hopes with a point from play in the 3rd minute, but Richie Bennis negated this with a point from a free in the 5th minute. Charlie McCarthy tried to blast a 21 yard free to the net in the 6th minute but his rising shot went over the bar. In the 8th minute Frankie Nolan with nobody to beat only Paddy Barry raised a white flag when a goal seemed certain.

Cork were hurling with renewed verve and dash at this period and visions of last year's sensational come-back at the Gaelic Grounds came vividly to mind when Charlie McCarthy blasted a 21 yard free through a wall of defenders in the 12th minute and two minutes later sent a similar effort between the uprights for a point. Cork were really prominent and held Limerick scoreless for 11 minutes, but when Richie Bennis broke the spell in the 19th minute with a point from a free, Limerick regained the initiative and finished in a flourish with three points from play registered by Liam O'Donoghue, Frankie Nolan and Michael Graham, who shot a beauty with the last stroke of the hour.

Rebel spirit

Although the Cork line-out bore no resemblance whatsoever to the selected fifteen, nevertheless they possessed rebel spirit and hurling ability in abundance and pushed Limerick to the extreme at times. There was a lot of merit in this Limerick success. The defence, a little unsettled on occasions, always managed to contain the strongest sector of the Cork team, midfield was ably manned, while the forwards moved with amazing cohesion and accuracy. All in all, Limerick look well equipped for that showdown in Enniscorthy with Wexford on Sunday next.

Séamus Horgan further enhanced his reputation as a goalie of the highest calibre with a courageous display of cool, confident play under severe pressure. He was fronted by a magnificent trio of Willie Moore, who is settling into his defensive role well; Eamonn Rea, who handled Ray Cummins in praiseworthy fashion, and Jim O'Brien, who allowed wily Charlie McCarthy very little scope.

The half-back line was a little disappointing, though Pat Hartigan, in the pivot position, was a dominant figure. A little prone to petty fouling, Hartigan more than compensated for the occasional lapse with a performance on par with his greatest in the green jersey. His lengthy clearances were a feature of the hour. His flankers, too - Jim O'Donnell and Seán Foley - were in rare form also, although Foley was often more spectacular. O'Donnell was his usual self, intercepting, covering up and clearing brilliantly until he retired seven minutes from the end to be replaced by Tom Ryan.

Scintillating

Éamon Grimes, in his first outing as captain of, the county team, turned in a scintillating performance at midfield. He chased every ball with deadly determination, placed accurate passes for his comrade and generally proved a great leader.

Bernie Hartigan obviously benefited from his rest and had a storming hour. He used his weight to much advantage while his crisp ground striking was a decided asset.

The forward division as a unit were the real success of the team. Eamonn Cregan was in sparkling form at centre-forward and was the launching pad for many of the attacks. He struck up a happy partnership with his wingers Richie Bennis and Michael Graham both of whom were in top form. Bennis got a "freak" goal from an acute angle free in the first half. Liam O'Donoghue showed courage, speed and skill when giving no less a man than blonde John Horgan a nightmare hour. To crown a great display young O'Donoghue picked of a lovely point and made several more. On the fringe of the square, Mossie Dowling was an eager full-forward. In tough luck for two goals in overhead clashes with Martin Doherty, Dowling showed drive and thrust that deserves further recognition. Frankie Nolan, who has been off and on the Limerick team for many years, staked his claim for a permanent berth in the left corner position when giving the established Tony Maher a severe roasting. The only players to impress for Cork were Gerald McCarthy, Seán O'Leary, Martin Doherty, George Webb, Mick Malone, Pat Moylan and Pat Doherty, who was surprisingly replaced.

Scorers

Limerick - R. Bennis 1-5 (1-4 frees); M. Graham 1-1; E. Cregan 1-0, F. Nolan 0-3; M. Dowling 0-2; E. Grimes and L. O'Donoghue 0-1.

Cork - C. McCarthy 1-5 (all frees); P. Doherty and M. Malone 0-1.

Teams

Limerick - S. Horgan; W. Moore, E. Rea, J. O'Brien; J. O'Donnell, P. Hartigan, J. Foley; B. Hartigan, E. Grimes; R. Bennis, E. Cregan, M. Graham; L. O'Donoghue, M. Dowling, F. Nolan. Sub. T. Ryan for J. O'Donnell.

Cork - P. Barry; T. Maher, M. Doherty, J. Horgan; D. Burns, G. Webb, G. McCarthy; J. Russell, P. Doherty; E. O'Donoghue, M. Malone, P. Moylan; C. McCarthy, R. Cummins, S. O'Leary. Subs.: N. Crowley for P. Doherty, S. Farrell for O'Donoghue, J.B. Murphy for Malone.

Referee - Noel Dalton (Waterford).

The Limerick team that beat Cork in the Athletic Grounds in March 1973.

Back Row (L-R): Mossie Dowling, Willie Moore, Eamonn Cregan, Pat Hartigan, Eamonn Rea, Jim O'Brien, Jim O'Donnell and Michael Graham.
Front Row (L-R): Séamus Horgan, Bernie Hartigan, Seán Foley, Éamon Grimes, Richie Bennis, Frankie Nolan and Liam O'Donoghue.

Cumann Luthchleas Gael.   N⁰ 24

CLAR OIFIGIUIL

NATIONAL HURLING LEAGUE

LUIMNEACH v.

LOCH GARMAN

AT BELLEFIELD, ENNISCORTHY

ON SUNDAY, 11th MARCH, 1973

Bellefield Grounds, formerly the property of the Starlights Football Club and presently of the Rapparees and Starlights Hurling and Football Club, will be undergoing a major, phased development over the next ten years. The reconstruction, when completed, will include covered stand, games hall, bar and restaurant, gymnasium and the most modern of dressingroom facilities. Your purchase of this programme will help finance this development.—Thank you.

This Programme is numbered—which means that you will participate in a draw for £5.00, the result of which will be announced at half-time.

PRICE :: :: :: 5p.

ECHO ENNISCORTHY

Horgan Stars As Limerick Go Into Last Four

(Limerick Leader, 12 March 1973)

Great Win In Wexford

By Seán Murphy

Limerick 4-11
Wexford 2-12

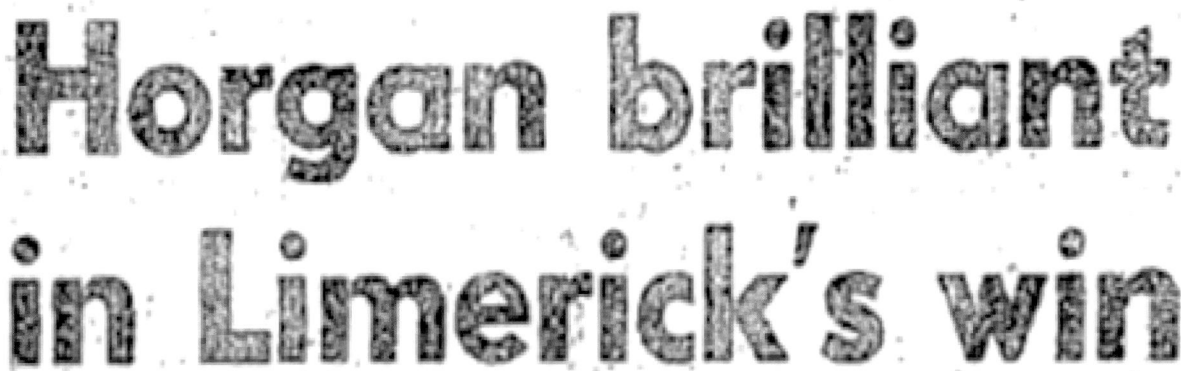

Limerick Senior hurlers "Rags to Riches" story in the current National League competition continues. At historic Enniscorthy on Sunday against all the odds they crushed the mighty challenge of Wexford in a high-scoring, spine-tingling hurling contest on the scoreline: 4-11 to 2-12 to cruise into the League semi-final once more in company with front-runners Kilkenny. The scoreline tells its own story. This win was as deserved, as it was meritorious. Yet it was achieved by a Limerick team that never sparked on all cylinders together but on which all members had their moments of supremacy.

The Bellefield Ground under the shadow of famed Vinegar Hill is certainly one of Limerick's happy hunting spots. It was here two years ago that a makeshift team rose phoenix-like to spark off Limerick's latest excursion to the forefront of the camán game. Now, once again, Limerick conquered high-riding Wexford in their own surroundings. Conditions weather-wise at the venue were ideal as the big crowd (including an exceptionally large Limerick following) basked in sunshine that would do justice to Kilkee in June. The sod was dry, but was very dead with the ball not inclined to hop at all. This reduced ground striking to a minimum and favoured the Wexford style of pick and strike hurling. On a day when possession seemed to be worth even more than the proverbial nine points of the law to referee J. Dunphy, the homesters exploited their advantage to the fullest.

Downhill

Wexford played with the downhill advantage in the first half and in a dangerous early raid Phil Wilson was just wide. Richie Bennis opened Limerick's scoring after 90 seconds with a point from a free but the lead was shortlived. The defence was completely unsettled and the elusive Wexford forwards were revealing kinks in our armour which hitherto were not explored. In the 3rd minute pint-sized Joe Purcell waltzed his way through a hesitant wall of defenders before parting to burly Tom Byrne, who shot a goal from close range. Limerick recovered well from this setback and two points from frees by Richie Bennis and Éamon Grimes (70 yards range) levelled matters once more after 5 minutes. Seán Kinsella who threatened danger every time he gained possession shot a fine point from play in the 8th minute but the equaliser came when Pat Hartigan lofted a 75 yards free straight between the uprights a minute later. Wexford continued to force the issue and in an overhead clash in the square veteran Phil Wilson, who had a fine game all through, raised a white flag.

LOCH GARMAN

(1) P. Nolan

(2) E. O'Connor   (3) P. Kavanagh   (4) J. Quigley

(5) C. Doran   (6) M. Jacob   (7) J. Pender

(8) M. Quigley   (9) D. Bernie

(10) S. Kinsella   (11) T. Doran   (12) P. Wilson

(13) J. Purcell   (14) T. Byrne   (15) J. Berry

Subs.—(16) J. Parle, (17) E. Murphy, (18) J. Browne, (19) P. Kehoe, (20) W. Murphy, (21) C. Kehoe, (22) M. Butler, (23) H. Goff, (24) J. Murphy.

Loch Garman	Cúil Goals	Cúiliní Points	Treasna Overs	70sl. 70's	Puch Saor Free Pucks
Iadh Leath 1st Half					
2adh Leath 2nd Half					
Iomlán Total:					

LUIMNEACH

(1) S. Horgan

(2) W. Moore (3) E. Rea (4) Jim O'Brien

(5) Jim O'Donnell (6) Pat Hartigan (7) John Foley

(8) Bernie Hartigan (9) Eamonn Grimes

(10) Richie Bennis (11) Pat Fogarty (12) Ml. Graham

(13) L. O'Donoghue (14) M. Dowling (15) S. Nolan

Subs.—(16) J. Hehir, (17) Tom Ryan, (18) Andy Dunworth, (19) Phil Bennis, (20) Jim Allis, (21) J. Grimes, (22) J. Quinlan, (23) Jim Hogan.

Luimneach	Cúil Goals	Cúiliní Points	Treasna Overs	70sl. 70's	Puch Saor Free Pucks
Iadh Leath 1st Half					
2adh Leath 2nd Half					
Iomlán Total:					

Wexford Supremacy

Then followed a period of complete Wexford supremacy as the right flank of their team - Colm Doran. Martin Quigley, Seán Kinsella and Joe Purcell had the edge on the opposite numbers. They also proved the old maxim "attack is the best form of defence" correct by using their half-backs in an attacking role from midfield and the Limerick forwards were lured almost to a defensive role thereby reducing their scoring threat. All-star centre back, Mick Jacob, a dominant figure in the Wexford rear-guard, pointed a '70 in the 12th minute and Seán Kinsella added another minor from play.

Limerick, although failing to reach top gear, continued to stay in a challenging position. Liam O'Donoghue, who was having a rough passage from John Quigley, came strongly into the limelight in the 13th and 14th minutes when in two delightful movements he placed Richie Bennis, who notched 2 beauties from play. Wexford's dominance continued with a hand-passed point by Jack Berry, and another point from Tom Byrne, who had now adapted a roving attitude. A wonder save by Séamus Horgan from Phil Wilson deprived Wexford of a certain goal in the 20th minute and despite further pressure they failed to raise another flag until the 27th minute when Mick Jacob pointed a free. Two minutes from the interval Richie Bennis pointed a 21 yard free to reduce the deficit. So after a very indifferent first half, Limerick, despite many limitations, were only trailing by 3 points - 1-7 to 0-7. This happy position was due more to the poor finishing of Wexford than to any effective measure of Limerick. The supremacy of Wexford in the opening 30 minutes is clearly mirrored when one records that Wexford shot 13 wides as against Limerick's 2.

Memorable

The second half produced some memorable hurling with superb striking by both sides, and great man to man pulling. Limerick were a rejuvenated side on resuming with the selectors making a few switches which had a telling effect. Richie Bennis shifted to centre-forward and immediately the dominance of Mick Jacob faded. Realising that ground hurling was a futile exercise on the prevailing surface, Limerick used the rise and strike hurling in the second half Pat Fogarty shot a point from play in the 1st minute, and Pat Hartigan pointed a free from fully 85 yards in the 3rd minute to give Limerick a lively start. They were now moving fluently, and Richie Bennis put the followers in high spirits when he superbly flashed a 21 yard free to the Wexford net in the 5th minute, and within 60 seconds Éamon Grimes shot a powerful point from play out on the left wing.

In the 8th minute, Limerick were pulled to reality when, following a defensive mix-up, Tony Doran availed of the opportunity to place Tom Byrne who palmed a great goal to bring the teams level once more. Andy Dunworth replaced Pat Fogarty on the Limerick team, and once more consolidated his rating as "the best substitute in the land," although my sympathy goes to Fogarty on this occasion.

Magnificent Points

Wexford forged to the front with two magnificent points from play by Tom Byrne and Tony Doran, who had now exchanged positions. Andy Dunworth showed his capabilities when, in a typical swing, he raised a white flag from the wing, but Tony Doran did likewise and the Slaney men were still in front 2-10 to 1-11 with fifteen minutes remaining. Richie Bennis tried to goal a close-in free but failed, and Limerick's task looked tougher. The signal for Limerick's victory came in the 17th minute when Andy Dunworth flashed a pass across the square where Frankie Nolan outwitted a vigilant Teddy O'Connor, juggled his way goalwards, and picked his spot in the Wexford netting to flash home a real gem of a goal. Nolan was again a prime mover in the next Limerick move a minute later when his speculative centre was fastened on to the net by Mossie Dowling.

Wexford were far from finished at this stage as Tom Byrne pointed a free and only a miraculous dive by Séamus Horgan turned a Seán Kinsella pile-driver over the bar when a goal seemed certain. The clincher for Limerick came in the 22nd minute when Éamon Grimes lofted a side-line puck from 35 yards all the way to the net. Limerick now scented victory and withstood a severe Wexford bombardment in the final five minutes. Wexford forced three '70s and a close-in free but all to no avail as a resolute Limerick defence held firm.

Disastrous

So after a disastrous start to the League campaign, Limerick have recovered from the floor boards and are now strongly in contention to regain a title they lost to Cork last year. Their performance on Sunday, although below par again, showed that they have the craft and skill to match the best in the country.

This latest win over Wexford will always be remembered as Séamus Horgan's hour, as the daring Tournafulla goalkeeper gave a display that had old-timers drawing comparisons with the halcyon days of Ahane's Paddy Scanlan. He again showed amazing courage in the face of fierce onslaughts while his ability to drive drew much admiration. He brought off at least three saves bordering on the miraculous variety, while his long puck outs are a decided asset to the team.

Éamon Grimes again played a captain's part with a methodical performance at midfield. Always foraging for the ball and ever anxious to help the distressed he was always on the spot to capitalise on the loose ball. His point from play was a magnificent effort.

Others to shine for Limerick were Pat Hartigan, Richie Bennis, Jim O'Brien, Seán Foley, Mossie Dowling and Frankie Nolan although the remainder were only slightly in arrears.

Wexford were best served by Colm Doran, Mick Jacob, Martin Quigley, Seán Kinsella, Tony Doran, Phil Wilson and Tony Byrne, their scorer in chief.

Scorers

Limerick - R. Bennis 1-5 (1-3 frees); E. Grimes 1-2 (0-1 free); F. Nolan, M. Dowling 1-0; P. Hartigan 0-2 (0-1 free); P. Fogarty and A. Dunworth 0-1.

Wexford - T. Byrne 2-3; J. Kinsella 0-3; A. Doran 0-2; P. Wilson, A. Jacob, J. Berry and D. Bernie 0-1.

Teams

Limerick - S. Horgan; W. Moore, E. Rea, J. O'Brien; J. O'Donnell, P. Hartigan, S. Foley; B. Hartigan, E. Grimes; R. Bennis, P. Fogarty, M. Graham; L. O'Donoghue, M. Dowling, F. Nolan. Sub: A. Dunworth for Fogarty.

Wexford - P. Nolan; T. O'Connor, P. Kavanagh, F. Quigley; C. Doran, M. Jacob, J. Pender; M. Quigley, D. Bernie; S. Kinsella, A. Doran, P. Wilson; J. Purcell, T. Byrne, J. Berry.

Referee - Jim Dunphy (Waterford).

CHAPTER 4
1972-73
NATIONAL HURLING LEAGUE (iii)

KNOCKOUT STAGES

Limerick played Tipperary twice in the knockout stages of the National Hurling League (NHL) of 1972/73. Firstly, in a double-header with the quarter final replay between Wexford and Waterford in Kilkenny on 15 April, the week before Easter. Two late goals saved Limerick from defeat. It was Limerick's second draw with Tipperary in this league campaign, 2-11 each. A call was made that weekend by the ICTU for the government to introduce legislation to prevent women from being sacked from most public service jobs when they married.

The replay against Tipperary was two weeks later, in Birr; a game of mythical proportions in the memory of many who were in attendance. It had everything. Sixty minutes of normal time followed by extra time, which was two periods of 15 minutes, to make up a total of 90 minutes of playing time. A third normal-time draw resulted between the two teams in a little under three months! Limerick eventually saw this epic game out after extra time, 5-10 to 3-14.

It is said that a number of supporters left at the end of normal time, thinking that the game was going to a second replay and only heard the result at 11PM that evening when Seán Óg Ó Ceallacháin announced it; others heard it on the sports news at 7PM if they had a radio in their car. It also snowed in Birr that bitterly cold afternoon. There is a wonderful set of black and white photographs from the game, produced by a *Limerick Leader* photographer (most likely AF Foley or John F Wright), on the FromLimerickWithLove website.

From a programme-collecting perspective, it is pretty certain that no programme was produced for the replay. Is it possible that the programme from the drawn game was distributed outside the ground instead? Peace was breaking out in the latest rent war with tenants of Limerick Corporation that weekend.

The league final was played in the middle of May, in Croke Park, with Wexford providing the opposition. It would be Limerick's fourth NHL final in a row. Wexford won the game after a hard battle, to annex only their fourth ever NHL title. It remains their last NHL success at the time of writing. Much of the game was captured by RTE cameras and shown afterwards in their sports highlights' programme, not to be seen again for many years. It is now up on YouTube, in all its colour glory, not the complete game, but three decent excerpts from it.

The incident that stands out for most people from the game is the injury to Michael Graham, who suffered a freak leg break after a dozen minutes of the first half. It would seem that the Wexford goalkeeper went to clear the sliotar and innocently made contact with Michael's lower leg. He went down immediately and was urgently dealt with by the available medics, all the while the game went on around him.

Quite why Frank Murphy, the referee, did not stop the play when there was a severe injury being tended to remains unrecorded, but is remarkable to the modern eye. Limerick were in the game for long periods before conceding a number of late scores to lose 4-13 to 3-7. It was also the weekend of a large fire in the new shopping complex on William Street, Limerick. It was also a week after Leeds United lost the FA Cup Final to Sunderland, in what was probably the biggest giant-killing act in final history.

It was Limerick's third NHL final defeat in four seasons (1969/70 to 1972/73). It was potentially a very demoralising setback, given the circumstances of the recent epic series of games with Tipperary, and the injury to regular starter Michael Graham. As Cormac Liddy prosaically said in his report of the final, "…if Sunday's defeat could be used as the stick to beat out some of the more obvious faults [of the Limerick team] then, perhaps, a return to Croke Park on 2 September to bid for a more supreme prize might yet be possible." Indeed!

Cumann Luth Chleas Gael

Sraith Comortas Naisiunta Iomanaiochta

Loch Garman v

Port Lairge 2.15 in

REITEOIR   FRANK MURPHY   Corcaigh

Tiobrad Arann v

Luimneach 3.45 in

REITEOIR   NOEL DALTON   Port Lairge

i bPairc Ui Nuallain
ar 15u Aibrean 1973

CLAR OIFIGIUIL   5p

Original programme cover for drawn Limerick v Tipperary NHL Semi-Final game.

Limerick Recover To Snatch A Draw
(Limerick Leader, 16 April 1973)

By Seán Murphy

Limerick 2-11
Tipperary 2-11

After having been virtually over-run by a rampant Tipperary team for most of the second half, Limerick made a dramatic do-or-die recovery in the last five minutes to score two goals and so snatched a draw in the National Hurling League semi-final at Nowlan Park, Kilkenny on Sunday.

So, Limerick remain in contention for league honours, but only barely! Their amazing fight back against such adversity could be aptly described as a modern day hurling miracle, or as one disgruntled Tipperary man called it "The Great National League Robbery."

The scenes prior to Limerick's larceny act are worth recalling. The Shannonsiders, in racing parlance, made all the early running and maintained their advantage score-wise until a goal by J. Flanagan in the 10th minute of the second half knocked the heart out of Limerick. Tipperary midfielders, P.J. Ryan and Séamus Hogan, were running riot due to loose marking, and when Francis Loughnane went on a scoring fiesta things looked black for Limerick as time ticked away, with the scoreboard showing Tipperary six points in front.

Downhearted Limerick fans were streaming through the exits discussing the "same old story" and the pros and cons of another unexpected setback, when the team made a concerted effort to stave of impending defeat.

Wily

Limerick stormed to attack, and the Tipperary defence, under pressure, conceded a free. Crack marksman, Richie Bennis, flashed in a sizzling shot, which the defence saved, but wily Liam O'Donoghue jabbed the rebound to the net. Limerick were back in business with 3 minutes remaining, and so determined were they to garner the sweet fruits of victory that the entire fifteen, with the exception of goalie, Séamus Horgan bombarded the Tipperary goal.

Even full-back Eamonn Rea led an assault into Tipp. territory with a solo run. In the 28th minute the Tipperary defence again fouled. Jim O'Donnell lobbed a high shot from 50 yards into the square and in a fierce melee Liam O'Donoghue became the new pin-up idol of Limerick followers when he smashed home a vital goal past a bewildered Tipperary back-line.

The sides were level and then Limerick nearly completed the grand larceny when a rising shot from Richie Bennis took the whitewash off the right hand Tipperary upright, and barely wide. But the drama did not end there! On the stroke of the hour Len Gaynor stood poised to give Tipperary victory from a '70, but the Limerick relief as his "score direct" shot fell short and referee Noel Dalton signalled time up was expressed in one of the loudest cheers of a thrill-packed game. The long last blast of the referee's whistle never sounded more sweetly in Limerick followers' ears than it did at Nowlan Park.

Stalemate

So the stalemate between Limerick and Tipperary continues and this draw again emphasises that there is very little between those evenly matched sides. This latest meeting in the Marble City before a big attendance was contested with characteristic vigour and determination in which no quarter was given or taken. Limerick started off as if they were going to annihilate Tipperary. Richie Bennis opened their tally after 3 minutes with a point from a free, and Frankie Nolan raised another white flag from play 30 seconds later, while Richie Bennis pointed a 60 yards to put them 3 points clear after 5 minutes. Even at this early stage it was obvious that Limerick's forward finish was extremely weak as several scoring chances were smothered after spectacular approach work. A slackness and lack of authority about a Limerick free from the back line eventually struck by Jim O'Brien let J. Flanagan through for a Tipperary point against the run of play. In the 11th minute, Francis Loughnane tried to blast a 21 yard free to the net but his effort was saved at the expense of a '70. Limerick continued to play swift and joyful precision hurling but were unable to consolidate their advantage with scores,

Frustration

In the 13th minute, Liam O'Donoghue, who was a constant cause of frustration to the Tipperary defence with his daring thrusts, centred to Eamonn Cregan, who funnelled a characteristic pass to Richie Bennis, who shot over an impeccable point. Shortly afterwards, Bennis tried to goal a free but failed, and at the other end Francis Loughnane pointed from a similar position. This pair exchanged two points apiece from frees between the 14th and 21st minutes. One of these points by Bennis was from over 65 yards out. Len Gaynor pointed a free to keep Tipperary in touch in the 23rd minute, but Richie Bennis pointed a free and Eamonn Cregan returned the puck-out straight over the bar to keep Limerick three points in front. Roger Ryan, who kept compounding the worries of the Limerick defence with his burly tactics delivered a K.O. blow in the 27th minute. He grabbed a high ball to the left of the goal-mouth and with amazing ease, waltzed through the defence to shoot from close range. His shot was saved by Séamus Horgan but dropped over the line for a goal. Richie Bennis nosed Limerick ahead once more with a point from a free in the 28th minute to leave the score at the interval, Limerick 0-9; Tipperary 1-5.

Limerick players Jim O'Brien, Ned Rea and Willie Moore are in control of this situation at Nowlan Park.

National Hurling League Semi-Final

LIMERICK RECOVER TO SNATCH A DRAW

In Trouble

It was apparent at the break that Limerick were in trouble. After doing all the hurling and providing most of the thrills they had a mere point to show for their advantages, while Tipperary, with limited possession, were breathing down their necks. When the teams resumed it came as no surprise to see Pat Hartigan back at corner-back after an unhappy sojourn in the No. 5 spot, which was now filled by Willie Moore.

Richie Bennis roused Limerick's sagging hopes with a point from a free in the opening minute but Francis Loughnane did likewise for Tipperary in the seventh minute. In a cheeky bit of opportunism Liam O'Donoghue pointed from play in the eighth minute and this, unbelievably, was to be Limerick's last until that dramatic recovery.

Pat Fogarty replaced Andy Dunworth in another of their replacement series, but gradually Limerick faded from the scene, The Tipperary midfielders were now "freemen" of the midfield sector and throughout the entire field Tipperary began to stamp their authority on the game. Any hopes Limerick had of staying in front were quickly and emphatically extinguished in the 10th minute when a long free by Len Gaynor into the square was dropped by Pat Hartigan, and John Flanagan availed of the slip-up to give Tipperary the lead for the first time with a goal. Tipperary exerted complete control and were it not for the Limerick defence, who stuck like leeches to their men, the issue would have been well and truly clinched.

Scoring Safari

Francis Loughnane went on a scoring safari as he pumped over points with the authority of a crack marksman, and Len Gaynor landed a '70 between the uprights. Tipperary were coasting to victory and the shadows of defeat were rapidly enveloping Limerick when that sensational rally saved the bacon for the boys in green. That Limerick could force a draw on an afternoon when many of our top players struck an off day must be a source of comfort to all concerned with the team and must give renewed hopes for the replay. One thing is certain, Limerick will never be as inept again.

On Sunday the troubles stemmed from midfield, where Bernie Hartigan and Éamon Grimes were never able to cope with P.J. Ryan and Séamus Hogan, while Eamonn Rea was completely at sea in his bid to thwart the hustling Roger Ryan. The switch of Pat Hartigan to the half-back line also proved an error and it must be now clearly seen that he is definitely the best full-back in the game. This is already recognised everywhere only in Limerick. One cannot solve a problem by creating two.

Uncertainty

Séamus Horgan could not be blamed for the shots that beat him, but he displayed a little uncertainty on this occasion. He was not his usual cool self, but perhaps the jittery defence did not help. Pat Hartigan in the second half produced the hurling of which he is capable, while throughout the hour Jim O'Brien was equal to his task.

Jim O'Donnell, in the pivotal position, was a towering figure with amazing ball control and lengthy clearances. His imperturbable coolness under pressure gave his colleagues the confidence they needed. Seán Foley emerged as my star of the hour with a whole-hearted and tenacious performance of clever defensive tactics.

In a forward division that showed deft touches in the first half but lacked drive and penetration, Liam O'Donoghue. Richie Bennis, Frankie Nolan and Eamonn Cregan donned the role of danger men. O'Donoghue, in particular, was most impressive, despite constant harassment by the Tipperary defenders.

1973 Keeping the Dream Alive

Bernie Hartigan showed his class in spasms, but Éamon Grimes faded completely out of the picture after a glorious opening spell.

Scorers

Limerick - R. Bennis, 0-8 (0-7 frees); L. O'Donoghue 2-1; E. Cregan and F. Nolan 0-1.

Tipperary - F. Loughnane 0-8 (0-6 frees); J. Flanagan 1-1; R. Ryan, 1-0; L. Gaynor 0-2 (0-1 free, 0-1 '70).

Teams

Limerick - S. Horgan; W. Moore, E. Rea, J. O'Brien; P. Hartigan, J. O'Donnell, S. Foley; E. Grimes, B. Hartigan; R. Bennis, E. Cregan, L. O'Donoghue; A. Dunworth, M. Dowling, F. Nolan. Subs: P. Fogarty for Dunworth (38th minute), Dunworth for Nolan (injured 58th minute).

Tipperary - T. Murphy; J. Fogarty, J. Kelly, J. Gleeson; J. Crampton, T. O'Connor, L. Gaynor; S. Hogan, P. J. Ryan; F. Loughnane, N. O'Dwyer. J. Ryan; P. Byrne, R. Ryan, J. Flanagan. Sub: M. Esmonde for O'Connor (injured 15th minute).

Referee - Noel Dalton (Waterford).

TIPPERARY		BLUE & GOLD	LIMERICK		GREEN & WHITE
	1. TADG MURPHY (21) Roscrea			1. SEAMUS HORGAN (23) Tournafulla	
2. JIM FOGARTY (22) Moyne/Templetouhy	3. JOHN KELLY (25) Kilruane	4. JOHN GLEESON (30) Moneygall	2. WILLIE MOORE (22) Doon	3. EAMONN REA (27) Faugh's	4. JIM O'BRIEN (27) Bruree
5. JIMMY CRAMPTON (22) Roscrea	6. TADG O'CONNOR (25) Roscrea	7. LEN GAYNOR (29) Kilruane	5. PAT HARTIGAN (22) Sth. Liberties	6. JIM O'DONNELL (30) Doon	7. SEAN FOLEY (24) Patrickswell
	8. SEAMUS HOGAN (25) Kildangan	9. P. J. RYAN (26) Carrick-Davins		8. EAMONN GRIMES (25) Sth. Liberties	9. BERNIE HARTIGAN (27) Old Christians
10. Francis Loughnane (28) Roscrea	11. NOEL O'DWYER (25) Borrisoleigh	12. JACK RYAN (24) Moneygall	10. RICHIE BENNIS (27) Patrickswell	11. EAMONN CREGAN (27) Claughan	12. LIAM DONOHUE (21) Mungret
13. PAUL BYRNE (22) Thurles Sars.	14. ROGER RYAN (29) Toomevara	15. JOHN FLANNAGAN (25) Moycarkey-Borris	13. ANDY DUNWORTH (26) Faugh's	14. MOSSY DOWLING (25) Kilmallock	15. FRANK NOLAN (22) Patrickswell

SUBS: 16. Jimmy Doyle Thurles Sars., 17. Jimmy Keogh Silvermines, 18. Martin Esmonde Moyne/Templetouhy, 19. Joe Kennedy Carrick-Davins, 20. Dinny Ryan Sean Treacy's, 21. J. Cunningham Roscrea.

SUBS: 16. Phil Bennis Patrickswell, 17. Jim Allis Doon, 18. Jim Hogan Claughan, 19. Pat Fogarty Ballybrown, 20. Joe Grimes Sth. Liberties, 21. Dan Connolly Kilmallock, 22. John Quinlan Doon, 23. Tom Hehir Bruff.

THIS PROGRAMME HAS COME TO YOU THROUGH THE EFFORTS OF THE BOYS OF THE O'LOUGHLIN'S G.A.A. CLUB

Teams from drawn Limerick v Tipperary NHL Semi-Final programme

CLÁR OIFIGIÚIL

National Hurling League
Semi-Final (Replay)

TIOBRAID ÁRANN v LUIMNEACH

St. Brendan's Park, Birr

April 29th, 1973

Luach - 3p

Seán Ó Síocháin
Árd Rúnaí

*Mocked-up programme cover for Limerick v Tipperary NHL Semi-Final replay programme.
Courtesy of Tom Morrison.*

Off-Form Limerick Mastered Tipperary
(Limerick Leader, 30 April 1973)
Thrills Abounded In Extra Time

By Cormac Liddy

Limerick 5-10
Tipperary 3-14

A blistering finish to a thunderous ninety minutes of full-blooded hurling saw Limerick storm into the National League final for the fourth successive year at a cramped St. Brendan's Stadium, Birr, on Sunday. The tag "lucky" can be added to Limerick's memorable triumph but it is gratifying that a side which had at least five players totally off-form can still survive in thrilling fashion.

Wexford provide the final opposition on Sunday week but until then Limerick supporters will have plenty to discuss about the memorable extra-time success over an extremely tough Tipperary side. Limerick goalie Séamus Horgan must still be wondering how a man can almost have his head knocked off and still concede a free.

Fortunately Horgan's head remains in an unaltered and uninjured position, but it is no fault of at least one Tipperary man that this is so. Then, having been at the receiving end of some over-aggressive strokes, the Tournafulla man had a free given against him. It was the second strange decision within minutes of referee Mick Spain, who otherwise handled the "needle" affair in very commendable fashion. Shortly before this, Pat Hartigan had brought off one of his spectacular clearances as he leaned over a Tipperary forward. He did not appear to be doing anything wrong, but the referee thought otherwise and gave a free to Tipp.

This was a contest that will be spoken about for many a day. It was furious stuff right front the very beginning and there was a Munster final atmosphere prevailing all through. There was some extremely hard pulling by both sides, and at times it seemed that it might prove too much for some of the combatants. Fortunately almost all kept their "cool."

It was brawny stuff all the way, and the wonder of it all was that nobody was seriously injured.

For years the whole affair will be talked about - and there was scope for discussion from the very minute the teams appeared on the field.

There, wonder of wonders to behold, was Claughaun man, Michael Graham, occupying the "A.N. Other" berth. The County Board Appeals Committee met on Saturday night to hear an appeal from Graham against the two months suspension imposed on him by the City Board last Tuesday night.

After lengthy discussion, the Appeals Committee reduced the suspension to two weeks.

Tom Ryan of Ballybrown also appealed his six months suspension, and this was reduced to two months.

Many and varied are the comments amongst Limerick club members at the swift sitting of the Appeals Committee. No doubt there will be questions asked and comments made on the matter at the next County Board meeting.

But back to Sunday's thrills, and while excitement was at fever pitch all the time and tackling was of a bone-crushing nature, the standard of hurling for too long was sub-standard. Limerick's Eamonn Cregan, Éamon Grimes, Michael Graham and Willie Moore can hardly be as bad again and figure on a winning side. This is, of course, a healthy sign for the final, when one hopes, all will be back to form when a much better display can be expected.

Tipperary, on Sunday, had their corner-back, John Gleeson, sent off after ten minutes for a very blatant foul on Liam O'Donoghue. This should have crippled Tipperary, but wise men that they are, they switched their forces to such a commendable degree that whereas the obvious(?) vacancy cropped up at corner-back they finished up by having the missing link at corner forward.

This meant that Limerick's Jim O'Brien was a loose man in the middle of the fray, and for long spells the Bruree man was completely out of things.

But while Limerick might have been a shade lucky to win, they once again displayed tremendous fighting qualities to force the extra time during which they were In complete control against an opposition that was by now restored to full complement.

Seconds

There were only 25 seconds remaining of actual time when Limerick were a goal down and forced a '70. Delightfully as he had done so many times earlier, Seán Foley lobbed in a glorious ball, which amid tremendous excitement Eamonn Cregan, in one of his rare good moments, flashed to the net to level matters again.

Few of the thousands of Limerick supporters could have hoped that what seemed inevitable defeat could have been avoided at such a late stage. But deservedly, equality had been restored and now followed half an hour of utter confusion. The teams retired for a "breather" and I imagine that some harsh words were spoken to many of the Limerickmen who had not been in any way responsible for getting yet another chance of advancement.

While the teams were away the rain began to pour. Even when the sides did return more confusion followed as Activities Committee chairman, Noel Drumgoole, called officials of both counties to the middle of the field. There was a problem about the crowd encroaching over the sideline and there was also some issue about who should supply sliothars. Eventually the matter was resolved and onward went the battle.

By now Leonard Enright came into the Limerick side in place of Graham and Paul Byrne was in action for Tipperary.

Limerick seemed doomed within seconds of the start of extra time. Francis Loughnane gained possession about fifteen yards out on the right, He battered his way through to the end line and then emerged from a flurry of Limerick men to race in from the end line to finish up a tremendous individual effort by palming the ball to the net.

It was a great re-start for Tipperary and when Jack Ryan and John Flanagan added Tipperary points without reply from Limerick it seemed that the great run of league successes was at an end. But with the rain by now drenching all, Limerick in super-style picked themselves together. Liam O'Donoghue, by now becoming the force all know he can be, rammed in a great goal from a Bennis cross and suddenly Limerick were storming back to life.

1973 Keeping the Dream Alive

Willie Moore gets in a hook against Séamus Power during the NHL semi-final replay in Birr.

Lead

Willie Moore helped a great effort by Frankie Nolan to the net to put Limerick in front and by now thoughts of defeat had almost disappeared. Richie Bennis tacked on a Limerick point to leave them two points clear and then Frankie Nolan cracked in a glorious goal to clinch the issue.

Frankie Nolan in action during the NHL semi-final replay.

Tipperary battled back though and the woodwork foiled them and then a lady spectator kicked a ball out that had apparently gone wide. This enabled Tipperary to remain on the offensive and Limerick were penalised. With seconds fading fast Loughnane stepped up to crash in a fine goal, but time had run out for Tipperary and Limerick were through.

But there will be many inquests by Limerick. It was a far from impressive display by the side whose effectiveness was obviously greatly blunted by the narrowness of the Birr pitch.

Not once did we see the characteristic displays of speedy teamwork from the attack and this unit of the side greatly disappointed.

Granted, they were up against a superb Tipperary defence in which Jimmy Crampton. Tadgh O'Connor and, most of all, goalie Tadgh Murphy, were brilliant. Len Gaynor was very little behind and with these in such form it was clear early on that Limerick would have to win it the hard way.

Of the Limerick attack, only Frankie Nolan did well and he had some terrific scores to his credit. The remainder of them were all a big disappointment though each worked very hard. Limerick's star on this occasion, to my mind, was left-half back Seán Foley. His display was superb and he made some powerful clearances.

There were other stars, too, for Limerick, and in this category must be Pat Hartigan, Jim O'Donnell and Jim O'Brien, when he had opposition which he could outhurl.

Eamonn Rea and Mossie Dowling both got through a great deal of good work and played their part in the win. Bernie Hartigan did well in patches, but many others will have to do a great deal better. Liam O'Donoghue did particularly well on his return during the interval of ordinary time after his early punishment.

Limerick had an array of substitutes in action, including the ever-reliable Phil Bennis, Len Enright, who achieved nothing; Pat Fogarty, of whom the same can be said. Michael Graham went off and came on again, but was equally ineffective each time, and there is great consolation that he and so many others were off form and that success was Limerick's lot.

From the very opening we had clear indications that a bone-shaking contest was "on." So hard did Éamon Grimes and P.J. Ryan pull to win possession from the referee's throw-in that Mr Spain had to speak to the two of them and then have a second throw-in before the contest got under way. While Tipperary had won the initial break-away, it was Limerick who were first to threaten. Then Richie Bennis lost a chance after a '70 had been dropped close in. A few minutes later it seemed as if the disadvantage of playing on such a confined pitch might not count as in a delightful movement Foley cleared his lines to Cregan, who in turn parted to Bennis, who however, took too much time in planning his stroke and his effort was easily cleared.

All that was inside two minutes, but a minute later Tipperary went in front when Loughnane pointed a free. Sixty seconds later the sides were level when Bennis tapped over a Limerick free.

Limerick supporters roared in anticipation of a goal shortly afterwards, but John Gleeson had his moment of glory when he scraped the ball off the line from a Cregan effort.

There was a five-minute spell of no scoring following Bennis' point, but that is not to suggest any lack of activity. Rather is it an indication of how close and exciting the exchanges were at this early stage.

Tipperary went back in front after nine minutes when John Flanagan had a point.

Sent off

Then followed the tenth minute drama when Liam O'Donoghue was at the receiving end of a foul stroke which upset Mr Spain to such a degree that he had little hesitation in sending Gleeson off. Now it seemed that Limerick were "good things." With fifty minutes to go and Tipperary so reduced one thought that this would be easy for Limerick but, if anything, the opposition was the ease.

After twelve minutes Bennis again levelled for Limerick from a free.

Once again Tipperary edged in front after fourteen minutes when Roger Ryan pointed and at this stage Andy Dunworth was in the game for Limerick in place of the wounded O'Donoghue.

By this time Tipperary had sorted themselves out in a big way. Right through the field they had altered their side so that whereas the original vacancy arose at left corner back by now the vacancy was at corner forward. This meant that Jim O'Brien was the unmarked Limerick man and nothing could have upset Limerick to a greater degree. Of all the players on duty O'Brien was the one whose effectiveness is always at his best when the opposition is at its strongest. Now the Bruree man was on his own and quite frankly for long stages he looked absolutely lost. He did not seem to know whether he should move forward, remain loose, or stay behind to cover off.

Tense moments around the Tipperary goalmouth at St. Brendan's Park, Birr.

1973 Keeping the Dream Alive

Éamon Grimes in action against Jimmy Crampton during the NHL semi-final replay in Birr.

As it was, what should have been a big advantage completely upset Limerick's fluency - such as it was up to then.

But now Limerick were already coming bedraggled and upset, but the fierceness of the exchanges prevented one from immediately noticing this, and it was only when one had time to think it all over during the interval that one realised that Gleeson's sudden departure was almost as big a handicap to Limerick as it was to Tipperary.

Limerick were fortunate to escape in the 17th minute. Tom O'Dwyer seemed sure of a goal, but a hurley had been thrown in his path by a panic seized defender, and the referee awarded a free, from which Loughnane tried to over-punish the defender by trying for goal, and his effort was cleared. In the eighteenth minute Loughnane had Tipperary two points in front, but three minutes later Limerick took the lead for the first time. A Bennis cross was finished to the net by Frankie Nolan.

Seconds later Limerick were back in scoring line again. But on this occasion Bennis tried for a goal, which was blocked and the ball rebounded to him. He was too slow to avail of the chance, but he did work the ball to Andy Dunworth, whose effort under extreme pressure went inches wide.

In the 24th minute Bennis had a point, but seconds later the same player had a very bad miss. This time the chance was again from a 21-yard free, but I am not sure whether Bennis intended to try and drop his effort just under the bar or whether he intended to have a point. But whatever his intentions, the ball dropped short and was cleared.

Once again it was the Patrickswell man who had a chance a minute later, when he was too slow to react to a line pass from Grimes. But in the 28th minute, Bennis hit over a very fine point from a free to leave Limerick three points in front. But a minute from the interval Tipperary got on terms. Séamus Horgan did well to stop a 21-yard free from Loughnane, but Jack Ryan stormed in to push the ball to the net. During the break we had time to think over Limerick's short-comings. In the first half five wides had been hit by Limerick, whereas Tipperary had only two wides. Liam O'Donoghue resumed for Limerick after the interval and Dunworth retired. But it was Tipperary who set off in front again, when Loughnane had a point.

A group of Limerick hurling supporters enjoying the action during the county's National Hurling League semi-final clash with Tipperary in Birr.

Second Half

Within a minute of the restart, Tipperary were once again in front, when Loughnane had a point. Seconds later, Bennis hit a bad wide and Graham was off target soon after. In all, Limerick had four wides within three minutes of resuming. In the sixth minute the sides were once again level with a splendid point from Frankie Nolan. Loughnane had a glorious point for Tipperary, but again in the eighth minute equality was restored when Bennis pointed a Limerick free.

Then followed a nasty foul by Loughnane on Foley, and the Roscrea man, in the tenth minute had another Tipperary point. That once again put his side in front, and Jack Ryan added another point in the 13th minute. Bennis pointed a Limerick free, but Loughnane had another point for Tipperary to have his side two points in front with a quarter of an hour remaining. In the 19th minute, Grimes floated in a great side-line cut which enabled Willie Moore to have a fine Limerick point. Eight minutes from the end Loughnane had another Tipp. point, but a minute later, Bennis had a beautiful point for Limerick who by now were struggling badly.

Pat Hartigan brought off a great clearance but was penalised for some unknown reason and Loughnane added another Tipperary point and defeat seemed certain. Bennis hit a hopeless wide and Nolan was also off target before Dinny Ryan pointed to leave Tipperary three points in front. But then came Foley's great late '70 which Cregan goaled to bring it to extra time. Of the Limerick attack Nolan was clearly most effective and O'Donoghue was next in the honours list.

The remainder were bad and must do better. But, while Richie Bennis did miss many chances, he also scored many vital points and his overall performance was fair. He can, and will, do much better.

While all their defenders were the stars, Tipperary also had a brilliant Francis Loughnane in action. Roger Ryan, I thought, also did well and the others all had their moments, although the front men should have capitalised more on the big advantage won for them by midfielders Hogan and P.J. Ryan. Tipperary, too, brought in many substitutes including a late and probably final appearance of the former star, Jimmy Doyle, who did not hit one ball when in the game.

Scorers

Limerick - F. Nolan 3-1; R. Bennis 0-8 (0-5 frees); E. Cregan and L. O'Donoghue 1-0; W. Moore 0-1.

Tipperary - F. Loughnane 2-8 (1-4 frees); J. Ryan 1-2; J. Flanagan 0-2; R. Ryan and D. Ryan 0-1.

Teams

Limerick - S. Horgan; P. Hartigan, E. Rea, J. O'Brien; M, Dowling, J. O'Donnell, S. Foley; E. Grimes, B. Hartigan; R. Bennis, E. Cregan, M. Graham; L. O'Donoghue, W. Moore, F. Nolan. Subs: A. Dunworth for O'Donoghue (injured), L. Enright for Graham (at the start of extra time), P. Bennis for Dowling, P. Fogarty for Enright, Graham for Foley.

Tipperary - T. Murphy; J. Fogarty, J. Kelly, J. Gleeson; J. Crampton, T. O'Connor, L. Gaynor; S. Hogan, P.J. Ryan; F. Loughnane, N. O'Dwyer, J. Ryan; J. Flanagan, R. Ryan, T. O'Dwyer. Subs: D. Ryan for T. O'Dwyer, P. Byrne (at start of extra time), J. Doyle for Flanagan.

Referee - Mick Spain (Offaly).

Front cover of the official programme of the 1973 NHL final.

Front cover of the pirate programme of the 1973 NHL final.

1973 Keeping the Dream Alive

The Limerick team that lost to We...
Back Row (L-R): Eamonn Rea, Eamonn Cregan, Pat Hartigan,
Front Row (L-R): Frankie Nolan, Michael Graham, Liam O'Do...

...73 National Hurling League final.
...n O'Brien, Jim O'Donnell, Willie Moore and Bernie Hartigan.
...s Horgan, Éamon Grimes, Richie Bennis and Mossie Dowling.

1973 Keeping the Dream Alive

The Limerick team who beat Tipperary, 5-10 to 3-14, after extra time in the replayed semi-final in Birr on April 29.

LUIMNEACH

Dathanna: Glas is Bán
(Green and White)

(1) P. Ó hArgáin
F. Horgan
(Tournafulla)

(2) P. Ó hArtagáin   (3) E. Ó Riabhaigh   (4) S. Ó Briain
P. Hartigan   E. Rea   J. O'Brien
(South Liberties)   (Faughs, Áth Cliath)   (Bruree)

(5) M. Ó Dubhlainn   (6) S. Ó Dónail   (7) S. Ó Foghlú
M. Dowling   J. O'Donnell   J. Foley
(Kilmallock)   (Doon)   (Patrickswell)

(8) B. Ó hArtagáin   (9) E. Ó Greacháin (Capt.)
B. Hartigan   E. Grimes
(Old Christians)   (South Liberties)

(10) R. Bennis   (11) E. Ó Criagáin   (12) M. Ó Greacháin
R. Bennis   E. Cregan   M. Graham
(Patrickswell)   (Claughaun)   (Claughaun)

(13) L. Ó Donnchú   (14) L. Ó Mórdha   (15) P. Ó Nualláin
L. O'Donoghue   W. Moore   F. Nolan
(Mungret)   (Doon)   (Patrickswell)

Fir Ionaid: (16) P. Bennis (P. Bennis, Patrickswell); (17) S. Allis (J. Allis, Doon); (18) S. Ó hOgáin (J. Hogan, Claughaun); (19) P. Ó Fógartaigh (P. Fogarty, Ballybrown); (20) L. Mac Ionnrachtaigh (L. Enright, Patrickswell).

LUIMNEACH	Cúil Goals	Cúilíní Points	Seachaí Overs	70 Sl. 70's	Saor-Phocanna Free Pucks
1adh Leath (1st Half)					
2adh Leath (2nd Half)					
Iomlán (Total)					

1973 Keeping the Dream Alive

● *The Wexford side who beat Waterford by 2-16 to 4-7 in the quarter-final replay in Kilkenny on April 15.*

LOCH GARMAN

Dathanna: Corcora is Ór
(Purple and Gold)

(1) **P. Ó Nualláin**
P. Nolan
(Olygate/Glenbrien)

(2) **S. Piondar**   (3) **E. Ó Murchú**   (4) **T. Ó Conchúir (Capt.)**
J. Pender   T. Murphy   T. O'Connor
(Oulart/the Bealach) *(Ferns)*   *(Rathnure)*

(5) **C. Ó Deoráin**   (6) **M. Iácób**   (7) **L. Ó Murchú**
C. Doran   M. Jacob   W. Murphy
(Buffers Alley)   *(Oulart/the Bealach)* *(Faythe Harriers)*

(8) **D. Bernie**   (9) **P. Mac Liam**
D. Bernie   P. Wilson
(Ferns)   *(Ballyhogue)*

(10) **C. Mac Eocaidh**   (11) **M. Ó Coigligh**   (12) **T. Ó Broin**
C. Kehoe   M. Quigley   T. Byrne
(Raparees)   *(Rathnure)*   *(Oulart/the Bealach)*

(13) **E. Mag Eochaidh**   (14) **A. Ó Deoráin**   (15) **S. Ó Béara**
H. Gough   A. Doran   J. Berry
(Raparees)   *(Buffers Alley)*   *(St. Annes/St. Patricks)*

Fir Ionaid: (16) P. Mac Eochaidh (P. Kehoe, Oulart/the Bealach); (17) S. Ó Coigligh (J. Quigley, Rathnure); (18) S. Pearail (J. Parle, Oulart/the Bealach; (19) P. Caomhánach (P. Kavanagh, Buffers Alley); (20) E. Ó Bogaigh (E. Buggy, Faythe Harriers).

LOCH GARMAN	Cúil Goals	Cúiliní Points	Seachaí Overs	70's 70's	Saor-Phocanna Free Pucks
1adh Leath (1st Half)					
2adh Leath (2nd Half)					
Iomlán (Total)					

Limerick Battered To Defeat In Thrilling League Final
(Limerick Leader, 14 May 1973)
Now Is The Time for Changes...
Time For A Big Re-Think

By Cormac Liddy

Limerick 3-7
Wexford 4-13

Throw in all the what might-have-beens and speculate all you like but when all things are brooded on and all calculations made it must be agreed that on the day Wexford were superior to Limerick in Sunday's extremely entertaining National Hurling League final. To claim that Limerick were unlucky would not be accepting the cruel, hard fact of hurling life which is that on final occasions Limerick just cannot shake off the position of being "second".

Referee Frank Murphy about to throw the ball in at the 1973 NHL final.

Pity Michael Graham who ended up with a broken leg in Jervis Street Hospital. Others, too, carry scars or big-day action but if Sunday's defeat could be used as the stick to beat out some of the more obvious faults then, perhaps, a return to Croke Park on 2 September to bid for a more supreme prize might yet be possible. A win then would fittingly atone for the three defeats out of four League final appearances. It is abundantly clear now that there are certain players on the present side who might he bettor suited to grandstand seats on big occasions.

No longer can it be said that such and such a man had an "off-day" and will be better the next time. It is a pity, but true, that certain members of the present side are just not up to the required standard. Accordingly the place for them should, and must, be on the sideline. Sunday's final was a stormer, full of life and vigour with hard slogging being the order of the day. At times there were the spectacular bursts of individual brilliance but for the greater part it was "hit first and ask questions later." That was the policy of both sides. Wexford implemented the plan much mere successfully and accordingly went home with the battered League trophy which someone might consider replacing.

All the cleaning and polishing of the present trophy would not be sufficient to entice me to sip champagne from it . . . even were I so disposed and should the opportunity present itself!

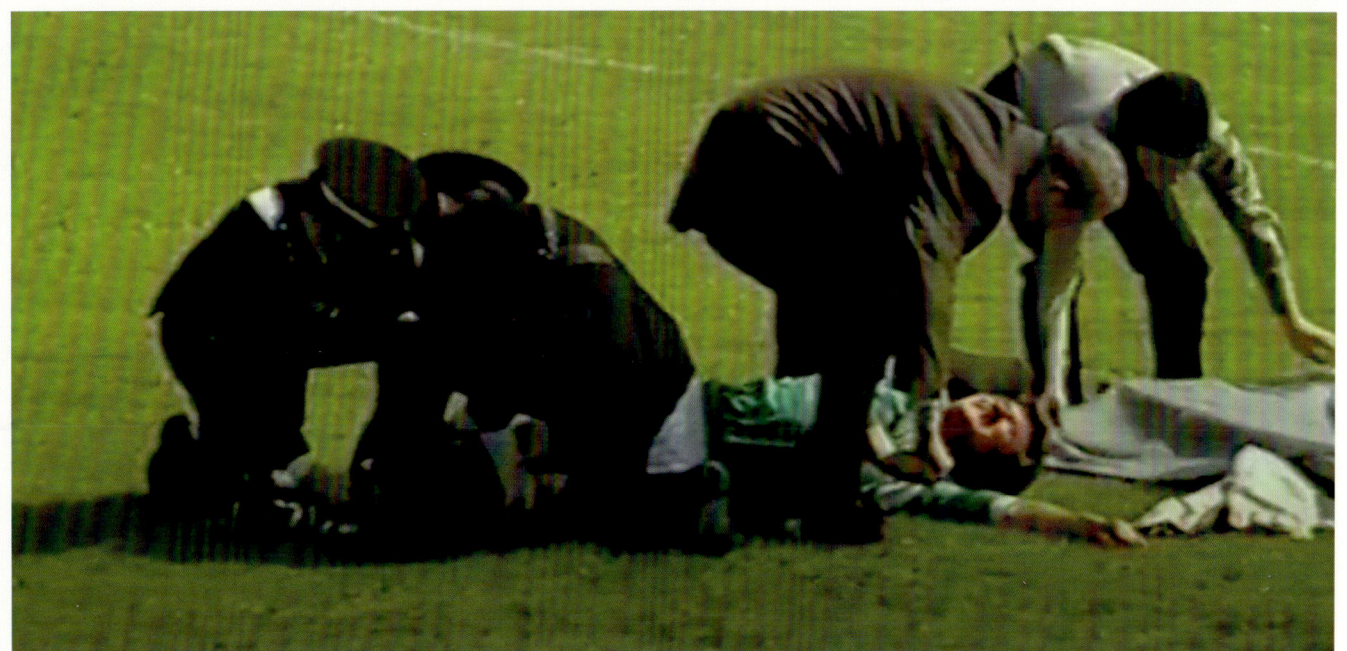
The pain etched on Michael Graham's face tells its own story as a double leg break sustained during the 1973 NHL final rules him out of action for the rest of the campaign.

Granted had Wexford's Pat Nolan not effected some super saves the prize might have come Limerick's way. But had such been the case it would have been very hard on Wexford and to a neutral follower justice would not have been seen to be done. Had a scorching effort by Mossie Dowling, which whizzed inches wide at a time when Limerick trailed by four points, gone in, I have not the slightest doubt it would have brought victory to Limerick. It was that type of an occasion, and while three goals might appear a substantial beating, Limerick were not that much inferior.

Few of the all-important "breaks" came Limerick's way. Indeed, if anything, Wexford won handsomely in the collection of "soft" opportunities and to their very great credit, they capitalised to a very successful extent on the "stray" chances that came their way. Had Limerick done likewise, then Éamon Grimes might have brought the trophy back in the train with him. But, had Limerick triumphed on Sunday I am convinced that it would have ended what hopes there are of the All Ireland championship being won. Success on Sunday would naturally have given the impression that Limerick are "tops."

If under such an illusion the Limerick selectors could be pardoned for not wielding the "big stick" for this is essential if any major title is to be won.

Pitch Size

Before Birr many Limerickmen opined that the small pitch could be all against Limerick's style of play. It was in many respects but those who thought that the wide open spaces of Croke Park would lead to a demolition of any opponents were sadly disappointed. Only on very rare occasions could Limerick set up a combined attack with a number of players figuring. At no stage was there a return to the golden era when three or four players would combine in a speedy move which would terminate with a top class score.

This time it was painfully clear once the second quarter was entered that Limerick could not be able, or allowed, to create the necessary opportunities to bring those delightful scores which were managed two years ago. But then it was Tipperary who were the opposition! Wexford were an entirely different proposition whose leading attribute was physical force. They used their size and weight to full advantage to beat Limerick into subjection.

Most times their brawny efforts were within the meaning of the rules. On rare occasions certain individuals stepped outside the letters of the law and committed indiscretions that merited more serious attention from referee Frank Murphy of Cork who, it must be stated, nevertheless, handled the game with top class efficiency. It was a thrilling affair for most of the time and even though Wexford went into a huge lead too often there was always the feeling that Limerick would come from behind to snatch success.

But the nearest they could get was within four points, about five minutes from the end after Richie Bennis had slammed in a glorious goal. Almost immediately came Dowling's great effort which rolled just wide with Nolan appearing beaten. Had it gone in Limerick could not have been stopped but Wexford shrugged off the sudden challenge and in the closing stages Tony Doran palmed in a glorious goal and that was that as far as Limerick were concerned.

Séamus Horgan pucking out the ball during the 1973 NHL final.

Doran, at times, looked as if he were conferred with the freedom of the park so much in the clear did he appear. He gave Eamonn Rea a merciless pounding and hard as did the Faughs man try he just could not cope with the bustling man from the Buffers Alley club. With Doran in such devastating form, he had the Limerick defence at full stretch throughout. Rea could not cope sufficiently with Doran, and as a result the others, a lot of the time, had to overlap to bridge the blatant gaps.

Once more it was fairly obvious that Limerick need Pat Hartigan on the verge of the square and in the full-back role, the side just cannot afford to have him operating on the flank. He must be where the action IS, and is LIKELY to be.

On Sunday, Hartigan had a fine game, but had he been at full-back I am convinced he would have blunted Doran and company to a far greater extent than was done.

Goalkeeper Séamus Horgan again brought off some fine saves, and his lengthy goal pucks were a feature. But too often his colleagues allowed him to be "crowded," with the result that I am sure he could not have had a proper view - in sufficient time - of two of the shots that beat him.

Game's Star

But Limerick did, provide the game's star in corner back Jim O'Brien. His was truly a memorable display, and the pity of it all was that his finest hour was not rewarded with victory. Many times O'Brien averted major crises and certainly it was no fault of his that Limerick are not champions.

Faults

Limerick's half-back line was not near as efficient as it might have been. Jim O'Donnell in the centre did achieve a good deal of success but there were times when he was left standing by the speed of the opposition.

Martin Quigley was very effective for the winners but even more so were half-forwards Christy Kehoe and Tom Byrne. This pair all too often were able to avoid the attentions of Seán Foley and Mossie Dowling. The former tried extremely hard but too often his opponent was in possession and he had to try and block him instead of he getting possession and forcing the opposition to try and deprive him of the ball.

Foley did make some fine clearances but too often he overdid the individualism and might have been better off had he made the ball do more of the work.

While at half back Mossie Dowling was not very successful although at all times he tried hard. When the Kilmallock man was moved to full forward he met with much more success and had he been in attack throughout he might well have brought Limerick victory. His strong, bustling style was most effective up front and in future he must be in attack.

Return

Limerick brought in the ever-dependable Phil Bennis as a substitute and the Patrickswell man once again acquitted himself with distinction. His was a fine effort and once more he showed that his heart is in the right place.

Limerick had their troubles at midfield, though, and for all that Bernie Hartigan and Éamon Grimes achieved it was near not enough.

Hartigan could only get into the game in spasms. When he did he was extremely effective but there were times when he seemed to be "missing."

Grimes tried extremely hard. In traditional style on occasions he "flew" past opponents but as was the case with Seán Foley I felt that at times he overdid the individualism. I hope I am not being too critical for I fully appreciate how Grimes might have felt towards those in front of him.

When one sees such little headway being made by others then the natural reaction is to try and go it alone. Grimes, had he had the necessary support, might well have been in a position to turn the tide Limerick's way.

That Limerick have many problems in attack is all too obvious. Not one of the original sextet made any lasting impression and, indeed a big re-think about the merits of some of them might not be out of order.

Front Three

The full-forward trio in particular achieved little. Willie Moore was never a serious danger to the Wexford defence, and far too often he was on the wrong side of his opponent. Liam O'Donoghue, of whom so much was expected, was never a real threat, but it would be unwise to write him off on the strength of one bad display.

In the other corner, too, Frankie Nolan did little right, and it was only when Mossie Dowling was moved into that area, that Limerick seriously threatened. Dowling prods, pokes and strikes in such a manner as to create many opportunities for himself and others. It was a great pity that he was not in a position to do so earlier on. Once again Eamonn Cregan was unable to turn in the performance of which we know he is capable. Apart from his well-taken goal, he did nothing, and this must rank as even a worse display than he gave at Birr.

Many Claughaun men are adamant that Cregan is a far better centre-back than a centre-forward. Now might be the ideal opportunity to test fully this theory, as Jim O'Donnell does appear to have lost a lot of his class. On Sunday he did bring off some vital clearances, but he, too, has often done better.

Richie Bennis was once again a disappointment. He did, of course, slam in a glorious goal, and he also hit over valuable points from frees. But Bennis seems to lack the "killer" instinct on the big occasion. Frequently he seemed to be moving - and thinking - at too slow a pace. On a number of occasions he seemed to be set to gain possession but too often he did not catch cleanly and he had to prod and poke to try and win back a ball that should have been his in the first place.

Crowd shot from the 1973 NHL final.

Bunching

As has been the case on too many sad occasions in the past, Limerick were once again on Sunday guilty of far too much bunching. Many times, two or even more members of the side went for the same ball. This allowed Wexford have a clear man and so crisply were they operating that this proved fatal. Again, too, Limerick were guilty of trying to raise the ball too often when it might have been far more rewarding had first-time pulling along the ground been the tactic.

Surprise

Wexford surprised many and, I am sure, some of themselves by their deeds. They certainly moved with a far greater degree of urgency than Limerick and they fully demonstrated the benefits to be gained by first time, hard pulling.

Their speed caught Limerick by surprise and their teamwork was infinitely better than that of Limerick, who too often were bedraggled and disorganised. It was a memorable occasion for John Quigley. When his club-mate Teddy O'Connor was ruled as unfit the Rathnure men brought in the play-anywhere Quigley to left corner-back. He had a brilliant game there and fittingly he became captain of the side.

His sturdy clearances were a feature and this was never more clearly emphasised than in the closing stages when he frequently burst clear from defence to set his colleagues at the other end in motion.

Pat Nolan in goal for Wexford was superb. He brought off some tremendous saves and had it not been for him Limerick, despite all their shortcomings, might have won.

It must be recorded, too, of course, that the woodwork foiled Limerick of a certain goal, but, of course, the timber is there to be avoided and it was not.

All the Wexford defenders looked classical this time, such poor impact did the Limerick attack make.

The half-back trio of Mick Jacob (centre), Doran and Willie Murphy were outstanding, while Dave Bernie and substitute Ned Buggy did very well at midfield.

Up front, Doran was superb and Jack Berry, Tony Byrne and Christy Kehoe were others to do much too good from a Limerick viewpoint.

But overall Wexford were too strong and too speedy for a Limerick side that had weaknesses in most sectors.

RTÉ still from the 1973 NHL final at Croke Park.

Fortunately there are games coming up at the Gaelic Ground against Cork (May 24th) and Kilkenny (May 31st) and these can he used to introduce new talent. Perhaps former Offaly man Joe McKenna, might be worth a try and also last year's London star, Mick Smith. Once again Christy Campbell might, with justification, be given another chance, and John Quinlan and some of the others might also be given sufficient "airing" to see their full potential.

This applied, too, to Andy Dunworth, who achieved little on Sunday during his brief stay but, perhaps, if he was told he was being given a full match he might be able to achieve more. I think that the haunting feeling that you are to be hauled off must adversely affect a player.

Support

Limerick had a huge amount of support on Sunday and I imagine that for every Wexford enthusiast there were four from Limerick. What a pity that the successful start could not be maintained.

After the first half top rate showing by Jim O'Donnell many were surprised to see that he had been switched to corner back on the resumption. Pat Hartigan was then at centre back, but the move did not bring the hoped-for success.

Willie Moore made no headway and it was left to Jim O'Brien, Séamus Horgan, Éamon Grimes, Mossie Dowling, Pat Hartigan and to a lesser extent O'Donnell and Foley to win what merit marks there were for Limerick.

Scorcher

There was a blistering fast start of skill, pace and sweet striking and it was obvious that one or other of the combatants would be unable to maintain the fierce pace. Éamon Grimes won the toss for Limerick who had five of their side wearing headgear. It was four minutes before we had the first score - a point from a free by Bennis after Moore had been fouled. Grimes had a glorious point for Limerick two minutes later after the move began deep in the Limerick territory and was carried on by Richie Bennis.

Scorers

Limerick - R. Bennis 1-4 (0-3 frees); M. Dowling 1-1; E. Cregan 1-0; E. Grimes 0-2.

Wexford - T. Byrne 1-6; T. Doran 2-2; M. Quigley 1-1; E. Buggy 0-2; C. Kehoe and H. Gough 0-1.

Teams

Limerick - S. Horgan; P. Hartigan, E. Rea, J. O'Brien; M. Dowling. J. O'Donnell, S. Foley; B. Hartigan, E. Grimes (Capt) ; R. Bennis, E. Cregan. M. Graham; L. O'Donoghue, W. Moore, F. Nolan. Subs: A. Dunworth for Graham (14th minute injured), P. Bennis for Dunworth (second half), L. Enright for O'Donnell (50th minute).

Wexford - P. Nolan; J. Pender, E. Murphy, J. Quigley (c); C. Doran. M. Jacob. W. Murphy; D. Bernie, E. Buggy; C. Kehoe, M. Quigley, T. Byrne; H. Gough, A. Doran, J. Berry. Subs: P. Kehoe for Pender (second half), J. Purcell for Gough (53rd minute).

Referee - Frank Murphy (Cork).

carrolls GAA allstars

Awarded to the 15 hurlers and 15 footballers who, throughout the year, have performed with outstanding skill and have consistently shown their superiority on the field.
The players are nominated and finally selected by the leading G.A.A. sportswriters. The result is the Carrolls Allstars. Two teams containing the very best of current G.A.A. talent.

Who will receive the honours this year?

'Bronntar Tabhartais Carrolls G.A.A. All Stars ar na hiománaithe agus ar na peileadóirí is mó cáil i rith na bliana ach 'sé an brí is mó atá leo ná aitheantas a thabhairt don tréithíocht sportúlachta is aoirde in ár gcluichí náisiúnta."

The magnificent trophy designed by leading sculptor Garry Trimble and awarded to each member of the Carrolls G.A.A. Allstars Hurling team.

Sponsored by:
P.J. Carroll & Co. Ltd.

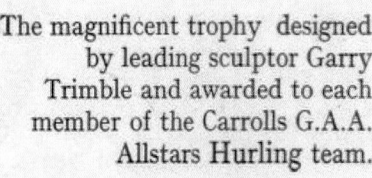

Back cover of the official programme of the 1973 NHL final

CHAPTER 5
1973
CHALLENGE GAMES

It is a pity that proper challenges games at senior inter-county level, for pitch openings or tournaments; are pretty much a thing of the past - contests that meant something to the teams that played in them. One of the last proper challenge games that Limerick played goes back to the opening of the Kilbreedy complex, which is mentioned later in this book as part of the 2013 celebrations of the heroes of 1973.

Traces have been found of five challenge games in 1973, one before the National Hurling League restarted in late January, another three between league and championship, and the last played after the championship had started. Mention was also found of a fascinating internal "A" versus "B" game played in early January. It was not publicised at the time but was mentioned by Séamus Ó Ceallaigh ("Camán") in his '1973 in Retrospect' article in the last *Limerick Leader* of that wonderful year.

It listed the men who must have been thought of as the top hurlers in the county at the time. An interesting list it makes too! Of the 21 men named in the All Ireland Hurling Final programme later that year, only Joe McKenna – still hurling for Offaly – was not mentioned in one form or another. Phil Bennis and Paudie Fitzmaurice were on the "common reserve panel," a term in vogue at the time in rugby union circles.

Offaly were played before the league restarted, with a win recorded. There were no teams printed in the meagre newspaper reports of the time, only the scorers. Local Offaly newspapers ignored the game completely. Eleven Limerick men who played that day have been recorded for posterity in the statistics chapter at the end of this book.

By May, Joe McKenna had made his inter-county transfer from Offaly to Limerick. He was already playing his club hurling with South Liberties and was part of the team that made its long-awaited breakthrough in 1972. He featured for the first time against Cork in a game won by the locals in the Gaelic Grounds. Joe had played the entire league campaign with Offaly and was even named for their championship opener only days before the actual transfer took place. The organisers produced a programme for this game. Matt Ruth made a big impression, the Kilkenny-born Christian Brother now being stationed in Sexton Street. He was to come unstuck later in the summer when his inter-county transfer floundered due to having lined out (in his pants) for a Kilkenny National Football League team a few months before. He did transfer to Limerick in 1974.

Limerick won another challenge match in the Gaelic Grounds soon after, against Kilkenny, where Ruth played well again. Paudie "Pat" Fitzmaurice also impressed that evening according to Charlie Mulqueen. Tony "Willie" Smith played that evening and starred for Kilmallock in the county final later in the year, before returning home to Clonmel a few years later.

Limerick travelled to Castlelyons for a return game with Cork 11 days later, two weeks out from the Munster Championship opener. The game marked the opening of a new community centre there. No programme is known from this game. Cork were "lucky" to get a draw according to newspaper reports. Jack O'Dwyer further impressed that evening. Cork would play Tipperary in the championship a week after Limerick faced Clare, in a rematch of their "disgraceful" late 1972 league encounter.

Not long after playing Clare in the championship, Limerick faced Waterford in a challenge match, again in the Gaelic Grounds. Waterford had been knocked out of the championship on 20 May against Tipperary and had nothing to play for. It was a high-scoring game, with 8 goals and 29 points recorded; Limerick securing the win, unimpressively so, after leading very well at half time. Eamonn Rea was deployed at full forward and made some impact but not enough for one well-known local reporter's liking. Jackie Power thought otherwise, as did others who saw the game. Michael Slattery refereed for obvious reasons. Such a game would be unthinkable these days.

Where Will Title Go This Year
(Gaelic Sport, January 1973)

By Mick Dunne of RTÉ who examines prospects for the upcoming year

We do not need the help of a crystal ball to declare, even at this early stage of the new year, that the '73 All Ireland hurling title will be won by one of four counties Kilkenny, Cork, Wexford or Tipperary. It is a fairly safe prediction and only a very significant shift of hurling power will show it to be incorrect. This is the way things have been in hurling in every one of the previous 13 years. Furthermore, in only nine of the last 50 years has the championship gone outside the four counties just listed - to Dublin in 1924, '27 and '38, Limerick in '34, '36 and '40, Waterford in '48 and '59, and Galway in '23.

And that is the most regrettable feature of hurling in modern times. Indeed, the real power in the game is so constricted and the championship as a consequence, so lacking in variety that it is a tremendous tribute to the four "Big Guns" that they can still consistently attract attendances to the final in excess of 60,000, sometimes less than 10,000 short of the crowds at the decider of the football championship in which there is not at all the same measure of predictability.

Just imagine, therefore, what a great response there would be if some new faces appeared in the hurling final. Reflect on what a welcome awaits Waterford, Clare, Limerick or Galway if they ever succeed in qualifying for the final again. Right now it does not seem as if they will be there in the immediate future, although all four have shown some encouraging signs in recent times. Clare, at the moment, appear the most promising.

They quickly purged themselves of the disappointment that followed last year's Munster final collapse and are doing well in the League. But some of the gloss is stripped from recent achievements by the very fact that the best of them were attained at home in Ennis. The real test will come when they go outside Cusack Park to play Kilkenny on March 4. After that game we will be in a much better position to say just how far they have advanced.

Waterford are also making some running in the League and they must be regarded as virtually certain to earn promotion back to the premier section. But it will take a little longer, I reckon, for them to become a force again among the top counties. Galway's triumph in the under-21 championship shows they are not devoid of young potential, but isolated as they are in the west as far as the championship is concerned - one wonders if they can ever make substantial progress.

As for Limerick, I believe they may have missed their chance. Even as they reached the last three League finals and the '71 Munster final they were not a young side — in the hurling sense. Now they cannot have been helped by internal trouble and disagreement over the training of the team.

Because of this, and the failure to make the big breakthrough in the past three summers, they may have left their spirit behind them. So it looks like the "Big Four" once again. The title is Kilkenny's and they are not going to relinquish it without a struggle even though several of their players are moving on in years. Their '72 triumph might, in this respect, be compared with the 1960 victory, which was the last, glorious effort for so many of the Wexford stars of the 1950s.

However, Kilkenny have shown they have a greater depth of talent now than at any time in latter years and this last has been emphasised by the fact that they remain happily placed in the League although not having a full team in action since the All Ireland final. Yet, it is a fact of history that although Kilkenny won the title seven times up to last year over the last four decades they never retained it in that period.

The last time they did so was when they successfully defended the championship in 1933. Tipperary will always be a danger — and their record shows that they are an even bigger danger if they get to the final against Kilkenny. But, most unusual for them, the replacements are not "growing on the trees" as they were in other decades.

This is not so with Wexford, who qualified for so many under-21 and minor finals in the past ten years that they should have a free flow of young talent coming along. Yet, they appear to be having difficulty welding it into a really sound striking force.

If I were a betting man - and 20 years of forecasting in sports journalism have taught me not to be - my money would be on Cork. Yes, despite their collapse in the '72 final. There was no doubt that when they played well in the past year they played superb hurling, but from experience they will have learned that there are no certainties in hurling. (Although, come to think of it, that is the lesson they should have learned in '69).

Moreover, they have an abundance of reserve talent coming from the under-21s and minors, but perhaps what they need most of all is weight in their attack, allied to the style, speed and intelligence. As one prominent hurler put it recently, "They play great hurling, but they've too many small men in the forwards."

The line-up at Pakie Hayes' Oyster Ballroom Dromkeen in early 1973, with the usual Bingo on Tuesdays!

"1973 in Retrospect"
(Limerick Leader, 29 December 1973)

This memorable year opened, appropriately enough, on the first Sunday (6th) of January, with a senior hurling trial, game, and the players named tor that encounter, will be of more than ordinary interest now, in view of subsequent developments.

"A" team
Séamus Horgan, Tournafulla; Mick O'Loughlin, Kilteely-Dromkeen; Pat Hartigan, South Liberties; Jim O'Brien, Bruree; Tom Ryan, Ballybrown; Jim O'Donnell, Doon; Seán (John) Foley, Patrickswell; Leonard Enright, Patrickswell; Richie Bennis, Patrickswell; Bernie Hartigan, Old Christians; Eamonn Cregan, Claughaun; Éamon Grimes, South Liberties; Andy Dunworth, Claughaun; Willie Moore, Doon; Frankie Nolan, Patrickswell.

"B" team
Jim Hogan, Claughaun; Joe Grimes, South Liberties; Eamonn Rea, Faughs; Jim Allis, Doon; Jamesy Carroll, Garryspillane; John Quinlan, Doon; John O'Dwyer, Pallasgreen; Con Shanahan, Croom; Dan Connolly, Kilmallock; John Neenan, Dromin-Athlacca; Mossie Dowling, Kilmallock; John O'Hehir, Claughaun; Liam O'Donoghue, Mungret; Mick Leahy, Bruff; Christy Campbell, Old Christians.

"Common Reserve Panel"

Phil Bennis, Patrickswell; Bill O'Gorman, Claughaun; Dan O'Connor, Tournafulla; Seán Kelly, Ahane; Denis O'Connor, Killeedy; Mike O'Leary, Dromin-Athlacca; John Ryan, Pallasgreen; Dominic Hayes, Kilmallock; Pat Fogarty, Ballybrown; Paudie Fitzmaurice, Killeedy; Mike Lundon, South Liberties; Eddie Franklin, Monaleen.

Hurlers Win
(Limerick Leader and Irish Press, 22 January 1973)

Limerick 4-9
Offaly 3-5

Limerick Succeed

Limerick successfully tried out five newcomers on their senior hurling team that travelled to Birr yesterday, where they defeated Offaly, 4-9 to 3-5, in a challenge match after leading 4-3 to 1-4 at the interval. Some very entertaining hurling was played in ideal conditions but the home team showed poor marksmanship and had 10 wides in the first half.

This contrasted with the sharper, keener hurling of the Limerickmen and the incisive play of newcomers, Pat Fogarty, Dan Connolly and Mossie Dowling was backed up in attack by such brilliant players as Frankie Nolan, Eamonn Cregan and, at centrefield, Bernie Hartigan.

However, Offaly did manage to come within a goal of the visitors in the second half, due entirely to the scoring of PJ Whelehan and improved hurling from Kieran Mooney, Seán Kennedy and centrefield Pat Moloughney.

Outstanding in the Offaly defence was Pat Corcoran while Limerick defenders, Jim O'Brien, Tom Ryan and Willie Moore caught the eye throughout the hour.

Scorers

Limerick - F. Nolan 2-3; M. Dowling 2-0; P. Fogarty 0-4; E. Grimes and J. Quinlan 0-1.

Offaly - P.J. Whelahan 1-3; P. Moloughney and K. Mooney 1-0 each; S. Moylan and J McKenna 0-1.

Referee: Gerry Kirwan (Offaly)

SENIOR HURLING TOURNAMENT

CORK

VERSUS

LIMERICK

REITEOIR: J. MOLONEY (Tipperary)

THURSDAY, 24th MAY

Commencing 7.30 p.m.

LUACH - - - 5p

The only programme known of Limerick's five challenge games of 1973.

Impressive Win by Limerick
(Limerick Leader, 26 May 1973)
Newcomers Ruth and McKenna can make big difference to c'ship prospects

By Cormac Liddy

Limerick 3-16
Cork 4-9

There was a tremendous amount of merit in Limerick's sparkling win over Cork at the Ennis Road Grounds on Thursday night. If that form could be repeated against Clare in the championship semi-final on June 24th at Thurles then there need be little doubt but that Limerick would be in final provincial action in July.

This was a Limerick display that had many in the huge crowd thrilled and quite a few dejected that the skills shown were not paraded against Wexford last Sunday week. Had that been possible, the battered League trophy would surely now be resting in the Grimes household. Limerick's selectors on Thursday night did the obvious and experimented. Brought in for his first game was Matt Ruth - scorer extraordinaire for Old Christians in his three games for them. He got 4-23 for them in three games.

Ruth came into the attack when Pat Fogarty had to retire because of aggravating his injured hand. It was hard luck on the sturdy Fogarty whom I hope to see given a further trial against Kilkenny, as I think he can still win a championship place. But Ruth jumped at his big chance. Delightfully he side-stepped opponents on many occasions, and he hit three of the nicest points that one could wish to see. Obviously he must come very much into future plans.

Former Offaly man, Joe McKenna, too, got his chance, and while he might give the impression of being a slow mover, he, too, impressed a great deal. But it was Éamon Grimes who shone most on this occasion, and his skills were a delight to watch. Limerick built up an interval lead of 2-8 to 1-6, and during the opening period they might have had as many scores again.

But in the closing stages, Limerick allowed an outclassed Cork team get far too near them for comfort and had Charlie McCarthy managed a goal from a last minute free, all Limerick would have had to show for such obvious dominance would have been a one-point winning margin.

Limerick were without Eamonn Cregan from the selected side and the selectors switched Seán Foley to centre-back and he had a fine game against Gerald McCarthy.

But there were some shock gaps revealed in Limerick's defensive set-up. Goalie Séamus Horgan did manage to make the odd good save but generally he gave rise to many anxious moments.

Pat Hartigan was finding Ray Cummins a handful until the Corkman had to retire with an injured hand, but once again Jim O'Brien had a splendid game - this time against Charlie McCarthy.

Jack O'Dwyer of Pallas was doing splendidly until injury forced him to retire prematurely but it is essential that he is tried again. He looked to have all the ingredients of solving a problem spot for Limerick.

1973 Keeping the Dream Alive

Impressed

His Injury afforded Christy Campbell the opportunity of coming into the side and the Old Christians man started slowly but by the finish he was hurling extremely efficiently. But the attack again had its shortcomings and while Richie Bennis did contribute some very vital scores from frees his efforts from play were also a marked improvement on recent efforts. But he is capable of even better. Liam O'Donoghue did reasonably in the top corner but through the field this was a most meritorious showing from a sweet-striking Limerick. Certainly the Claughaun Club deserve credit for making such an enjoyable game possible and I hope their bank manager is smiling today. Cork were short five of their chosen side but they, too, can be happy with their efforts. Paddy Barry made some superb saves in goal and Frank Norberg, Conn Roche, Jack Russell, Mick Malone and Donal Clifford all had their moments. Limerick will be in action again next Thursday when they play All Ireland champions, Kilkenny in what should be another entertaining outing.

Scorers

Limerick - R. Bennis 1-6 (1-4 frees); L. O'Donoghue 1-1; M. Ruth. 0-3; M. Dowling. 1-0; E. Grimes and B. Hartigan 0-2. F. Nolan and J. McKenna 0-1 each.

Cork - C. McCarthy 2-3 (all frees); S O'Leary and E. Kelleher 1-1; J. Russell, R. Cummins, G. McCarthy and P. Moylan 0-1.

Teams

Limerick - S. Horgan; W. Moore, P. Hartigan, J. O'Brien; P. Bennis, S. Foley, J. O'Dwyer; B. Hartigan, E. Grimes; J. McKenna, R. Bennis, P. Fogarty; L. O'Donoghue, M. Dowling, F. Nolan. Subs: C. Campbell for O'Dwyer, M. Ruth for Fogarty, M. Aherne for Nolan.

Cork - P. Barry; D. Burns, M. Doherty, F. Norberg; G. Webb, J. Buckley, C. Roche; D. Clifford, P. Moylan; J. Russell, G. McCarthy, M. Malone; C. McCarthy, R. Cummins, S. O'Leary. Subs: E. Kelleher for Cummins, M. Coleman for Russell.

Referee - John Moloney (Tipperary).

The teams for the game above - note Eamonn Cregan being named at Number 6.

Ruth Figures Prominently as Limerick Win
(Limerick Leader, 2 June 1973)

By Charlie Mulqueen

Limerick 3-14
Kilkenny 4-5

Last night's match at the Gaelic Grounds, in which Limerick beat Kilkenny by 3-14 to 4-5, served once more to confirm the considerable potential of Matt Ruth, a Christian Brother, based at Sexton Street, came on as a substitute the previous week against Cork and impressed when scoring three points from play. Last evening, he was brought in for the entire hour and was the shining light of what was otherwise a featureless game. Ruth was born in Ballyraggett. County Kilkenny, but has moved around the country quite a bit as a member of the Christian Brothers order. Last year while playing with St. Mary's, Clonmel, he won a Munster intermediate medal with Tipperary, and had a blinder in the final against Kerry. Since joining Old Christians in February of this year, he has notched 5-30 in competitive matches and numerous other scores in challenges. It was quite apparent that Ruth, a well built, wing half forward, isn't fully fit for he played only in patches last night. But in these spasms he proved his tremendous potential and had the crowd roaring with a hat-trick of points in the space of four minutes mid-way through the second half.

First

The first of these was a beauty, a cut up shot on the run from 35 yards sailing between the posts after the best movement of the match. Limerick had a number of other new faces on view and of these. Most impressive was another member of the clerical profession, Fr Paudie Fitzmaurice at right-half forward. Fr Fitzmaurice was a member of the Maynooth side that won the Fitzgibbon Cup this year and the highlight of his display last night was a thundering point from all of 80 yards 10 minutes into the second half.

Cautioned

Willie Smith, of whom much had been expected, was a big disappointment at centre-half forward and was cautioned by the referee on two occasions for over robust play. There will be worry, too, about the performance of goalkeeper Séamus Horgan, who could he faulted for some of the Kilkenny goals and whose all round display was not up to the standard of his league outings.

Last night's game was a disappointment in as much as both sides were depleted and Kilkenny were especially hard-hit. However, their more established players exposed weaknesses in the Limerick set-up and none more so than centre-half forward Kieran Purcell who looked a class apart.

Scorers

Limerick - M. Dowling 2-1; R. Bennis 0-5; M. Ruth 0-4; P. Fitzmaurice 1-1; B. Hartigan, F. Nolan and W. Smith 0-1.

Kilkenny - K. Purcell 1-2; M. Murphy, S. Cooke and P. Broderick 1-1; M. Brennan 0-1.

Teams

Limerick - S. Horgan; W.Moore, J. Allis, J. O'Brien; P. Bennis, C. Campbell, J. O'Dwyer; R. Bennis, B. Hartigan; P. Fitzmaurice, W. Smith, M. Ruth; L. O'Donoghue, M. Dowling, F. Nolan. Subs: T. Ryan for Nolan.

Kilkenny - N. Skehan; P. Larkin, N. Orr, J. Treacy; P. Butler, M. Fitzpatrick, E. Morrissey; L. O'Brien, S. Kiely; S. Cooke, K. Purcell, P. Broderick; M. Brennan, M. Murphy, J. O'Shea.

Referee - Jack Quaid (Limerick).

Cork Just About Deserved Draw
(Cork Examiner, 11 June 1973)

By Jim O'Sullivan

Limerick 1-12
Cork 2-9

It is debatable whether or not Cork deserved a draw in this senior hurling tournament game at Castlelyons last night in view of their gross inaccuracy in attack, but they certainly put enough effort into the last twenty minutes to merit it. Even allowing for the weakness up front, Cork had enough possession late in the game to have won it by half a dozen scores and they probably would have, had not full-forward John Rothwell been unfortunate to divert a well-directed shot from Willie Walsh wide at a crucial stage. Overall, however, a draw was a fair result and the manner in which it was achieved, with Eamonn Kelleher pointing just on time.

Cork, without seven of the selected team, including Tony Maher who broke his finger on Saturday night, once again looked unbalanced. They were strong in defence but unimpressive in attack in which Kelleher and Willie Walsh were the only players to stand out. Limerick, who were also missing several regulars, had few weaknesses in defence.

Jim Allis looked very convincing at full-back, in the absence of Pat Hartigan, and Eamonn Cregan hurled very well at right-half after an unsteady start. In attack they were much more direct and with Liam O'Donoghue excelling once again, they made far more use of their possession.

From Cork's point of view, the match proved a number of things. Firstly, Con Roche is back to his brilliant best, and the displays of Noel Dunne and an in-form Frank Norberg highlighted the richness of talent in defence, John Buckley now looks the player most likely to be picked at centre-back after another fine display, and notable too was the continuing good play of Donal Clifford and the sharpness of Willie Walsh, even though the centre forward was as inaccurate as the others.

Cork were slow to settle, but a goal from John Rothwell in the ninth minute and another from Ted O'Brien in the 24th (after he had shifted to left corner forward) enabled them to be a point in front at half time (2-4 to 1-6). Afterwards there was a doubt about whether or not Cork scored five points, but the game was officially a draw.

1973 Keeping the Dream Alive

Limerick played with more fire in the third quarter, but their attack got little scope. There was little between the sides at midfield, with Clifford and E. Grimes the best players, and D. Coughlan finishing more strongly than Richie Bennis. Defences dominated a great deal and Limerick did not score after Joe McKenna's 50th minute point left three points between the sides.

A minute later John Buckley pointed a '70, and E. O'Donoghue had another point with a minute and a half remaining. Then, as Cork's tally of wides mounted with each successive raid, Kelleher saved the day with his late equalising point.

Scorers

Limerick - L. O'Donoghue 0-4; J. McKenna 0-3; R. Bennis 1-1; F. Nolan 0-2; M. Dowling and E. Grimes 0-1.

Cork - J. Rothwell 1-1; T. O'Brien 1-0; E. Kelleher and D. Coughlan 0-2 each; E. O'Donoghue, J. Buckley, W. Walsh and R. Crowley 0-1.

Teams

Limerick - S. Horgan; W. Moore, J. Allis, P. Bennis; E. Cregan, S. Foley, J. O'Dwyer; R. Bennis, E. Grimes; P. Fitzmaurice, J. McKenna, M. Ruth; L. O'Donoghue, M. Dowling. F. Nolan. Subs: W. Smith for Ruth, C. Campbell for Nolan.

Cork - P. Barry; F. Norberg, M. Doherty, D. Burns; D. Coughlan, D. Clifford, T. O'Brien; M. Walsh, E. Kelleher; E. O'Donoghue, J. Rothwell, J. Barry Murphy, T. O'Brien, J. Buckley and W. Walsh. Substitute, R. Crowley for O'Brien (injured).

Referee - Derry O'Brien (Cork).

Cork Just Draw Level
(Limerick Leader, 11 June 1973)

Limerick 1-12
Cork 2-9

The Senior Hurling challenge game played at Castlelyons yesterday ended in a draw. The match was played on the occasion of the opening of the new community centre in Castlelyons. It was only a point in the closing minutes that brought Cork level. Cork led at half-time by 2-4 to 1-6. In the second half Limerick went ahead with four points in a row but Cork slowly closed the gap.

Scorers

Limerick - R. Bennis 1-1; L. O'Donoghue 0-4; J. McKenna 0-3; F. Nolan 0-2; M. Dowling and E. Grimes 0-1.

Cork - T. O'Brien and J. Rothwell 1-1; E. O'Donoghue and D. Clifford 0-2; W. Walsh, B. Crowley and E. Kelleher 0-1.

INTERNATIONAL HURLING/SHINTY MATCH
(Under Compromise Rules)

i bPáirc an Chrócaigh

19-5-1973

IRELAND v SCOTLAND
(40 minutes-a-side)

Referee: Mr. W. BATCHEN (Inverness)   3.30 p.m.

Juvenile Hurling/Shinty

BLESSED OLIVER PLUNKETTS
v OBAN HIGH SCHOOL

Réiteoir: T. Ó CONCHUIR (Ciarraí)   2.00 p.m.

Luach 8p

Seán Ó Síocháin
Ard Stiúrthóir

The Scottish and Irish teams line up together before the start of the International Hurling/Shinty match played in Bught Park, Inverness, on August 5th, 1972.

IRELAND

Dathanna: Glas is Bán
(Green and White)

(1) S. Ó Dúraic
S. Durack
(An Chláir)

(2) P. Ó hArtagáin
P. Hartigan
(Luimneach)

(3) S. Ó Treasaigh (Capt.)
J. Treacy
(Cill Chainnigh)

(4) T. Ó Murchú
T. Murphy
(Gaillimh)

(5) M. Iacób
M. Jacob
(Loch Garman)

(6) P. Ó hOráin
P. Horan
(Uibh Fhailí)

(7) E. Ó Greacháin
E. Grimes
(Luimneach)

(8) M. Mac Mathúna
M. Mahon
(Laois)

(9) S. Ó Foghlú
J. Foley
(Luimneach)

(10) S. Breathnach
J. Walsh
(Cill Dara)

(11) E. Ó Criagáin
E. Cregan
(Luimneach)

(12) C. Mac Eocaidh
C. Keogh
(Loch Garman)

(13) A. Ó Deoráin
A. Doran
(Loch Garman)

(14) P. Ó Fathaigh
P. Fahy
(Gaillimh)

Fir Ionaid: (15) D. Ó Máirtín (D. Martin, Uibh Fhailí); (16) P. Ó Lorcáin (P. Larkin, Cill Chainnigh); (17) C. Puirséal (K. Purcell, Cill Chainnigh); (18) M. Ó Coigligh (M. Quigley, Loch Garman).

1973 Keeping the Dream Alive

Limerick to Win All Ireland this Year
(Limerick Leader 14 July 1973)
Former US GAA President Predicts

By Richard Naughton

The Limerick hurling team will beat Tipperary and go on to win the All Ireland senior championship. This is the opinion of Mr John Hunt, past chairman of the GAA in the United States.

"I saw the match between Cork and Tipperary last Sunday week, and while the play was not up to Irish standards, if we had hurling of that calibre in the American Board it would be a tremendous source of strength to Irish exiles and make our heritage stronger than what it," he told me in the course of an interview in Cruise's Hotel.

"I think Limerick will beat Tipperary," he said. And then, having a second thought about it, he added, "I am actually sure of it."

Limerick, he pointed out, have the science, the hurlers and the ability to hurl. But he warned: "They have not got enough poison (sic!) at the moment". If they make good this deficiency, the All Ireland is theirs." Mr Hunt is back in Athea and on a vacation in Ireland with his wife, Kathleen, and fourteen-year-old son, John. He was elected chairman of the GAA in the United States in 1964 at a convention in Cleveland, Ohio, and was re-elected the following year at a convention in Syracuse, New York. He was elected president of GAA American Board at a convention held in Boston, Massachusetts, in 1966. He has represented the GAA at Congress in Ireland and at meetings of the Central Council held at Croke Park, and was chairman of the Young Ireland hurling who that toured here about 1956.

While he does not hold any executive position in the GAA at present, his interest in Gaelic games is as active as ever. He is a very pre-eminent worker in the United States for Northern Aid, and gives his support and encouragement to Irish cultural movements, including the Irish language, which he speaks. Visiting Ireland after a decade's absence, he sees big changes, and not all for the better. The Common Market is, he says, "a rich man's club," and the cost of living is too high for the working man. And the Common Market is no asset to Irish tourism: "Organisations are going abroad promoting Irish tours, and there is no need for them to do so." "Ireland is a land of beauty; where would you get anything to surpass the Cliffs of Moher or the Lakes of Killarney?

I believe the tourist business in Ireland would be good no matter what market you got into." Mr Hunt is in the United States for some 25 years. His wife is former Miss Kathleen Shinnors of Ballinahinch, Birdhill. They have three children, John, who is school-going; Edward, who is studying law at a university in Wisconsin, and Kathleen, who is with an insurance firm in Chicago.

John Hunt Jr., Kathleen and John Sr. on their visit home.

Limerick Seven Point Winners over Waterford
(Limerick Leader, 11 July 1973)
First Half Supremacy is Vital
Hurling Challenge: A Worthwhile Exercise

By Charlie Mulqueen

Limerick 4-18
Waterford 4-11

Tuesday night's eighty minute challenge in which Limerick beat Waterford by seven points, 4-18 to 4-11, was a worthwhile exercise in our build-up to the Munster final, now definitely scheduled for Semple Stadium, Thurles on Sunday, July 29th. In the final analysis, Limerick were not impressive in winning against a Waterford side having its first outing since losing to Tipperary in the championship six weeks ago.

At the same time, the five selectors, busily huddled together on the far sideline, and equally visibly unimpressed with much of what they saw, should have learned a little more from the encounter. Circumstances may have obliged them to do so, but it is difficult to applaud their decision to bring Eamonn Rea all the way down from Dublin - and then play him, not in his accustomed and selected position of full-back, but instead at full-forward. To give him his due, Rea tried for all his worth. and scored a well-taken goal and a point, but with the full-back position one of the problems in the side at present, surely he could have been given a chance to redeem his league final failure there at some stage of the game.

Notable absentees from the side were Pat Hartigan and Éamon Grimes, as well as Pat O'Brien from Bruree, who was surprisingly recalled to the panel for this game.

Style

Accordingly, Willie Moore came back at right-corner back, Jim Allis at full-back and Paudie Fitzmaurice at midfield. Of the three, Fitzmaurice looked full of style in the centre, and is a man deserving of consideration. Quite wisely, the selectors took the opportunity to bring in a few substitutes. One interesting alteration was the introduction of Christy Campbell in place of Phil Bennis at right-half back. Both these players have admirable qualities, and these were once more in evidence against Waterford. It is a toss-up which gets the No. 5 jersey against Tipp - it could be that both will eventually grace the Munster final arena.

The match took a fairly a predictable course. Limerick, quicker to settle down and with the strong wind at their backs, were completely on top in the first half and led by the over-powering margin of 3-14 to 5 points at the interval. A mixture of Limerick relaxation, Waterford improvement and defensive errors allowed the visitors to put a far more respectable appearance on the scoreboard, and the final score, 4-18 to 4-11, was testimony to the 100 per cent non-stop effort of the Waterford men.

Goalkeeper Séamus Horgan made some fine saves and typical clearances, but uncertainty on his part cost two goals that never should have been allowed by an inter-county 'keeper.

It is to be sincerely hoped that the Tournafulla man regains total confidence before the Munster final.

Scorers

Limerick - E. Cregan, L. O'Donoghue and F. Nolan 1-3; E. Rea, 1-1; B. Hartigan and M. Dowling 0-3; R. Bennis and P. Fitzmaurice 0-1.

Waterford - L. Canning, 2-1; F. Greene, 0-5; P. Egan and A. Heffernan 1-0; P. Enright 0-3; P. O'Grady and M. Geary, 0-1.

Teams

Limerick - S. Horgan; W. Moore, J. Allis, J. O'Brien; P. Bennis, J. O'Donnell, S. Foley; P. Fitzmaurice, R. Bennis; B. Hartigan, M. Dowling, L. O'Donoghue; E. Cregan, E. Rea, F. Nolan. Subs: C. Campbell for P. Bennis, J. O'Dwyer for Dowling, E. Grimes for O'Brien.

Waterford - P. Flynn; S. Hannon, P. Coady, S. Walsh; P. Morgan, J. Greene. P. McGrath; J. Galvin, P. O'Grady; P. Egan, M. Geary, P. Enright; S. Greene, L. Canning, A. Heffernan. Sub: J. Fraher for Walsh.

Referee - Michael Slattery (Clare).

The chairman of Limerick County Board, GAA, Mr Rory Kiely, smiles from his bed at Limerick Regional Hospital. He is recovering from injuries received when he was gored by a bull while working on his farm in Feenagh. He has damaged ribs but is expected to be discharged shortly.

FÁILTE GO DTÍ LUIMNEACH STAIRÚIL

The third annual Féile na nGael is being held in historic Limerick this year, and for months past the executive and various sub-committees have been working with great dedication and enthusiasm, to ensure the smooth running of the Féile. From Limerick County and City will come the hand of friendship and welcome to the many hundreds of young hurlers from every county in Ireland, and again on this occasion I should like to pay tribute to the many families in County Limerick who will play host to our young visitors.

The Féile this year is being extended to a full week and I am happy to say it will provide excellent entertainment for our tourists also. During the Féile the Shannonside Tourist Office in O'Connell Street, will be at your service, and we will be pleased to assist you with any enquiries you may have.

Tá súil agam go mbainfidh gach duine taithneamh as a cuairt chuig Luimnighe ach go hairithe lucht na n-óg, agus go mbeidh deis agaibh filleadh orainn aris gan ró-mhoill. Gabhaim comhgáirdeachas le Cumann Luthcleas Gael as ucht reachtail na Féile agus guim gach rath arimeachtaí na seachtaine.

Eamonn De Stafort,
Oifigeach Forbairt Fáilte.

Limerick Stage Féile
(Gaelic Sport, July 1973)

By Séamus O Ceallaigh

Limerick GAA clubs play the difficult role of hosts to the hurlers of Ireland over a colourful weekend this month, when the flags of all the counties will be hoisted on specially erected flag poles at Páirc na nGael, as the great parade of hurlers from each of the 32 counties ends its journey from the city centre, led by a massed display of bands, for the final ceremonies of Feile na nGael. Nine committees have been working hard for several months to ensure the success of the venture, and if enthusiasm counts for anything then the Gaels of Limerick seem intent on leaving their own special imprint on the occasion. A specially encased hurley will be carried in relays from Michael Cusack's birthplace at Carron, County Clare, for the symbolic opening of the Feile, which takes place on Friday, 20th July, with the arrival of the hurling teams from each of the 32 counties.

Thirty-three Limerick clubs, drawn from all over the county, are participating in the Feile and these, with the visiting clubs, will provide a grand total of 64 teams, who will play off in four sections for the Feile honours. A visiting county had been assigned to each of the participating Limerick parishes. The visiting party in all instances will consist of eighteen players and three officials, and the host parish will provide them with accommodation and meals for the duration of their stay - Friday evening to Sunday evening. General get-to-know-each-other Socials on a divisional board basis are being organised for the Friday night, and host clubs will arrange entertainment for their visitors on the Saturday night. The big match programme is set for the Saturday, with all first round games listed for 11AM at the venues of the host clubs. An elaborate communications system is being established to ensure that all second round games will commence at 2:30PM with third round fixtures listed for 7PM. In the case of a draw, extra time of twenty minutes must be played.

The big spectacular of the Feile will be the parade of all the participating teams, visiting and home, in their togs and bearing banners and placards, with an expected nine bands, commencing at 12 noon on Sunday and marching through the streets of Limerick city to Páirc na nGael, where the finals of the four sections will be staged. Prizes will be distributed to the winners of each section, and there will also be an award for the best turned out team and the most attractive banner.

A meal will be served at Páirc na nGael to all participants.

The Feile will in actual fact commence on 15th July with the launching of a seven-a-side inter-firm hurling tournament, in which 32 teams are being invited to participate. In conjunction with the Feile, a GAA museum is being organised, in which it is hoped to portray in tangible form the building up of the Association, and the honours won on the playing fields. The first medal presented for the All Ireland Senior Football Championship, and which Limerick Commercials won, will be on display, as well as all the Limerick trophies presently in competition and some historic ones of the past.

A collection of club and county team photographs is being arranged, and old scrapbooks and newspaper cuttings, ballads etc. dealing with important GAA events will also be on display. Limerick in the early GAA days had a great athletic tradition and some remarkable athletes who won Olympic titles and broke world records, notably in weight and field events, it is hoped to have on display many mementoes of those great days in our athletic history. The organisers are hoping that many other items of general GAA interest will be offered for display, and that this section of the Feile will prove most attractive and receive widespread patronage. Limerick Gaeldom in this Feile opens its doors to hurling lovers from every corner of the land for what promises to be a really great weekend.

1973 Feile na nGael

FIRST ROUND SATURDAY, 11 a.m.

		HOST VENUE			REFEREE	Feile Official
Division One		*GROUP A*				
	A	Cork	v	Adare	B. Nolan	T. Healy
	B	Dublin	v	Garryowen 10.30	G. Craughan	N. Whelan
	C	Kilkenny	v	Cappamore	J. Butler	N. Cafferky
	D	Tipperary	v	Kilmallock	P. McCarthy	C. Farrell
		GROUP B				
	E	Clare	v	Garryspillane	P. Kelly	S. Burke
	F	Wexford	v	Ahane 10.30	S. Scanlon	J. Kirby
	G	Waterford	v	Old Christians 11.30	T. Ryan	N. Whelan
	H	Galway	v	Doon	W. Hayes	J. McGrath
Division Two		*GROUP A*				
	A	Kerry	v	Patrickswell	J. O'Donoghue	G. Bennis
	B	Laois	v	Rathkeale	N. Duggan	T. McNamara
	C	Antrim	v	Dromin-Athlacca	P. Ryan	D. Ryan
	D	Offaly	v	Claughaun	M. O'Shea	M. Savage
		GROUP B				
	E	Kildare	v	Pallasgreen	M. O'Keeffe	T. Ryan
	F	Roscommon	v	Treaty Sarsfields	B. O'Gorman	J. Collins
	G	Down	v	Bruff	T. Moynihan	F. Greene
	H	Westmeath	v	Ballingarry	J. Quaid	D. Hourigan
Division Three		*GROUP A*				
	A	Leitrim	v	Feoghanagh	Jack Quaid	S. Sheehan
	B	Sligo	v	Ballybrown	S. O'Brien	S. Bennis
	C	Carlow	v	St. Patrick's	H. McNamara	M. O'Connell
	D	Wicklow	v	Kilteely/Dromkeen	D. Laffan	J. Breen
		GROUP B				
	E	Derry	v	Mungret	D. Burke	P. O'Donoghue
	F	Armagh	v	Castletown/Ballyagran	G. Moloney	S. Sexton
	G	Louth	v	Na Fianna	J. Bulfin	J. Moran
	H	Meath	v	Croom	M. Barron	J. Hickey
Division Four		*GROUP A*				
	A	Donegal	v	Kilfinane	M. O'Sullivan	L. Allen
	B	Tyrone	v	Newcastle West	B. Nash	M. O'Connor
	C	Cavan	v	Monaleen	V. Cobbe	C. Murphy
	D	Longford	v	Na Piarsaigh	L. Moloney	D. Hickey
		GROUP B				
	E	Mayo	v	Murroe/Boher 11.30	D. Mescall	J. Kirby
	F	Fermanagh	v	Glenroe	M. Carroll	P. Ryan
	G	Monaghan	v	Ballybricken	E. Wade	B. Crehan
	H	Askeaton	v	South Liberties	D. Nestor	E. Corbett

N.B.—REFEREES & FEILE OFFICIALS FOR THE FINAL

Draws, Fixtures & Venues

	REFEREE	Feile Official	Teams & Venues		REFEREE	Feile Official	FINAL
...D SATURDAY at 2.30 p.m.			**Third Round (Semi-Finals) Saturday 7 p.m.**				
...ll / ...ks	B. Nolan / V. Cobbe	G. Bennis / M. Connell	A or B v C or D	at Rathbane	B. O'Gorman	J. Power	at GAELIC GROUNDS 22nd JULY at 4.20 p.m.
...sh	D. Laffan / W. Hayes	F. Moore / J. Kirby	E or F v G or H	at Murroe	W. Hayes	J. Kirby	
	T. McNamara / S. Clancy	N. Duggan / D. Barrett	A or B v C or D	at Adare	J. Quaid	T. Healy	at GAELIC GROUNDS 22nd JULY at 2.20 p.m.
	B. Crehan / J. O'Brien	M. Connell / S. Sexton	E or F v G or H	at Bruff	J. Neenan	D. Barrett	
	R. Bennis / J. Butler	T. Healy / N. Cafferky	A or B v C or D	Na Piarsaigh	J. O'Grady	D. Hickey	at GAELIC GROUNDS 22nd JULY at 5.10 p.m.
e	D. Murray / G. Callaghan	S. Hickey / F. Greene	E or F v G or H	at Kilmallock	M. Dowling	C. Farrell	
	D. O'Connell / B. O'Gorman	D. Feehan / J. Power	A or B v C or D	at Croom	L. O'Brien	J. Hickey	at GAELIC GROUNDS 22nd JULY at 1.30 p.m.
...n	K. Walsh / D. Burke	P. Higgins / S. Bennis	E or F v G or H	Caherconlish	E. Wade	F. Moore	

...BE APPOINTED ON SATURDAY NIGHT 21st JULY

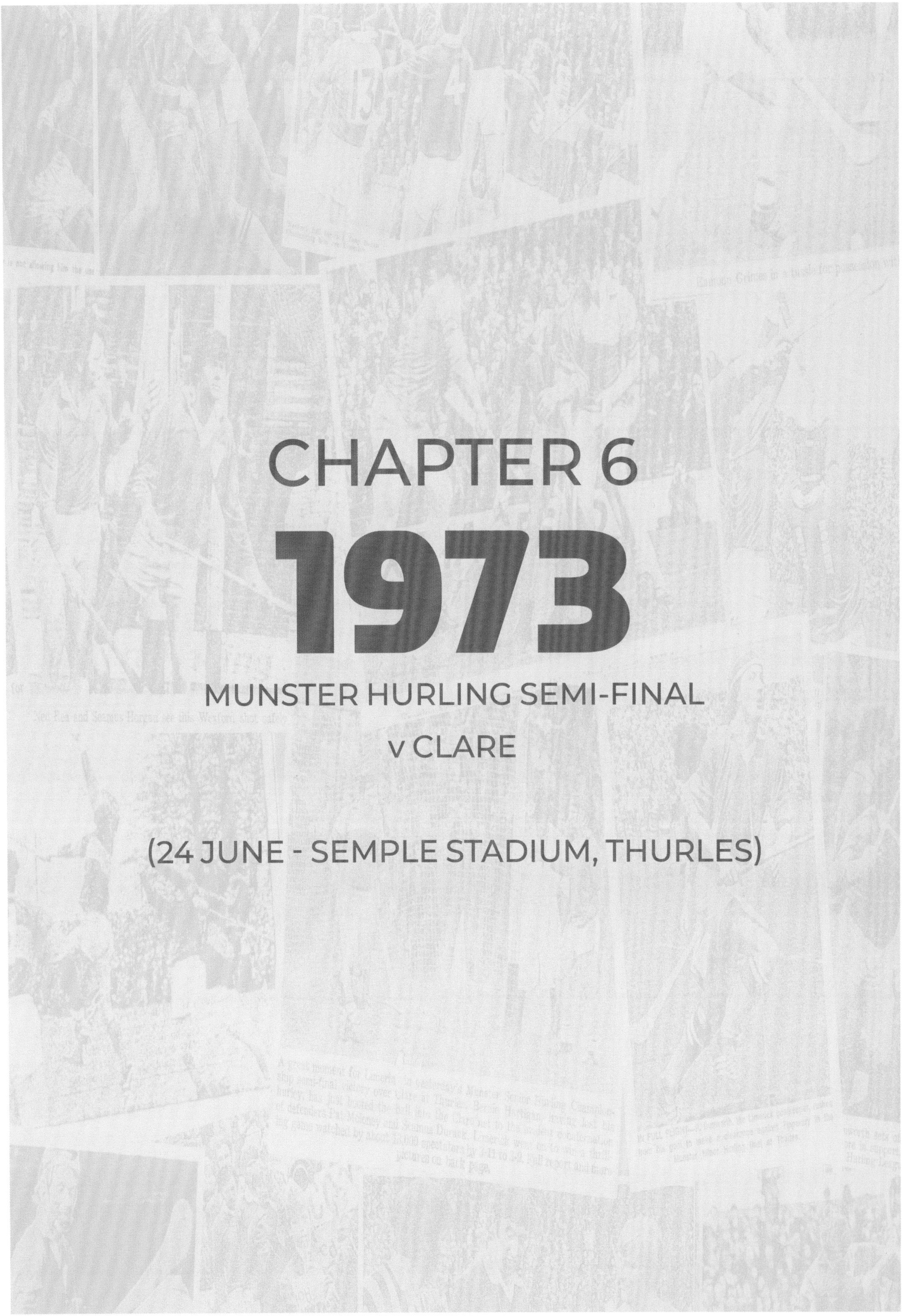

CHAPTER 6
1973

MUNSTER HURLING SEMI-FINAL

v CLARE

(24 JUNE - SEMPLE STADIUM, THURLES)

Limerick played Clare on Sunday, 24 June 1973 in the Munster Hurling Championship (MHC) at Thurles. It was the second part of a double header there that afternoon, the curtain raiser being the All Ireland Club Senior Football Final replay between Nemo Rangers (Cork) and St. Vincents (Dublin). Nemo beat Vincents by 4-6 to 0-10. This was the third full All Ireland club series played, in both hurling and Gaelic football, these competitions having started in 1971.

This MHC game was overshadowed by the previous year's clash between the same teams, in Ennis, that saw Clare surprisingly emerge victorious, as earlier referenced. (Clare would lose the subsequent Munster Hurling Final to Cork, 6-18 to 2-8.) This game would be the then standard 60 minutes in duration, as the rule at the time dictated that only senior provincial finals, All Ireland semi-finals and finals were to be 80 minutes in duration. This little-remembered rule was in place for five championship seasons, 1970-1974 inclusive, and was further modified at GAA Congress in Easter 1975. All senior inter-county championship games would be 70 minutes from then onwards.

There had been a lot of discussion as to where this game would be played, with Limerick refusing a home and away arrangement at an earlier Munster Council meeting. Limerick had played Clare in Limerick in the 1970 MHC replay, with a replay required before Limerick won for the first time against Clare since 1956. The replayed game in 1970 also saw four sendings off (two from each side) in what was described as a "farcical" game amid "a storm of ill-feeling", with Clare scoring only 0-4. The drawn game was in Thurles a week before, with Limerick scoring 2-12 to Clare's 3-9. The two teams' 1972 MHC encounter has already been referenced in an earlier chapter.

With only a few minutes to go in 1973, a surprise result was still on the cards. Clare had drawn level and threatened to take the lead. Limerick broke forward from a Clare error and scored the go-ahead point through Éamon Grimes. Clare threw the kitchen sink at Limerick but came up short multiple times, before a long-range point from Mossie Dowling gave the Shannonsiders a bit of breathing space, the game finishing, 3-11 to 3-9.

This was a close escape for a Limerick team who were possibly looking much further down the road, rather than at what was in front of them. Special mention must be made of Doon's Jim O'Donnell who came onto the field before half time for Pallasgreen man, Jack O'Dwyer. Jim was mentioned in all reports as being instrumental in Limerick's "lucky, lucky" success. It is a game that is looked back upon by many Clare people as another one that 'got away'.

No Limerick Leader report is available for the game – not on IrishNewsArchive.com, nor in the Limerick Leader's physical archive. The Clare Champion report is reprinted in this chapter instead. There was a Limerick Leader photographer at the game and an evocative set of images were produced and subsequently placed on the FromLimerickWithLove.ie website. Some of these photos have been freshened up and published in this chapter.

Erskine Childers was inaugurated as the fourth president of Ireland the day after the game. There are official (with Séan Mac Cártaigh's signature on the front) and pirate programmes known for this game, both covers are printed in this chapter. The (official) programme is doubly collected due to the All Ireland Club Football Final being part of this double header.

Cork and Tipperary would play 7 days later, with the prize of playing Limerick in the Munster Final on offer. They had played in a very nasty league game earlier that season, but the championship game was expertly handled by Michael Slattery, which probably helped in the selection process for the Munster Final referee a month later.

Official and pirate programme covers from the Clare game - Seán Mac Cárthaigh (Tralee) was secretary of the Munster Council from 1931 until 1977.

1973 Keeping the Dream Alive

5p Semi Final

Munster Hurling Championship

Semple Stadium, Thurles   24 - 6 - 1973

Clare v Limerick

Referee :- J. MOLONEY (Tipperary)   3.30 p.m.

All-Ireland Club S.F.C. Final Replay

Nemo Rangers v St. Vincents
(CORK)   (DUBLIN)

Referee :- M. SPAIN (Offaly)   2.15 p.m.

1973 Keeping the Dream Alive

Handwritten top-left:
Limerick 2-7
Clare 2-5

CLARE

	(1) **S. DURACK** (Feakle)	
(2) **P. MOLONEY** (Clarecastle)	(3) **V. LOFTUS** (Eire Og, Ennis)	(4) **S. HEHIR** (O'Callaghan Mills)
(5) **N. McINERNEY** (Sixmile Bridge)	(6) **M. McKEOGH** (Smith O'Brien, Killaloe)	(7) **J. O'GORMAN** (Cratloe)
(8) **M. CALLANAN** (Clarecastle)		(9) **P. RUSSELL** (Clarecastle)
(10) **N. RYAN** (Eire Og)	(11) **N. CASEY** (Sixmile Bridge)	(12) **M. CULLIGAN** (Crusheen)
(13) **T. RYAN** (Newmarket-on-Fergus)	(14) **G. LOHAN** (Newmarket-on-Fergus)	(15) **M. O'CONNOR** (Tubber)

Handwritten annotations next to players: G. Loughnane (by 5); M. O'Connor (by 13); Gilmartin (by 11); T. Ryan (by 12); M. Casey (by 15).

Handwritten scoring times (right margin):
3. M. Ryan pt.
4. Dowling pt.
7½ J. Ryan goal
8. B. Hartigan pt.
11½ R. Bennis pt (free)
13. R. Bennis pt.
15½ R. Bennis pt (70)
16½ O'Donoghue pt.
18. J. Ryan pt (free)
19½ Cregan goal
21. J. Ryan pt (free)
23. J. Nolan pt.
24. B. Hartigan goal
27. Russell pt.
28. Lohan goal
30. McKeogh pt (70)

Subs.—16, G. Loughnane (Feakle); 17, J. Power (Tulla); 18, B. Meehan (Newmarket-on-Fergus); 19, M. Gilmartin (do.); 20, M. Hegarty (Clarecastle); 21, E. O'Connor, (Tubber); 22, P. J. Keane (Sixmile Bridge); 23, G. McNamara (Newmarket-on-Fergus).

	An Chead Leath	An Dara Leath	
CUIL	IIII ④	IIII ④	⑧
CUILINI			

The team pages from the official programme - they show the team changes plus the times of the scores, something that is not officially available elsewhere.

1973 Keeping the Dream Alive

Handwritten top left:
Limerick 3-11
Clare 3-9

Handwritten top right:
2½ M. Callinan goal
3. J. Ryan pt (free)
4. Cregan goal
6. Grimes pt.
8½ J. Ryan pt (free)
13. Russell pt (cut)
15 E. Cregan pt (cut)
20. J. Ryan pt (free)
27½ E. Grimes pt.
29½ Dowling pt.

LIMERICK

(1)
S. HORGAN
(Tournafulla)

(2)　　　　　　(3)　　　　　　(4)
W. MOORE　**P. HARTIGAN**　**J. O'BRIEN**
(Doon)　(South Liberties)　(Bruree)
　　　　J. Allis

(5)　　　　　　(6)　　　　　　(7)
P. BENNIS　~~J. FOLEY~~　~~J. O'DWYER~~
(Patrickswell)　(Patrickswell)　(Pallasgreen)
　　　　O'Donnell　*O'Donnell / Foley*

(8)　　　　　　(9)
R. BENNIS　~~E. GRIMES~~
(Patrickswell)　(South Liberties)
　　　　Cregan

(10)　　　　　(11)　　　　　(12)
B. HARTIGAN　~~E. CREGAN~~　**L. O'DONOGHUE**
(Old Christians)　(Claughaun)　(Mungret)
　　McKenna　*Cregan / Jones*

(13)　　　　　(14)　　　　　(15)
~~J. McKENNA~~　**M. DOWLING**　**F. NOLAN**
(South Liberties)　(Kilmallock)　(Patrickswell)
Dowling / Donoghue　*McKenna / Dowling*

Subs.—16, John O'Donnell (Doon); 17, J. Allis (do.); 18, J. Grimes (Sth. Liberties); 19, C Campbell (Old Christians); 20, Paudin Fitzmaurice (Killeedy); 20, Jim Hogan (Claughaun).

	An Chead Leath	An Dara Leath	
CUIL	||||||| ③	|||||||| ⑨	⑯
CUILINI			

1973 Keeping the Dream Alive

The Limerick team that played C...
Back Row (L-R): Séamus Horgan, Joe McKenna, Seán Foley,
Front Row (L-R): Jack O'Dwyer, Mossie Dowling, Liam O'D

...ster Championship in June 1973.
...n O'Brien, Eamonn Cregan, Willie Moore and Richie Bennis.
...n Grimes, Phil Bennis, Frankie Nolan and Bernie Hartigan.

Lucky Limerick Just Pip Clare in Thrilling Finish
(Clare Champion, 29 June 1973)
Midfield Swing was Decisive

By Seán King

Limerick 3-11
Clare 3-9

Lucky, lucky Limerick. Dame Fortune may be a fickle old damsel with both benign and begrudging features, but what odds against her being elected the next Lord Mayor of Limerick. The City Council may have more exalted views on the subject, after watching Limerick pip a dour, workmanlike, Clare team in a traumatic and intensely exciting finish to the Munster Senior Hurling Championship Semi-Final, played in overcast conditions at Semple Stadium, Thurles, on Sunday, I can only surmise that the Old Lady has taken a distinct liking to the Limerick hurlers.

Never over-amorous when it comes to fraternising with Clare hurling teams, a band of sportsmen she has frowned upon more than a few occasions in the past, the Lady with the clairvoyant touch was certainly on Limerick's side when it came to stealing the laurels at Thurles on Sunday. In retrospect, this was far from an exercise in petty larceny. It was daylight robbery and Limerick hurling students were, I am sure, among the first to admit that their heroes were decidedly lucky to escape through to meet either Cork or Tipperary in the provincial final.

The thrills and spills of a Munster championship game between Limerick and Clare.

Clare, hardly reckoned with in ante-post opinion, were every bit as good as Limerick throughout a close, well-contested, but unspectacular game. The Claremen gave as good as they got for the greatest portion of the hour but the vital breaks which so often draw the dividing line between victory and defeat never came the way of the hard-battling Banner men.

This was never more in evidence than in the closing stages when, in some hectic goalmouth exchanges, the Clare forwards peppered the Limerick citadel only to be denied by a freakish bounce of the ball on the hard surface, last ditch defensive action, on the part of substitute Jim O'Donnell in particular, and the safety of the goalposts, which saved an almost certain Clare goal. Yes, this was the sort of luck which Clare experienced and Limerick enjoyed.

Upper Hand

There can be no doubt, however, that Limerick, held the upper hand in the opening half, when a marked superiority at midfield ensured that the Limerick forwards saw plenty of the ball. The Clare pairing of John Callinan and Paschal Russell, though they had their moment subsequently, found it hard to find their feet, and but for some heroic work on the part of Martin McKeogh and the towering Vincent Loftus, who played the full-back line almost on his own, and a series of scintillating saves from Séamus Durack, Limerick would have been much more than 2-7 to 1-3 in front after 24 minutes play.

Paradoxical, though it may appear, it was Clare who set the pace from the start when Noel Ryan, easily Clare's most polished forward, scored a gem of a point from play after four minutes. Limerick equalised through Liam O'Donoghue, but Clare again nosed in front when, after eight minutes, Michael O'Connor blasted a tonic goal from a rebound, after an earlier effort of his was saved by Séamus Horgan.

Noel Casey get his shot off but breaks his hurley against the block of Willie Moore.

The remainder of the first half, for the most part, belonged exclusively to Limerick who, though they went on to register five points without reply from Clare, failed badly when it came to applying the finishing touches. This was, in part, due to the brilliance of Durack and the stout resistance offered by Loftus, McKeogh and the spasmodic Jackie O'Gorman, who found Bernie Hartigan a hot handful.

The first signs of a Clare resurgence came to light in the 17 minutes when Tim Ryan slapped a fierce shot to the Limerick net from close range, but to the consternation of the large Clare following, referee John Moloney, whistled back and wait for it, awarded a free to Clare. This was a clear-cut case for the application of the advantage rule, but, instead, the man in charge, who, otherwise had a splendid game, took away whatever advantage there was when Tim Ryan obliged with Clare's second point from the resultant free.

Neutrals in the near 13,000 crowd, who had come more in search of a good game than with the intention of placing allegiance behind any particular team were, one felt, almost excited at the prospect of what a Clare goal do to enliven the contest from a competitive point of view. The goal came, true enough, but it was to Limerick and it only helped to imbalance the scales still further and send Clare hearts sinking into a state of near depression.

1973 Keeping the Dream Alive

1973 Keeping the Dream Alive

Frankie Nolan gets his shot off against Vincent Loftus.

Indecision

The goal came about when V. Loftus effected a timely clearance from the Clare goal which was obviously intended for Seán Hehir but the O'C Mills player, whose inexperience was shown up on more than one occasion allowed the ball to go over the end-line for a '70. Richie Bennis's shot landed in the square, but in a rare moment of indecision S. Durack appeared to mis-time his advance and Eamonn Cregan was left with the simplest of chance's in front of an empty, unguarded net. This put Limerick four clear points in front and the cat very much among the pigeons as far as Clare was concerned. Tim Ryan replied, briefly, with a pointed free, but back came Limerick with a Frankie Nolan point and a goal from Bernie Hartigan, who, after gathering a cross-field pass, from Nolan, careered his way through the Clare defence before kicking the ball to the net past Séamus Durack who made a valiant effort to dispossess the wing-forward.

This was in the 24th minute, but the remaining period up to half time highlighted a magnificent Clare fightback, Paschal Russell, who, by this time was faring much better against Éamon Grimes, blazed the comeback trail with a long-range point. A minute later Gus Lohan was on hand to finish off a Michael O'Connor centre to the Limerick net, and shoving up to half time Martin McKeogh left only two points separating the teams when he pointed from a '70, 2-7 to 2-5.

Mossie Dowling follows the ball while three Clare defenders converge on him, including a very young Ger Loughnane.

When one sits down to examine that entertaining first half, in which fortunes fluctuated like a yo-yo, it hardly bears reminding that the Clare midfield partnership never got off the ground when it came to matching the steely and skilful hurling of Richie Bennis, though his colleague in this sector, Éamon Grimes, offered precious little in support.

The flame-haired Patrickswell clubman was in commanding form, and in the circumstance it is hard to fathom how Clare, despite a mammoth fighting heart, got back into the game at all. However, unlike former years when Clare teams collapsed at the sight of defeat last Sunday's outfit kept battling to the last and thanks mainly to the efforts and lengthy clearances of McKeogh and O'Gorman, who grew in stature as the game progressed Clare managed to come within striking distance of Limerick by half-time.

The Clare full back line, too, did have its shaky moments in the first half when both Hehir and the usually reliable Pat Moloney were too often left trailing in the wake of the speedy Limerick forwards. Outside, Niall McInerney was giving far too much scope to Liam O'Donoghue, but the attack, when it got moving, showed that it had the ideas, with Noel Ryan, especially emerging as a shining star of the future.

What Clare's hopes needed most of all in the early minutes of the second half was a goal. And sure enough, it came after only two minutes when a speculative shot from John Callinan, from fully 50 yards, dropped into the Limerick net over the head of a bewildered Séamus Horgan. Now in front by a point, Clare stretched the lead to two points when Tim Ryan was on the mark from a free. But tragedy was to follow when after Durack saved smartly from Hartigan, Limerick struck again when Eamonn Cregan showed a clear pair of heels to the Clare defence before unleashing a stinging ground shot to the net to restore the lead for Limerick.

Nailbiting

The exchanges, forever of an intense variety, grew to nailbiting proportions as Limerick went back into the attack when Éamon Grimes, now moved to wing-forward, flighted over a point to leave two minors between the teams. Then followed bouts of fantastic hurling as the play swung from end to end. Limerick came close to increasing their lead but Durack and the steadfast Loftus were always on hand, while at the other end only the brilliance of Séamus Horgan deprived Noel Ryan and Michael O'Connor of pulling Clare back into the picture.

The final link in Limerick's defensive armoury, however, finally snapped in the seventh minute when Lohan was fouled going through and Ryan reduced the lead to a single point from a free. Richie Bennis saw a good-looking effort of his from a placed ball go narrowly wide, before, in the 14th minute, Paschal Russell levelled matters, again, with a picture point from a side-line ball.

This was definitely it. Had Clare got the mental aptitude to keep up the pace or would the fitter and more experienced Limerickmen finished the stronger.

These are the thoughts which flickered through the minds of the Clare supporters. Ger Loughnane was playing his heart out after coming on in the tenth minute, for an obviously out-of-touch Niall McInerney, and the Clare defence was much steadier because of his presence.

It was Limerick, however, who nosed out in front, again, with the help of an Eamonn Cregan point, but Tim Ryan redressed the balance in the 20 minute, when he scored his fifth and what proved to be Clare's final point from a free.

In between these scores, Clare had a golden opportunity of sealing the game, when in front, of an empty goal, Gus Lohan blazed inches wide. Goalkeeper Horgan, after saving a long range shot from McKeogh, was caught out of position but Lohan, with the goal at his mercy shot hurriedly and wide.

It was anybody's game approaching the 27th minute and, if anything, the Claremen were forcing the pace. Martin McKeogh, whose reputation as one of the country's leading centre backs grew a thousand-fold in this game, shot wide from a '70 and when offered another bite at the cherry chose, instead, to short pass the ball to Michael Kilmartin. Whether the Newmarket man, who had come on in the 20th minute of the second half for Michael Culligan, called for the ball or not, I am not in a position to say, but one thought that McKeogh would have been far better employed lobbing the ball into the crowded Limerick square where, with Pat Hartigan retired injured, anything might have happened.

1973 Keeping the Dream Alive

Bernie Hartigan gets in behind the Clare defence to kick a vital goal at Semple Stadium.

However, as events materialised Kilmartin was penalised presumably for holding onto the ball and from the free Éamon Grimes escaped the clutches of Ger Loughnane to put Limerick into a lead which they never, subsequently lost.

Clare tried hard for the elusive equaliser and Noel Casey was most unlucky when a sizzling shot of his was tipped round the post for a '70 and in another nerve-wrecking instance the ball rebounded off the butt of the Limerick post only to be cleared to safety by Jim O'Donnell. With the game at boiling point and excitement at fever pitch Clare threw everything into attack but a long-range point from Mossie Dowling almost in the stroke of full time secured a win for Limerick and a passage to the Munster final.

There are many who will argue, and with justification, that Clare could have won. There was that first half "goal" that wasn't, and the spate of misfortune in the closing minutes when Clare threw everything but the kitchen sink at the Limerick defence and almost came close to pulling off another surprise victory.

Pulsating

The second half was a pulsating affair. The Clare attack, which resumed with Noel Casey in the corner, Tim Ryan on the wing, and Culligan on the 40 yards mark, did have enough chances to pull the game out of the fire. But a combination of ill-luck and the signs of fatigue, particularly from Casey, who never hit the high spots expected of him, took much of the gloss away from some promising approach-work.

The game, I hasten to add, was won and lost at midfield, and why the Clare backroom boys did not transfer an obviously bang-in-form Noel Ryan to this department at half time is something that will be talked about in Clare hurling circles for many a long day. There were other equally noticeable deficiencies as well, but had Clare gained even parity at midfield when the Limerick pressure was at its peak in the opening half, heavens knows what might have happened on the change of ends.

Undoubtedly, the heroes of the hour for Clare were goalkeeper, Durack, full back, Vincent Loftus, and the National League half back line of Loughnane, McKeogh and O'Gorman, with McKeogh emerging as the lynch-pin of this division. Pat Moloney settled down considerably to play a steady second half, but Seán Hehir will need a full league campaign before his full potential is realised. Russell and Cullinan found the going anything but easy at midfield. The Clarecastle pair showed some neat touches at different intervals but, by and large, they played a poor second fiddle to Bennis and Grimes and finally, Cregan.

The Clare attack showed refreshing touches at times, though Casey and Culligan looked cumbersome in comparison to the spring-heeled Noel Ryan, O'Connor and Tim Ryan. Lohan, if one forgets that yawning miss, was a success at full-forward, taking his goal well but without reservation the pick of the attack was Ennisman, Noel Ryan, who proved that he is just as proficient with a hurley as he is with a soccer ball.

But, oh for a Michael Moroney, a Jim Cullinan or even a Pat Cronin. Memories, memories.

Scorers

Limerick - E. Cregan 2-1; B. Hartigan 1-1; R. Bennis 0-3; M. Dowling and E. Grimes 0-2; L. O'Donoghue and F. Nolan 0-1.

Clare - T. Ryan 0-5; G. Lohan, J. Cullinan and M. O'Connor 1-0; P. Russell 0-2; N. Ryan and M. McKeogh 0-1.

Liam O'Donoghue in action during his championship debut against Clare.

1973 Keeping the Dream Alive

1973 Keeping the Dream Alive

Mossie Dowling in a race for possession against Vincent Loftus of Clare.

Frankie Nolan tries to avoid the attentions of Niall McInerney (soon to transfer to Galway).

1973 Keeping the Dream Alive

Séamus Horgan clears despite Gus Lohan's attempted blockdown.

Teams

Limerick - S. Horgan, W. Moore, P. Hartigan, J. O'Brien; P. Bennis, S. Foley, J. O'Dwyer; E. Grimes (Capt) and R. Bennis; B. Hartigan, E. Cregan, L. O'Donoghue; J. McKenna, M. Dowling, F. Nolan. Subs: J. O'Donnell for O'Dwyer and J. Allis for P. Hartigan.

Clare - S. Durack, P. Moloney, V. Loftus, S. Hehir; N. McInerney, M. McKeogh, J. O'Gorman; P. Russell and J. Cullinan; N. Ryan, N. Casey, M. Culligan; M. O'Connor, G. Lohan, T. Ryan. Subs: G. Loughnane for N. McInerney and M. Kilmartin for M. Culligan.

Referee - John Moloney (Tipperary).

Back Row (L-R) S. Hehir, N. Casey, N. McInerney, M. O'Connor, V. Loftus, J. O'Gorman, N. Ryan and M. McKeogh.
Front Row (L-R) M. Culligan, T. Ryan, S. Durack, G. Lohan, P. Russell, P. Moloney and J. Cullinan.

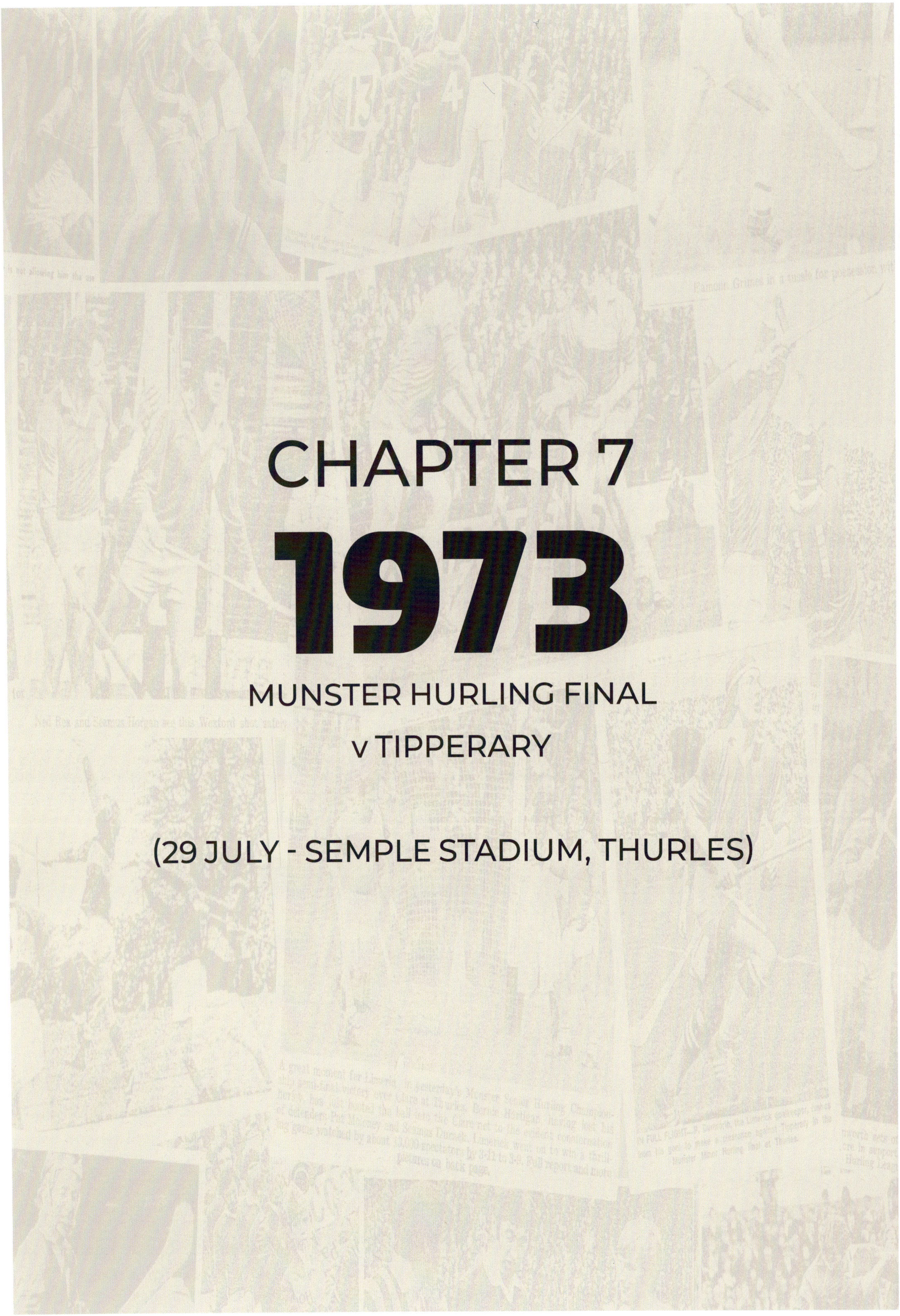

CHAPTER 7
1973

MUNSTER HURLING FINAL

v TIPPERARY

(29 JULY - SEMPLE STADIUM, THURLES)

1973 Keeping the Dream Alive

Limerick played Tipperary on Sunday, 29 July 1973 in the Munster Hurling Final at Thurles. This was a game for the ages and Raymond Smith gave it due respect in his Book of Hurling, published in July 1974. He dedicated many chapters of this fine work to Limerick's 1973 success, with small excerpts reprinted here. It is arguably the only book to date that has given extensive coverage to the 1973 Limerick campaign.

The game has taken on a mythical status in Limerick GAA folklore. Richie Bennis's last gasp '70 had many people openly weeping in the crowd, the home fans with disappointment and the travelling supporters with joy. It was to be Limerick's day after many years in the wilderness, Limerick's first Munster Hurling Championship success in 18 years, and only the second since 1940. It also avenged the grave disappointment of Killarney two years earlier against the same opposition.

The controversy of the very late point has been well ventilated since. Limerick people say that the sliotar was inside the post; Tipperary people say otherwise, obviously. Whether it was a '70 in the first place is a lesser, but no less contentious, issue for some. We have the benefit of good-quality YouTube footage of this game, the last 30 minutes of the second half being available on this ubiquitous media website. It is wonderful footage of a top-quality game played in dry and warm conditions. No quarter was given or taken that afternoon and it was described afterwards as a "stirring" game. Tom Semple would have been proud of his Thurles enclosure that afternoon.

This was the fourth time that these two teams had met in 1973, with two of these games finishing in draws and the third being won only after extra time by Limerick. This, together with the big games between the same opposition in 1971, meant that there was only the thickness of a very thin cigarette paper between these two teams; the 1971 NHL final was decided by a point, while the Munster Final was, as previously mentioned, a one-point game too. The 1973 Munster Final was a ding-dong encounter with Limerick getting a flyer of a start, but Tipperary came back into the game strongly before the short whistle to lead 2-9 to 3-2. The second half was just as exciting, which the available footage makes clear. Limerick were still stuck on two points after 50 minutes of the game. Limerick got goals to stay in touch, while Tipperary continued to get points to keep ahead.

The game looked destined to finish in a draw until the last few seconds, with Michael Slattery telling Richie that he would have to score direct from the '70, or else the game would finish level. What Michael 'Babs' Keating really said to Richie as he stood over the free is not recorded! Normally, Seán Foley would have just dropped the ball into the square. Richie had to go for it. Neither the referee nor his umpire had any doubt about which side of the right post the ball finished up crossing, the original '70 being called on the other side of the town-side goal.

None of the Limerick players in line with the ball had any doubts either! It was a point. The incident immediately after the score being white-flagged was very unfortunate. An official investigation was mounted by the Munster Council into it. Its findings were never published. Len Gaynor wrote about this incident in his book, taking responsibility for giving the unfortunate umpire a "jab." Both Len and the umpire became friends in later life.

The ecstatic scenes after the final whistle are still remarkable, even 50 years on, unbridled joy on every Limerick person's part, and all captured on film and radio audio - Micheál O'Hehir's commentary of Richie's '70 is transcribed in this chapter! A number of sidebars in this chapter capture this joy in other ways too. Tipperary easily beat Limerick in the minor final curtain raiser. As the penny Limerick Leader headlined the Cormac Liddy game report the following day, "We Are The Champions." A Peters & Lee's single was number one in Ireland that weekend, "Welcome Home". Quite appropriate!

Limerick Close to the Breakthrough
(Gaelic Sport, August 1973)

By Jay Brennan

Did they but know it, Limerick are probably closer now to that longed for breakthrough than they ever were. And it must be even a surprise to themselves. There was not much hope - more recrimination in the atmosphere of lost opportunity - at the end of the year when that controversy was whipped up about their selection of a trainer.

It was with faltering steps that they picked up the threads after Christmas in a League which seemed to be slipping out of their control. When eventually they qualified it was not a performance full of confidence when they met Tipperary at Kilkenny in the semi-final. A draw was satisfactory in the circumstances and the victory in extra time of the replay was a morale-booster. Yet, the final was lost and again they were brought to earth with something of a bump by a bustling Wexford.

In their semi-final against Clare, there were times when Limerick showed the confidence debt they have accumulated as a result of the years of trying fruitlessly. Not ten minutes from the end, when their best endeavours had failed to break Clare and establish a winning lead, they almost gave up the ghost. For some minutes, they seemed to run out of moral resource; the game was almost there for the taking by Clare at that time.

But, Clare were unable to take it, and after five minutes of this flaccid physical and mental impotence, Limerick stirred themselves again and won. Now, without reaching their best or playing with anything like the authority they sometimes showed in other years, they are in the Munster final. And the opposition is Tipperary which showed itself to be vulnerable (if not lucky) against Cork. Limerick must have noted the obvious lack of command of Tipperary in that game; the shortcomings in several positions, the fact that teamwork and determination are more vital than hurling mastery in bringing Tipperary into this final. They must have noted that, with a little improvement here and there, with a greater effort for full fitness, they will have the same chance of imposing themselves on Tipperary in the championship as they had in the League.

Both teams - Limerick and Tipperary - will, of course, be better for the final. Limerick, perhaps, will have regained the courage and belief in their ability to dominate which they so lacked in the semi-final. Now, having got off the hook, and not altogether by their own doing, they will take mighty great care never to slacken their resolve when they play Tipperary. Throughout the year, and even against Clare near the end, it must have seemed to them that they were still on the old road without a turning. And suddenly, they find themselves in the Munster final - and against opposition that has given no evidence to believe that it is anywhere in the class of that which Tipperary provided in 1971. Is this the sudden bend in the road that was not visible until the last moment? Round it is there, perhaps, the promised land?

Tipperary, against Waterford and again against Cork, have failed to prove that they have anything greater than their character and their traditional stout-hearted refusal to accept defeat. They had to struggle mightily and draw on their depth of experience to contain the "devil" in Waterford's challenge; and they were truly reduced to a sad state with only 1-4 to their credit, a dozen missed opportunities, gaps in technique, fitness and ability, and only their courage to keep them going eight minutes from the end of the Cork game. It so happened that four goals came in the last minutes, but they did nothing to obscure the happenings earlier in the game.

Tipperary are not certain that they have a goalkeeper that answers the specification for Munster championship stuff. The remarkable thing is that neither Waterford nor Cork were able to fire enough quick shots at Doyle or Murphy to prove which or whether. That says a lot, of course, about the staunch qualities of the full-backs and halves or else it is a fair estimate of the Cork and Waterford forwards.

Well, I think it is partly one and partly the other; but the Tipperary full-backs are no pushover, that's clear enough. They still are unable to command the game under the dropping ball, if Limerick would care to note this point and play it accordingly. And the halves are tenacious and tough and marvellously courageous, yet they seldom dominate, because O'Connor is not really happy in the middle, Crampton is still feeling his way on the right, and Gaynor is bothered with having the burdens of responsibility heavy on his shoulders in case the others make a mistake.

Players like O'Dwyer and Jack Ryan or Mick Roche and John Flanagan like to move freely in search of space and they capitalise on Loughnane's headline. And I speak altogether irrespective of what they are actually scoring or achieving: they were (all three) mostly dreadful against Cork for most of the second-half, yet the play was pitched in Cork's half most of the time.

Inside, massive Roger Ryan is always a threat, especially when he encounters a referee who does not recognise that a full-back has any rights; but the corners are neither settled nor especially thrustful.

If Tipperary are to be beaten it will be by a half-back line that will dominate them; not so much that it will contain them, for that is what Cork did in a negative and unproductive sort of way, but that it will drive its clearances with punishing depth. They must be backed by a midfield of consistent and combative endeavour; by full-backs who stick to their task; by a goalie of courage; and by forwards who keep flying and piling on pressure in waves, and never allowing open clearances by backs.

How do Limerick meet the requirements? Doubtfully, it must be admitted. But, they have the talent, if they employ it and give it the right orders. I wonder about the half-back line; I wish they could run Seán Foley through a copying machine and get one of him for left-half; another of him for right-half and another for centre-field. O'Donnell can do it at centre. Bernie Hartigan can disrupt the Tipperary half-backs; Cregan should have the skill; Grimes, flashing in and out of a corner could, if he would, get scores galore. It is a fascinating prospect.

Limerick Leader, SATURDAY, JULY 28, 1973

G.A.A.: SUNDAY CAN BE MAKE OR BREAK DAY FOR LIMERICK
Ground hurling can bring success

SPORTING VIEW

Limerick Minors deserve your support

Limerick senior hurlers will not be short of support in Thurles on Sunday, when they pit their skills against mighty Tipperary in the 1973 Munster final.

It would be a nice gesture were fans to arrive at Semple Stadium in time to lend vocal support to the county's minors in their bid for glory against the blue-and-golds.

After all, our future as a hurling force, rests with our under-age players. They are very much the underdogs on Sunday, but with plenty of encouragement from the sidelines, they might upset pre-match calculations.

Not since 1965, have Limerick won the provincial crown in this grade. Cork and Tipperary have dominated the scene over the years, and it is like a breath of fresh air to see the green and whites making one of their all-to-rare appearances in a decider.

The panel of players have trained rigorously for this contest, and the trainers and

THERE ARE MANY who remember the afternoon in 1936 when a panic stricken and bombarded Tipperary side used three goalkeepers in a miserably unsuccessful bid to avoid a Munster championship trouncing by Limerick. Could it be an indication of fear that for Sunday's final Tipperary have three 'keepers in their panel?

Limerick don't care a thrawneen at having to play in Thurles and there is every confidence that the title can be won for the first time since 1955. It is a relief to all that in the build-up to what promises to be a tremendous 80 minute battle there is no moaning or whinging from officials in either county.

If enthusiasm and spirit count for anything then Sunday should be Limerick's day. It is indeed a very long time since such a thorough preparation was made by a Limerick side and the big crowds who watched the concluding training sessions early in the week were thrilled to observe the zeal shown by the players for action.

In recent years, all contests involving Limerick and Tipperary at senior level have been thrillers and this one should certainly be in keeping with that trend. In League contests, Limerick have a tremendously successful record in clashes in the past few years.

But Tipperary took the "big one" two years ago when, after a tremendous battle they beat Limerick at Killarney in the championship final. That win is to boost Tipperary's confidence this time. They must, too, be pleased that the game is being played on their home pitch.

But it has been pointed out more than once that any side capable of doing so can hurl at Thurles, it would be unrealistic to believe that Limerick are not at something of a disadvantage in having to do battle at Semple Stadium.

Tipperary have been training hard there for several weeks, but where "home" advantage will help them most I think, is the fact that their free-takers will have had all the time they wished to practice from every angle with placed balls.

This, I think, is the only real way that playing at Thurles will

HURLING by Cormac Liddy

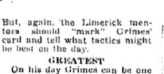

Liam O'Donoghue, now at right half-forward

believe in adding a little "weight" to their endeavours. Limerick can expect a tremendous amount of hustling and bustling from Sunday's rivals. That is the way they set about their business. Most of the time their efforts come within the meaning of the hurling rules. There is nothing—and this heavens for it—in the rules to prevent the giving and taking of ruthlessly hard-knocks.

Limerick had better be prepared for it this way and I have no doubt that they will into the bargain. I hope that the sturdy ones in the Limerick side will be capable of using their avoirdupois to best advantage.

A hardy shoulder charge can upset the best of men and knock them out of their stride, that will certainly be the aim of some of the Tipperary side.

I am sure that all will be pleased that Mick Slattery of Clare has been appointed to referee the game. He is a man who believes in allowing the play to flow in so far as possible. He does, too, believes in the strictest observance of the rules.

Both sides know this and will be anxious for as rousing a game as possible that within the scope of the rules.

Never has there been such an enthusiastic response from the players to training. Each and every one of them gave his very best and the Dublin-based members of the panel had no hesitation in ensuring that they were present at the Gaelic Grounds for practice.

Jim O'Brien, Limerick's corner-back, has a vital role to play if his side are to win.

But, again, the Limerick mentors should "mark" Grimes' card and tell what tactics might be best on the day.

GREATEST

On his day Grimes can be one of the greatest players in the country. But all too often we have seen him too long inactive. He should make it his business to be in the thick of things throughout on Sunday.

He and Richie Bennis face mammoth tasks. If in form, they can both, be brilliant. Yet both of them can also appear to be serving no useful purpose. It is the hope of all that Bennis can show his undoubted talents once again. He is capable of being brilliant and his assets as a freetaker are something that every county would hope to have in their side.

There should be a great battle between Bernie Hartigan and Tipperary's Jimmy Crampton who is without doubt a powerful defender if allowed to be so. Crampton's lofty clearances have turned many a game in Tipperary's favour. But if he is constantly kept in action he may not be able to maintain his calm composure which is one of his greatest assets. In even the most stirring of contests Crampton keeps his "cool" and he is certain to be one of the strong men in the Tipp. defence.

TASK

The Limerick player who perhaps has the greatest task will be Liam O'Donoghue. A brilliant hurler, he will have to shake off the tenacious Len Gaynor.

It will not be easily done, but Gaynor against Cork was another who never played as we know he is capable. Invariably he is at his best against Limerick.

ATMOSPHERE

The more one writes the more one gets caught up in the atmosphere that only a Munster final can generate. Limerick have been "sitting it out" so to speak for a long time now. A great deal has been achieved in recent years. But the "big one" has yet to be accomplished.

Sunday could well be the day of the big break-through. Certainly, it will not be for want

Jim O'Donnell back to his best at centre half-back

fectly fair deal.

Tipperary were so terribly poor for most of the time against Cork that they could not be a and again. Limerick must make them even worse to do. But they can do so—and so go on to meet either Galway or London a week later in the All-Ireland semi-final.

TENNIS

£200 tennis challenge

Tennis enthusiasts from all parts of Munster will converge on Lattin, Co. Tipperary, on Sunday night. The two progressive local clubs have arranged what promises to be a tremendous attraction when Ireland's Davis Cup player, Michael Hickey, of Limerick, will play twenty years old South African Bob Millington.

But this will be no ordinary round-the-mill challenge that, as the winner, in fact, will receive £200 and so every shot of the five sets should be carefully played.

Millington last Saturday played some delightful strokes when winning the South of Ireland

CLAR OIFIGIUIL

CUMANN LUITH-CHLEAS GAEDHAEL

MUNSTER HURLING FINALS

SENIOR:

TIOBRAD ARANN v LUIMNEACH

at 3·30. Referee—M. SLATTERY, (Clare).

MINOR FINAL:

TIOBRAD ARANN v LUIMNEACH

at 2 pm. Referee—N. DALTON, (Waterford).

LUACH :-: 10p

Nº 7884

S. Mac Cárraig

Runai

(TIPPERARY STAR, THURLES)

THURLES SARSFIELDS CLUB

This programme is compiled by Thurles Sarsfields club in association with Thurles CBS, two bodies that have given, and are giving sterling service to the Association. Sarsfields have won the Tipperary senior hurling championship on twenty seven occasions, the junior hurling championship, three times and the minor hurling championship on four occasions.

In fact, in the years 1955 and 1956, they had the distinction of winning the county minor, junior and senior hurling titles together.

The club at present fields a senior team, two junior teams, under-21 and minor sides and its players play with St Patricks in juvenile grade. The club is also actively involved in the plans for a Social Centre at Semple Stadium.

Receipts from programme sales go towards the financing of these activities.

KEEP THIS PROGRAMME

Because, as you will notice, the programme is numbered, and at half-time in the senior game, **there will be a raffle for two All-Ireland hurling tickets.**

We thank you for your support.

FOR NORTHERN RELIEF

A percentage of the gate receipts from today's games will be donated to the Northern Relief Fund.

Tipperary Senior Team
(Blue & Gold)

(1)
T. MURPHY
(Roscrea)

(2) **J. FOGARTY** (Moyne) (3) **J. KELLY** (Kilruane) (4) **J. GLEESON** (Moneygall)

(5) **J. CRAMPTON** (Roscrea) (6) **T. O'CONNOR** (Roscrea) (7) **L. GAYNOR** (Kilruane)

(8) **S. HOGAN** (Kiladangan) (9) **P. J. RYAN** (Carrick-on-Suir)

(10) **F. LOUGHNANE** (Roscrea) (11) **M. ROCHE** (Carrick-on-Suir) (12) **N. O'DWYER** (Borrisoleigh)

(13) **J. FLANAGAN** (Moycarkey) (14) **R. RYAN** (Roscrea) (15) **M. KEATING** (Ballybacon-Grange)

Subs: (16) P. Byrne (Sarsfields); (17) D. Ryan (Sean Treacys); (18) J. Ryan (Moneygall); (19) S. Shinnors (Newport); (20) J. Doyle (Sarsfields); (21) M. Esmonde (Moyne); (22) J. Keogh (Silvermines); (23) P. Williams (Kilruane).

Tipperary named 23 while Limerick named a bare 21!

Limerick Senior Team
(Green & White)

(1)
S. HORGAN
(Tournafulla)

(2)　　　　　　　(3)　　　　　　　(4)
W. MOORE　　**P. HARTIGAN**　　**J. O'BRIEN**
(Doon)　　(South Liberties)　　(Bruree)

(5)　　　　　　　(6)　　　　　　　(7)
P. BENNIS　　**J. O'DONNELL**　　**S. FOLEY**
(Patrickswell)　　(Doon)　　(Patrickswell)

(8)　　　　　　　(9)
R. BENNIS　　**E. GRIMES**
(Patrickswell)　　(South Liberties)

(10)　　　　　　　(11)　　　　　　　(12)
L. O'DONOGHUE　　**M. DOWLING**　　**B. HARTIGAN**
(Mungret)　　(Kilmallock)　　(Old Christians)

(13)　　　　　　　(14)　　　　　　　(15)
F. NOLAN　　**E. REA**　　**E. CREGAN**
(Patrickswell)　　(Effin)　　(Claughaun)

Subs: (16) **J. Allis** (Doon); (17) **J. McKenna** (South Liberties); (18) **P. Fitzmaurice** (Killeady); (19) **A. Dunworth** (Faughs); (20) **T. Ryan** (Patrickswell); (21) **J. Hogan** (Claughaun).

1973 Keeping the Dream Alive

The Limerick team that pla[yed]
Back Row (L-R): Jim O'Brien, Eamonn Cregan, Eamonn Rea, P[...]
Front Row (L-R): Liam O'Donoghue, Séamus Horgan, Seán Fo[...]

...n the 1973 Munster Final.
...O'Donnell, Willie Moore, Bernie Hartigan and Richie Bennis.
...mes (Capt.), Frankie Nolan, Mossie Dowling and Phil Bennis.

1973 Keeping the Dream Alive

The Tipperary team that p[...]
Back Row (L-R): Noel O'Dwyer, John Kelly, Roger Ryan, Séamus [...]
Front Row (L-R): Len Gaynor, PJ Ryan, John Gleeson, Fra[...]

in the 1973 Munster Final.
che, Jimmy Crampton, Tadhg Murphy and Michael 'Babs' Keating.
(Capt.), Jim Fogarty, John Flanagan and Tadhg O'Connor.

Munster SH Championship Winners

1887	TIPPERARY	1930	TIPPERARY
1888	UNFINISHED	1931	CORK
1889	CLARE	1932	CLARE
1890	CORK	1933	LIMERICK
1891	KERRY	1934	LIMERICK
1892	CORK	1935	LIMERICK
1893	CORK	1936	LIMERICK
1894	CORK	1937	TIPPERARY
1895	TIPPERARY	1938	WATERFORD
1896	TIPPERARY	1939	CORK
1897	LIMERICK	1940	LIMERICK
1898	TIPPERARY	1941	TIPPERARY
1899	TIPPERARY	1942	CORK
1900	TIPPERARY	1943	CORK
1901	CORK	1944	CORK
1902	CORK	1945	TIPPERARY
1903	CORK	1946	CORK
1904	CORK	1947	CORK
1905	CORK	1948	WATERFORD
1906	TIPPERARY	1949	TIPPERARY
1907	CORK	1950	TIPPERARY
1908	TIPPERARY	1951	TIPPERARY
1909	TIPPERARY	1952	CORK
1910	LIMERICK	1953	CORK
1911	LIMERICK	1954	CORK
1912	CORK	1955	LIMERICK
1913	TIPPERARY	1956	CORK
1914	CLARE	1957	WATERFORD
1915	CORK	1958	TIPPERARY
1916	TIPPERARY	1959	WATERFORD
1917	TIPPERARY	1960	TIPPERARY
1918	LIMERICK	1961	TIPPERARY
1919	CORK	1962	TIPPERARY
1920	CORK	1963	WATERFORD
1921	LIMERICK	1964	TIPPERARY
1922	TIPPERARY	1965	TIPPERARY
1923	LIMERICK	1966	CORK
1924	TIPPERARY	1967	TIPPERARY
1925	TIPPERARY	1968	TIPPERARY
1926	CORK	1969	CORK
1927	CORK	1970	CORK
1928	CORK	1971	TIPPERARY
1929	CORK	1972	CORK

1973 ....

'They are not balanced enough'
(Evening Press, 25 July 1973)

Paddy Scanlan, one of the all-time greats of Limerick hurling, is not too hopeful of the prospects for Sunday next. "I feel that they have too many passengers and are not balanced enough to win a Munster or All Ireland title," he commented.

"They are not well balanced enough," is Paddy's view." Mind you Tipperary are no great shakes, but they can improve whereas I am not too sure that Limerick can."

Paddy Scanlan will be in Thurles to see the big game. His last visit to a Munster Championship final was in Killarney in 1971, when Limerick lost a memorable match to Tipperary by just one single point. Paddy recalls the game vividly.

"Limerick threw it up in the air that day." They were six points up at half-time, and thought that they had it in the bag. The backs were found wanting that day, and I'm still worried about the defence." Paddy has strong views on the standards of hurling today as against those in his day. Not surprisingly, he thinks the men of the thirties and forties were far superior.

"The players today wouldn't be in it at all," he says." They are not in the same class, and it is ridiculous to say that the game today is faster. I often remember pucking out a ball, it would be doubled on at midfield and sent flashing over the bar at the other end."

Scanlan feels that there is far too much poking and lifting nowadays. And when they do get it in their hands, they only hit it thirty or forty yards.

The great Ahane man has strong views on fitness also.

"Ah, sure, they don't train at all these days. In my time, we had very little money and we had little else to do but train, practice and play. Nowadays, there is plenty of money, motor cars and so on, and too many distractions," says Scanlan.

He recalls his own training days." We used to go into Limerick every night for a fortnight before a Munster Championship match up to three nights beforehand. And there would be no messing . . . wholehearted stuff all the way and then home at 10:30PM or 11PM."

Paddy Scanlan of Ahane will long hold a special place in the hearts of Limerick hurling followers. Paddy won two All Ireland medals in the Limerick goal - in 1936 and 1940, both times under the captaincy of his even more famous Ahane team-mate, Mick Mackey.

The number of times he saved Limerick are legion, and he was goalkeeper in the side that won the National League five years in a row in the thirties.

He was easily recognisable by his big cap which he wore down over his eyes to block the sun and it was a characteristic trait of his to fling the headgear into the goals when he felt the pressure was off!

Although Paddy Scanlan is not particularly impressed by the modern-day hurler, there is little doubt but that he will be cheering lustily for a Limerick triumph in Semple Stadium on Sunday next.

"We Are The Champions" - They Roared
(Limerick Leader, 30 July 1973)
Bennis The Hero of Superb Final as Title Won After 18 Years

By Cormac Liddy

Limerick 6-7
Tipperary 2-18

Never before can there have been such a dramatic ending to a Munster senior hurling championship final than that at Thurles on Sunday. With the last stroke of a stirring contest Richie Bennis slammed over the winning point from a '70. It was a superb stroke by the Patrickswell man who emerged the hero of the day as he erased memories of squandered chances earlier on.

Tense moments before the throw-in. Referee Michael Slattery, Clarecastle, has a word with the Limerick captain Éamon Grimes, and his Tipperary counterpart, Francis Loughnane, prior to the start of the Munster Final in Thurles. Tipperary's County Board PRO and Development Officer, Séamus Ryan, is also in the picture.

It might have taken eighteen years to win back the title but Sunday's pulverising finish will long be remembered by those fortunate to have witnessed a game that produced some brilliant passages, some poor play, but overall, an occasion which saw Limerick finally breakthrough for a win that all Ireland was pleased to hear about.

The excitement of the occasion was quite fantastic. First Limerick stormed into a seven point lead inside fourteen minutes. A landslide win looked a possibility but then by the interval it was Tipperary who were clear leaders as they had four points to spare.

On a number of occasions in a superb second half the sides were level and, indeed, practically all in the 41,000-plus crowd would have settled for a draw. But Limerick, per Richie Bennis, forced a last second '70. Referee Michael Slattery of Clare told Bennis that he must score direct from his effort. Tension was almost unbearable as the red-haired Patrickswell man drew a monstrous swipe and as confusion was stirred up in the Tipperary goalmouth by some of the home players the umpire waved his flag.

Thus Bennis had won the championship for Limerick. Two years ago he won the League for the county and now he had tacked on the biggest prize of all. He deserves the congratulations of thousands for a truly outstanding contribution to Limerick's hurling fortunes. Many times criticised, Bennis can have the last laugh. He silenced his critics with that super stroke and while he might be faulted for not taking points from frees throughout the game all can truly he forgiven because of that great match-winning effort.

Never can there have been such excitement. It was incredible to think that two teams who had played each other so often in recent years, could again be separated by only a point after eighty minutes.

Insignificance

That League win of two years ago pales into insignificance after this super-show. Granted, some of the hurling was not of purist quality but who cared, Limerick had won. Eighteen years was a long time to wait and it only added to the thrills on Sunday. It was an occasion that thousands scarcely believed possible. All had hoped for victory, but, deep down, few could really have been over-confident.

That lightning start by Limerick set the tempo for a fast and furious eighty minutes. Hard knocks were given and taken for the most part, in tremendous sporting fashion. But the glory-scenes at the finish will be a memory for a life-time. For thousands of Limerickmen and women, this was a "first" breakthrough; many had never before experienced such a victory. Many of those present could not go back the eighteen years to the last big win. "Now, all can join with the celebrated old-timers, in talking of great days of Limerick hurling.

Many a heartbeat was missed at various times on Sunday. Indeed, many Limerick supporters were too tired at the finish to give full vent to their feelings. Essentially it was a glorious triumph for Limerick teamwork. But some more than others played parts which had a greater impact. To many, Bennis will be the number one, hero. But there are others who will insist that Eamonn Rea was the real star.

Tipperary's Francis Loughnane and Seán Foley with the old embankment at Semple Stadium in the background.

1973 Keeping the Dream Alive

The pressure cooker atmosphere of a Munster hurling final is plain to see in the faces of the players during the pre-match parade in Thurles.

1973 Keeping the Dream Alive

The players make ready as the Seán Treacy Pipe Band from Moycarkey Borris marches away.

Selectors Abu!

To the oft criticised selectors must go considerable credit for what proved a master-stroke in picking Rea at full-forward. Many beforehand felt it was an unjustified risk. Others accepted it on the grounds that he could hustle and bustle the Tipperary backs. This he did, but all were happily surprised by the skills happily he displayed. His truly was a polished performance as he caught, stopped and struck some delightful balls. He had a part in some of the Limerick goals and his performance was truly outstanding.

Back at the other end, goalkeeper Séamus Horgan turned in a superb display. He made a string of brilliant saves which completely wiped out one bad error which gave Tipperary a soft goal. Yes, Horgan is here to stay and so are many of his colleagues.

The Limerick full-back line must also take considerable credit. Pitted against three of the greatest forwards in modern hurling they effectively coped with them and in the end had come out on top.

It was tremendous to see Willie Moore put in a storming finish. He had a very difficult task in policing Mick Keating, but he accomplished a great deal.

Pat Hartigan had a bustling, hard eighty minutes in coping with Roger Ryan, but he effectively subdued the powerful Tipperary man. In the other corner, Jim O'Brien was once more superb. His powerful clearances were a feature of this epic occasion, and he must rate very high in the honours list.

The bloodied warrior Eamonn Rea makes a break through Tipperary's John Gleeson (left) and John Kelly (right).

Brilliant

Limerick were brilliant on occasions . . . that was definitely true when they played the ground hurling which they were exhorted to do. Their speedy, crisp ground striking was a sheer delight to watch. Tipperary floundered under these tactics and it was indeed a great pity that they could not sustain the effort throughout. Or maybe, in retrospect, it wasn't. Had they done so, Tipperary would have been wiped into the ground and we would not have had that super-charged and exciting wind-up.

Who can forget the second half hurling artistry of Bernie Hartigan. He had a great start, like others he faded, but what a storming finish he put in. It was magnificent to see him burst out from a deep-playing midfield role with the ball in his possession and then shake off Tipperary's efforts to stop him. Yes, Bernie, this was what we knew you were capable of, but had not seen for all too long.

Then who will forget the hurling skills shown by Seán Foley? As a wing back and then a centre-back he was brilliant. He faced a powerful challenge which he met in stirring manner and he, too, played a major part in the win. Phil Bennis got through a vast amount of work as a right and left-half back. He was always very much in the thick of things and while he may often have appeared to be doing better, his efforts this time were very worthwhile.

The Limerick selectors were, to my mind, a little slow in making a change in defence. It was obvious from very early on that Jim O'Donnell just could not get going. Such things happen to all great players from time to time. While one might tend to be over-critical this time, it must not be forgotten that were it not for O'Donnell's superb display against Clare, Limerick might not have been involved at all on Sunday. Ballybrown's Tom Ryan was drafted into the side at the interval and he, too, played a big part in the win. But his tendency to foul gave Tipperary a number of valuable points from frees.

Midfield

Limerick, in the opening quarter of an hour were brilliant at midfield. Éamon Grimes and Richie Bennis made the opposition look very poor indeed, but then for some unknown reason the Limerick pair lost the initiative and Séamus Hogan and P.J. Ryan took control for Tipperary. But over the eighty minutes, Grimes did well. Brilliant on occasions he, however, did a lot of fumbling and foostering on others. Nevertheless he played a captain's part and some of his deeds were worth going a very long way to see.

What can one say of Richie Bennis - hero extraordinary? All the jubilant roars could not have been but for his match winning stroke but there were many times during the game when he achieved little. He can do considerably better in play than he did on Sunday. Indeed, he will have to in future games if the successful march is to be continued. Up front, Rea was the undoubted hero, but Frankie Nolan cannot be much behind. He achieved a great deal, while Eamonn Cregan was out of the game for far too long.

Switched

The Limerick front men switched positions cleverly during the second half and this distracted the Tipperary defenders even if, at times, it also seemed to confuse themselves. Bernie Hartigan, as stated, achieved wonders when he moved to a deep-lying midfield role. There was also a very creditable performance by Mossie Dowling at centre-forward, and the Kilmallock man struck one great goal and chased every ball as if his very life depended on it.

Éamon Grimes leaves three Tipperary players in his wake: PJ Ryan, Séamus Hogan and Mick Roche.

1973 Keeping the Dream Alive

Finally, I come to Liam O'Donoghue and he, too, achieved a great deal in what must have been a very trying occasion for one so young. He put in a top-class showing and played his part in the win. But while we all join in this glorious occasion it would be very unwise to think that it was a super performance. There were many occasions when Limerick could be faulted. At times it seemed as if they were going to be swamped so much did they allow Tipperary take control. But the home side had no answer to Limerick's persistent forages and their full-back line of Fogarty, Gleeson and Kelly were made look quite ordinary this time. None of the Tipperary defenders were allowed to show the authority they stamped on other games. All were given a very tough task to do and while some were better than others, none was really outstanding. Goalkeeper Tadgh Murphy did make some tremendous saves but those in front got a very tough passage - mainly due to the brilliance of Rea.

Séamus Hogan and P.J. Ryan got through an amount of good work for Tipperary at midfield but Francis Loughnane was the only forward to meet with great success. While the others threatened a lot they did not achieve a great deal so well were they "policed" by the Limerickmen. Mick Keating did strike some grand points but the others were beaten into subjection. Limerick's defenders had the sun glaring into their eyes as referee, Slattery, blew for proceedings to start. It was Tipperary's Mick Roche who had the first scoring opportunity, but he was wide from about 40 yards. Almost immediately came Limerick's first chance, but Bernie Hartigan was unable to utilise possession, and he, too, shot wide. It was three minutes before the first score came, but a glorious one it was. Limerick won a sideline cut about 50 yards out. Éamon Grimes cut in a beauty and Frankie Nolan slammed in as first rate a goal as one could wish to see.

Spurred on by that great effort, Limerick burst into action. A Tipperary defender was penalised, but to the horror of the thousands of Limerick supporters, Richie Bennis was badly wide with the free. To many it seemed he had tried for a goal and failed miserably . . . others around thought that he lofted the ball too far in front of him and could not connect properly to take the obvious point. Whatever the reason, it was a bad miss. But the miss was forgiven after ten minutes when the red-haired Patrickswell man clattered in a goal from a 21-yard free after Rea was pulled by a defender as he made inroads on the Tipperary goalie. At the other end in the eleventh minute, Horgan made a fine save, but Limerick were moving slickly and speedily now and were in total control. Grogan lost a chance, but in the fourteenth minute Bennis pointed another free to put Limerick seven points clear, and Tipperary had not yet managed a score.

It was a truly superb opening by Limerick, who hurled magnificently and had Tipperary in a terrible mess.

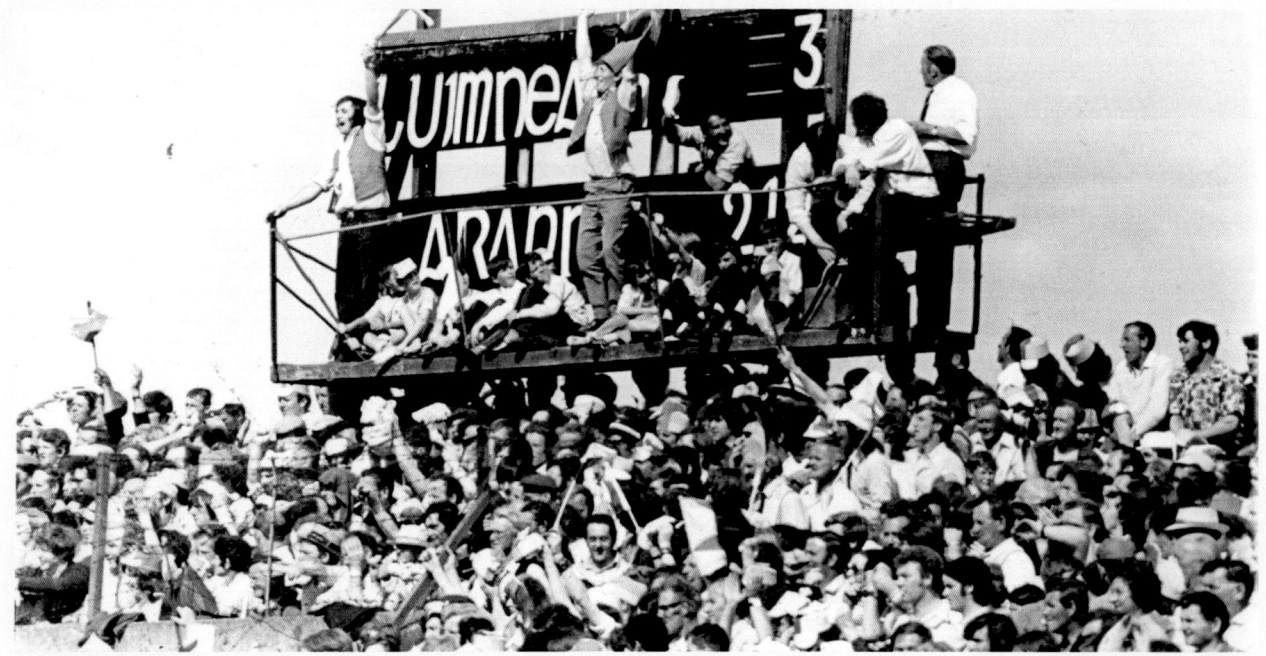

The old scoreboard at the Town End about to record another Limerick goal.

Fourteenth

Not until the fourteenth minute did Tipperary open their account, and then it was a point by Francis Loughnane from a free just after a delightful overhead flick by Bernie Hartigan had gone wide at the other end. But even at this early stage it was becoming apparent that Jim O'Donnell was struggling at centre-back for Limerick. Roger Ryan might have been spoken to for retaliating in an uncomplimentary manner to Pat Hartigan after the Limerick man had gone over to inquire as to his well-being after he had been stretched on the verge of the square.

Tipperary began to edge their way into the game, and a lot of the gloss of Limerick's sparkling opening was gone after Loughnane (free) and Mick Keating had points before the seventeenth minute. Again Tipperary crowded down on Limerick's terrain, and Roger Ryan had an eighteenth minute point to leave only a goal in it at that stage. Indeed seconds later Tipperary seemed certain to get on terms. From 20 yards Noel O'Dwyer sent in a bullet-like drive, but in superb fashion Horgan brought off a wonder save. Surprisingly, Loughnane fluffed a chance from a free in the 20th minute, but he made no mistake when narrowing the gap still further a minute later.

By now Tipperary were very much in the game, but in the twenty-fourth minute Limerick cracked in another goal. Grimes lofted in the ball from midfield, and it seemed to be Dowling who worked it to the net. After twenty five minutes Séamus Hogan had a Tipperary point. Immediately at the other end, Nolan had a Limerick point after Liam O'Donoghue created the chance. Limerick were once again five points clear, but Tipperary showed their true fighting spirit by coming right back into proceedings. Firstly, Mick Keating had a twenty-seventh minute point, and two minutes later Horgan was badly beaten for a very soft goal when he seemed sure to clear the effort. With only a point in the difference, there followed six minutes of thrilling fare without a score until Keating levelled the scores with a 35th minute point.

Tipperary goalkeeper Tadhg Murphy (far right) and his defence struggling to deal with the aerial threat of Eamonn Rea, with Frankie Nolan (far left) in support.

1973 Keeping the Dream Alive

Éamon Grimes is watched by Séamus Hogan and Mick Roche with Michael Slattery in the background.

1973 Keeping the Dream Alive

"*The 1973 Munster Hurling Final was by far the most intense and exciting match that I ever played in*" (Quote by Éamon Grimes).

Fight-back

It was the culmination of a tremendous fight-back by the home side, who stunned the Limerick thousands by going in front with a well-taken goal four minutes before the interval by Loughnane, though I thought two of the Limerick backs had the chance to block the effort.

Limerick should have levelled in the 37th minute, but Cregan was unable to touch home a great opportunity created by Grimes. Two minutes from the interval, Loughnane had another Tipperary point, and just before the break, Bennis tried for a goal from a 21 yard free when he would have been considerably better off taking a point. Thus Limerick found themselves four points behind at the interval after they had been seven points in front after 12 minutes.

It was certainly poor reward for all Limerick's skilful play early on but, as had been the case so many times before on big occasions, they failed to capitalise on the great advantage they gave themselves. It was some minutes before the four Limerick selectors made their way across the field to go into the dressing room.

Obviously, they had debated making changes, but there are many who think that Jim O'Donnell should have been withdrawn from the scene long before the interval. The Doon man was completely out of touch and Mick Roche was allowed the virtual freedom of the park. During the interval the sun faded and the Tipperary backs began the second half without the sun being in their eyes. It was vintage Tipperary in the latter part of the first half. Once a player seemed to have done enough he drifted to the corner of the attack and another stepped in for his share of the limelight . . . or so it seemed.

It was no surprise when O'Donnell did not re-appear and Tom Ryan made a re-appearance for the county. He took over at right-half-back with Seán Foley as centre-back and Phil Bennis on the other side. During the first half too, Limerick made several temporary alterations in attack and at midfield, There were many Limerick supporters who would not have given tuppence for the prospects of a win at the interval. It was being trotted out that they had built up sufficient of a match winning advantage and that having lost it they had, accordingly, no hope of advancement.

Pat Hartigan, Willie Moore and Tom Ryan deal with the threat posed by Roger Ryan of Tipperary.

Certainly prospects were not bright at that stage. The twelfth minute 2-1 to nil lead had been transformed into a four-point deficit and Tipperary were now in front by 2-9 to 3-2.

It seemed that Limerick were destined for certain defeat when even the sun disappeared at the start of the second half. The announcer on the public address system asked for half a dozen sliothars to be made available "otherwise it might not be possible to finish the match." It seemed a most unusual possibility but there were some Limerick supporters who would have settled for an ending at that stage so remote were prospects of success.

Ninety seconds into the second half Limerick went further behind when Loughnane pointed a Tipperary free to extend their lead. In the third minute Séamus Hogan from a free stretched their advantage to six points.

But Limerick pulled themselves together again. Seán Foley lofted in a '70, which his clubmate from Patrickswell, Frankie Nolan, finished to the net after Eamonn Rea had helped in the move. Mick Keating lofted over a glorious point for Tipperary from way out, but in the ninth minute Limerick were right back in the picture. Éamon Grimes sent the ball goalwards from the centre of the field. Rea was prevented from striking but he managed to work the ball clear and Eamonn Cregan stepped in to crack it to the net to put Limerick only a point behind, 5-2 to 2-12.

Jim O'Brien of Limerick just misses his clearance as Tipperary's Mick Roche closes in.

1973 Keeping the Dream Alive

Richie Bennis won the coveted Irish Independent 'Sport Star of the Week' following the Munster Final.

Almost immediately Cregan lost a scoring chance but after ten and a half minutes Richie Bennis lofted over a point to level proceedings. Thus as Tipperary had done in the first half so had Limerick fought back from six points in arrears.

Limerick supporters went wild with delight in the fourteenth minute, when again, Eamonn Cregan crashed in a goal. This time Bernie Hartigan had sent in a delightful sideline cut. Once more, Rea had a part in proceedings, before Cregan gained possession and slammed it past Tadgh Murphy.

A minute later, Richie Bennis yet again tried for a goal from a free, when a point should have been taken. The effort was blocked, at the expense of a '70, but Seán Foley's fine effort was inches wide. Loughnane cut the deficit for Tipperary with a point from 40 yards, and Dinny Ryan came in for the home side in place of Jack Ryan, who had earlier come in for Jim Crampton.

Limerick hearts fluttered as Loughnane burst his way goalwards, past a number of defenders. The Roscrea man lost his hurley in the process, but he delightfully palmed the ball over the bar, only to be called back to take a free. He tried for a goal from the free, but he had to be content with a '70, which yielded nothing.

Seconds later, Loughnane was inches wide after Keating had created the chance.

Excitement was at a tremendous level now, and in the 21st minute, Liam O'Donoghue had a point, as Rea and John Kelly were spoken to by the referee. Loughnane had another Tipperary point from a free, and then followed a superb double save by Horgan from point blank range, and Willie Moore - who was now a formidable foe - effected a powerful lengthy clearance.

Éamon Grimes had a wide after Nolan gave him possession, and yet again Horgan made a tremendous save. Then followed two points by Loughnane to level for Tipperary, and practically everyone in the 41,722 crowd would have settled for a draw at that stage.

Francis Loughnane takes a second half free into the Killinan End goal.

Fluffed

Limerick fluffed a goal opportunity and then Loughnane had a point to put Tipperary once again in front, and it seemed Limerick were once again destined to be losers. But Bennis pointed a free to level and the Patrickswell man then pointed to put Limerick in front. It was absolutely stirring stuff at this stage, and John Flanagan had a Tipperary point from fully 65 yards to again bring equality.

All now would have settled for another day, but Limerick forced that never to be forgotten '70. Over moved Richie Bennis; Seán Foley also moved in his direction to wish him the best, as referee Michael Slattery told him he must score direct. Bennis lifted, struck, the umpire moved forward to lift his flag, he seemed to be knocked over by a Tipperary man. But the flag had gone up, Limerick had won, and bedlam with full justification had broken loose. Players jumped into the air, others hugged each other, some threw themselves on the ground in one of the greatest moments of jubilation ever for a Limerick sporting side. In years to come there are many who will be talking and debating about Sunday's contest.

Scorers

Limerick - R. Bennis 1-5; F. Nolan 2-1; E. Cregan 2-0; M. Dowling 1-0; L. O'Donoghue 0-1.

Tipperary - F. Loughnane 2-10; M. Keating 0-4; S. Hogan 0-2; N. O'Dwyer and J. Flanagan 0-1.

Teams

Limerick - Séamus Horgan; Willie Moore, Pat Hartigan, Jim O'Brien; Phil Bennis, Jim O'Donnell, Seán Foley; Éamon Grimes, Richie Bennis; Liam O'Donoghue, Mossie Dowling, Bernie Hartigan; Frankie Nolan, Eamonn Rea, Eamonn Cregan. Sub: Tom Ryan for Jim O'Donnell (HT).

Tipperary - T Murphy; J. Fogarty, J. Kelly, J. Gleeson; J. Crampton, T. O'Connor, L. Gaynor; S. Hogan, P.J. Ryan; F. Loughnane, M. Roche, N. O'Dwyer; J. Flanagan, R. Ryan, M. Keating. Subs: J. Ryan for Crampton, D. Ryan for J. Ryan.

Referee - Michael Slattery (Clare).

BENNIS THE HERO OF SUPERB FINAL AS T

Limerick's crucial three second half goals which rocketed them to a memorable triumph ... the first, on Eamonn Cregan's double thrust se

"WE ARE THI

LIMERICK, 6-7;   TIPPERARY, 2-18

NEVER BEFORE can there have been such a dramatic ending to a Munster seni hurling championship final than that at Thurles on Sunday. With the la stroke of a stirring contest Richie Bennis slammed over the winning point from "70". it was a superb stroke by the Patrickswell man who emerged the hero the day as he erased memories of squandered chances earlier on.

It might have taken eighteen years to win back the title but Sunday's pulverising finish will long be remembered by those fortunate to have witnessed a game that produced some brilliant passages, some poor play, but overall, an occasion which saw Limerick finally break through for a win that all Ireland was pleased to hear about.

The excitement of the occasion was quite fantastic. First Limerick stormed into a seven point lead inside fourteen minutes. A landslide win looked a possibility but then by the interval it was Tipperary who were clear leaders as they had four points to spare.

On a number of occasions in a superb second half the sides wede level and, indeed, practically all in the 41,000-plus crowd would have settled for a draw.

But Limerick, per Richie Bennis, forced a last second "70". Referee Mick Slattery of Clare told Bennis that he must score direct from his effort. Tension was almost unbearable as the red-haired Patrickswell man drew a monstrous swipe and as confusion was stirred up in the Tipperary goalmouth by some of the home players the umpire waved his flag.

Thus Bennis had won the championship for Limerick. Two to the last big win. Now, all can join with the celebrated old-timers, in talking of great days of Limerick hurling.

Many a heartbeat was missed at various times on Sunday. Indeed, many Limerick supporters were too tired at the finish to give full vent to their feelings.

Essentially it was a glorious triumph for Limerick teamwork. But some more than others played parts which had a greater impact. To many, Bennis will be the number one hero. But there are others who will insist that Eamonn Rea was the real star.

Selectors Abu!

To the oft criticised selectors must go considerable credit for what proved a master-stroke in picking Rea at full-forward. Many beforehand felt it was an

Hartigan. He had a great start, like others he faded, but what a storming finish he put in. It was magnificent to see him burst out from a deep-playing midfield role with the ball in his possession and then shake off Tipperary's efforts to stop him. Yes, Bernie, this was what we knew you were capable of, but had not seen for all too long.

Then who will forget the hurling skills shown by Sean Foley? As a wing back and then a centre-back he was brilliant. He faced a powerful challenge which he met in stirring manner and he, too, played a major part in the win.

Phil Bennis got through a vast amount of work as a right and left-half back. He was always very much in the thick

At times it seemed as i were going to be swamp much did they allow Tip take control. But the hom had no answer to Lim persistent forages and the back line of Fogarty, G and Kelly were made look ordinary this time.

None of the Tipperary c ers was allowed to sho authority they stamped or games. All were given tough task to do and while were better than others was really outstanding. keeper Tadgh Murphy di some tremendous saves bu in front got a very toug sage — mainly due to th liance of Rea.

Seamus Hogan and P. J got through an amount o work for Tipperary at m

WON AFTER 18 YEARS

...wling makes sure that Frankie Nolan's shot reaches a happy resting place; in centre, and on right, ... fans into raptures.

"CHAMPIONS" — THEY ROARED

Gallant bid by minors not sufficient

BY SEAN MURPHY

TIPPERARY, 5-12;   **LIMERICK, 5-4**

CONCEDING HEIGHT and weight to their opponents, Limerick, after much promise midway through the hour, had to surrender to the greater all-round combination of a hard-hitting Tipperary side in the Munster minor hurling championship final at Thurles on Sunday. Tipperary thus won their first title in this grade since 1962.

It was a richly deserved success achieved by a determined team using first time tactics and magnificent team work. They got off to a dream start in the opening minute when Limerick goalie, Pat Dunworth, pulled down a shot sailing over the bar, but his clearance was flashed to the net by Seamus Waters. A point from play by John Grogan and a simple goal by Paschal Ryan in the 6th minutes left Tipperary leading 2-1 to nil and a disastrous beating looked all "on." However, the picture changed as Paddy Kelly, even with limited support, began to gain the initiative at midfield and the overall stature of the team improved.

much of the play in the remaining 17 minutes but they seemed obsessed with the idea of rising the ball and their "pick and poke" tactics paid no dividends against the first time striking of Tipperary.

Limerick possessed many fine individual players but they lacked the cohesion and composure of Tipperary. The Limerick forwards in particular were very selfish in possession and this cost many scores.

For Limerick, Tom Lawlor tried his heart out in defence with able assistance from Pat Ryan and Mike Barron. Pat Kelly ploughed a lone furrow at mid-field, while in the forwards, Brendan Flynn, John

---

...ck's defenders had the ...ing into their eyes as ... Slattery, blew for pro- ... to start. It was Tip- ... Mich Roche who had scoring opportunity, but wide from about 40 ... Almost immediately came ...'s first chance, but Ber- ...tigan was unable to ...ossession, and he, too, ...

... three minutes before ... score came, but a glor- ... it was. Limerick won ... cut about 50 yards ...nonn Grimes cut in a ... and Frankie Nolan ... in as first rate a goal ...ould wish to see. ... on by that great ... Limerick burst into ... A Tipperary defender ...alised, but to the horror ... thousands of Limerick ...ers, Richie Bennis was ...ide with the free. To ... seemed he had tried ...al and failed miserably ...ers around thought that ... the ball too far in ... him and could not ... properly to take the ob- ...point. Whatever the ... it was a bad miss.

...he miss was forgiven ... minutes when the red- ... Patrickswell man clat- ... a goal from a 21-yards ...er Rea was pulled by a ... as he made inroads on ...perary goalie.

...e other end in the ... minute, Horgan made ...ave, but Limerick were ... slickly and speedily

nificently and had Tipperary in a terrible mess.

Fourteenth

Not until the fourteenth minute did Tipperary open their account, and then it was a point by Francis Loughnane from a free just after a delightful overhead flick by Bernie Hartigan had gone wide at the other end.

But even at this early stage it was becoming apparent that Jim O'Donnell was struggling at centre-back for Limerick. Roger Ryan might have been spoken to for retaliating in an uncomplimentary manner to Pat Hartigan after the Limerickman had gone over to inquire as to his well-being after he had been stretched on the verge of the square.

Tipperary began to edge their way into the game, and a lot of the gloss of Limerick's sparkling opening was gone after Loughnane (free) and Mick Keating had points before the seventeenth minute.

Again Tipperary crowded down on Limerick's terrain, and Roger Ryan had an eigthteenth minute point to leave only a goal in it at that stage.

Indeed seconds later Tipperary seemed certain to get on terms. From 20 yards Noel O'Dwyer sent in a bullet-like drive, but in superb fashion Horgan brought off a wonder save. Not surprisingly, Loughnane fluffed a chance from a

1973 Keeping the Dream Alive

King George IV Scotch Whisky say **K.G. 4**	**SPEEDI-CABS** **4-88-44** ANYTIME! ANYWHERE!

Limerick

Vol. 84.   No. 15586   Price 1p

MEMORABLE DAY FOR FANS

IT WAS A MEMORABLE day for the many thousands of Limerick hurling supporters who went to sunny Thurles on Sunday and saw their heroes conquer the home county in a blistering game.

On the famous bank facing the stand supporters of both teams not only saw a memorable encounter but at the same time got a sun tan as good as anything they could acquire in Spain or the Riviera.

The minor bickering between fans of both teams was generally of good natured variety and most of the Tipp supporters accepted defeat gracefully except for some cribs about the legality of Limerick's winning point.

ROARING

Hawkers did a roaring trade and so great was the demand that minerals and fruit ran out in most sections by the start of the second half of the senior game. Then it was ice-cream or nothing from the young sellers which included a lady with the strange name of "Spanner".

It was generally accepted that the Limerick selectors had made a master move by shifting Ned Rea to full forward, that Babs Keating is still deadly accurate with half a chance, as is the redoubtable Roger Ryan who was well held by a Pat Hartigan probably steeled by an underhand blow: Foley, Cregan and Moore—who got away with one very judicious push at a crucial moment—were mentioned as other Limerick heroes.

CONGRATULATED

After the game Mayor Mick Lipper congratulated the winners and both teams on a sporting display. He

"Are You Right There Michael Are You Right quested by a B.B.C. listener who must have bee chic.

A token stop of a few seconds was then ma Goolds Cross for some peculiar reason, as it cer was not long enough to pick up passengers.

CONTRAST

The return journey was in complete contra least on the first train out. It left Thurles at a qu to six and arrived back around 6.30 p.m. Great and ample compensation for the outward trip.

Goolds Cross was ignored, there was no an at Solohead Beg, neither was there a Dromkeen ' fle."

Residents angry over fire at city dump

THE RESIDENTS in the Thomondgate and Ki areas are angry with the Corporation becau the annoyance being caused by a fire which has alight at the Longpavement dump, since Thurso

One of the residents, Mr. Joe Daly, 76 New Road, Thomondgate, said they were "pestered" by the smell and the smoke which has been coming from the dump over the week-end.

"The fire started on Thursday morning and the Corporation said it was the second biggest

Good and B NEWS

1973 Keeping the Dream Alive

Leader

MONDAY, JULY 30, 1973

BEE MOYNIHAN & Co.
2 O'CONNELL ST
Limerick
JEWELLERS
Tel. 45385
Watches Repaired

METRO 4-hour Cleaning
now at
61 William St.

A section of the huge crowd which watched the epic Munster Hurling Final in Thurles yesterday.

ESSO PAY F ORKERS

SO Teoranta will shortly their 35-year association Foynes harbour... but four locals who have loyal service to the comy—Messrs. Ned Nestor, O'Sullivan, Willie O'Connd Tony Davitt—will reamounts varying from en £3,000 to £6,000 in ndancy money plus a ly pension of £15 each.

four have been emd with Esso for over 20

of era

xt Monday will see the f an era in Foynes when ast tanker will arrive jet fuel for Esso.

Continuous general education is desirable

IT IS NOW generally accepted that a continuous process of general education during working life is desirable for employees.

This is the view taken by the new AnCO document on training in industry.

Dealing specifically with the question of apprenticeship, when much of a man's training occurs, the statement says:

If an apprentice is to be successful, he must have achieved a good standard of basic gen-

If during working hours, who bears the cost—the employer, the employee, or the State?

"Credits"

Should people, during their working lives, build up "credits" based on service, which they could use to take time off from

Warmer houses

A BOOM in central heating in the past ten years has brought extra warmth to thousands of Irish homes. It has also brought the problem of how to keep the heat in the house and keep the fuel bills down.

There is in Limerick city since last October, a company called Irish Insulation, the first in the county, doing the job of insulating cavity walls with plastic foam with great success.

Basically, the foam can be "injected" into the cavity walls of a house through a small hole bored from the outside: its role is to reduce the movement of air inside the cavity and thus produce an insulation.

It is claimed that fuel bills can be reduced by one-third, as well as eliminating dampness and reducing noise and

1973 Keeping the Dream Alive

Munster Hurling Final Winning Point

Radio Commentary by Micheál O'Hehir

The sides are level and the stopwatch says about a minute left in the game. Blow the whistle, referee, we want to see this again. Ball out over the sideline, here. Looking at the watch, the referee looking at his watch, we're doing the same. He's going to throw in the ball; the linesman throwing in the ball, just down in under us. It goes in… Richie Bennis, Richie Bennis going up along the right wing. He's on the 21 yard line. He sends it into the centre. To Frankie Nolan. Frankie Nolan takes his shot. His shot is blocked down. Ball goes out the far side. Another shot by Eamonn Rea. Blocked down. They're pulling in, they're pulling out. The ball comes out into the wing.

And it's gone wide…it's a '70, a '70.

Éamon Grimes, took a shot that was defected round the post by Tadhg Murphy for a '70.

And, I think, this could well be the last puck of the game.

The referee, signalling, back to the taker of the '70. Richie Bennis, the taker.

The score Limerick 6-16…6-6, Limerick 6-6, Tipperary 2-18.

…inaudible announcer in the background…

Richie Bennis!

There's someone announcing something over the public address system. But nobody seems to care. Limerick have all moved up around the Tipperary goal. If Richie sends this one over the bar, well, they have won the Munster title. If he doesn't, well, we live to fight another day.

[Only '70 scored all year by Limerick]

Referee gone down into the parallelogram.

Richie Bennis, lifting, striking, sending the ball high, and sending it to, the, right…no IT'S OVER THE BAR!

IT'S OVER THE BAR.

IT'S A POINT.

…wild cheering…

IT'S A POINT.

…wild cheering…

And one of the umpires, the umpire who put up the white flag, has been struck.

…wild cheering…

The game is over, the game is over.

Gallant bid by Minors not Sufficient
(Limerick Leader, 30 July 1973)

By Seán Murphy

Tipperary 5-12
Limerick 5-4

Conceding height and weight to their opponents, Limerick, after much promise midway through the hour, had to surrender to the greater all-round combination of a hard-hitting Tipperary side in the Munster minor hurling championship final at Thurles on Sunday. Tipperary thus won their first title in this grade since 1962.

It was a richly deserved success achieved by a determined team using first time tactics and magnificent team work. They got off to a dream start in the opening minute when Limerick goalie, Pat Dunworth, pulled down a shot sailing over the bar, but his clearance was flashed to the net by Séamus Waters.

A point from play by John Grogan and a simple goal by Paschal Ryan in the 6th minute left Tipperary leading. 2-1 to nil and a disastrous beating looked all "on." However, the picture changed as Paddy Kelly, even with limited support, began to gain the initiative at midfield and the overall stature of the team improved. In the 18th minute a '70 taken by Gerry Mullane was finished to the net by John Ryan and Limerick were now there with a chance.

Tipperary No, 5 J. O'Meara in action during the Munster minor hurling final.

1973 Keeping the Dream Alive

When Bernard Berkery connected with a John Flanagan centre in the 28th minute to shoot a spectacular goal they were only three points in arrears. Tipperary were reduced to fourteen men when full-back Martin Loughnane received "marching orders" just before half-time.

Action from the 1973 Munster Minor Hurling Final between Limerick and Tipperary.

Limerick started in lively fashion on resuming when Eddie Barry shot a point from play after two minutes but they flattered only to deceive. They failed to use their "loose" man to advantage and in the next four minutes Tipperary had increased their lead to eight points in a sudden scoring spree. Limerick's sagging hopes received a boost in the 13th minute when Pat Kelly goaled a 21 yard free but Tipperary's reply was fast and decisive.

In a great passing movement, Jim Ryan, son of former Limerick midfielder, Timmy Ryan, raced through a hesitant Limerick defence for a spectacular goal, and Limerick's fate was doomed. They enjoyed much of the play in the remaining 17 minutes but they seemed obsessed with the idea of rising the ball and their "pick and poke" tactics paid no dividend against the first time striking of Tipperary,

Limerick possessed many fine individual players but they lacked the cohesion and composure of Tipperary. The Limerick forwards in particular were very selfish in possession and this cost many scores. For Limerick, Tom Lawlor tried his heart out in defence with able assistance from Pat Ryan and Mike Barron. Pat Kelly ploughed a lone furrow at midfield, while in the forwards, Brendan Flynn, John Ryan and Eddie Barry were most prominent.

On a well-balanced Tipperary side, goalkeeper Tom Doran, John Doyle, Jim O'Meara, team captain, Michael McCormack, Kenny, Johnny Ryan, Paschal Ryan and Tom Shore were the stars.

Scorers

Tipperary - P. Ryan 2-1; J. Ryan 1-4; J. Grogan 0-5; S. Waters and T Shore 1-1.

Limerick - P. Kelly 2-2; B. Berkery 2-0; G. Moloney 1-0; E. Barry and B. Flynn 0-1.

J. Grogan takes a sideline for Tipperary during the minor final.

1973 Keeping the Dream Alive

Teams

Tipperary - T. Doran; S. O'Brien, M. Loughnane, J. Doyle; T. Barry, M. McCormack, J. O'Meara; J. Grogan, P. Kirby; S. Hennessy, B. Kenny, J. Ryan; P. Ryan, S. Waters, T. Shore. Subs. N. Fleming for Hennessy and P. Ryan for J. Ryan.

Limerick - P. Dunworth; M. Ryan, M. Barron, P. Ryan; W. Nicholas, G, Mullane, T. Lawlor; T. Ryan, P. Kelly; B. Berkery, B. Flynn, E, Barry; J. Flanagan, J. Ryan, G. Moloney. Subs: J. Chawke for P. Ryan, J. Quane for Barry and D O'Keeffe for Mullane.

Referee - Noel Dalton (Waterford).

The Tipperary team that won the 1973 Munster Minor Hurling Final.

Back Row (L-R): Tom Doran. John Doyle, Stephen O'Brien, Jimmy Ryan, Brendan Kenny, Pascal Ryan, Jim O'Meara and Tom Barry.
Front Row (L-R): Séamus Waters, Martin Loughnane, Tommy Shoer, Séamus Hennessy, Pat Kirby, Michael Cormack (Capt.) and John Grogan.

The Limerick team managed by Seán O'Connor that played Tipperary in the 1973 Munster Minor Hurling Final.

Back Row (L-R): John Chawke, Tom Lawlor, Pat Ryan, Ger Moloney, Terence Murray, John Flanagan, Ger Mullane, Joe Ryan, Eddie Barry, Ger Hayes and Mike Barron.
Front Row (L-R): John Quane, Davy O'Keeffe, Willie Nicholas, Tom Ryan, Bernard Berkery, Brendan Flynn, Paddy Kelly, Michael Ryan, Seán Burke and Paddy Dunworth.

1973 Munster Hurling Final

At Semple Stadium, Thurles, in the year of '73,
Limerick played Tipperary and did not show any fear;
They pulled on the ball with skill and might,
They give poor Tipp. a hell of a fright.

Horgan in goal, a plucky man from the West,
Blocked raspers and gave a display of the best;
Full-back, Pat Hartigan, a hurler so fine,
In his helmet he put the burly Roger Ryan.

Willie Moore in the corner, a hard hurler is he,
When marking Babs Keating he showed no fear;
Jim O'Brien from Bruree, on the banks of the Maigue,
Out-hurled John Flanagan from Moycark-e-y.

Jim O'Donnell in the centre on Roche he did play,
He landed every ball right into the square;
Phil Bennis on the right, a plucky hurler is he,
He gave plenty of the stick to the man from Borrisoleigh.

Seán Foley from the 'Well gave a manful display,
He outhurled the one-sided hurler, Loughnane, from Roscrea;
At centre-field there was Richie, who scored the point of the day,
Tipperary can stay at home now and save the hay.

Éamon Grimes the great, the Mackey of today,
Showed the ball to Tipperary and ran like a hare;
Mossie Dowling at centre-forward, a hurler to the end,
Showed the great Tadgh O'Connor the way to bend.

On the right was Liam O'Donoghue, the find of the year,
Len Gaynor from Kilruane at the end shed a tear;
All praises to Bernie Hartigan, he hurled so great,
He stopped Tipperary so they met their fate.

At full-forward there was a hurler called Eamonn Rea,
He rattled the Tipperary full-back line in their own square;
Frankie Nolan in the corner, no mistake did he make,
Any ball that he got he gave it a flake.

Eamonn Cregan from Claughaun, a hurler of renown,
Slammed the ball into the net and, did not even frown;
This is the year, boys, we will drink a sup,
Out of the long-awaited, cherished, the MacCarthy Cup.

Vincent Donnelly

Magical Thurles 1973

By Tom Aherne

I will always remember attending my first Munster Hurling Final in Semple Stadium, Thurles, on Sunday 29 July, 1973. I will never forget the colour, glamour, and excitement of Semple Stadium, and how it turned out to be an historic day for the Shannonsiders. We experienced the build-up to the big day in the media, all that week. We attended the early morning Mass, in Carrigkerry followed by the Chapel gate chat, and a glance at the *Sunday Press*, for the latest news about the game. The breakfast was digested quickly, and the sandwiches packed and out the door for a short walk to meet my drive. "It's a long way to Tipperary" goes the song, and it certainly was from Glensharrold in West Limerick.

The journey by Volkswagen car with friends and neighbours, took up to three hours. (Michael Kiely was the young driver, his sister Mary (nee Kiely), their father Mike, and neighbour Dan Flynn were the others). The last few miles were slowed to a snail's pace as the crowds converged on the historic town that gave birth to the GAA in famed Hayes Hotel in 1884. A car park was found, and we tucked into the sandwiches which never tasted better.

We quickly made our way into Liberty Square and joined the excited crowd on the way to the grounds. The stalls were overflowing with hats, flags, and rosettes, in Limerick green-white and Tipperary purple-blue-gold colours, as the cries of the programme sellers could be heard above the noise. Nearer the ground the music of the banjo player, Pecker Dunne, and the blind fiddler filled the air with a blast of "Slievenamon" and "Where the Mulcair River flows."

A place was secured underneath the scoreboard behind the goals, which would be a talking point even to this day. The atmosphere was electric, and the sun from the azure sky intense and the heat from the sardine packed crowd was overwhelming. Bottles of Cidona, orange, and red lemonade, cones and choc ices were consumed by the shirt-sleeved crowd around us, and the fruit sellers had a field day with sales of apples, pears, and oranges soaring as people quenched their thirst.

The minor match passed quickly as we shaded our eyes from the sun with the match programme, and as the throw-in time approached you could cut the tension with a knife. The teams ran on to the field to a deafening roar from both sets of supporters. It was spine tingling for all as the teams marched behind the band, and the National Anthem was drowned out by the roar as it came to an end. Referee Michael Slattery from Clare got the action under way and the drama began to unfold, like a page from a book.

A great start by Limerick saw us seven points ahead after ten minutes, with Frankie Nolan, and Richie Bennis getting goals. Tipp fought back with captain Francis Loughnane in top scoring form, to lead by four points at the short whistle. The half-time break gave us a chance to draw our breath, suck some Silvermints, and to down some more liquids. A buzz was going around the ground as the fans discussed the action, and we wondered could Limerick bridge the 18-year gap to the last title and wipe out the agony of 1971 in Killarney, or would Tipperary deny us again.

Tipperary increased the pressure from the throw-in and took a 6 point lead, but a Frankie Nolan goal kept Limerick in contention. With Pat Hartigan taking the puck outs and putting intense pressure on the Tipp half back line, and Eamonn Rea keeping the dust flying around the Tipp goalmouth, Limerick became fired with ambition. Eamonn Cregan cracked home his first goal, and Richie Bennis levelled with a point from play as things hotted up. Eamonn Cregan scored one of the finest goals seen in a Munster final to put Limerick ahead.

Tipp pulled it back to one point as the temperatures soared amongst the crowd. Babs Keating broke clear and his shot for the winning goal was parried by Tournafulla's Séamus Horgan, who also saved the rebound from the late great John Flanagan, who had broken Limerick's hearts in Killarney by scoring the winning point. Francis and Richie scored two points each to leave Limerick still ahead with five minutes left. John Flanagan hits over a beauty from 70 yards to level, and our nails are now bitten to the quick.

Éamon Grimes shot wins a 70 off goalie Tadhg Murphy's hurley and we were about to see history being made, but we did not realise it at the time. You could hear a pin drop as Richie Bennis lined up his shot, and we didn't know he had to score direct as the ball took flight. The crowd swayed forward for a better view, and from our good vantage point behind the goals it looked a point, but only just.

The raising of the white flag, and the final whistle, was greeted with great euphoria as the crowd invaded the famed pitch to mob their heroes. The cup presentation to captain Éamon Grimes was cheered until our throats were dry and hoarseness set in.

A few very enjoyable hours were spent around the town, as we revelled in our success with all the other supporters. The journey home passed swiftly as we replayed the game and recounted the great moments of a memorable match. The bonfires burnt bright late into the night, at every crossroads in the county and I still had enough energy to attend the carnival dance in the Marquee in Carrigkerry village.

Now 39 years later (this was written on the 25 September 2012) I can still recall the wonderful moments from my first Munster Final. It was great to see the star players in action that I got to know from listening to Micheal O'Hehir's commentaries. Players like Mick Roche, Michael "Babs" Keating, Francis Loughnane, John Flanagan, Len Gaynor, Noel O'Dwyer, from Tipperary, and the more familiar Limerick players, that I had seen before. It was certainly a magical day in Thurles in 73 and hopefully the bonfires will soon be burning again.

FOOTNOTE

50 years later Dan Flynn and Mike Kiely who were in the car with me that day have passed to the sporting arena in the sky. They were loyal supporters of Limerick, and it was nice that we could share that special day together. In April 2023, Mary McNamara (nee Kiely) was laid to rest in Mungret Cemetery after a short illness.

She was a massive Limerick supporter with her family, and they attended all the recent Limerick hurling successes. Michael still attends the matches, and I am now an armchair supporter. Up the Green and White!

The Cups (GAA Family Silver, Humphrey Kelleher - published in 2013)

Munster Hurling Cup

The First Munster Senior Hurling Championship final won on the field of play was in 1890 when Cork beat Kerry by 2-0 to 0-1. The present trophy, referred to as the Munster Hurling Cup, is the second. The first trophy was presented by the Munster Council in 1928 and was won by Cork who beat Clare in a replay by 6-4 to 2-2.

That cup was replaced in 1991. In 1990 Cork were the last team to win the old trophy and Tipperary were the first recipients of the new trophy, beating Cork in the 1991 final replay by 4-19 to 4-15. Neither cup bears the name of a person.

(The original Munster Hurling Cup was agreed to be named after Dan Fraher but the name never stuck, reason unknown. The second Munster Hurling Cup was replaced by its latest incarnation in 2022, now named the Mick Mackey Cup. It was fitting that it was first lifted by Declan Hannon in Limerick's extra time win over Clare in Thurles in June.)

John Comyn on GAA - Did You Know?
(Sunday Independent, 29 July 1973)

Limerick and Tipperary will be meeting for the fourth time this year when they line out for the Munster final at Thurles today and with two draws and a two-point win for Limerick in the third game, it seems certain that a bounce of a ball one way or the other will decide Kilkenny's opponents in the All Ireland final. (I simply can't take Galway or London as serious contenders.)

This, in fact, will be the tenth game between the counties since 1971 and Limerick hold the edge 4-3 with two draws, but if we go back to 1969, Tipperary take over 6-4 with two draws.

Here's the run-down:

1973
Limerick 3-7; Tipperary 2-10 - League.
Limerick 2-11; Tipperary 2-11 - League.
Limerick 5-10; Tipperary 3-14 - League.

1972
Tipperary 4-7; Limerick 2-11 - League.
Tipperary 8-7; Limerick 4-12 - Wembley Games.

1971
Limerick 0-13; Tipperary 1-8 - League.
Limerick 3-12; Tipperary 3-11 - League.
Limerick 3-12; Tipperary 3-11 - League Final.
Tipperary 4-16; Limerick 3-18 - Munster Final.

1969
Tipperary 2-6; Limerick 2-3 - Challenge
Tipperary 4-10; Limerick 4-4 - Challenge
Tipperary 0-14; Limerick 2-5 - League.

Strangely perhaps I can find no record of a match between Tipperary and Limerick in 1970.

Now take those last nine outings between the sides with Limerick 4-3 to the good, the odd fact is that Tipperary have the higher score, 28-99 to 24-109, but that's a margin of only two points over nine games. If we include the remaining three matches, the margin stretches to 14 points, but the average is still very close indeed at 2-13.2. to 2-12.1 in favour of Tipperary.

So far this year, this method of assessing scores has not been as successful as in previous years, but that is precisely because of my failure to work out the difference between the 80-minute and 60-minute games. Of course, results haven't worked out too well on form either.

Anyway, all things considered, It will be very surprising if the contest isn't decided by a point or two, perhaps something like 3-19 to 3-18 in favour of Tipperary.

Remember 1965

The last time Limerick and Tipperary met in the Munster minor hurling final was in 1965, a game which Limerick won by 5-6 to 3-9, and it's interesting to note that of the Tipperary team that played in that game, John Kelly, Seamus Hogan and John Flanagan are now regular seniors, while on the Limerick side, Eamon Grimes is the only member of the Limerick side in action with the seniors today.

It will be recalled that Tipperary looked set for victory when two great goals by red-haired Sean Bourke swung the game in Limerick's favour and they went on to win by three points. Bourke has figured on Limerick senior teams in recent times. The teams were level at half-time.

The teams that played that day were: **Limerick**—T. Brennan, M. O'Flaherty, D. Manning, A. Cronin, S. Toomey, E. Boland, J. Hehir, P. Doherty, D. Foley, E. Grimes, W. Hayes, C. Shanahan, M. Grace, B. Murnane, S. Bourke.

Tipperary—P. Kennedy, M. F. Ryan, J. Kelly, E. Bourke, S. Hogan, D. Fahy, J. Mescall, B. Dwyer, D. Kennedy, J. Flanagan, M. Loughnane, K. Fogarty, B. Crosse, E. Morrissey, O. Ryan.

Limerick went on to the all-Ireland final but lost to Dublin. The Limerick win came during the great run of Limerick CBS in the Harty Cup competition.

From the official programme of the 1973 Munster Hurling Final.

J. LEAHY & SONS LTD.

PLASTERING   CONTRACTORS

Charleville and Mallow.

***

Cumann Luith-Chleas Gael

Munster Under 21 Hurling Final

CORCAIGH v LUIMNEACH

Dr. Mannix Park, Rathluirc

Wednesday, 8th August, 1973

At 7.30 p.m.   Referee: John Moloney.

PROGRAMME   5p.

***

JOHN DESMOND

Phone (063) 476

GARAGE
REPAIRS PANEL BEATING
SPRAY PAINTING

New Line, Charleville.

PRINTED BY ORIEL PRESS LTD. CHARLEVILLE.

Cork Can Still Win an All Ireland Title
(Cork Examiner, 9 August 1973)

Cork 4-11
Limerick 2-7

By Michael Ellard

Cork's hope of one All Ireland hurling title is still alive and vibrant. But they can thank their lucky stars that when disaster struck for them at rain-swept Rathluirc (Charleville) last evening, they had built up a considerable early lead which played the principle part in carrying them through to their Munster under 21 hurling championship victory over Limerick. Magnificent in the first half, this Cork side looked as if they were going to wipe Limerick off the face of the earth on this fine sod of Bishop Manning Park. They led 3-8 to 0-2 at the interval, but when right half back Vincent Twomey was sent to the line by referee John Maloney 11 minutes after the resumption, Limerick struck back with all the tenacity at their disposal, and though they made up considerable leeway, Cork were still 10 points to the good at the close of the game. There was really only one team in it in the first half, when Cork played a spectacular brand of hurling.

Limerick had no answer to the power of their hurling, and two magnificent goals by right corner forward Dan Relihan had them 2-5 to 0-2 in front after the first quarter. True, Limerick had missed four chances of scoring from 21 yard frees, but there was no question about it but that Cork were the vastly superior team. Their defence, in which the entire sextet were outstanding, experienced no trouble in curbing a rather weak Limerick attack. Tim Crowley and Brian Cotter gave them a major share of the midfield exchanges and their forward line, in which Relihan, Tommy Sheehan and Séamus Farrell played starring roles, were much too talented for the Limerick rear-guard. Taking their points with aplomb, they made a mockery of Limerick's bid to get into the game, and when Tommy Sheehan goaled a minute from half-time, they seemed to be coasting to a huge victory. The Mallow left half forward seemed to hammer home the final nails in Limerick's coffin when within minutes of the resumption he first pointed a free and then notched his second goal.

But with Twomey's dismissal after which there was a brief flare-up involving several players, Limerick took advantage of their numerical superiority and they came at Cork with a vengeance. Liam O'Donoghue, the only member of their champion winning senior team, came out of his shell and sparked off their recovery with a point. Throwing everything at the Cork rearguard, in which goalkeeper Frank O'Sullivan, Michael Corbett, Liam Kelly, Brian Murphy, John Buckley and Denis Burns did everything in their power to weather the storm, Limerick still succeeded in getting through for two goals via Denis O'Sullivan and Fintan Ryan, but time ran out for them and so Cork regained the title they relinquished last season.

Scorers

Cork - T. Sheehan 2-5; D. Relihan 2-2; J. Barry-Murphy, S. O'Leary, J. Buckley and T. Crowley 0-1 each.

Limerick - F. Ryan 1-2; D. O'Sullivan 1-0; V. O'Donoghue 0-3; J. Curtin and B. Neenan 0-1 each.

Teams

Cork - F. O'Sullivan; M. Corbett, L. Kelly, B. Murphy; V. Twomey, J. Buckley, D. Burns; T. Crowley, B. Cotter; P. Kavanagh, S. Farrell, T. Sheehan; D. Relihan, J. Barry-Murphy, S. O'Leary. Sub: T. Canavan for Kavanagh.

Limerick - T. Hehir; J. Grimes, P.J. O'Shea, P. Ryan; M. O'Leary, J. Quinlan, P. Herbert; D. Connolly, F. Connolly; L. O'Donoghue, L. Enright. F. Ryan; J. Moynihan, D. O'Sullivan, B. Neenan. Subs.: J. Coughlan for Neenan and M. Daly for Ryan.

Referee - John Maloney (Tipperary).

Reflections of a Dramatic Game at Thurles
(Gaelic Sport, September 1973)

By Eamonn Young

Eighty minutes of remarkable entertainment. That to me was the Munster final when grim, manly yet stylish Tipp were beaten by Richie Bennis's seventy - the last puck of the game. Eight goals we saw, and twenty-five points; a beautiful ciotog stylist called Loughnane shot two goals (one of them from a crisp spot of anticipation) and ten points; Mick Keating scored four smart points on the turn without changing feet. All were good, the last, excellent. Mossie Dowling and Frankie Nolan doubled on falling balls and whipped them to the net with a precision of a machine, the well-trained human. Séamus Horgan, the goalie from Tournafulla, hammered back two fine shots to the Tipp forwards, ones that had 'goal' written all over them.

The final climax when forty thousand watched, prayed hoped, held the breath and then erupted in delight or despair was a moment in one's sporting life which I think only hurling can produce. Firm straight reffing by black-clothed Michael Slattery, grim virility between hard men like Roger Ryan, John Kelly, Pat Hartigan and Eamonn Rea … all this was served up to us a multi-coloured audience pulverised at times into silence, goaded to groans of despair or fired to pinnacles of delirium. As we went down in the pints over at the Jockey afterwards I felt happy to be a member of this sporting community.

It is only natural in the days after this great match when the intoxication of unusual sport is still in the blood, that one is likely to look at the prospects of this Limerick team through rose-tinted glasses. I do hope they will win the All Ireland. Apart from being a Munster man, the sympathy a sportsman feels for a side which bestrode the hurling world like a colossus over thirty years ago, and which since has often cried like a lost child asks for a Limerick win. But there will be no scoreline for sympathy on Sunday, 2 September and it won't be much use showing your opponent the press notices of the Munster final when he's breathing down your neck.

Liam O'Donoghue causing great concern for Tipperary's Len Gaynor and PJ Ryan in Thurles.

Just how good are Limerick?

To win any good hurling game a side needs great individual skill, adequate collective understanding, a capacity for analysis as each ball comes, a judgement on what one should do with the thing when one has possession, a bunch of men on the line who can direct, and an emotional stability among the whole team party which will ensure that each man is well-prepared, that each man plays fairly well and that each man keeps his head for the full eighty minutes. Add to that the superb fitness needed in an All Ireland, fitness far beyond what is needed in the earlier games and this is essential to the player as the admission fee is to the spectator . . . without it he's not even in the game. And finally add power, real old-fashioned strength applied with snappy concentration by hard men, just as the shot-putter skips across that circle and then explodes to send the iron ball careering beyond the mark of ordinary men.

To start where I ended, Limerick beat Tipp because of power. Roger Ryan beat Cork on his own; Pat Hartigan fought him man to man in fair combat for the eighty minutes, though the hardy Tipp man had a spot of real bad luck when he connected with a lightning-fast ground ball for it was Hartigan's bash that sent the sliotar flying up over the bar when no goalie would have stopped it. On the other side it was Eamonn Rea's power that tormented the gallant John Kelly, until the lighter Tipp man hurled himself into a frenzy.

There's power too in Mossie Dowling, Jim O'Brien and Seán Foley. That's not to say these chaps can't hurl or that the others are weak. Far from it.

Eamonn Cregan, still below his exciting best, quick-striking earnest Éamon Grimes, Bernie Hartigan of the flashing pace, Richie Bennis, audacious and level-headed, skilful Frankie Nolan and Liam O'Donoghue, and straight, crisp Jim O'Donnell ... there's a lot of good hurling there. Add the tenacity of Willie Moore and Phil Bennis to the added confidence which Séamus Horgan must feel after his great day in Thurles and you see that this is a good team. There's power in the puck-out and skill in the frees; there's speed in the feet and a swift clarity in the heads.

Mick Cregan has been working with this team for some months. They showed no signs of slack in the end of the eighty-minute game, and one can expect that they won't be beaten for fitness, a factor which took on a new emphasis after the '72 All Ireland.

So Limerick are skilful enough, have fair power, and should be very fit. How are they for match analysis before and during the game?

That I don't know but this I do: Kilkenny are formidable here. They have things pretty well worked out and only careful planning and endless discussion by men who know the thirty pretty well can ensure that when the unexpected happens - as it surely will - a sensible solution will be applied quickly.

There's one aspect in which Limerick must be superior to Kilkenny and that's in motivation. Not only did none of the present bunch not play in an All Ireland for Limerick, they weren't born for the last one of thirty-three years ago when Mick Mackey, who had just then joined the army along with half the virile young men of the country, led the men from the Shannon to a great win. Limerick need this win very badly: I feel they're dreaming about it, whether that's a good thing or not remains to be seen.

Steadiness on the day doesn't always spring from extreme eagerness. Motivation, so valuable in any human effort sometimes starts men off at a really fierce rate, but the valley period comes after about twenty minutes when the intense burst drains energy. Will nerves set Limerick off like a released spring while Kilkenny come to full power more gradually, maintaining it over the eighty minutes as they did last year?

1973 Keeping the Dream Alive

"Kilkenny will beat Tipp; they'll destroy Limerick." That's what a few sound men said to me BEFORE the Munster final. At half time they hadn't changed but at the end they were not so sure. After an afternoon of exposure to Limerick's dash the statement sounded intemperate.

A moment from the end of the Munster final Len Gaynor and Richie Bennis line up for a slap ball on the side-line. Ref. Slattery looks at the watch. It's almost time by us. A draw and back to Thurles for the replay. Two hard whipping players raise their sticks and my bet is on the relentless Gaynor. As the sliotar reaches the ground the red head of the Limerick man bends, the stick guarding the hand and he has the leather. Darting away down the wing he slaps it across the goal twenty yards out, where they pull and dodge, until the sliotar is belted low and hard towards the upright. Tadhg Murphy gets the stick to it and its over for a seventy. Richie Bennis gets the message from Michael Slattery and turns away to place the ball. Pause, legs straight, a look goalwards and the sliotar is raised, stick swung and 'way she goes.

Then the place goes suddenly mad. They run on from the line, Bennis tears away across the field towards us, leaps ecstatically four feet into the air, is grabbed by a comrade and embraced, bursts out again from the delirious knot of worshippers and runs leaping downfield where another green-shirted man grabs him and they roll like small boys gambolling on the grass embracing each other in a madness of delight. Tipp players wending their way grim and silent towards the dressing-rooms can hardly join in the joy just then. Later even they who fought the good fight to the end may take a little pride in their role which brought such sporting joy to a county which needed it. And that's what life is all about, isn't it?

Victory in the Sun.
This picture captures the joy of the Limerick team and supporters on Munster Final Day, 1973, as Éamon Grimes displays the cup after receiving it from P.A. (Weeshie) Murphy, Cork, Chairman of the Munster Council, who was to die suddenly on the evening of the All Ireland Final.

Excerpts from Raymond Smith's Player's No. 6 Book of Hurling
(Pages 19-22)

In hurling Limerick teams of recent years, as Richie Bennis will be the first to tell you, began to discover that the glories of the Mackey era had become like a millstone around their necks, for in defeat cruel comparisons were invariably made. All right, they were aware that what Mick Mackey and his team of all the talents had achieved had made Limerick in the minds of the hurling public one of the foremost strongholds of the game, had given a distinctiveness to the Green and White, especially when the dust was flying around the goal at Thurles that could never fade. But as the seasons out of the championship honours list began to build up in number - first a decade, then two, then three - it happened that some despaired that Limerick would ever make it back to the top again and in their desperation, they became more and more carping in their criticisms of players who were trying their best but who knew that in the minds of these critics they could never measure up to the standards set in the thirties and early forties.

So Richie Bennis and the others became determined that they could create their own traditions. And they would make men talk of 1973.

Yes, men will talk now of the Limerick team of 1973 and how Richie Bennis scored the winning point from the '70 in the Munster Final at Thurles with the last puck of the game and of the wonderful victory scenes in the sun that day how they swarmed on to the field to overwhelm him in their enthusiasm, how others were shouldered high from the pitch as the swaying throng surged across to the Stand, waving the Green and White flags and banners high as Éamon Grimes received the Cup and the shirt-sleeved crowd rose in spontaneous applause to the Limerick team as they went in, rose also to Tipperary who had helped to make it the memorable contest it was, and how Limerick supporters danced in the streets and outside the hotel where the team took their after-match meal that became a victory celebration. Not to have been in Thurles on that evening was to have missed one of the great hurling occasions.

The All Ireland week-end was unforgettable too. They poured into Dublin on Friday and Saturday from all the strongholds of Limerick hurling - from Bruree, Dromcollogher, Fedamore, Castleconnell, Patrickswell and Cappamore. And they smelt victory in the air.

In the swirl of smoke and the talk and the arguing in the establishments where hurling men gather on these week-ends, they were debating if the Limerick team of 1936 was the greatest of all time and recalling again the individual deeds of Mick Mackey and Jackie Power, who was coach to the 1971-73 side. But they were able to look back now, these Limerick followers, not in a lengthening twilight as it were for the glories of other days, but with the knowledge that they had a team in this 1973 season that could challenge and take on the best - for after Thurles and the defeat of Tipperary they needed no sympathy from anyone, not anymore.

A man, who had flown in from the States, tossed a wad of notes, eighty pounds in all, on the counter of O'Dwyers of Leeson Street and asked that it be covered at 5/4 against Limerick. And there was one there, who had followed Limerick through thick and thin, not just in the sun but on miserable wet days in League matches which meant that he had to hit out from Dublin after a rushed lunch, or maybe no lunch at all, to make it in time to see them play and without hesitation he went in and took forty pounds of it. And the rest was as quickly taken and the chap in from the States was asked if he wanted to have more on Kilkenny and at that he shied away, for he had never seen such fearless confidence.

The Limerick men did not gamble normally on hurling or football matches. That was not their style, but now I guessed they were betting not so much for the money but because they were insulted that someone who had missed Thurles and did not have to endure what they had to suffer on the bank as Richie bent and lifted and hit the last stroke on which everything rested, should cross the Atlantic and show the temerity to lay 5/4 against the men in the Green and White.

"But they are not champions yet?" "What is written, is written," he replied.

They broke a dozen bottles of champagne with the money that was won and all were one now - no matter what county they hailed from-with the Limerickmen, joining with them in lifting their glasses to the champions of 1973 and there was a man from Athlacca who composed a ballad as he went along in memory of the occasion, a parody about a bunch of the boys whooping it up in the back of a saloon in Bruree!

And there was no sign of the man in from the States to be seen anywhere.

I said to myself, coming down from the Hogan Stand after Éamon Grimes had received the Liam MacCarthy trophy on that first Sunday in September, 1973, that even if the Shannonsiders were not to win another All Ireland title in the seventies they had accomplished an outstanding feat for hurling in breaking the monotonous sameness of the Final pairings. We were beginning to take it almost for granted that it would be Cork or Tipperary against Wexford or Kilkenny.

It confirmed an opinion I have always held that it would be foolhardy in the present state of hurling to try and concentrate on too broad a front in endeavouring to preserve and foster the national game. Better in my view to put the main emphasis and the bulk of the resources into keeping it alive in Tipperary, Cork, Limerick, Waterford, Clare, Kilkenny, Wexford, Galway, Dublin, Offaly, Laois, Antrim and possibly Kildare, Wicklow, Westmeath and Kerry, the four counties that completed Group B (Division Two) of the National Hurling League in 1973-74. This makes a total of sixteen counties in all, but personally I normally think in terms of twelve real hurling counties at most.

If Limerick in winning their seventh All Ireland senior title, could make the 1973 season so memorable, what would our seasons not be like if Clare and Waterford could challenge at the same level - getting there on sheer merit and not on the sympathy of the crowds.

A Players No. 6 statuette being presented to Éamon Grimes with other Limerick players in close attendance.

1973 Keeping the Dream Alive

The Players No. 6 statuette that appeared in 'The GAA in 100 Objects' book published last year. John Egan of Fiddown produced them in large quantities in the 1960s and 1970s but they are now extremely rare and very collectible.

CHAPTER 8
1973
ALL IRELAND HURLING SEMI-FINAL v LONDON

(5 AUGUST - CUSACK PARK, ENNIS)

Limerick played London on Sunday, 5 August 1973 in the All Ireland Hurling Semi-Final at Ennis. London? Yes, London! London won the All Ireland Intermediate (Junior until 1961) hurling championship in 1968 and "graduated" to the senior ranks as a direct result. They played in All Ireland senior hurling semi-finals from 1969 until 1972, losing all of them by wide margins. In 1973, it was decided that London would play Galway at the newly-created All Ireland quarter-final stage. They created a considerable shock by beating Galway in Ballinasloe on the same day that Limerick beat Tipperary. This game was 60 minutes in duration. The Connacht Tribune solemnly headlined an article in the aftermath of this defeat, "The Day Galway Hurling Died." That there were 6 Galway men on the starting London 15 was very cold comfort to the locals. Kilkenny had already qualified directly for the All Ireland final by beating Wexford in the Leinster Hurling Final on 8 July.

The London team flew into Dublin Airport for the game very late on Saturday night, having been delayed for 7 hours in Heathrow due to a baggage handlers' strike that afternoon. The team also had problems getting adequate transport down to Ennis early on Sunday morning. A number of the team had remained in Ireland after beating Galway the previous Sunday. This did not make for great preparation for the massive task ahead of them. The curtain raiser was the minor semi-final between Galway and Tipperary. Galway recorded a famous victory over Tipperary, 3-14 to 3-10.

Limerick made a few changes for the London game, with Jim Hogan (born 1937) coming into goals for the injured Séamus Horgan. It was a popular selection as Jim had started his inter-county career a full 15 years before in 1958, making only 23 championship appearances, though he was an ever-present starter until the start of 1973. At the other end of the Limerick player age scale, Liam O'Donoghue (born 1952) was only starting his inter-county career, one that finished a full 15 years later, in June 1988. Between the two men, they spanned 30 years of inter-county duty in the green and white of Limerick. Eamonn Cregan was injured (knee cartilage) late in the game but was successfully treated by John St. George in the Regional Hospital (now known as UHL) soon afterwards.

Most of the media coverage in the run-up to the game centred on the novelty of brother playing against brother, in the form of Limerick-born Gerry Rea of London (also captain of the team) playing at full back against Eamonn Rea of Limerick playing at full forward. Their father was reported in local media before the game as wanting London to win. There was some speculation that they would not go into direct opposition with each other, but this proved to be unfounded. Eamonn Rea was started in the corner but reverted to the full forward position as the original positional change did not work.

There are a number of photographs of Gerry and Eamonn in direct opposition, even though there was an NUJ strike in place at the time. Limerick played in blue (Munster GAA) while London played in white (Kildare) as there was a clash of usual colours. The game itself was competitive up to half time but Limerick were much the stronger combination during the second moiety, with the game being described as "disappointing". London's travel problems plus their lack of 80 minute games must have had negative effects on their chances.

There was a nice six page fold-out official programme printed for the game. Even though a crowd of 12,000 attended the game the item is rare, the scarcest of the four Limerick championship game programmes of 1973. There was no Limerick Leader published on the bank holiday Monday and no report was filed for the game in later editions. There is no known team photo of either senior team that day, though a Galway minor team photo from that day exists. Luckily, photos of the London team were taken when they played Galway the previous Sunday. The headline in the weekend Limerick Leader was about the increase in maximum prices for many basic foodstuffs. Kerosene went from 15p to 16p a gallon, for instance. This era was in the run-up to the first oil crisis later in 1973.

ALL-IRELAND HURLING

1973

AT CUSACK PARK,

On SUNDAY NEXT, 5th

SENIOR AT 3.30

LIMERICK v L

Referee: M. Sp

MINOR AT 2 P.M

TIPPERARY v C

Referee: S. Ran

OFFICIAL PROGRAMME

ALL-IRELAND HURLING SEMI-FINALS
1973

AT CUSACK PARK, ENNIS

On SUNDAY NEXT, 5th AUGUST, 1973

SENIOR AT 3.30 P.M.

LIMERICK v LONDON

Referee: M. Spain

MINOR AT 2 P.M.

TIPPERARY v GALWAY

Referee: S. Rankins

☆

OFFICIAL PROGRAMME - - - - 5p

LIMERICK

(BLUE)

1
T. Hogan
(CLAUGHAUN)

2	3	4
W. Moore	P. Hartigan	J. O'Brien
(DOON)	(S. LIBERTIES)	(BRUREE)
5	6	7
P. Bennis	J. O'Donnell	S. Foley
(PATRICKSWELL)	(DOON)	(PATRICKSWELL)

8	9
R. Bennis	E. Grimes
(PATRICKSWELL)	(S. LIBERTIES)

10	11	12
L. O'Donoghue	M. Dowling	B. Hartigan
(MUNGRET)	(KILMALLOCK)	(OLD CHRISTIANS)
13	14	15
F. Nolan	E. Rea	E. Cregan
(PATRICKSWELL)	(EFFIN)	(CLAUGHAUN)

SUBS.: 16 J. Allis (Doon); 17 J. McKenna (South Liberties); 18 P. Fitzmaurice (Kileady); 19 A. Dunworth (Faughs); 20 T. Ryan (Patrickswell).

PLEASE SUPPORT OUR ADVERTISERS

CUSACK PARK, ENNIS — AD

NOW AVAILABLE

Firms interested should apply for term

County Treasurer

MR. JIM McMAHON, FRANCIS STR

LONDON

(WHITE)

1
E. Walshe
(KILKENNY)

2   **3**   **4**
B. Twoomey   **J. Rea**   **J. Barrett**
(CORK)   (LIMERICK)   (TIPPERARY)

5   **6**   **7**
P. Cronin   **M. Connolly**   **D. Lawlor**
(KERRY)   (GALWAY)   (WEXFORD)

8   **9**
R. Cashin   **S. Kinsella**
(WATERFORD)   (WEXFORD)

10   **11**   **12**
L. Corless   **T. Connolly**   **P. O'Neill**
(GALWAY)   (GALWAY)   (TIPPERARY)

13   **14**   **15**
M. Linnane   **F. Canning**   **L. Burke**
(GALWAY)   (GALWAY)   (GALWAY)

SUBS.: 16 M. Butler (Wexford); 17 D. McCarthy (Cork); 18 M. Walshe (Kilkenny); 19 T. Frehill (Galway); 20 V. Gantley (Galway).

PLEASE SUPPORT OUR ADVERTISERS

SING SPACE

particulars to:

- ENNIS

✲ EIRE OG BINGO

Every Sat. - New Hall, Ennis

At 9 P.M.

£1,500 WON IN THE LAST 3 WEEKS

OVER 2,000 PLAYERS

☞ JOIN THEM SAT. NEXT

All Ireland Hurling Semi-Final
(Cork Examiner, 6 August 1973)

Limerick There After 33 Years

Limerick 1-15
London 0-7

Munster champions Limerick are through to the All Ireland Senior Hurling final for the first time since 1940, thanks to this big win over London at Ennis yesterday. But supporters of the winners will readily admit that the side will have to play considerably better if Kilkenny are to be beaten on 2 September.

Absent yesterday was the fire and spirit shown against Tipperary in the provincial final a week earlier. Granted it was apparent early on that London were no world beaters, but still there was a lot of slipshod play by Limerick.

Indeed the red hot favourites found things difficult enough during an entertaining first half in which London were at their best. In that spell Limerick could not shake off the determined efforts of the visitors who however, could not maintain the effort and it was obvious long before the finish that an upset was unlikely.

Limerick in blue

Limerick will be playing in the blue of Munster on Sunday, because both counties normally wear green.

Sean Kinsella comes into the London team, and Gerry Rea has been chosen to play in direct opposition to Eamonn.

London will be playing in white.

While Limerick wore blue, London wore white, using a borrowed set of Kildare jerseys.

Limerick took steps before the start to avoid the direct confrontation of the Rea brothers. They switched Eamonn to left corner forward, moved Eamonn Cregan out to centre forward and had Mossie Dowling at full forward. The changes had an adverse effect as the front line found scoring a very difficult proposition against a hard tackling London defence. Indeed Limerick were faring so poorly that before the interval, the side was back to that which was chosen.

Limerick's Eamonn Rea versus his brother London's Gerry Rea, with Frankie Nolan on hand to help his teammate.

1973 Keeping the Dream Alive

Brother v brother

It's brother v. brother as Eamonn Rea (Limerick), No. 14 and his brother Gerry (No 3), the London full-back, make a determined attempt to gain possession in the goalmouth clash in the All Ireland semi-final.

1973 Keeping the Dream Alive

This meant that Rea was marking his brother Gerry who fared much better than did the Tipperary fullback of a week previously.

London went in front after 45 seconds with a point by Frank Canning but Richie Bennis levelled for Limerick after two minutes. A minute later London again went in front with a point by Pat McDermott, Again Bennis brought equality. Liam O'Donoghue put Limerick in front for the first time after six minutes and they were never subsequently headed.

However, London were faring quite well at this stage and they were on terms at five points each after 22 minutes.

Limerick were far from impressive at this stage and the selectors moved Jim O'Donnell from centre back to left half back and brought Seán Foley to centre back. This made for considerable improvement by Limerick and they went on to lead by 10 points to five at the interval.

Bernie Hartigan runs for possession near the London goalmouth during the All Ireland hurling semi-final.

Wonderful fielding by Eamonn Cregan against Tom Connolly with Richie Bennis in the foreground.

Mastered

What entertainment the game had to offer was crammed into that first half. It was apparent at the interval that London had been mastered and the second half was too one-sided to be entertaining. All told it was a disappointing contest but Limerick will no doubt be happy to be through to the All Ireland final for the first time in 33 years. On yesterday's display it was difficult to understand how London had beaten Galway but difficulty in travelling from Heathrow Airport might have upset them somewhat.

Limerick had the long-serving Jim Hogan back in goal and he brought off four splendid saves. Indeed it is a very long time since Limerick went through a game without conceding a goal and the selectors will have a difficult task in deciding whether Hogan or Séamus Horgan should be in goal for the final. Pat Hartigan was outstanding at full back and Jim O'Brien again shone at corner back. The Limerick half-back line had its share of troubles and three centre backs were used during the game with Phil Bennis finishing up in the position. But of the three, Seán Foley was clearly the pick and he had an excellent overall game.

Éamon Grimes did well at times at midfield where he was joined by Bernie Hartigan for a good part of the second half. But of the Limerick forwards only Liam O'Donoghue played to his usual form and the remainder will have to do better. Eamonn Cregan had to retire after 28 minutes of the second half and before he did so he had switched positions with Richie Bennis. Cregan's injury is not a serious one.

Easily London's outstanding player was Larry Corless who operated at midfield and in the half forward line. Tom Connolly was another forward to impress but like Limerick the visitors had their best players in defence.

Goalkeeper, Eamon Walsh, made several spectacular saves and John Barrett excelled at corner back. Dave Lawlor was another to shine and Gerry Rea did very well at full back.

Scorers

Limerick - R. Bennis 1-7 (1-5 frees!!); L. O'Donoghue 0-4; E. Cregan 0-2; B. Hartigan and F. Nolan 0-1.

London - F. Canning and P. O'Neill 0-2; P. McDermott, L. Corless and T. Connolly 0-1.

Referee - Mick Spain (Offaly).

The London senior hurling team and substitutes who defeated Galway on the same day that Limerick beat Tipperary in the Munster Final.

Hartigan Opts out of Discus
(Irish Press, 21 June 1966)

By John Redmond

Never on Sundays - that is all rounder Bernie Hartigan's attitude towards athletics. Sunday he devotes exclusively to Gaelic games, and he is willing to forego the chance of winning the All Ireland N.A.C.A. discus title to pursue his favourite sport. Explained Hartigan, "Although I like athletics, particularly the discus, hammer and javelin, my real loves are football or hurling. It is impossible to have a Sunday free with Gaelic games, but that is the way I like it. Unfortunately the discus event is being held on a Sunday so I will not take part." But the Limerick inter-county and Old Christians player will be in two N.A.C.A. Championship events, the hammer and javelin. They are on Saturday, July 30, the first day of the meeting.

Although Old Christians or Limerick have not arranged a game for July 31, Hartigan said: "I expect there will be either a football or hurling game on that Sunday so, therefore, I am making no arrangements to take part in the discus." However, it is likely that Hartigan will win an All Ireland title. He competed in a hammer event for the first time in Grounds (sic") last Saturday and shocked a good entry by winning the event with a throw of 165 ft. This notable success was achieved after only six months training.

An hour later Hartigan completed a double by winning the discus with a throw of 143 feet 11 inches and then he took third place in the javelin. Hartigan, who played in the Cardinal Cushing Games in America, played a leading role In Limerick's shock Munster hurling championship win over Tipperary.

Bernie to Break Barrier
(Sunday Independent, 29 May 1977)
Now He Hurls Hammer Only

By Seán Diffley

At least twice a day, on his journeys to and from Shannon Airport where he works, Bernie Hartigan drives past the statue of John O'Grady in the city of Limerick.

Limerick may not be unique but is certainly unusual in having a monument to the memory of a famous athlete. The significance is certainly not lost on Bernie Hartigan, particularly as O'Grady from Caherconlish, was a weight-thrower. Hartigan, like all Limerick sportsmen, is fully conscious and proud of the remarkable Limerick athletic heritage. O'Grady was a mammoth man who putted weights, 16 lbs., 28 lbs. and 56 lbs., quite prodigious distances. He was at his best just before and during the first World War.

And O'Grady was by no means the most famous Limerick athlete of the quite astonishing past. It was said that just before the turn of the century the winning performances in many a national championship abroad "would not be capable of winning a parish sports event in the county of Limerick."

Host of Champions

From a relatively small area came Olympic Champions and world record holders - John Flanagan from Kilbreedy (three times winner of the Olympic hammer title), Paddy Ryan from Pallasgreen (Olympic hammer title and world record holder for 24 years), the Leahys of Cregane and the Ahearnes of Athea (Olympic champions in the triple jump and world record holders in the high jump).

That is the heritage to which Bernie Hartigan is heir to. This year is the centenary of the Limerick Athletic Club and Hartigan is chairman of the club. The club is promoting the international Ireland v Greece match in Limerick next Wednesday and Thursday which means that Hartigan, between training for the hammer and chairing club meetings, has little free time. It also means that he has given up hurling. He was a member of the Limerick team that won the All Ireland hurling championship in 1973 but this summer he has cut the knot. "As an active athlete and an administrator I simply have not the time to give to hurling - so I've had to make a choice," he explains.

The specialisation in the hammer has begun to pay off. Last weekend in the trials in Limerick he got away a personal best throw of 194 feet 10¼ inches. That puts him third best in the all-time Irish rankings behind John Lawlor (213' 10") and Dr Pat O'Callaghan (195' 4 3/4"). And ahead of John Flanagan and Paddy Ryan.

Breaking The Barrier

And when he throws for Ireland at Plassey this week his ambition is to beat 200 feet. He is not at all concerned that he is now 34 years old. As he points out, Bondarchuk of Russia was 32 when he won in Munich and four years later he was still good enough to take a bronze medal in Montreal.

Bernie Hartigan's good form this season in the hammer is no accident. He has worked pretty hard on his technique and last September he travelled to Bedford to participate in a British hammer-throwers squad training session. A few weeks ago he was in Aldershot on a similar course. All that came through a meeting with Carl Johnson the British national hammer coach, whom he met when Johnson was at Gormanston at a Bears A.C. course. Since then Bernie has been in regular contact with Johnson.

Bernie Hartigan throwing the discus in the mid-1970s after his inter-county retirement.

The Hartigan Brothers' Athletic Achievements

Bernie Hartigan

NACAI National U20 Discus [1.75kg]
1962 (1st)

NACAI and BLE National Discus
1966 (1st) (NACAI)
1968 (1st) (BLE)
1971 (1st)

BLE National Hammer
1968 (1st)
1974 (1st)
1975 (1st)

Pat Hartigan

IJAB National Shot Put U16 [4kg]
1966 (1st)

Irish Schools Shot Put and Discus competitions
1967 Intermediate (1st)

Irish Schools Shot Put and Discus competitions
1968 Senior (1st)

BLE National U20 Shot Put [6kg]
1968 (1st)

BLE National Indoors Shot Put
1988 (1st)
1989 (1st)

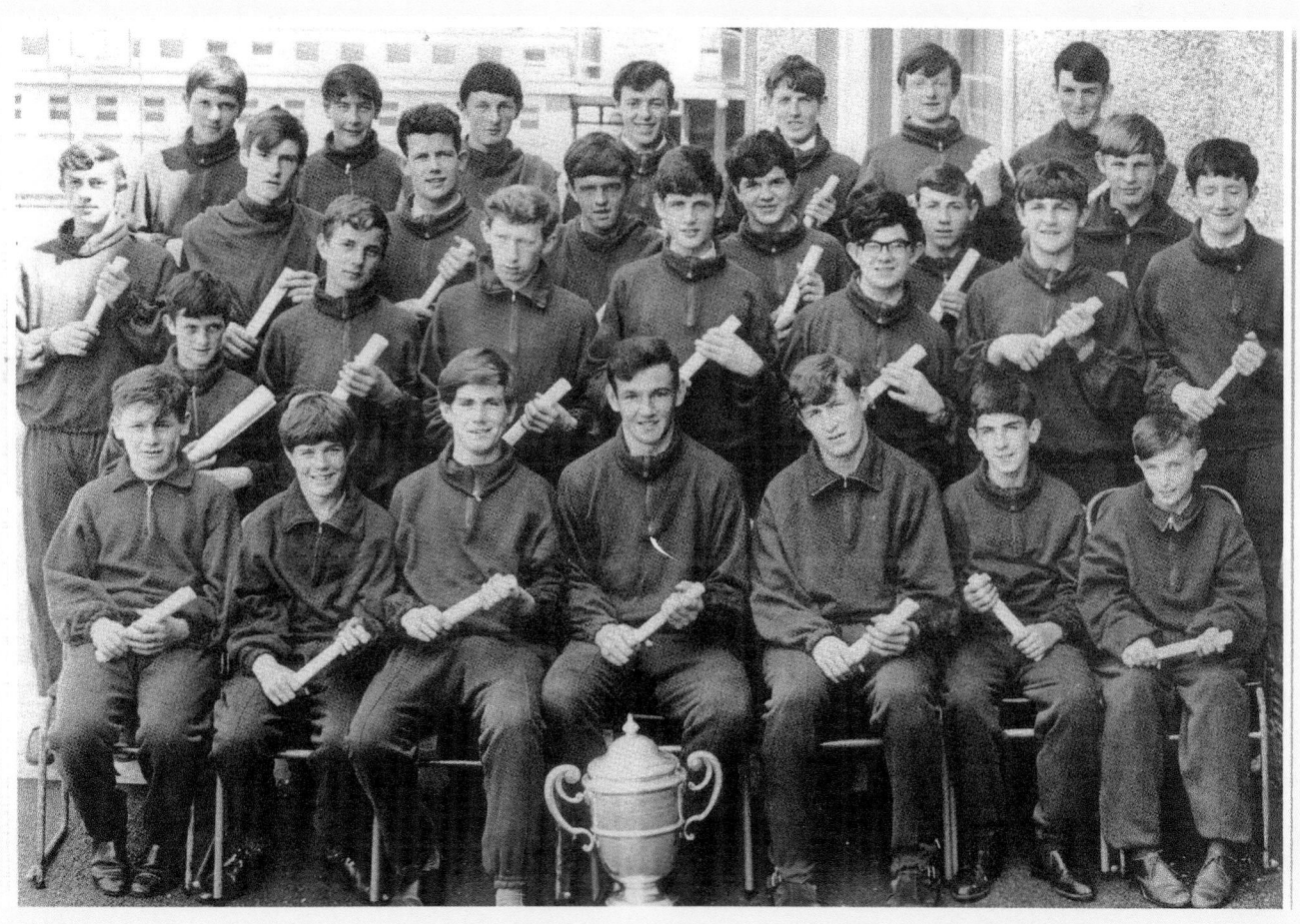

Limerick CBS was awarded the College of Science trophy for being the best secondary school at the Senior U-19 grade at the 1968 All Ireland Secondary Schools championships.

Back (L-R): Ger Brazier, Pat O'Callaghan, Derek Casey, Noel Ryan, Eamonn Morrissey, Martin Sheehan.
Third row (L-R): Tommy Scanlan, Martin Moloney, Pat Doherty, Tony Dwane, John O'Grady, Liam O'Donoghue, Pat Griffin.
Second row (L-R): Damien O'Brien, unknown, Gerry Ryan, Tim O'Neill, Charlie Flynn, Pat Neville, Tim Phelan.
Front (L-R): Jack Dillon, Gerard Croke, Joe Adams, Pat Hartigan, captain; Tommy O'Carroll, unknown, Tony Malone.

CHAPTER 9

1973

ALL IRELAND HURLING FINAL (i)

PRE-MATCH

After beating London, Limerick had qualified for their first All Ireland Final since 1940. The county went mad. The successful era of the Mackeys, Scanlan, Power and Stokes was recalled in the weeks before the final, but Limerick supporters were also looking forward to a new generation of heroes making their mark on the national stage. The panel for the final started training the week after the London game, with different players coming into and going from it all through the championship, as was usual at the time. The era of 36-man training panels was a long way away and only the 21 on that "final" panel would be named in the programme. The likes of Michael Graham would surely have made it, if he remained injury free, while some others must have been in hard luck not to make the shake-up too.

Club championship games impacting the panel were discontinued until later in September. There would be no more challenge games, though Kilkenny did play Wexford in a Walsh Cup game on 12 August. That game proved fateful as it resulted in another injury for Kilkenny. Eddie Keher broke his collarbone. Kieran Purcell's appendix was removed the same week, while Jim Treacy acquired an Achilles injury in an earlier tournament game, and Eamonn Morrissey's imminent emigration could not be delayed. Limerick, on the other hand, had no injury worries once Eamonn Cregan's cartilage problems cleared up. The team masseur, Vincent O'Connor, did a good job keeping these men fit and limber! Kilkenny were going for their second All Ireland title in a row, having beaten Cork in 1972.

They would win again in 1974 and 1975. Kilkenny were still considered hot favourites for the 1973 game, even with the four substantial personnel setbacks. Only one national newspaper tipped Limerick to make the long-awaited breakthrough. Kilkenny had beaten Wexford very impressively in the Leinster final played on 8 July – they would not play their next championship game for eight full weeks. Training was open and many supporters attended the last few sessions at the Gaelic Grounds, another tradition that has been quietly discontinued in more recent times. This was a time before widespread sponsorship, though a few canny companies were able to associate their products with the Limerick team and acquire some cheap advertising in the process, years before the Kerry footballers were 'whitewashed' by Bendix washing machines. One company, for example, provided the panel with new boots, and some players wore them for the final. Hard but traditional training continued apace for two weeks after the London game, with all heavy preparations completed with 10 days to go. Mick Cregan's job was done.

Trains were still a heavily-used mode of transport to matches, with relatively few possessing motor cars. The trip from Dromkeen to Heuston Station on the morning of the game (9:55AM) took a little over two hours and would have set one back the grand total of £2.60 return. The homeward train departed Heuston Station at 8:05PM, a full three hours and seven minutes after the final whistle. A reserved seat (with associated ticket) for the upper deck of the Hogan Stand cost £2.50, while the Cusack Stand lower deck was a snip at £1. Both stands sold out well beforehand. The terraces were pay-on-the-day, with entry for as little as 50p via cash-only turnstiles. A packet of 20 Player's No6 cigarettes was 24½p, while a decent bag of Tayto was a mere 3p. The official programme for the final was 10p. The unofficial programme was cheaper, but much inferior, at 5p. A Lady Lavery dark blue £10 note did go a long way in 1973!

The paper of record in Limerick, the Limerick Leader, did a wonderful job previewing the final with a 7,000+ word article the weekend of the final entitled, "Meet the Players". Camán summoned all his knowledge, gleaned in the county over many years, to give informative synopses of the 21 men who would represent the county on the big day. He did a similar article on the selectors and trainer in the Limerick Leader the week afterwards. Both are required reading for those who, otherwise, might only know these great men by name. Remember, Séamus Ó Ceallaigh was a Kilkenny native, though he had been in Limerick since the 1920s. He died in Limerick in 1988, having written for the Limerick Leader since 1944, working for the Kerryman newspaper before that. Finally, who was 'The Man Who Came To Cheer'? Could it have been Tim Lloyd, a prominent Limerick player in the early 1900s from Caherline?

What The Fans Think!
(Limerick Leader, 1 September 1973)

What do Limerick's supporters think of the team's chances? Reporter Seán Murphy and photographer Dermot Lynch went into the highways and byways to meet the man in the street. Here's their report...

Whatever else Limerick hurlers will lack when they face Kilkenny in the All Ireland final at Croke Park on Sunday, it certainly will not be support.

For every man, woman and child capable of making the journey to the Big Smoke are on the move.

From the hillside village of Tournafulla, homestead of goal-keeper, Séamus Horgan, to Doon, on the extreme East and, and from Kilbehenny to Coonagh, a new generation of hurling fans are preparing to give their heroes a welcome of flags, hats, scarves and rosettes not witnessed at Croke Park since Down carried off the Sam Maguire Cup in 1960.

Yes, indeed, Limerick will be "The Deserted County" and perhaps some budding poet might pen the words to match Oliver Goldsmith's "The Deserted Village."

The golden era of Limerick hurling ended in 1940, and so after 33 years in the wilderness, the Shannonsiders are back challenging strongly for the Blue Riband of the hurling world. Throughout the county there is an air of confidence in the ability of the team to take the crown, but in my tour of the various towns and villages, I found great respect for Kilkenny, who are considered All Ireland final specialists.

In Patsy Flannery's Tavern in Upper William Street, it was like a re-union of the old-timers. Jimmy Close, a stalwart attacker in the 1934 Limerick team which defeated Dublin, got the ball moving by saying, "If Limerick play ground hurling, like they did in the opening ten minutes of the Munster final, there is no team in Ireland to beat them." And the opinion was strongly supported by former Limerick League of Ireland player, Kevin Holman.

Coveted

Dave Clohessy, who proudly showed me the coveted Celtic Cross medals won in '34 and '36, deplores the absence of a Fedamore representative from the panel, but says that if Limerick play the hurling they are capable of, the bonfires will be blazing.

Mick Grace, a Kilkenny man domiciled in Limerick for many years, whose sons, Richie and Matt, won Harty Cup medals with Limerick CBS and later figured in various Limerick teams, was studying The *Kilkenny People's* preview of the game in company with Micky Cross, a legendary figure from the golden days. Cross feels the game today is much slower because players are too fond of picking the ball. "In our time, it was first-time pulling," said Micky.

"The present team are a speedy and crafty combination, and if they get the lucky breaks they will just about pip Kilkenny, who always produce great teams," concluded Cross. Mick Grace was in a cautious mood, "Kilkenny are badly hit by injuries," he said, "and despite our great reserve talent, I think we have only a 50/50 chance." Grace, whose brother-in-law, Mark Marnell, won an All Ireland medal with Kilkenny in 1947, remarked that if Limerick did win it would do immense good for hurling. "We must have new teams and new heroes," concluded Mick, a charge-hand in the drapery firm of Denis Moran and Co., William Street.

(L-R): Micky Grace, a Kilkennyman pictured with Micky Cross of the successful Limerick teams of 1934 and 1936.

Willie Doyle, a bus driver from Murroe, was in a confident mood, "We have the power and determination to match any team," he told me during a break from duty on the Ballynanty route.

Pat Walshe, a supervisor with Coca Cola and native of Clare, maintains that Limerick on the Munster final form must be favourites to win. "If they do, and I sincerely hope they will, Clare will be the second best team in Ireland," laughed Pat, who lives at 201 Woodview Park, Moylish.

In a busy John Street stores, owned by John Naughton, a renowned hurling follower told me that interest in the game was just amazing. He thinks that Kilkenny are using the injuries to upset Limerick's approach and warns the selectors and players not to fall for the trap. Having seen the panel in training, he feels that Limerick are in excellent trim and capable of winning the MacCarthy Cup.

Fiery

Pat Horgan, a fiery forward with Tournafulla, and a brother of goalkeeper Séamus, was in a lively discussion with customers of various sporting allegiance on the pros and cons of the hurling final in Kennedy O'Brien's Bar, where he is employed, when photographer Dermot Lynch and myself arrived on the scene.

"This will be no pantomime," quipped Bart Dillon from Kennedy Park, a well-known performer with the Panto Frolics Group. "Limerick will win by 3-10 to 3-6," forecasts Dillon.

John Naughton of John Street Stores with his daughter Geraldine, hoping for a Limerick victory.

Con Carey, who captained Garryowen to beat Dolphin in the 1940 Munster Senior Cup final and also witnessed Limerick's All Ireland win in the same year, thinks it will he very close and victory will come to Limerick.

Phil Carroll, who lives in Bruff and lines out with Na Fianna, a Hospital-Herbertstown combination, exclaimed "It's now or never."

Sunday next will certainly be a day to remember for one Limerick fan - Thomas Cross from Lower Park - who will be watching his 41st consecutive All Ireland Hurling Final. He has not missed a hurling decider since Kilkenny beat Clare in 1932. Thomas recalls his first All Ireland final in 1923 with regret for Limerick, captained by Paddy McInerney, lost to Galway.

"I have watched all the greats of the hurling scene - Christy Ring, Mick Mackey, Jimmy Langton, Nicky Rackard," the genial Thomas told me, "but I am looking forward to Sunday's game as if it was my first All Ireland.

"How do you rate Limerick's chances?" I asked. "Very good", came the rapid reply. "You see", said Cross, "Limerick have several utility players who can play in various positions and can be shifted if the occasion demands. This is most important, especially against Kilkenny, who are masters in the art of switching."

A hurley used in the 1940 decider by Paddy McMahon, the towering full-forward from Kildimo, and which spent many years in exile in the custody of his sister in America, is now back once more in the McMahon household at Annacotty. Designed by Nearys of Kilkenny, the bás is much longer and very narrow in comparison with present day hurleys.

The hurley is in immaculate condition after all those years. In the nicely kept flower gardens surrounding the McMahon home, Paddy recalled nostalgic memories of the 1940 campaign for me.

"I won't say the standard of hurling has dropped," he told me, "because one cannot compare two eras, but certainly the game has speeded up considerably, but rising is too prevalent. In our day Mick Mackey was the only man who would attempt a solo run. It was all ground hurling and first time pulling."

Good Combination

McMahon's opinion of the present Limerick team - a good all-round combination with plenty of hurling talent and loads of guts as we saw against Tipperary in the second half. His advice for Sunday's game, "Settle down early, pull on the ground and forwards pick off points at every opportunity." His verdict on the outcome, "A narrow win for Limerick after a hurling classic."

At Ballysimon, well-known Monaleen administrator, Leo Morrison, was demonstrating to a customer how to play the Burmah All Ireland game and in a quick comment said, "It must be Limerick, but I would prefer to see Kilkenny at full strength," and Paddy Lyons, chairman of Kilteely-Dromkeen GAA Club nodded in agreement. At Cappamore I met Richie Campbell, Jack Ryan and Michael McNamara sitting on the bridge below the town and hurling was again the topic. They all agreed that Limerick should win but felt Kilkenny will not be beaten easily. In Doon, hometown of Willie Moore, Jim O'Donnell and Jim Allis, everywhere we went the All Ireland was debated.

In Gerry Moore's Bar (father of Willie Moore), Willie's sisters - Louisa, Mairéad and Anna, were busy serving local hurling fans. Amidst applause, local undertaker - Michael Danaher - gave the verdict, "We'll bury Kilkenny."

Con Birrane, who won a minor All Ireland hurling medal with Limerick in 1940, was one of the few people interviewed who favoured Kilkenny. "I am hoping Limerick will win but I don't think they will do it," he said. Asked to elaborate, Birrane, a nurse at St. Joseph's Hospital, said he based his assessment on form. "Limerick were well and truly beaten by Wexford in the National League Final. Kilkenny later trounced Wexford in the Leinster final, so where do Limerick fit in?" he quizzed me.

In Old Pallas, Jim Quirke, who won a county hurling championship medal with Cappamore did not relish the idea of facing an All Ireland final with a changed line-out. "Cregan will be missed in the forwards - he is the only goal getter we have," he said. The defence is now on trial but if things work out Limerick could finish on top.

In Herbertstown the feat of Na Fianna, the local junior side in reaching their second successive South Limerick final had to take second place to an inquest on the Limerick vs. Kilkenny clash. Local farmer, Christy Scanlon, a hard-tackling defender in his day, thought Limerick would, "Just about manage to win," while Mike McCarthy, a commercial traveller who learned his hurling at Belcamp College, opined that Limerick, especially with Eamonn Rea on the edge of the square carried too many big guns for a weakened Kilkenny outfit.

Dromcollogher's Donal Broderick, a CIÉ bus conductor on the Broadford route and a member of the Limerick side which surprised Clare in that sensational 1955 Munster final, feels that Limerick have the talent and ability to at least win an All Ireland title. "If they use their speed to exploit the open spaces and play fast ground hurling, the Limerick supporters will certainly chant, "We are the champions" around 5 o'clock on Sunday, he said.

In Croom, Jack English, hon. secretary of the local club for many years, recalled how he made the trip to Dublin in 1940 to see Limerick win their last All Ireland title for 8/6d!

"I had a shilling each way on the winner of the Galway Plate at 100/8, and my winnings covered the entire expenses," declared the talkative Jack.

Jack, who won a county minor hurling medal with Croom in 1936 is sceptical about the alleged Kilkenny injuries. "I think this is all a publicity stunt," he said, "I know Jim Treacy and Eamonn Morrissey are definitely out, but I think the others will line out at the start."

"33 years is a long time to be out of an All Ireland final, it is a big occasion. I hope the lads will not suffer from Croke Park nerves," said Peter Cregan, who played at left half-back on the Limerick team which defeated Kilkenny 3-8 to 1-7 in 1940. Peter's task that day was marking Kilkenny's wizard Jimmy Langton - while in the Munster final of the same year his opponent in both the drawn game and replay was none other than Christy Ring. "It's no wonder I remember 1940 so vividly," remarked Peter.

Peter is loud in his praise for the present Limerick side, and feels that if they concentrate on ground hurling - like the stuff that mesmerised Tipperary, in the opening ten minutes at Thurles, that Kilkenny will have no answer, although he admits that, "Kilkenny in an All Ireland final are a law unto themselves."

Peter, whose son, Séamus, a well-known athlete, was recently married to Miss Sheila Grimes a sister of Sunday's team captain, Eamon - feels that Limerick will have to pace their effort for the full 80 minutes. "Remember Kilkenny's finishing rally against Cork last year?" he asked me. "They are great championship fighters."

Need Points

"Our forwards will have to start scoring points," warned Peter Cregan. Although we scored six goals against Tipperary, we could have lost the match, because of Tipp's ability to raise white flags."

The hurling fever which is sweeping the county had reached epidemic proportions when we touched down in Patrickswell, where I was informed that the entire population of the parish were heading for Croke Park to cheer Limerick to victory. Local publican, Dom Punch, who is treasurer of the Patrickswell GAA Club since its inception, feels that with such support the team cannot fail.

Pa Foley, a brother of star half-back, Seán, told me during a break in a ballad session at the Cú Chulainn Lounge, where he is employed, that the spirit and determination of the entire panel in training was a revelation. "Don't forget to come out when we have the MacCarthy Cup here", quipped young Foley, a hurler who looks like following in his brother's footsteps.

The ladies are keen followers and judges of hurling in the 'Well, and well-known inter-county camogie player, Phil Darcy, a great admirer of Seán Foley and Richie Bennis, forecast a Limerick win by four points.

Meet The Players
(Limerick Leader, 1 September 1973)

Séamus Horgan

The uprise of Séamus Horgan, can in great measure, be attributed to the decision of the special commission that enquired into the state of Limerick hurling a few years ago, to insist on each division organising a senior hurling championship with a minimum of six teams. The west had only a single senior team, and no championship in 1971; but the 1972 competition turned up trumps, and produced a great final, in which Tournafulla defeated Killeedy. In the subsequent play-off for the county crown, the Tournafulla boys beat a fancied Ahane and were only ousted from the competition, following a replay, with Patrickswell. It was in this series of games that the real worth of Séamus Horgan as a net minder, came to light, and when called to the county colours last autumn, he was an immediate success - continuing to improve through the National Hurling League campaign, in the final of which, he made his first Croke Park appearance last May, with Wexford providing the opposition.

His display in the recent Munster final against Tipperary, at Thurles, was his best to date, and some of his saves were bordering on the unbelievable - despite the handicap of playing with a bad shoulder injury, which was aggravated in that game, and which kept him on the sideline against London, when Jim Hogan proved a great deputy. Educated at Tournafulla NS, and Newcastle West Vocational School, Séamus played on the Limerick Intermediate team, defeated by Kerry in 1972, his initial game in county colours. Séamus is only goalkeeping with his club since 1970, previous to which he played half forward. On the home front, he helped Tournafulla win the West Junior Hurling Championships of 1970 and 1971, and the senior crown last year, when he was also goalie of the Mountcollins team that won the West Junior Football Championship.

Two brothers, Pat and Tim, were colleagues of his on the Tournafulla side in all their successes since 1970.

Willie Moore

The first appearance of Willie Moore in the Limerick colours was on the county minor hurling team of 1968, it was three years later when he pulled on the senior jersey in that year's National League campaign and he played his part in bringing Limerick to the final in which, however, he was a spectator, because of injury. "The most exciting game I have ever watched," he said afterwards. He was back in the side for the Oireachtas Cup final which Limerick won, and, of course, he figured in the recent Munster championship success, but in the corner-back berth, as opposed to his earlier full-forward assignments.

Willie first came to the forefront with that great hurling nursery, Doon CBS, whom he helped to a Rice Cup success in 1963. He then graduated to Mungret College, once the home of great hurling, where he turned to the college game, rugby, and helped in the winning of the Limerick Schools City Senior Cup.

It was back to hurling when he went to UCC and he had a most successful run with them, winning the Quinlan Cup in 1968-9, the Cork senior league and championship runner-up spot in 1969; the Cork County Senior Hurling Championship the following year and the Fitzgibbon Cup in the two seasons, 1971 and 1972.

Willie has the remarkable total of fourteen East Limerick championship trophies - two in juvenile hurling, 1963 and 1965; three in minor hurling, 1965, 1967 and 1968; two in minor football with Oola, 1967 and 1968; five under 21 hurling, 1966, 1967, 1968, 1970 and 1971; one in junior hurling, 1967; one in junior football, 1968. Add to that a half dozen county championship medals - four secured with Doon - minor hurling, 1965 and 1967; under 21 hurling, 1966 and 1967; two got with Oola - minor football, 1967 and 1968 - and the extent of his participation will be all the better appreciated - not counting at all his senior appearances in the Doon jersey.

Pat Hartigan

This Donoughmore-born lad was very prominent in hurling, football and athletics at Limerick CBS, with whom he won Munster under 15 hurling in Ryan Cup, 1966: Dr Harty Cup, 1965, under 16 football and Dean Ryan Cup 1966, Dr Harty Cup 1966 and 1967, and the All Ireland Colleges Cup, 1966.

In athletics, he had, like his brother, Bernie, a distinguished career. Starting off with the All Ireland shot put under 16 in 1966, he secured the colleges discus the following year, and intermediate shot put and in 1968 won the colleges senior shot put and the junior under 19 shot put championship. He represented Ireland in shot put on four occasions - twice against Spain, 1968, in Dublin, where he won; 1969 in Spain, where he was second. He also competed in the British School Championship in Wales in 1968, and represented Ireland at the Catholic Student Games in Lisbon the same year. Also that season, by winning the All Ireland colleges senior shot put and discus, he brought the College of Science trophy to Limerick for the first time. This trophy is the blue riband of Irish college athletics and goes to the school with the most points. Pat has East Limerick medals for juvenile football won in 1963 and 1966; minor football, 1965, and senior hurling, 1971 and 1972. Runners-up in two county senior hurling finals 1967 to Kilmallock on a replay: 1971 to Claughaun. He helped his club, South Liberties, win the coveted crown last year.

Pat must have almost a record for under age appearances in the county colours. He played minor hurling for Limerick for four years from 1965 to 1968, and minor football all three years, 1966 to 1968; was first picked in under 21 hurling in 1966, and played for six successive years, plus five in football from 1967 to 1971. He won on both intermediate hurling and junior football teams in 1968, and later that season gained promotion to the senior sides in both codes, in which he has figured since, helping Limerick to win the National Hurling League and Oireachtas Cups in 1971, and the Munster Championship this year.

A member of the Munster Railway Cup teams for the past two seasons, he also got the Carrolls All-Star hurling award and two very enjoyable trips to San Francisco. His most memorable occasion was a day in 1968 when he played three games - intermediate hurling and junior football against Waterford and a county senior cup game with his club South Liberties.

Frankie Nolan

Frankie Nolan served a good apprenticeship on County minor and under 21 fifteens before being called to the senior panel, on which he seems assured of a very bright future. He had his first really big game in the 1972 National hurling League final against Cork, but it was at Birr in the semi-final of the 1973 League that he really hit the jackpot against Tipperary, scoring 3-1 in that encounter. He was again to the fore in the recent Munster final against the same opposition. Educated at Adare CBS, where he was to the fore in schools hurling and figured in winning the local league, Frankie was very early called to the assistance of his club, Patrickswell, and at the age of twelve we find him and his twin brother, Benny, helping in under age competitions.

They shone on the team that won the Ballybrown juvenile tournament in 1966, and in the City minor championship of the following year. In 1969 they won both City and county minor Crowns. It is almost a unique position for Frankie to have played five years running in under 21 championship competition, winning the City honours in all five seasons, and crowning with county successes in 1968 and 1970. In football, for good measure, he helped in winning the under 21 City league in 1968, and the championship the following year. Quickly earning promotion to the senior club fifteen he helped Patrickswell win the county hurling championships of 1969 and 1970; and he was a member of the club junior team that won the football championship of City and county in 1970. Other honours to come his way include Duggan Cup and New Ireland Shield wins. His twin brother, Benny, who is a dedicated referee, got the City Board senior hurler of the year award for 1972.

1973 Keeping the Dream Alive

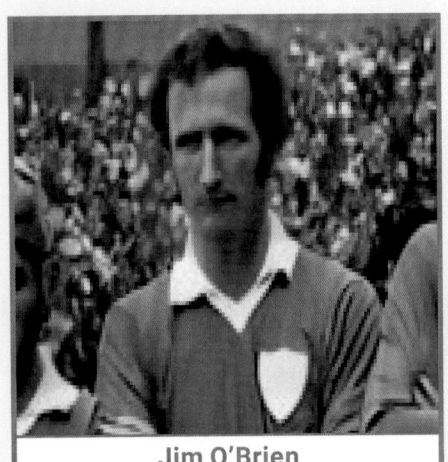

Jim O'Brien

One of the best corner backs in hurling just now, Jim O'Brien came to senior notice at a very young age, when he figured in goal for the South Limerick Selection against the West in the Inter-divisional Championship for the Thomond Cup in 1961. Two years later he helped Limerick win the Munster minor hurling championship, and he went into goal in the All Ireland final against Wexford when Andy Dunworth was injured.

One of his great games was at Dungarvan in 1965 against Waterford in the intermediate hurling championship, another was his unforgettable display against Leinster in the 1972 Railway Cup final. His recent game against Kilmallock in the South Limerick senior hurling semi-final was another notable one. All round schools champion with Rockhill NS, he earned that title by winning the 220 yards, 440 yards, the high jump at the South Limerick School and the best performance medal at the South Limerick School Sports in 1958.

When Bruree beat Bruff in the final for the Canon Kelly Cup under fourteen championship he was full-back; with his club, Bruree, he also won South and county junior hurling honours, and South medals in under 21 hurling. With Knocksouna he won a South minor football championship in 1962, and at present plays junior football with Bruree.

Jim figured for three years on the county under 21 team and for two years on the intermediate side before graduating to senior ranks, in which he has been one of the most consistent performers since Limerick fought back to the limelight in late 1969. He played in four National Hurling League finals, but was only on the winning side in one - that for 1971 - in which year he also helped in securing Oireachtas Cup honours.

Seán Foley

When Limerick were last in the full glow of the All Ireland spotlight, Seán Foley of Ballybrown was lurking in the wings and rather unlucky not to gain inclusion in the senior side, for earlier that season he was a member of the panel that defeated Kilkenny, then All Ireland champions, in the first Oireachtas Cup final, and the following year figured on the Limerick team to win All Ireland junior hurling honours, defeating Galway in that war time final at Ennis, 8-2 to 4-1.

Another John (Seán) Foley, his son, is now one of our great Limerick hurling hopes. We saw his potential when he helped Limerick CBS, win an under 15 Munster medal, which he followed up with a Dean Ryan Cup, two Dr Harty Cups and an All Ireland Colleges (Croke Cup) trophy.

With his club, Patrickswell, he won four City under 21 hurling championships and two county titles in the same grade; a City and county junior football championship success in 1970 and three senior hurling county crowns, 1966, 1969 and 1970.

A member of the Limerick minor hurling team in 1967 and 1968, he played in the latter year also on the under 21 side and continued with the under 21 team until 1970, in which year he also played on the underage football side.

Incidentally his brother, Liam, who also plays on the Patrickswell senior team, following a distinguished spell in minor and under 21 ranks, travelling a like road as far as inter-county is concerned, having donned the Limerick jersey in minor and under 21 hurling.

Seán, since his graduation to senior ranks, has helped Limerick win National Hurling League and Oireachtas medals in 1971 and the Munster senior title this year. He was on the Munster Railway Cup sides of 1972 and 1973.

Éamon Grimes

Éamon Grimes is undoubtedly the man for the big occasion, and a worthy captain of the side. He never plays better than when the stakes are really high, and he really demonstrated this on an historic occasion, in April, 1964, when he was one of the outstanding figures on a grand Limerick CBS team that beat St. Peter's of Wexford, 6-7 to 4-5, to win All Ireland Colleges hurling renown. Before that, he was the dominant figure on a Limerick CBS side that recaptured Dean Ryan Cup laurels, later graduating to the colourful team that won three storied Dr Harty Cups, and two All Ireland College triumphs, that mark another golden interlude in the hurling story of a great Gaelic school.

The great work the city primary schools are doing for Limerick hurling, is typified in Eamon, who, with St. John's CBS, showed very early promise, and was in the winning of two great competitions - the "Olo" and "*Limerick Leader*" Cups. The intense pride the boys of St. John's have taken in his subsequent prowess, is reflected in a number of colourful presentations which they have made to him, and which must be almost unique of their kind. With South Liberties from his schooldays, he showed his versatility early on, by winning with them, two East Limerick titles in juvenile football, and another in minor football. He played for "Liberties" in four county senior hurling finals, and it was a proud moment last December, when, as skipper, he carried away in triumph, the John Daly Cup, putting his club back on top in Limerick hurling, following a gap of eighty years.

Called to the county colours, to win two Munster minor hurling medals with Limerick, he was later on the senior team that won National Hurling League and Oireachtas Cup renown in 1971. Recently, he captained the Limerick team that regained the Munster Senior hurling title, the first such success in eighteen years. Eamon hails from Donoughmore, and in addition to his hurling and football capabilities he has shone in athletics, collecting county crowns in the 200 metres and 440 yards flat event and picking up prizes also in the 100 yards and 880 yards - and a fine achievement, one notable evening at Clarina where he collected the Matt Hayes Cup for the best all round athlete at the meeting.

Joe McKenna

The great spate of senior football successes the county deservedly enjoyed over the past few years took the spotlight somewhat off the Offaly hurlers, who at the commencement of the great football run were giving every indication that it was they who might actually break the barrier and crash to All Ireland success with the caman. Offaly might be written the most unlucky team of the recent League campaign, for they rose to great heights against some of the finest teams in the competition and were considered on most occasions unfortunate to suffer very narrow defeats, resulting in their relegation.

An extra tall, well-built, strapping lad from Shinrone caught the practised hurlers eye fairly frequently in those encounters, and on enquiring further one learned that he was Joe McKenna, who had played in all grades for the county, after he had been to the fore with St. Flannan's College in Munster schools hurling, with a junior medal as a souvenir of his stay there. With the home club, Joe won an Offaly county junior hurling championship in 1967, but no further trophies came his way until he transferred to South Liberties last year on coming to live in the district. With the 'Liberties, he was an immediate success, and he figured in the double senior triumph in the East, when Ahane were overcome, in both the hurling (2-13 to 2-8) and football (2-6 to 0-8) divisional finals. His great thrill, however, was in helping to win the county senior hurling final, in which South Liberties beat Patrickswell, 4-8 to 1-5. In fact, his contribution of 1-2 from play to that win was the best of the game.

Joe is a first cousin of Mackey McKenna, who had some great games in the big time with Tipperary during their commanding spell of the early 'sixties.

1973 Keeping the Dream Alive

Phil Bennis

The old saying that "the best of goods are in small parcels" is well borne out in the case of Phil Bennis. Small of stature, he has the heart of a lion, and reminds one in this regard of two of Limerick's greatest ever hurlers - both light and lithesome in appearance, but hurling demons when the chips were really down: Jimmy Humphreys, who captained the Ireland team in the 1924 Tailteann Games, and Mick Fitzgibbon, Limerick captain in the unforgettable 1933 All Ireland final against Kilkenny.

One of a distinguished family of seven boys - all of whom have given great service to hurling Phil, whilst still a lad of tender years attending Lurriga NS, helped his club, Patrickswell, win the City and county juvenile hurling championships of 1954. Three years later he was in the winning of junior hurling honours for Patrickswell. He then he showed himself more than useful with the big ball too by winning City and county junior football honours in 1964 and again in 1970.

His big moment, however, was when he captained Patrickswell to its first ever senior hurling championship success in 1965, and the ornate Seán Daly memorial cup again decorated his sideboard the following year. He was to win two further senior hurling medals with the club in 1969 and 1970, as well as figuring prominently on the teams that brought Duggan Cup, Kerryman Cup and New Ireland Shield honours to the parish. Phil was a member of the Limerick senior hurling side that first came to prominence in 1970, when it worked its way to the National Hurling League final - and he has missed very few of Limerick's engagements since - in fact, the occasional days he was absent showed up more than anything else his value to the side, for he was sorely missed. Phil is a player of great resource, limitless courage and tenacity, whose grit and determination has to he admired by friend and foe alike.

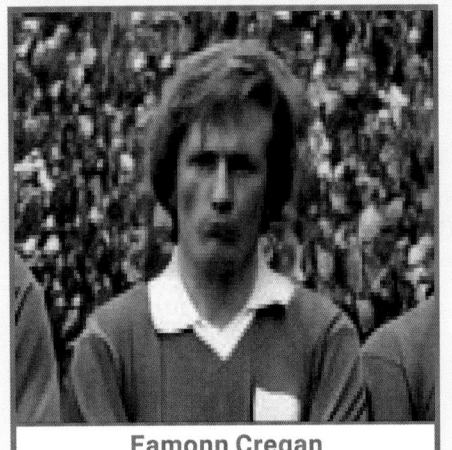

Eamonn Cregan

I think it was Eamonn Cregan who first re-lit the Limerick hurling fire and set it ablaze that memorable 5 June, 1966, at Cork Athletic Grounds, when he gave his greatest ever performance, scoring 3 goals and 5 points against then All Ireland champions, Tipperary, to inspire Limerick to a sensational 4-12 to 2-9 win, in the opening round of the Munster championship. He has been shining in-county colours ever since, putting in some very colourful hours - and often, too, turning over to the sister code, football, in which he could, if the opportunity offered, be also a first class exponent.

He had a very happy experience that very few players in any sporting code in Limerick has enjoyed in recent decades, when he arrived at Limerick Railway Station on 27th April, 1964, bearing aloft the All Ireland Colleges Cup won the previous day against St. Peter's, Wexford, 6-7 to 4-5. As he, and his team-mates, stepped off the train, bonfires blazed, fog signals were exploded, while all the time five bands played rousing martial airs and ten thousand people roared themselves hoarse.

The Mayor and Corporation were there to add their congratulations, the Mayor saying: "Your magnificent win has given to hurling a transfusion of interest if ever the game needed one, for hurling, above all other games, has been synonymous with the name of Limerick for longer than any of us can remember." Eamonn, who captained the Claughaun team that won the 1968 County Senior Hurling Championship, also skippered Limerick CBS, in their great successes of 1964, and the Limerick side that won the Munster Minor Hurling Championship in 1963. Winning with Claughaun, City and county medals in both hurling and football in juvenile and minor grades, he also helped them win senior hurling and football honours in both championship and cup.

Besides playing on Limerick hurling and football teams in minor, under 21 and senior grades, he figured with Munster on a Railway Cup winning hurling side, and in both 1971 and 1972 got the Carrolls All-Star hurling award.

Richie Bennis

Tipperary folk by now regard Richie Bennis as a strange type of a hurling wizard, the possessor of a second head, which he takes out of an ice box at vital stages in a game, and with cool and calculated mastery, devastates the fond hopes of a whole hurling county, and their countless followers.

It has the reverse effect, of course, of turning nearly every man, woman and child that Limerick must ever have reared - and very many from outside the confines of the county - into stark raving lunatics as they throw all discretion and decorum to the winds, in a vast outpouring of their innermost feelings - and even to the people they scarcely know, if at all, but all equally intoxicated by the common joy of what appears a once in a life-time triumph.

In two unforgettable hurling finals - the National League win of 1971, and this year's Munster success - Richie grasped victory with the last stroke of the game - all the more remarkable in that they looked unscorable. But these great feats are only the veneer, covering a whole series of scoring successes that has kept his name high in the national charts all through the past four seasons, with contributions that have played a very big part in the Limerick success march.

Educated at Lurriga NS, Adare CBS, and Limerick Vocational Schools, success came to him early, when he captained the team that won the All Ireland Vocational Schools' Championship in 1961. Later, he figured on minor and under 21 Limerick county sides, before making the senior team.

With his club, Richie has won four county senior hurling and two county junior football championship medals, as well as numerous tournament trophies.

Liam O'Donoghue

The name O'Donoghue has been associated with Mungret and Limerick hurling for longer than most of us care to remember, and the subject of our sketch, Liam O'Donoghue, has an uncle and four cousins, all of whom won All Ireland hurling medals in some grade with Limerick.

His father, Joe, after winning a hard-earned *"Limerick Leader"* Cup medal with Mungret NS, was a member of the great Mungret team of the 'forties, with whom he won several trophies.

Liam has two brothers, Ger and Josie, the former the winner of Dr Harty and All Ireland Colleges hurling medals with Limerick CBS in 1966; the latter collecting an under 15 and a half award and Dean Ryan Cup junior hurling medal in the same colours the following year. Liam played both hurling and football at CBS and under age awards gained there in 1964 and 1965 mark the start of a very large collection of trophies that must be only very much in the making, considering that Liam, at twenty, is the youngest member of the present Limerick side.

With Mungret, Liam won the City juvenile hurling championship in 1968, and in the county semi-final when playing against St. Mary's, Rathkeale, he had a personal tally of 6-5, which must be a Limerick championship record for any individual player. Mungret were most unfortunate in that championship, for after winning the county final 3-3 to 2-2, an objection deprived them of the title. However, Liam had some compensation the following year when he helped Mungret win the county junior hurling championship.

A member of the county under 21 side in the three years since his first appearance in 1971, this is his first season playing with the senior team but he has been showing exceptional promise and gives every indication of becoming a great scoring forward. His anticipation is very sharp, and his accuracy and "will o' the wisp" tactics can be a nasty thorn in the side of any defence.

Mossie Dowling

Mossie Dowling has made a very successful comeback to the senior team, after a lengthy absence. His first appearance in premier county colours was in 1968, the direct result of some great displays in the 1967 county series, which his club, Kilmallock, won out, following a great drawn game with South Liberties in the final - rated by many as one of the best club games the championship has known.

Educated at Kilmallock NS, and Rathluirc Vocational School, Mossie came to the fore in the Kilmallock jersey, when they won South and county juvenile hurling honours in 1962. Two years later, in the same colours, he helped in the winning of South and County minor hurling renown; and since then has won with Kilmallock, several other South championship and tournament trophies, in both hurling and football.

He got his first call to county colours in 1964, when he was selected on the minor hurling team. Limerick were Munster title holders at the time. They beat Clare in the opening round, 6-5 to 2-6, and then faced Tipperary, whom Limerick had ousted in the 1963 final, 4-12 to 5-4. On this occasion, the Premier County boys had revenge, winning 4-9 to 3-7.

Mossie later played with the county under 21 side, before his first call to the senior colours. On his return to senior county favour early this season, he impressed in the full forward position, but the selectors moved him to right half back, in which sector he usually figures with his club, in an effort to strength then the defence for the National Hurling League final bid against Wexford. He is now successfully operating in the half line of forwards.

Eamonn Rea

South Limerick contributes three members to this Limerick selection and longest serving of these is Eamonn Rea, a native of Effin, who first came to hurling notice when winning with that club the South minor hurling championship in 1957 and two years later winning South and county minor hurling honours in 1959. He was on the county minor hurling side in 1962, by which time he was in the "leaving class" at St. Munchin's College, of course, he was on the school hurling team, and where he is remembered as a "strong hard man."

Against Kerry the minors put up a big score, 12-16 to 1-0, and when they beat Galway 8-12 to 7-2. Hopes of championship success were very bright, but Tipperary beat them in the next outing 7-9 to 4-7. So Limerick had to wait until the following year for that title by which time Eamonn was outside the age limit. He was called to the county senior colours however, in 1963 and continued a regular member of the side until 1968 when he went out of favour. In 1963 he played for Emmets against Feenagh-Kilmeedy in the county senior Hurling final, which the latter won.

A graduate in Dairy Science from UCC, he helped them win two Fitzgibbon Cup finals and in local Cork hurling he won a senior hurling trophy with UCC and a runner-up award in the 1965 County Senior hurling championship.

After parting with the green and whites in 1968 he was inclined to lose interest but a fortunate decision to join the Dublin Faughs club was the remaking of him hurling wise. He found congenial company in Faughs, and plenty of match play in the Dublin leagues and championship rebuilt his appetite for hurling and with Faughs he won, Dublin senior hurling championship medals in 1970 and again in 1972.

The Limerick selectors then got interested again and he returned to the defence for the 1973 National Hurling League campaign, but his great spectacular with the side was when he played full forward in the recent Munster final against Tipperary - a gamble that really paid off.

Bernie Hartigan

Bernie Hartigan first hit the headlines when helping his home club, South Liberties to the East Limerick juvenile hurling honours, in 1957; a success they repeated the following year, and capped with county honours defeating Claughaun decisively in the final, 9-0 to 1-0. Two years later, they were Eastern minor hurling champions, and again faced Claughaun in a county final, and once more triumphed: this time by 5-10 to 2-1. As a student at Limerick CBS, Bernie hit the headlines in hurling, football and athletics. He was rated the outstanding college hurler in the province, and he played a prominent part in winning the Munster Colleges senior football championship in 1960.

It was at Limerick CBS, too, that his bent for athletics came fully to light. His shot putting was a revelation, and he was honoured with selection on the Irish team, for the Catholic Student Games. He won the decathlon championship of County Limerick, in 1962, breaking two county records - the discus at 129 feet, and the javelin at 157 feet - figures he considerably improved later at the County Senior Athletic Championships, when he scored a first class treble in the 16 lb. shot, 40 ft. 5 ins; discus, 134 ft. 2 ins; javelin, 165 ft. 7 ins. He represented Ireland in 1969 and 1971 at hammer and discus throwing, and won the All Ireland discuss title in 1966, 1968, and 1971; and the hammer in 1968. He also represented Limerick CBS in handball, and was beaten in the Munster Colleges doubles final of 1961.

Bernie was in the founding of the Old Christians club, who had a fantastic first year, when they won the City senior football championship, defeating Claughaun, 2-5 to 0-5, in a colourful final at Páirc na nGael, on 4th November, 1962. They crowned this achievement by defeating Ballysteen on a replay to collect the County Senior Football Cup for the same season. Called to the County Minor colours in 1960 and 1961, in both hurling, and football, he was on the Munster championship intermediate team of 1962, and the under 21 teams in hurling and football in 1964. A member of the senior hurling and football sides without a break since 1962, it is a fair commentary on the lean period Limerick suffered, that his only inter county successes before this year, were secured in 1971, when the National League and Oireachtas Cups were won. He holds the rare distinction for a Limerick man, of having played on both Railway Cup teams - hurling in 1966, 1967, 1968, 1970 and 1971; football in 1969. He was selected for the Ireland hurling team in 1966, in which year he also played in the Cardinal Cushing Games in New York. With Aer Lingus teams, he has played in Rome, Boston, Chicago and Hartford; and with Limerick, at Wembley in 1972.

Tom Ryan

Ballybrown - a stronghold of GAA for very many years, has come more and more into the picture in recent times, and this season, they have realised a cherished ambition in winning the City Senior Hurling final, and qualifying for a place in the county play off. One of the big figures in the success story of Ballybrown, is Tom Ryan, whose father, Willie, was a founder member of the sister parish club, Patrickswell, in 1948, and who has now an active interest in Ballybrown management, where the development of the splendid sports grounds at Clarina is a big priority.

Tom Ryan is hurling in the Ballybrown colours since he was twelve years of age, but was before his time as far the winning of honours was concerned, for the under age grades were not strong in that part of the parish then - a matter that has been more than rectified of late, as very amply demonstrated in the recent Feile na nGael when national honours were bought to the parish.

Tom Ryan played in all grades of hurling for his club, and he has a more than useful foot too. He figured with distinction on city divisional teams, when they competed as a group in the county hurling championship, he has played under 21, intermediate and senior for Limerick.

He was a sub on the side that lost to Cork at Croke Park in the 1970 National Hurling League final, lost favour with the selectors at the time, but returned to the fold for the current championship and really made his presence felt, when he replaced Jim O'Donnell in the recent Munster Final against Tipperary.

With his club, he won three junior hurling titles in a row; a county junior hurling title; two Dean Punch Cup titles, a New Ireland Shield success, and numerous tournament trophies. He is also a keen administrator, and was Ballybrown club secretary for three years and is now very closely associated with developing the under age activities.

Enthusiastic supporters look on from the Old Hogan Stand at a Limerick training session ahead of the All Ireland final.

Andy Dunworth

Andy, son of former Munster champion, Stephen Dunworth, first came to the notice of hurling fans, when he won Limerick under 14 hurling championship honours with his native Banogue, in 1959.

He was still of tender years, when he helped the Banogue lads to junior hurling championship success, three years later. In 1963, he figured as the keeper with the Emmets that contested the county hurling final with Feenagh-Kilmeedy, with the latter winning 3-6 to 3-1. In 1965, he was on the Bruree side that won the South Limerick under 21 hurling title.

Joining Claughaun shortly afterwards, he won with the club, the county senior runner-ups for 1966 and 1969; the senior hurling championships in 1968 and 1971, and the Duggan Cup in 1970. He helped Faughs win the Dublin Senior Hurling Championship last year. Andy was a member of the Limerick team that won the Munster Minor Hurling Championship in 1963.

On the road to success, they beat Galway who were playing in Munster, in the opening round, 2-11 to 4-4; drew with Waterford, 2-6 to 1-9, beating them in the replay, 2-10 to 1-9, and then overcoming the Tipperary challenge in the final, 4-12 to 5-4. In the All Ireland decider, they lost to a great Wexford side. Andy had to retire injured in that game.

He was again "between the sticks" on the minor hurling team the following year, and his display against Clare in the opening round, was out of the top drawer. Tipperary, however, beat them in the Munster semi-final, only to lose themselves to Cork, later. Andy as a goalkeeper, looked an exciting prospect at this stage, but he opted for an outfield berth, and secured his place on the county Intermediate hurling side as a half forward in 1966, and put up a scoring total of 4-3, which, however, was not sufficient to avert a defeat by Clare, 8-6 to 8-3.

This display gained him promotion to senior ranks, and he has been on and off the panel ever since. He helped Limerick win the Oireachtas Cup in 1971, and came in as a sub in the National Hurling League finals of 1970 and 1973, as well as the recent All Ireland senior hurling semi-final against London.

Jim Allis

Jim Allis learned his hurling at Doon CBS, and he helped them win the "*Limerick Leader*" and Dr Rodgers Cups, collecting also a few medals in school athletics. Jim played in all grades from juvenile to senior with Doon club, and he was on the under 21 hurling side that blazed a trail in winning the Eastern and County Championships of 1966. They beat Bruff, 3-12 to 2-4, in the final for the county crown at Pairc na nGael on 24th September, 1967. The following season he displayed his prowess in football when helping to win the Eastern Junior Football Championship.

Jim's first inter-county recognition came in under 21 ranks, His initial outings were quite successful - wins over Kerry, 3-4 to 1-3, and Tipperary, 2-6 to 1-7. This qualified them for the Munster final against Cork, who had a great team that year, and who won 3-12 to 2-6. He later played in intermediate ranks before getting the call to senior colours, in which he has given sterling service.

Jim has played on some of the best forwards in the game today, notably Tony Doran, Babs Keating, Charlie McCarthy and Ray Cummins, and the experience so gained has proved of immense value. His preference is for the full-back line, in which he has given some very satisfactory performances for both club and county: His greatest thrill was in winning the 1971 Oireachtas Cup final, in which Limerick beat Wexford 4-12 to 3-8. He was on the Limerick team the following year beaten by Cork, 3-14 to 2-14 in the National Hurling League final.

Jim Hogan

Jim Hogan, who hails from Kilgobbin, Adare, opened his hurling account as early as 1951, when he was only fourteen years of age, when he played a really great game in goal against Dromcollogher, in the West Limerick minor hurling final. The following year saw the revival of juvenile hurling in the west, and Jim, playing outfield, this time had the distinction of captaining the Adare side that won the title. As a pupil of Adare CBS he helped his school reach the Dean Ryan Cup final of 1953, in which they were beaten by Waterford De La Salle.

1957 was a year of great achievement for the Adare youth, now resident in Cork, for, besides winning a coveted Cork County Senior hurling medal, with the renowned Sarsfields, he figured in many tournament successes with them, between 1955 and 1958. During the same period, he played with the far-famed Lees footballers usually in the left half forward position.

Lees hit the high spot, too, in 1957, and reached the Cork senior football final, only losing on a replay, to St. Finbarrs. On his return from Cork, Jim joined the Claughaun club, and helped them win the 1959 county senior championship, and many tournament trophies.

When his native Adare embraced senior ranks, after winning the 1964 county junior hurling crown, he helped them for a few seasons, and gained a county senior hurling cup medal. Back to Claughaun in 1968, he collected a Limerick senior hurling championship trophy, playing in the final against his native parish, figuring for the first time in an encounter of such importance. He won another county championship souvenir with Claughaun in 1971, as well as county cup and Duggan Cup laurels.

Jim Hogan's first appearance with Limerick was a winning one. It was in the Rose Cup, on Easter Sunday, 1958, in which Limerick beat a Waterford fifteen, then in their hey-day. Jim has been with Limerick ever since, and starred in the two great successes of 1971 - National Hurling League and Oireachtas Cup.

In addition, he played with Munster in the Railway Cup final of 1964, and on the Rest of Ireland team against Kilkenny the same year. He was five times in Rome with the Aer Lingus hurling club, between 1962 and 1967, and has visited Chicago several times in recent years also to play there.

Jim O'Donnell

Old timers say that Limerick hurling is never really flourishing unless it is strong in East Limerick. Castleconnell, Caherline, Cappamore, Murroe, South Liberties and Pallasgreen were the areas one looked to in the past for the hurling stars from the East to grace Munster and All Ireland fields.

Now, thanks to the dedicated work of the Christian Brothers in Doon, a new dimension has been added to East Limerick hurling with the boys from the parish very much to the fore as expert wielders of the camán.

The founding of the East Limerick Board in 1944 really set the ball rolling for them and two years later they won their first of a dozen minor divisional titles. Then, in 1964, they invaded both juvenile and junior ranks and they have now seven titles in each of these grades to their name. But their most spectacular performance was in under 21 grade, and since their initial success in 1966 they have won this title on five occasions.

Jim O'Donnell is the senior of the three Doon representatives on the present selection. A product of the local CBS, after figuring very successfully through his schooldays with the school hurling fifteen, he collected juvenile and minor trophies with the home club before departing for a spell in America during which he participated in many exciting Gaelic Park clashes.

On his return, he quickly picked up the hurling thread again with the Doon Club and soon earned county recognition, to be acclaimed on many occasions for some very spectacular hurling, his high catches and long clearances being a particular feature of his play.

Jim played in three National Hurling League finals - 1970, 1971 and 1973, gaining the coveted medal in the middle year, but he was unfortunate later that season to miss the Oireachtas Cup win due to injury.

Paudie Fitzmaurice

Paudie Fitzmaurice comes from good Gaelic stock; his father, the late Liam Fitzmaurice, N.T., was an ardent devotee of native games, and was chairman of the West Limerick Board, and vice-chairman of the County Board, for many years.

Paudie spent five years in St. Munchin's College, where he played both hurling and football. A colleague of his there said of him: "He was very clever, and he had a fierce interest in hurling."

When he graduated to Maynooth, Paudie continued his interest in hurling and did a tremendous lot for the game there so it was no empty gesture that he was captain of the Maynooth side that won the Fitzgibbon Cup for the first time, this season. In one game for them, Paudie had the splendid total of eleven points, all scored by that deadly left hand. His brother, Willie, recently ordained, and now C.C., St. John's, was also on that Fitzgibbon cup winning side. Paudie was also honoured with inclusion on the Combined Universities side that participated this season in the Railway Cup series.

With his brothers, Willie and Mick, Paudie has been figuring prominently in local competition with his home club, Killeedy, but, it was only when they reluctantly went senior in 1972, at the promptings of the Western Board, that the brothers really came to the notice of hurling fans. In disposing of a sturdy Adare challenge, Willie at midfield, and Paudie as left half forward - the latter deadly accurate from both frees and play - were both outstanding and again, when they contested the western final with Tournafulla and afterwards in the County Championship against ultimate winners, South Liberties.

One of the 10 laps that training usually started with!

Some Limerick Player Statistics
(Limerick Heroes)

SÉAMUS HORGAN is 25, stands 5 foot (ft.) 11 inches (ins.) [1.80M] and weighs 11 stone (st.) 7 pounds (lb.) [73KG]. He played with the county in last year's Intermediate Hurling Championship, and earned his big chance in the senior grade against Kilkenny in Kilkenny in a National League game in October 1972, when regular goalkeeper Jim Hogan was in the U.S. His first important senior medal win was forged in the Munster final last July.

WILLIE MOORE is 23, 5ft. 11ins. [1.80M] and 12st. 10lb. [81KG]. A county minor in 1968, he won a Cork senior medal with UCC in 1970. Missed the 1971 National League Final win through injury, but helped Limerick to the Oireachtas Cup final win of 1971, and to the 1973 Munster title triumph.

PAT HARTIGAN is 23, 6ft. 4ins. [1.93M] and 14st. 10lb. [93KG]. An All Ireland Colleges' medalist in 1966, he has played with Limerick in all grades of football and hurling, and shared in the county's major successes of recent times - the National League, Oireachtas Cup and Munster title - that preceded the Liam MacCarthy Cup win.

JIM O'BRIEN is 28, 6ft. [1.83M] and 12st. 4lb. [78KG]. He won a Munster minor medal in 1963, and is another who has figured in all of Limerick's top triumphs.

PHIL BENNIS is 31, 5ft. 7.5ins. [1.71M] and 11st. 2lb. [71KG]. Led Patrickswell to their first County senior hurling final win in 1965, and was captain again in 1966, when the club retained the crown. He is another who has been prominent in all of the county's glory days in recent seasons.

EAMONN CREGAN is 28, 5ft. 11.5ins. [1.82M] and 12st. 2lb. [77KG]. Captained the Limerick CBS team that won the 1964 All Ireland Colleges' title, and made his senior inter-county debut that year. He has also represented Limerick in football, and holds two Railway Cup hurling medals, as well as playing in the 1971 National League and Oireachtas Cup winning teams, and the recent Munster final side.

SEÁN FOLEY is 23, 5ft. 11ins. [1.80M] and 12st. 8lb. [80KG]. Won an All Ireland Colleges' medal with Limerick CBS in 1966, was a county minor in 1967 and 1968, and played in the Under-21 inter-county grade. Has been prominent in all of Limerick's recent successes in the top competitions.

RICHIE BENNIS is 27, 6ft. [1.83M] and 13st. 3lb. [84KG]. Captained the Limerick team that won the 1961 All Ireland Vocational Schools' title, and played minor, junior and Under-21 as well as senior, with the county. His last-second point that won the Munster title last July will long be remembered, and he has helped the county to all of their top title wins over the past three seasons.

ÉAMON GRIMES is 25, 5ft. 8ins. [1.72M] and 12st. 7lb. [79KG]. A bright star of the All Ireland colleges' title wins of Limerick CBS in 1964 and 1966, and a former county minor, he is another with League, Oireachtas Cup and Munster senior medals to his name. A county senior since 1966.

LIAM O'DONOGHUE is 21, 5ft. 7ins. [1.70M] and 10st. 7lb. [67KG]. Has appeared with Limerick in the minor and under-21 grades, and wore the Limerick CBS colours in colleges' competitions. He was called up to the premier grade early in 1973 for a National League game with Tipperary, and was in the Munster final team.

MOSSIE DOWLING is 27, 5ft. 10ins. [1.78M] and 12st. [76KG]. He made his debut with the senior county side in 1967, and has played in the defence, at midfield and in the attack. He did not play in the 1971 League and Oireachtas Cup finals, but was a star of the win over Tipperary at Thurles.

BERNIE HARTIGAN is 30, 5ft. 11ins. [1.72M] and 14st. 9lb. [93KG]. A dual interprovincial player, he won Railway Cup hurling medals in 1966, 1968 and 1970, has represented the county at minor and Under-21 in both codes and at intermediate hurling. In the premier county side since 1962, he is a further prominent link with the 1971 League and Oireachtas Cup wins, and last summer's memorable win against Tipperary.

FRANKIE NOLAN is 23, 5ft. 8ins. [1.72M] and 11st. 7lb. [73KG]. A comparatively new arrival to the side when playing against Cork in the 1972 League final, he graduated after playing in the minor and under-21 grades. Won county senior hurling medals in 1969 and 1970.

EAMONN REA is 29, 6ft. [1.83M] and 14st. 8lb. [92KG]. His transfer from full back to full forward will rank as one of the most astute moves of the year in hurling. He has appeared with the county in all grades of hurling, and has got among the Dublin hurling medal winners with the Faughs club.

JOE McKENNA is 22, 6ft. 3ins. [1.91M] and 14st. 1lb. [89KG]. Played with his native Offaly at minor, under 21 and senior before joining the Limerick side. Won a Limerick senior medal with South Liberties last year, and played against Clare in the first round of the Munster senior championship.

The powerful hands of Vincent O'Connor are still fondly remembered by the 1973 panel.

All Ireland Special - Meet the Backroom Boys
(Limerick Leader, 8 September 1973)

Mick Cregan - Trainer

At twenty-nine, this Limerick-born army officer, son of a great All Ireland hurler of the early 'thirties, the late Ned Cregan of Monagea, must be one of the youngest to train an All Ireland winning team.

Mick, of course, hurled with Limerick, and he played no small part in bringing the 1971 National Hurling League title to the county, as well as giving many other big hearted and extra plucky displays in the green and white.

Mick captained the Claughaun team that won the senior hurling championship in 1971, and he had as colleagues on the team two brothers - Eamonn, who gave rousing performances in the centre-half-back berth, and Conor, who may now hit the headlines and fulfil the great promise he showed as a schoolboy.

Mick was prominent in hurling and football ranks for Limerick CBS and was on county minor teams in both codes before gaining promotion to the senior colours. With his club, Claughaun, he won city and county juvenile medals in hurling and football in 1958 and 1959.

In minor ranks he won a city and county title in 1962, winning hurling and football, after having led city and county football earlier in 1961. Some senior successes with Claughaun include cup and championship in both codes, with Gleeson and Duggan trophies included for good measure.

Jackie Power - Selector

Recipient of the Cúchulainn Award of 1969, an outstanding hurling star of the past, Jackie Power had the proud distinction of playing for many years on the hurling fields of Ireland, during which he played in every position, even goalman, and clashed with the greatest hurlers of the period.

Monaleen born, fifty-seven years ago, Jackie captained his local school team in the *"Limerick Leader"* Cup competition before helping St. Patricks in the 1931 minor county championships.

In 1932 he joined the famed Ahane club, wearing their colours in minor, junior and senior ranks, reaching the latter stages the following year, and continuing to do so for well over a dozen seasons, amassing a load of successes not easily surpassed.

He was a promising athlete but it was unfortunate that his preoccupation with hurling and football engagements prevented him devoting more time to the track. His first senior game for Limerick was in the 1935 Thomond Feis, and he later played in the Munster final of that year. He was then 19.

He was a first class footballer and wore the Limerick jersey at both junior and senior level for many seasons, and captained the Shannonside junior fifteen that defeated Kerry at Killarney in 1939, in the Munster final.

Jackie's lifetime of hurling was punctuated with a galaxy of glory spells from which he extracted all the honours the world had to offer - All Ireland, National League, Railway Cup, Munster Championship, Oireachtas and Thomond Feis with tournament successes galore, including victories in London and New York and then county titles almost beyond count in both hurling and football.

Jackie wore the Munster jersey in nine Railway Cup hurling finals and was on the winning side on seven occasions.

Seán Cunningham - Selector

When the present South Liberties hit the headlines two years ago to win the first ever East Limerick senior hurling title they took home with them a grand new trophy - the Seán Cunningham Cup.

It is indeed fitting that Seán's name should be permanently associated with this new premier hurling competition in East Limerick, for no man played a bigger part than he in the establishment of the divisional board.

Since its foundation in February 1944, Seán has been closely associated with it - for nearly a quarter of a century as secretary, and recently completing a three years' term as chairman. Indeed, it might be said that under his wise guidance the board has gone from success to success until it is now a most efficient unit, with well organised competitions and a very fine spirit indeed.

Seán was introduced to the games when as a schoolboy he figured in a Munster Colleges win with Doon CBS over St. Colman's College, Fermoy. He played Dr Harty Cup hurling for two seasons running and his talents were spotted by the county selectors and he played in both Munster minor championships - hurling and football - in the Limerick colours.

He played In all hurling grades with Doon Club, and was prominent, too, on the administrative side, for he held the position of club secretary for a decade, only relinquishing it on his appointment as secretary of the Eastern Board.

In 1964 he became acting secretary of the County Board, and was elected secretary two years later, also becoming a Limerick representative on the Munster Council. For many years a member of the County Appeals' Committee, he has served on many selection bodies, and is the senior member of the present "Big Five," to which he was first elected in 1964.

(L-R): Jim Quaid, Seán Cunningham, Denis Barrett, Jackie Power and Dick Stokes.

Jim Quaid - Selector

When Father Tim Culhane went to Feohanagh in the early 'fifties, football was the parish game, and the cult of the camán was not very familiar there. The subsequent progress of hurling in Feohanagh is one of the greatest success stories associated with Limerick hurling, and it was a high tribute to the dedicated work of a devoted priest, and the deep interest of the Gaels of Feohanagh, that, in 1952, they established their Junior Hurling Club, and two years later had progressed to such a degree, that they were able to win both western and county crowns.

I think I saw five Quaid brothers figure on winning Feohanagh teams - the twin boys, Jim and Jack, with Liam, Tom and Oliver. Jim and Jack quickly gained promotion to county colours, and they spearheaded a grand fifteen that won All Ireland Junior Hurling honours in 1954. The following year, they were members of the county senior side that had a sensational win over Clare, to capture the Munster crown - only to lose to a great Wexford team in the All Ireland semi-final. The pair continued to help Limerick for many years; and played their part too in further strengthening the game in the home parish, with the result that Feohanagh won Western juvenile crowns for 1957, 1958, and 1959. With Western Gaels, they participated in the county Senior Hurling Championship, and had two great successes when winning the county titles for 1961 and 1962. As twins, they look alike, and on Gaelic fields, their careers have been almost identical. They are good referees, still a lot in demand, and always ready and willing to oblige; and both have served as members of Limerick Senior Hurling Selection Committees: Jack, some years ago - Jim now.

Dr Dick Stokes - Selector

When the name of Dr Dick Stokes is mentioned, in Limerick Gaelic circles, the fact that he was one of our greatest hurlers is not the first thought to come to mind. Rather, the memory comes crowding of his wonderful loyalty, and the journeys he made across the sea - to line out with Limerick. And Dick never worried what kind of a team he turned out with, all the rest of them might be taking a day off, but Dr Dick was always there. I was going to say: "filling his accustomed position," but, sure, he never minded where he played, and must have figured in almost every berth since he first togged off for his initial outing - as goalkeeper with Doon CBS in a Dr Harty Cup tie.

By 1938, he was starring at midfield, to such effect that he was a reserve on the Munster Colleges' team. Twelve months later, he was partnering Vin Baston of Waterford, in the All Ireland Colleges' final, and played a big part in bringing the title back to Munster. The Limerick selectors also had their eyes on the up-and-coming star, and he wore the green and white in minor hurling and football before the call to senior colours came in early 1940, when he was selected as a half forward, to participate in Limerick's last great glory campaign.

Beating Waterford in a replay - a thrilling meeting too - before Cork were deprived of their Munster crown, and Limerick went on, via a great win over Galway at Ennis, to meet and beat All Ireland champions, Kilkenny, in the Blue Riband decider. When the great deeds of that campaign were re-told, and the hurling heroes of the great Limerick success were acclaimed, the knowing ones spoke of a fair-haired half forward, that might, one day, eclipse them all - and that lad was Dick Stokes.

Dick wore the Munster jersey from 1940 to 1946, and, himself, played no mean part in winning the Railway Cup five years running. With UCD, Dick won Dublin County Senior Football honours in 1943, and County Senior Hurling renown in 1947 and 1948. He helped UCD sides to win Fitzgibbon Cup honours from 1941 to 1944, and Sigerson Cup medals from 1944 to 1947. And maybe the greatest honour paid him was in 1952 - a dozen years after he won his All Ireland medal, when he captained the Combined Universities side that played Ireland for the first time, in hurling. Dick flew to Dublin from overseas, through fog and winter winds, to take his place against Kilkenny, and contribute materially to the Limerick success in the 1947 National Hurling League final. Three years later, he filled another role for Limerick, when he helped the footballers win a Munster Junior crown.

Denis Barrett - Selector

The Denis Barrett Cup is the prized trophy for the new South Limerick Senior Hurling Championship - the two first holders of which were Garryspillane and Kilmallock. And the popular donor must be hoping it will change hands again this year, with his club, Bruff, participating in the final.

Denis, who is a native of Ardpatrick, was educated at Effin NS and Rathluirc CBS and had played some hurling with Effin before moving to Bruff, where he participated in juvenile and minor ranks before his playing career was cut prematurely short by serious illness, which however, he very gallantly overcame, and returned to active Gaelic ranks, this time as a top-rate referee, who took charge, of many important county championship ties including finals; and a number of inter-county engagements and appears to have given general satisfaction for he never encountered any real trouble or hostility.

Six years ago he faced another health crisis, for which he underwent successful surgery in America, and on his return he was back in the thick of things Gaelic, and was soon shouldering the increasingly heavy responsibilities of treasurer of the South Limerick Board, and has proved a most dedicated and hard-working official and most obliging, as anyone who has reason to contact him on Gaelic matters will undoubtedly vouch.

As selector, Denis can claim worthwhile experience, having served at County selection committees at all levels - minor, under-21, intermediate, and senior. He is a member of the latter since 1970 and saw Limerick contest four National Hurling League finals - and his greatest thrill of all - seeing them for the first time in an All Ireland senior final last Sunday.

These boots were made for hurling! Éamon Grimes, Limerick captain, receiving a presentation of Adidas boots on behalf of the team from Pierce O'Farrell, Limerick Sports Store, and Michael O'Connell, Three Stripe International.
Inset: Eamon on his way up to collect the Liam MacCarthy Cup.

How To Save Hurling ...The Cregan Way
(Irish Press, 12 September 1973)

GAA Talking Point by Tom Tobin

Army Captain Mick Cregan, the 28-year-old hurler from Claughaun who brought about a revolution in training methods, sharply silenced his many critics when the Limerick senior hurlers brought home the 1973 All Ireland title - the realisation of a 33 year dream.

Seldom, if ever, was an exhibition of superb physical fitness seen in Croke Park to equal that of Limerick, when they defeated Kilkenny on that memorable Sunday 2 September. But Mick Cregan is not happy with present day hurling in general. "I am afraid it is a dying game and the main reason is - the skills of hurling are dying," he told me in an exclusive interview yesterday.

"There is no reason why this should happen. The problem, in my view, lies in how to improve the skills of the game and, by skills, I mean striking the ball. Cregan went on to say that the manner in which the ball was struck would always remain the main skill in hurling. "During the 'thirties and 'forties, we have been led to believe, the standard of hurling was exceptionally high.

"If we stop to analyse why, you will see, very clearly, that it was due to the social and economic conditions of the period. Our young men had little to do except go down to the most suitable field in the evening and play hurling. They played the game for a few hours every night for seven nights a week. With such constant practice, it is no wonder that their skills were at their highest."

CAUSE AND EFFECTS

The Claughaun star, who played no small part in bringing the 1971 National Hurling League title to Limerick went on to say: "Since the early 'fifties, we have had the effects of emigration; a serious decline in the rural population; an economic development that continues to grow and we have seen the price of hurleys become too costly. "Then we must take into account the many inroads made by other forms of sport. We must make provision for the dramatic changes in the social life of the community. We saw the rapid expansion in the number of cars throughout the country; we saw the growth of new forms of entertainment and especially television, Yes, it can be said that it has been the affluence of recent years that has been the cause of the biggest drain of all.

"People in the towns and cities do not have the space to practise the skills of hurling as their fathers did in the 'thirties and the 'forties, but many young men continue to play with their various clubs, but there has been little or no individual effort to practice the real skills of the game. Hence the serious decline of hurling." Capt. Cregan, on the present standing of other games, pointed out that most showed a clear improvement, and gave a few examples why. "Lew Hoad, one of the greatest tennis players of all time practised his tennis by painting a line the height of the net on a wall and then kept on banging the ball over that line against the wall for hours every day."

APPLYING THE SKILLS

"So much so, as I have said, he finished up one of the greatest players of all time. He simply applied the principle of maximum activity to the full. He would have been a very foolish man if he had gone into the tennis court and kept hitting the ball over the net wasting valuable practice time retrieving each ball.

"Now, let us take a look at golf. Any young golfer who wants to be a successful player will place one hundred balls down in front of him and practice his driving, chipping or putting, by striking these balls every five or six seconds. He is also applying the principle of maximum activity. He, too, would be a very foolish man if he only used one ball, struck it and then walked 150 yards or more after it, to strike it again.

"The same applies in soccer where the young lads in towns and cities improve their skills by getting a ball and then keep on banging it against a wall with the right foot, the left foot, and the head. It is by constant use of these methods that you produce such stars as George Best, Bobby Charlton and Johnny Giles.

"This can be applied also to squash. Present-day top players simply go into a court and practice by striking balls against the wall for hours. Jonah Barrington has long since reached the stage when he can place his feet on the ground of the court and strike 500 balls off the front wall and sidewalls without moving his feet.

"It can be seen quite clearly that the same principle of training is being used by participants in all these different games. Why not hurling?

"Let us now examine what goes on out on the local club field. Let us say that we have twenty players and three sliothars. Normally, these sliothars will be pucked around from player to player, but with no great urgency. The player will stop the sliothar; pick it up and strike it with his best, his strong side, to the next player. Very few skills are practised when using this method of training from my experience, such is the common method used when practising hurling throughout the country.

"On top of this, it is worth taking into account that in one hour's practice a player would be lucky to strike the ball fifty times, with no great improvement in the other vital skills of overhead hurling, doubling the ball left and right, and volleying.

"The problem is how to improve this archaic system of training? How can we apply the basic principles and the methods of training adopted so successfully in tennis, golf, soccer and squash? In other words, how do we adopt the principal of maximum activity?

"The answer lies in the handball alley, with the usual four walls and lattice wire on top. The hurler should use a Dunlop softball and keep on hurling that ball against the walls. This will soon improve his striking skill in every way. In other words, let us play handball with hurleys."

EVERYTHING NEEDED

Capt. Cregan went on to add: "If we examine this method in theory we will find that if you strike this ball every three seconds, you will have struck it 1,200 times in one hour, as against fifty or so in the playing field and, as well as that, you will have practised every skill that is needed in top class hurling.

"Now, compare the method of practice in the handball alley to the more widely used method on the field. Straight away it will seem that the alley has its drawbacks in that you do not learn how to mark an opponent, how to hook and a few other things, but these can be taught on the field at a later stage. The vital requirement is to improve in hurling skills.

"To make this system more enjoyable I would suggest that two hurlers should go into the alley and compete against each other. It would have tremendous benefits, yet it is simply a game of handball using hurleys instead of the palms of your hands. The obvious remark would be that there is a shortage of alleys.

"I firmly believe that every hurling club throughout the country should have its own handball alley and even more than two, if the members can afford to meet the cost.

"It should be borne in mind also that hurling, as a game, could very quickly spread internationally if this method of learning the skills of the game was adopted. May I say right away that it is nonsense to say that hurlers are born and not made. They are made through the right kind of practice, and plenty of it."

When I asked Capt. Cregan how he knew that such a method would prove successful, he promptly recalled Capt. Tony Wall of Tipperary. "Tony spent four or five hours every week using this method of practice, and he developed into a most safe and skilled half-back, winning three All Ireland medals with Tipperary . . . and Tony will be remembered as a perfectionist.

"Christy Ring's heels were worn in handball alleys all over Munster using the same system of training, and there are countless others who use it also, but I feel the two stars I have mentioned are good enough examples.

NATURAL IMPROVEMENT

Going back to my suggestion of having two hurlers competing against each other in the handball alley, it is worth remembering that the ball comes to them at various speeds and angles off the front wall, the two side walls, and off the back wall, with the result that they have to develop all the skills that they will ever use on the hurling field.

"It is only natural that their skills, will improve dramatically, the longer they practice hurling in this way.

Following many hours of this, I can envisage many great hurlers of these years to come surpassing in skill the great heroes of the 'thirties and the 'forties.

"There are moves afoot in the Southern Command to get this form of competition established as an annual event with the ultimate aim of raising the standard of hurling in the Army. I feel I should point out that this is the only hope for the young player of today, if he is to win the fine skills of hurling.

"They will not get a better method of training, because there is no way we can turn the clocks back. Young men will not devote every evening of the week to practising the skills of hurling today and we cannot expect them to do so. We are living in a different age.

"The handball alley method would be of tremendous benefit to our camogie players also. Their striking is far from what it should be and they could gain a great deal. I would strongly recommend this method to every school and college throughout the country.

"My advice to anybody who wants to become a truly skilled hurler is to get into your nearest handball alley with a team mate. Using the soft ball, you should belt away with your hurleys as much as possible, and as often as possible. The speed of the action will soon improve your reflexes and your reactions.

"It may seem strange now," concluded Capt. Cregan, "but the important fact to remember is that the future of hurling lies in the handball alleys of Ireland, and the Southern Command of our Army will lead the way in restoring the best in hurling skills."

The Man Who Came To Cheer
(Limerick Heroes)

By Pádraig Puirséal

The man who came to cheer for Caherline was a faithful Limerick hurling supporter of whom I first wrote many a long year ago. Indeed it was in the early 1930s I first became aware of his tallish, lean figure. In those days when Mick Mackey and his mighty men had only recently begun to climb the long, hard road to hurling greatness, and I was only starting out to follow the Munster hurling circuit, you would, when Limerick were playing, be sure to find this man somewhere near the radio commentator's box. There, at unpredictable intervals, he would raise his voice in his one and only battle-cry, "Up Limerick! Come on Caherline!"

Eventually I began to watch out for him at any of Limerick's games that I attended, and rarely did he fail to appear. Even when I could not attend some Munster matches, and had to be content with listening to the commentary, I formed the habit of paying particular attention to the background noises on the 'Effects' microphone of any game in which Limerick were playing. Sure enough, sooner or later that familiar voice, and that familiar shout, was bound to come over the airwaves, "Up Limerick! Come on Caherline!"

Come the Emergency Years when to those of us based in Dublin it was rarely possible to attend any games at all at down-the-country venues. But I still listened to the commentaries and, whenever Limerick were on the field, that familiar voice and that familiar slogan was still to be heard from time to time in the background. With the passing of the years, however, there came a subtle change in the wording of the war-cry which eventually became "Up Limerick! Good man Jackie Power! Come on Caherline! "

Sadly, Limerick's hurling glories faded as the 1940s waned, until at last I heard that voice no more, either at Munster games or on the radio. Then, some few years ago, I received a letter from a County Limerick reader giving me the name of the Man Who Came to Cheer for Caherline, and telling me that he had passed away some weeks before.

I wrote, at the time, that I hoped he would be remembered when Limerick hurling stars shone bright again. On the Monday morning after this year's All Ireland final, I came downstairs to find that, at some stage during the previous night or morning, a note had been slipped into my letterbox.

It read as follows - "If my memory serves me right, it was back in the 'fifties you had a write-up in the Irish Press about the great Limerick teams of the 'thirties and a man who used to attend all their matches in Croke Park, stand by the broadcasting box, and say 'Come on Caherline'. "When he died, you wrote you hoped that, when next Limerick appeared in an All Ireland final again, someone would stand there and say, 'Come on Caherline' in remembrance of that old man. "I am here at the match, and I will not forget him." The letter was dated 2 September, 1973 and signed "William Cantillon, Meelick, County Clare."

Well, William Cantillon, I have never met to my knowledge yet, but may God reward him for his kindly thought in remembering the Man From Caherline who followed Limerick so faithfully through good times and bad. Indeed, when on the night of the homecoming, Jackie Power stood there on the flag-bedecked platform on Charlotte Quay among a new generation of Shannonside hurling heroes, I could not help but feel that, somewhere beyond the glare of the arc-lights, and the flame-lit smoke of the bonfires, there hovered the shadow of a tall and lean man.

And I could well believe that, if the blaring car-horns and the bands and the riot of cheering would only subside for a few seconds I might again hear the faint echo of a once-familiar voice shouting "Up Limerick! Good man Jackie Power! Come on Caherline!" But above all, after all the years, it was heartening to discover that, amid the tens of thousands of dedicated followers sporting Limerick's green and white at Croke Park on the first Sunday in September there was at least one spectator who did not forget The Man Who Came To Cheer For Caherline.

GETAWAY
ON A DAY TRIP

BY TRAIN TO

DUBLIN
SUNDAY, 2ND SEPTEMBER 1973

ALL-IRELAND HURLING FINAL

LIMERICK v. KILKENNY

			Day Return Fare
NEWCASTLEWEST	Depart	08.35	£3.00
RATHKEALE		08.54	£2.80
BALLINGRANE		09.01	£2.80
ADARE		09.14	£2.80
PATRICKSWELL		09.24	£2.60
DROMKEEN		09.55	£2.60
HEUSTON STATION	Arrive	12.02	—

Return train at 20.05.

 CIE great people to go with

What some experts predicted

SUNDAY INDEPENDENT—September 2: "It Must be Kilkenny"—John Comyn.

IRISH INDEPENDENT—August 31: "Final Vote for Kilkenny"—John D. Hickey.

SUNDAY WORLD—September 2: "It Must be Kilkenny"—Joe Lennon.

SUNDAY PRESS—September 2: "Going for Kilkenny"—Eugene McGee.

IRISH TIMES—September 1: "Kilkenny Can Overcome Setbacks"—Paddy Downey

THE IRISH PRESS on September 1 was the only National paper to predict a win for Limerick.

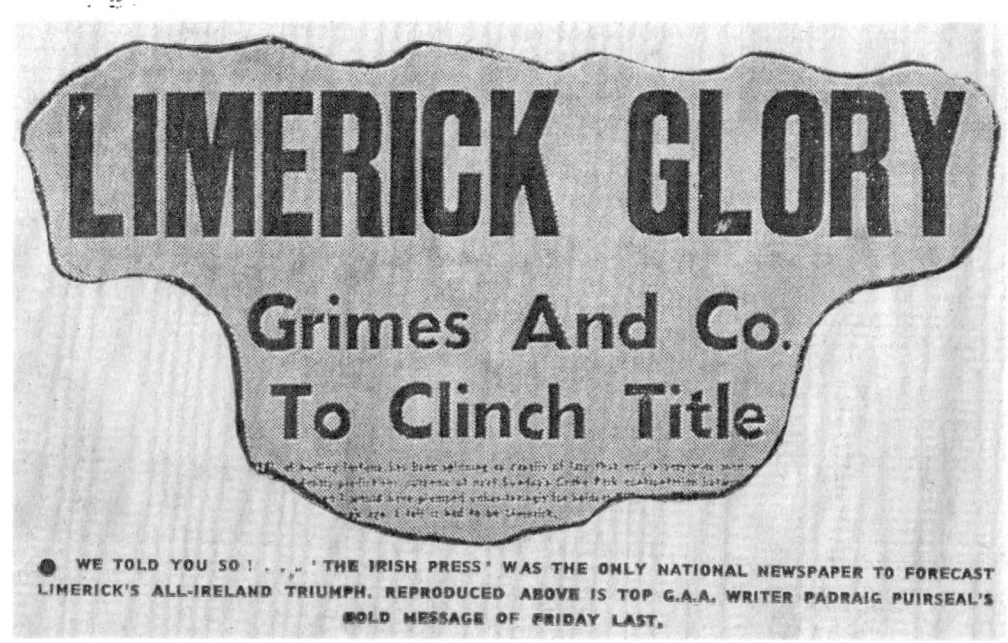

Energetic County Secretary
(1972 Limerick GAA Yearbook)

Tom Boland, the energetic Secretary of Limerick County Board GAA and county delegate to the Munster Council is a much respected official who goes about his work with quiet dignity and determination and with the reputation of getting things done effectively and without fuss. Tom came to Gaelic notice first with that fine *alma mater* of many first-class camán wielders, Adare CBS, with whom he starred in school and college ties.

He was a founder member over a quarter of a century ago of Patrickswell club, and figured with them in many of their early games. He was first the captain of the club's junior hurling team and a committee member the same season. They won the city junior hurling championship on three occasions - 1949, 1955 and 1957, going on to collect county honours in the two latter years.

With the Limerick team that won the Munster Junior hurling title in 1948, he was again on the side that regained the trophy in 1952. In between he figured in the ill-starred Munster Senior hurling final of 1949 against Tipperary. In a preview of that game he was described thus: Tom Boland, twenty years of age, eleven stone weight, red haired, and one of the fastest members of the team. He is a civil servant, who won the Munster Junior Hurling championships last year. He played his first Senior Championship game recently against Waterford."

Tom figured in what was probably the most dramatic incident of that game. Again let us quote the newspaper report: "Tom Boland swiftly crossed to Jackie Power, who went off on a grand solo run amidst tremendous excitement and bashed to the net for what looked like Limerick's crowning goal. Hats, caps, coats were in the air, but the Shannonside jubilation was stifled when the referee ruled that Power had carried the leather too far and awarded a free to Tipperary. To my mind the game was lost and won in that tragic moment."

Appointed Assistant Secretary and Registrar of the City Divisional GAA Board in 1956, he was appointed City Board Secretary in 1963, a post he resigned a few years later when elected to his present position of County Board Secretary.

Have you a ticket?
Well Tom Boland, Limerick county secretary, has his hands full of them,
but he also has a big headache sharing them out.

Experts' Views on the Hurling Final
(Gaelic Sport, September 1973)

By John O'Shea

The clash of a side noted for its guile and experience and one, characterised by youthful exuberance and dogged determination, has brimful of possibilities. Such is the appeal of the meeting of Kilkenny and Limerick in this year's All Ireland Senior Hurling final.

Who will win? The bulk of noted personalities in the game whom I discussed the matter with, favoured Kilkenny, but let no one tell you there's not a whale of an amount of money on the Shannonsiders.

Here then are the opinions of men who know their hurling.

Séamus Power (Waterford):

On all known form it must be Kilkenny. Word has it that knowledgeable Kilkenny folk consider this the best side to leave the county for fifteen years. This is saying something.

As a Munsterman, naturally I would like to see Limerick get through, but I have grave reservations about their half back line. Quite honestly I can't see them holding the likes of Keher, Delaney, and when he is moved out, Purcell. Limerick's only chance is to maintain a fierce pace throughout and keep the ball moving. But as I didn't think they were over impressive in Munster, I would have to give my vote to Kilkenny.

Dave Bernie (Wexford):

Kilkenny looked unbeatable against Wexford, and as I feel Limerick are as yet, not ready for the big breakthrough, it must be another Kilkenny victory. Had we beaten Kilkenny we would have believed Limerick were an "easy thing" in the final.

I suppose like most followers of the game I would love to see Limerick win, if for no reason other than to see a change at the top. But frankly I see no way the Limerick defence can hold Delaney and his men. Jim Treacy will be missed, but with such as Pa Dillon in the "full line" there will be little looseness.

Pat Fanning (Waterford):

I have seen Limerick produce hurling over the last few years which would win any All Ireland, and I'm reasonably sure that provided they play to their full capacity, they will triumph on this occasion. The players must know that it's a case of "Now or Never", and I feel that the occasion will produce the effort. If success is to come, it will be from a sustained effort through the field, with every player putting in a full 80 minutes. They cannot afford to relax or falter: their very best will be required.

Gerald McCarthy (Cork):

A big doubt about the ability of the Limerick attack to get the necessary scores, prompts me to plump for Kilkenny. What worries me about Limerick is that while they seem to be able to grab quite a few goals, they find points difficult to get. Against Kilkenny, few teams manage to crack home many goals.

I consider too that Limerick have a definite weakness at midfield where Bennis is more suited to a half forward position and Grimes tends to fade from the scene for long periods during the game. Kilkenny can be relied upon to play solidly for the full 80 minutes, and for Limerick to have any chance, they will have to rise above the form they have previously shown.

1973 Keeping the Dream Alive

Mickey Birmingham (Dublin):

Keher, Purcell and Brennan will inspire Kilkenny to another success. The Kilkenny attack simply carries too much fire power for Limerick, who although their defence is reasonably sound, their forwards are not capable, in my view, of as big a total as Kilkenny.

There is probably no better side in the country than Kilkenny for pacing themselves through a game. They proved this countless times and I expect they will really hit out during the last ten minutes of the All Ireland when perhaps Limerick will have given their best.

Kilkenny are also better prepared in that they emerged from a championship where the standard was of a higher quality than in Munster. It's a long time since a side took a Munster title scoring seven points. Limerick have not proved that they have the ability to get a big points' tally. Kilkenny have no worries in this regard.

Tom Neville (Wexford):

If Kilkenny were at full strength, I would tip them. In the circumstances, I'm going for a Limerick win.

Basically I believe they are stronger up the middle, with Hartigan, the real king-pin of the side. They have sufficient players to hold Kilkenny's key men, Purcell and Delaney. In brief, I would suggest that Limerick are a more evenly-balanced side.

The fact that this particular group will be contesting their first All Ireland final is of no significance. They have enough experience, gained from "knocking at the door" over the past few years, and with 80 minutes to play, they should settle down before the game is very old.

Treacy's absence represents a huge blow to Kilkenny, and I feel the full back line could prove quite porous in the event.

Tommy Barrett (Tipperary):

It's not an easy match to forecast. With Treacy in the side, Kilkenny would have been my choice, now I'm not so sure. Kilkenny must be strong favourites as besides the craft and experience, they have the ability to knock up substantial points' totals. I'm not certain Limerick can match them here. It's not an easy match to forecast. With Treacy in the side, Kilkenny would have been my choice, now I'm not so sure.

Limerick's own brand of tea, from 1886 to 1984.

Shannonsiders to Sweep MacCarthy Cup?
(Solo, September 1973)
'Cats' Chase Two-In-The-Row

Kilkenny want to be underdogs in this All Ireland Final. Not, of course, that there is any honour in the role but it is a notorious fact that in recent years whenever Kilkenny were fancied they invariably went down - indeed often in a most inexplicable manner. What's the sense in making either side favourites? When two teams reach the All Ireland Final it must be taken that they got there on merit and that, consequently, they most have an even chance. Forecasting is a commentator's forte but I prefer to row in with famous Cork star of the past, Jim O'Regan. When I asked him last year about the Cork-Kilkenny final he remarked, "How the hell does anyone know who is going to win?"

Win, lose or draw Kilkenny have problems that do not present an easy solution. Missing from his usual left full back position is Jim Treacy, while the left flank has been further affected by Eamonn Morrissey's emigration to Australia. The obvious answer to the left full back problem is to play Pa Dillon at full back and Nicky Orr in Jim Treacy's place. Nicky Orr has shown a steady improvement in his recent games and he impressed me by his showing against Tipperary when they played Kilkenny in a challenge to mark the opening of the new GAA field in Windgap (County Kilkenny).

That was some weeks before the Leinster final in which he had what was, perhaps, the most outstanding game in his career. In that game he was at left full back. He has had, in the meantime, an opportunity of adapting himself to the position. But the left half back position is a much more difficult problem. Last year's minor captain, Brian Cody, has already had some experience in senior ranks and it is beyond question that he has the skill and ability. The only thing is that does not seem fair to ask a player not yet 20 to take on such responsibility in an All Ireland Final.

Martin Coogan is still playing quite well as he proved in a club match recently when he matched wits with Kieran Purcell and suffered no loss of prestige in this exacting assignment. Then, could Martin Coogan be expected to stand the strain of an 80 minutes contest? Jim Lynch, the Mooncoin man has shown a return to form and has filled many different roles for his club and for the county. There may be others worthy of consideration but you just cannot put a man into an All Ireland Final without some experience in top class hurling - no matter how good he is.

These are some of the imponderables about the Kilkenny lineout, but there are others. In last year's final Kilkenny stayed the pace better than Cork but Limerick showed at Thurles that they can endure the gruelling test just as well and it would be futile to count on the Shannonsiders failing to stay the distance. Even with Jim Treacy off, the Kilkenny defence is reasonably sound, at its best and despite the big tally of goals that Limerick men hit against Tipperary they may not find it quite as easy to penetrate the Kilkenny defence. A lot will depend on the half back line and it is here that Kilkenny have their most pressing problem.

The midfield exchange could play a decisive part in the game and Kilkenny followers will be hoping that Frank Cummins will strike one of his best days. When he does he can have a devastating effect. The Kilkenny attack proved very effective against Wexford but they will have a much tougher proposition in this final and they will have to be on the watch for every possible chance. Kilkenny are not going to have their work made any easier by reason of the fact that they are attempting to win their second title in successive years, a feat which the Noremen have not accomplished since 1932-33. But significantly when they won in 1933, their victims were Limerick.

The counties have not met in an All Ireland Final since 1940 when Limerick won. Limerick won when the sides met in the 1936 final but Kilkenny already had notched up two wins over the Shannonsiders, in 1933 and 1935. Kilkenny were in America in 1934 and were not in the final that year. The two occasions on which Kilkenny won were among the greatest finals ever played.

Kilkenny won by four points in 1933 but the 1935 final was an even closer affair when the black and amber men got home by a point in a scintillating game played in a downpour.

The teams of those days included such noted hurlers as Mick and John Mackey, Paddy Clohessy, and men like Scanlan, Cooke, McCarthy, Ryan and other wonderful hurlers, while Kilkenny had Lory Meagher, Podge and Eddie Byrne, Paddy Phelan, Jimmy Walsh and Matty Power in a galaxy of stars.

The teams of both Limerick and Kilkenny of this period must rank as among the greatest the game has known. Will the present teams live up to such a great tradition? The game itself will tell but if they can give as anything like the 1933 or 1935 finals they will have earned a niche in the annals of the game.

Fundraising Letter

Sir,

Now that Limerick hurlers are in an All Ireland and have bridged a gap of 33 years, I think it only right that everyone should get behind them. I was disappointed to see that the County Board had to make an appeal for funds. There should be no need to. Firms and other big businesses should come to their aid and help by their contribution to have our team at top form for Sunday.

Maybe some garages could do their bit by supplying car stickers and flags etc. Let's not allow the occasion to slip by and let no-one be able to say that "we let down the team".

Finally, it is a pity that we haven't some short rallying song that we could sing in Croke Park. I feel that it often helps to lift a team. However, if no one comes up with a suitable one soon, then at least we can all take part in the chant, "Limerick, Limerick" that was so nice to hear at Thurles.

I know very well that the *Limerick Leader* will do more than its share to make this an extra big occasion.

Thanking you, Mr Editor.

S Hennessy

C.L.C.G.—COISDE CHO. LUIMNI

A TRAINING FUND

to finance the additional expenses involved in the preparation of our team for the All-Ireland Final has been launched. Subscriptions may be sent to any of the following:—

Ruairi O Cadhla, Feenagh, Kilmallock.
Sean O Faolain, Newcastle West.
Seamus O hIci, Banogue, Croom.
Sean Mac Craith, Doon.
Sean O'Grada, Cloughkeating, Patrickswell.
D. O Maolain, 37 Beechwood Drive, Greystones, Limerick.
T. O Beolain, Patrickswell.

All subscriptions will be acknowledged.

Taken from the Limerick Leader in the weeks before the 1973 All Ireland Hurling Final.

FINAL LINE-UP

NUMBER SEVEN FOR LIMERICK

PAT HARTIGAN

A star of the South Liberties team that won the Limerick senior hurling title last December for the first time since 1890, he has been in the county senior side since 1968. Now 22, he won a National League medal and an Oireachtas Cup souvenir in 1971, and was chosen for the Carrolls All-Stars selections in the past two seasons.

LIMERICK bridge a 33 year gap with this final outing. It was on September 1, 1940, that the county, captained by the legendary Mick Mackey, last had a direct interest in the showpiece game of the year. The opposition was provided by Kilkenny, and Limerick emerged champions for the sixth time on the score, 3-7 to 1-7.

Since then, Limerick have won only two Munster titles — 1955, when they lost the All-Ireland semi-final to Wexford, and last July.

LIMERICK'S LAST NATIONAL TITLE

LIMERICK'S last national title was won at Cork in May, 1971, when they beat Tipperary 3-12 to 3-11 for a first National League crown since 1947 with the following team:

J. Hogan; T. O'Brien, P. Hartigan, J. O'Brien; C. Campbell, J. O'Donnell, P. Bennis; J. Foley, M. Graham; R. Bennis, B. Hartigan, E. Grimes; D. O'Flynn, M. Cregan, E. Cregan. Sub: E. Prenderville for Campbell.

Limerick 3-11; Clare 3-9

A power-packed display by Richie Bennis at centre-field was a key factor in this two point win at Thurles. In a grand game, he received strong support from Eamonn Cregan, who bagged two goals, Mossy Dowling and Jim O'Brien.

Limerick 6-7; Tipperary 2-18

That man Richie Bennis again. A great point with the last puck of the game from a "70" by the Patrickswell player brought the title back to the county after an absence of 18 years. But good goalkeeping by Seamus Horgan, progressive back play from

FORM GUIDE—

John Foley, a top form Bernie Hartigan at midfield in the second half were among the factors that led up to that dramatic win.

Limerick 1-15; London 0-7

An adequate rather than impressive showing this from Limerick, who struck the decisive blow fifteen minutes into the second half when Richie Bennis goaled from a 21 yards free. Pat Hartigan, Phil Bennis, Frankie Nolan and Liam O'Donoghue were other key figures in shaping a win that clinched a first final appearance since 1940.

From the Gaelic Sport Hurling Final Special edition, September 1973.

By Owen McCann

OR NINETEEN FOR KILKENNY

PAT DELANEY

Now 30, he won an All-Ireland minor medal in 1960, and made his senior inter-county championship debut in the 1968 Leinster campaign. This Johnstown club man helped Kilkenny to their 1969 and 1972 All-Ireland senior title wins, has three Railway Cup medals (1971-72-73), and he was honoured by the Carrolls All-Stars selection last year.

KILKENNY, probably the most classical exponents of all in hurling, are in line to accomplish a feat that has eluded the county since 1933. That was the last year they won the All-Ireland senior championship two seasons in succession.

The county was first represented in a national final in 1893, when they lost to Cork. Their first success was in 1904, and last year they boosted their total of titles to 18 by beating Cork. This is Kilkenny's third final in a row — they lost to Tipperary in 1971.

1973 CHAMPIONSHIP

Kilkenny 2-19; Dublin 2-11

Short men of the calibre of Frank Cummins, Pat Henderson and Jim Treacy because of injuries, Kilkenny had some anxious moments before pulling away in the last eight minutes. Brian Cody, Mick Brennan and Pat Broderick were among their brightest stars.

Kilkenny 4-22; Wexford 3-15

Nicky Orr's great full-back play — he was in command against Tony Doran, and in the final minutes against Jack Berry — and clever forward play and spot-on finishing by Pat Delaney, who hit 2-2, and set up another goal, were decisive factors in fashioning this third Leinster title on the trot. Another to catch the eye was Pat Broderick, making his Leinster final debut.

FINAL MEETINGS

Final Meetings: Limerick beat Kilkenny in 1897, 1936 and 1940.

Kilkenny beat Limerick in in 1933 and 1935 — 3-2 in favour of Limerick.

LAST YEAR'S TITLE WINNERS

THIS is the side that won the title last year for Kilkenny: N. Skehan (capt.); P. Larkin, P. Dillon, J. Treacy; P. Lalor, P. Henderson, E. Morrissey; L. O'Brien, F. Cummins; M. Crotty, P. Delaney, J. Kinsella; E. Byrne, K. Purcell, E. Keher. Subs.: M. Murphy for Byrne (at half-time); M. Coogan for Larkin (49 minutes); P. Moran for Kinsella (74 minutes).

CHAPTER 10
1973

ALL IRELAND HURLING FINAL (ii)

v KILKENNY

(2 SEPTEMBER - CROKE PARK, DUBLIN)

Limerick played Kilkenny on Sunday, 2 September 1973 in the All Ireland Hurling Final at Croke Park. The game was dominated by the weather: rain and more rain. According to the weather forecast printed in that weekend's newspapers, a frontal trough was moving south-easterly from the Atlantic through the country, mostly clear but with some showers. Dublin got mostly showers, starting soon after noon that early September day. It affected the attendance at the game by as much as 7,000, with the official attendance recorded as 58,009, substantially down on the previous year. Bookmakers made Kilkenny favourites at 1/2, while Limerick were generously priced at 7/4. It was not the first time that the Limerick hurlers were shown live on television, that honour going to the Wembley Games contest against Tipperary in May 1972. Kilkenny won the minor game with a last-minute goal to "foil" Galway, who were in pursuit of their first-ever minor title, something they would not secure for another 10 years. Seán O'Brien did most of the damage for Kilkenny that day, scoring 4-2 of the winning team's 4-5. The "better balanced" team lost. Cyril Farrell cut his inter-county teeth with this Galway team, as its trainer.

The senior final started soon after 3:15PM (the move to 3:30PM only occurred in 1987) and the constant rain that had been experienced during the minor game continued as a downpour for the rest of this glorious afternoon. It was one of the last occasions where the Bishop of Cashel and Emly was presented on the pitch to the two captains and referee before the throw-in. Kilkenny were without four of their stars but started confidently. Limerick were in the lead by two points by the short whistle, even though Kilkenny had gotten the first goal of the afternoon. The game had ebbed and flowed during that half, with Liam O'Brien of Kilkenny suffering an accidental head injury in the throw-in, this being the era before compulsory helmets. A number of players on both sides did wear protective headgear though, mostly basic Coopers. They protected the skull but not the face, unlike modern equipment. One Kilkenny player, Paddy Broderick, even wore ordinary eyeglasses with his helmet. Some of the Limerick players changed their jerseys at half-time, while the entire Kilkenny team swopped theirs. Conditions visibly deteriorated during the second half, as can be seen in the available footage on YouTube. (The entire 80 minutes can be streamed from there.)The Munster Final referee, Michael Slattery of Clare, refereed his only All Ireland Hurling Final that year, and managed the game very creditably. He took a number of players' names and awarded all frees judiciously. This was the era before three-men-in-goal penalties: that rule change was only introduced the following spring at the annual GAA Congress, together with the addition of the large parallelogram in both hurling and Gaelic football. There would have been at least four penalties in this game if that rule has been brought in a year earlier! The 'Thou Shall Not Pass' edict was in force in both defences. Pat Hartigan took over the puckouts after Séamus Horgan took the first one of the day.

The key moment in the game was six minutes into the second half when Mick Crotty attempted to play a point-blank handpass past Séamus Horgan and into the goal. Séamus' quick reflexes prevented the goal, but Kilkenny now had the lead, as this was their third unanswered point of the half. Mick Cregan had specifically targeted the possibility of attackers handpassing past the goalkeeper in pre-match drills. Richie Bennis scored a free to level matters again very soon after. The Limerick goal arrived two minutes later. In a melee in the small square, Mossie Dowling, aided and abetted by Eamonn Rea, handpassed the ball over the line past a despairing Noel Skehan. Bernie Hartigan soon added his signature point to stretch the lead to four. With 10 minutes to go, Limerick were still leading by those four points, 1-17 to 1-13. Over the next six minutes, Limerick added four more points, some of them wonderful strikes, with other good chances spurned. Kilkenny were a beaten docket. The final whistle blew, and the ecstatic crowd ran onto the Croke Park pitch, another tradition that winning supporters (and teams) no longer get to experience. The winning captain, Éamon Grimes, gave a short but very impassioned speech. His totally impromptu speech is reprinted hereabouts. He was awarded the man-of-the-match accolade afterwards, followed closely by Seán Foley, with Richie Bennis not that far behind. "It's Ours" was one of the Limerick Leader headlines that week. At Last! Two facts from the day: (1) There were 31 handpasses in the 1973 All Ireland Hurling Final and (2) The then 22-year-old JP (John Patrick) McManus finished up in the Limerick dressing room after the match; he came in through an outside window!

THE RIVAL CAPTAINS

EAMONN GRIMES

BRILLIANT stars of schoolboys' competitions do not always make the grade as seniors, but this is certainly not true of Eamonn Grimes. The great potential that was evident in the mid-'Sixties when he was producing sparkling hurling with Limerick C.B.S. in Colleges' competitions, and with the county minor side, has been amply fulfilled.

Indeed, his non-stop hurling, deft touches and creative distribution mark him out as one of the most gifted members of the Limerick side. A very enthusiastic worker, he also has the temperament and the experience for the role of team leader in a game of this importance.

Experience ? This may be his debut in an All-Ireland senior decider, but a couple of Munster finals, National League and Oireachtas Cup medal wins, and a power-packed display when leading his county in their National League final last May against Wexford at Croke Park are among the important high points that have helped the 25-year-old South Liberties hurler to acquire the expertise and to perfect the skills that could mean so much to the county in this breakthrough bid.

It is a great distinction for any player to lead his county in a bid to link a proud — if now long-gone—glory era of other days, and the present with a title win. It is a big challenge, too, but Eamonn Grimes has had such a thorough schooling on the way up, and is applying his talents so successfully that he can be depended on to discharge his duties of leadership, and at the same time, play his part as a hurler of more than ordinary class.

PAT DELANEY

THIS year will go down as a particularly memorable one for Pat Delaney if Kilkenny retain their All-Ireland title. The man who leads the defending champions has already this season captained two important title winning sides—Leinster to their Railway Cup success in March, and, of course, Kilkenny in the recent provincial final.

Delaney can take much satisfaction from both wins. Against Munster on St. Patrick's Day he only scored a point, but his all round progressive hurling had much to do in shaping the title win, and in the provincial decider he highlighted another good display by scoring two vital goals and a couple of points for good measure.

These victories further emphasise that Pat Delaney is well equipped for the role of captaincy.

Since joining the county senior team against Wexford in 1968, Delaney has given sterling service to the county—and Leinster in the interprovincial series. Skill he has in plenty. And, those two goals against Wexford are a timely reminder to Limerick that this wholehearted and determined worker is a forward who must be closely and constantly watched.

Now one of the older members of the side, this Johnstown (The Fenians) club-man is yet another brilliant graduate from the minor ranks. His tenure in the senior side enables him to bring to his role of captain the type of experience that, allied to genuine talent, is invaluable in the make-up of any player leading a side in the top game of the year.

In short, Kilkenny, a county that has produced some great captains down the years, has in Pat Delaney a man well qualified to take his place among the best of them.

Captains' page from the official programme.

CILL CHAINNIGH

Dathanna: Dubh is Buí
(Black and Amber)

(1) N. Ó Sceacháin
N. Skehan
(Bennettsbridge)

(2) P. Ó Lorcáin
P. Larkin
(James Stephens)

(3) N. Orr
N. Orr
(Fenians, Johnstown)

(4) P. Ó Cuilinn
P. Cullen
(Bennettsbridge)

(5) P. Ó Leathlobhair
P. Lawlor
(Bennettsbridge)

(6) P. Mac Einrí
P. Henderson
(Fenians, Johnstown)

(7) B. Mac Óda
B. Cody
(James Stephens)

(8) L. Ó Briain
L. O'Brien
(James Stephens)

(9) P. Ó Cuimín
F. Cummins
(Blackrock, Cork)

(10) C. Ó Duinn
C. Dunne
(Mooncoin)

(11) P. Ó Dúláinne (Capt.)
P. Delaney
(Fenians, Johnstown)

(12) P. Ó Bruadair
P. Broderick
(Fenians, Johnstown)

(13) M. Ó Crotaigh
M. Crotty
(James Stephens)

(14) S. Ó Loingsigh
J. Lynch
(Mooncoin)

(15) M. Ó Braonáin
M. Brennan
(Castlecomer)

Fir Ionaid: (16) M. Ó Mórdha (M. Moore, James Stephens); (17) P. Ó Diolúin (P. Dillon, St. Lachtans); (18) M. Ó Cuagáin (M. Coogan, Castlecomer); (19) S. Cinsealach (J. Kinsella, Bennettsbridge); (20) S. Mac Cuag (S. Cooke, St. Senans); (21) L. Ó hAirt (L. Hart, Galmoy).

CILL CHAINNIGH	Cúil	Cúilíní	Seachaí	70 sl.	Saor-Phocanna
1adh Leath (1st Half)					
2adh Leath (2nd Half)					
Iomlán (Total)					

LUIMNEACH

Dathanna: Glas is Bán
(Green and White)

(1) S. Ó hArgáin
S. Horgan
(Tournafulla)

(2) L. Ó Mórdha
W. Moore
(Doon)

(3) P. Ó hArtagáin
P. Hartigan
(South Liberties)

(4) S. Ó Briain
J. O'Brien
(Bruree)

(5) P. Bennis
P. Bennis
(Patrickswell)

(6) E. Ó Criagáin
E. Cregan
(Claughaun)

(7) S. Ó Foghlú
J. Foley
(Patrickswell)

(8) R. Bennis
R. Bennis
(Patrickswell)

(9) E. Ó Greacháin (Capt.)
E. Grimes
(South Liberties)

(10) L. Ó Donnchú
L. O'Donoghue
(Mungret)

(11) M. Ó Dúllaing
M. Dowling
(Kilmallock)

(12) B. Ó hArtagáin
B. Hartigan
(Old Christians)

(13) P. Ó Nualláin
F. Nolan
(Patrickswell)

(14) E. Ó Riamhaigh
E. Rea
(Faughs, Áth Cliath)

(15) S. Mac Cionaoith
J. McKenna
(South Liberties)

Fir Ionaid: (16) S. Ó Dónail (J. O'Donnell, Doon); (17) T. Ó Riain (T. Ryan, Ballybrown); (18) S. Allis (J. Allis, Doon); (19) P. Mac Muiris (P. Fitzmaurice, Killeedy); (20) A. Donnuartaigh (A. Dunworth, Claughaun); (21) S. Ó hOgáin (J. Hogan, Claughaun).

LUIMNEACH	Cúil	Cuilíní	Seachaí	70 sl.	Saor-Phocanna
1adh Leath (1st Half)					
2adh Leath (2nd Half)					
Iomlán (Total)					

1973 Keeping the Dream Alive

The men behind the cameras at the 1973 All Ireland Hurling Final.

1973 Keeping the Dream Alive

1973 Keeping the Dream Alive

The Kilkenny team that st
Back (L-R): Nicky Orr, Phil Cullen, Brian Cody
Front (L-R): Paddy Broderick, Pat Lawlor, Mick 'Cloney' Brennan, Liam

All Ireland Hurling Final.
...n, Mick Crotty, Frank Cummins and Jim Lynch.
...en, Pat Delaney (Capt.), Noel Skehan, Claus Dunne and Phil 'Fan' Larkin.

The Cups
(GAA Family Silver, Humphrey Kelleher - published in 2013)

Liam MacCarthy Cup

The Liam MacCarthy Cup is without doubt one of Irish sport's most famous trophies and has been presented to the winners of the All Ireland Senior Hurling Championship since 1921. Modelled on the ancient Irish mether (a drinking vessel), it is instantly recognisable, it has inspired some of the nation's most memorable sporting occasions and it has been presented to many of hurling's greatest players.

Like its football counterpart the Sam Maguire Cup, it has a strong connection to London and the GAA scene in the British capital. Liam MacCarthy was born in London on May 21, 1853, of Irish parents Eoghan and Brigid who had arrived from Ballygarvan, Co Cork two years earlier. He grew up in Peckham in a close-knit Irish community and in a home where Irish was the first language. At over six feet and weighing 18 stone, MacCarthy was a keen athlete and developed a passionate interest in Gaelic games and a love of hurling in particular. He regularly practised his stick and ball skills on Clapham Common.

After leaving school Liam spent some time earning his living as a blacksmith's hammer man working on the railways. In 1875, at the age of 22, he married Alice Padbury and went to work in her father's cardboard box business. Having served his apprenticeship there he then set up his own business called William MacCarthy and Sons Cardboard Boxes in Peckham which proved to be a very successful enterprise.

A prosperous businessman, Liam MacCarthy channelled much of his energy and profits into Irish causes. He became heavily involved in GAA circles in the city, served as the first treasurer of the London County Board, and later was chairman for 10 years. He also acted as vice-president of the Gaelic League. MacCarthy was a fervent Catholic and a teetotaller, and he championed Irish causes at a time when it was not always safe to do so. His home often became a halfway house for Irish emigrants when they arrived in England. In 1921, together with his sons William and Eugene, Liam paid £50 (current value: €7,800) to purchase 10 certificates in the Irish Loan set up by Michael Collins. When the loan was redeemed Liam used the money to buy a cup based on an ancient Gaelic design. It was made by Edmund Johnson Jewellers of Grafton Street in Dublin. The cup was offered to the Central Council of the GAA with the intention of awarding it to the winners of the All Ireland Senior Hurling Championship. Liam MacCarthy died in London on 28 September , 1928. The pitch in Ballygarvan, Co Cork was named in his honour in 1984.

The first six Liam MacCarthy Cup finals were won by six different counties – Limerick, Kilkenny, Galway, Dublin, Tipperary and Cork. The GSWR Cup, donated by the Great Southern and Western Rail company, preceded the MacCarthy Cup and Johnny Leahy, as Tipperary captain in 1916 and 1925, was the only man to lift both cups. Limerick were the first winners of the Liam MacCarthy Cup. They won the 1921 final, which was played on March 4, 1923, by beating Dublin 8-5 to 3-2. The first captain to receive the cup was Bob McConkey who scored four goals for Limerick in that final. In 1992, as a result of wear and tear, the first Liam MacCarthy Cup was replaced and a replica was commissioned by the GAA. It was created by goldsmith James Kelly in Kilkenny. The last captain to be presented with the original cup was Tipperary's Declan Carr in 1991 and the first player to receive the new one was Liam Fennelly of Kilkenny in 1992.

The original Liam MacCarthy Cup is now in the GAA Museum in Croke Park.

Michael Slattery

Slattery was Man of The Match (Evening Herald, 4 July 1973)

Judging by the explosive opening to last Sunday's blood-curdling Munster Championship semi-final in Limerick (Tipperary and Cork), the man who may have been directly responsible for preventing it from developing into another nasty blood-bath was referee Michael Slattery whose positive action during those opening minutes had the desired effect of upsetting whatever plans some of the contestants may have had of dragging the game into further disrepute.

Indeed, even after making it quite clear that he would NOT stand for any nonsense, or more to the point dirt, referee Slattery still had his hands full in maintaining law and order. But he did so in such a manner that one could not help but admire the courage and guts by which he delivered his findings, and while always appearing to have the game under his control, he was, on the other hand, not overpowering in his sense of fair play.

Munster Final Preview (Limerick Leader, 28 July 1973)

Finally, let us hope that it will be a contest in keeping with the great occasion it is. Both sides should play their part in helping Clare referee Michael Slattery make this as enjoyable and sporting an affair as was the Tipp-Cork game. Certainly it is gratifying that a man of Slattery's calibre will be in charge. Both sides can expect a perfectly fair deal.

First for Michael (Irish Press, 15 August 1973)

Michael Slattery, of Clare, will referee the All Ireland senior hurling final between Kilkenny and Limerick on 2 September. Limerick's Seán O'Connor will have charge of the minor final, in which Galway will play Kilkenny.

Slattery has been in the top flight of referees for the past few years, but this will be his first All Ireland senior final. Coincidentally, 2 September is also his 36th birthday.

A native of Clarecastle, he has been prominently identified with GAA activities since boyhood. He his been actively associated with referees' courses at national, provincial and club level, is on the Clare County Board's Disciplinary Committee and is one of the driving forces behind the Clarecastle Club. O'Connor is another established knight of the whistle and controlled the Kilkenny-Cork senior final in 1969.

Michael Slattery - Some QUESTIONS and ANSWERS (Limerick Heroes)

Q. What chance did you give the Limerick team to win the All Ireland at the beginning of the year?

A. Little chance. The controversy regarding team selection and team trainer seemed to the outsider a formula for failure. The fact that the team surmounted these divisive attitudes is an indication of the wonderful leadership, sincerity and dedication, of all involved in getting Limerick to the top of the hurling world.

Q. What did you think of their performance in the Munster final?

A. Good, but not great. Some obvious weaknesses and some unfit players. One always had the feeling that the power hurling of Kilkenny would again prevail, as the Munster standard seemed low.

All Ireland Hurling Final
(Limerick Leader, 3 September 1973)
Super Show by Limerick
Fitting Champions of Ireland
Kilkenny Overpowered in Thriller

By Cormac Liddy

Limerick 1-21
Kilkenny 1-14

Seldom, if ever, can a team of champions have been battered to such total submission as were Kilkenny in Sunday's superb All Ireland senior hurling championship final. A fantastic display thrilled thousands in what was surely one of the greatest sporting triumphs ever by any Limerick team in any code. The blistering pace set and maintained by Limerick was a revelation as the side tore Kilkenny to shreds.

The ecstatic scenes at the finish were fitting evidence that Limerick were champions once again. That it had taken thirty-three years to regain the title made success all the sweeter. It was an occasion that will be remembered for ever by thousands who could hardly have anticipated such a classical performance in such conditions.

Mist and rain could have ruined the game. But Limerick, principally, and Kilkenny, also, by their total dedication and skill, made the thousands forget that they were drenched as they provided all the "goodies" which makes hurling the greatest game in the world.

This surely was a performance that stunned many by its brilliance. Granted there were times when a great deal of messing and mis-hitting was given by both sides. But taken overall this was a superb final and Limerick were worthy champions. Kilkenny, too, deserve great credit for playing their parts in making the game such a classic.

Many other champions would have resorted to destructive tactics when their "empire" came crashing down but Kilkenny, to their great credit, battled as skilfully as they were allowed right up to the end. They proved once again that when it comes to sportsmanship they are "tops."

But this was Limerick's day, and the thousands who had waited so long for the opportunity left all and sundry know just how they felt about being champions once again. Delirious scenes marked the finish as thousands raced on to the field to roar approval of a magnificent win.

Players who seemed super men only minutes before were thrown into the air like confetti by their delighted supporters, and it was a considerable time before team captain, Éamon Grimes, was able to receive the Liam MacCarthy Cup from GAA President, Dr Donal Keenan.

When he did so, the thousands went wild all over again in what must surely have been one of the most exciting victory scenes ever witnessed at the venue.

There were many who had dreamed and hoped for a Limerick win. But even the most confident could hardly have bargained for such a convincing win.

Every point of the winning margin was thoroughly deserved and, indeed, so utterly supreme were Limerick in those closing stages that Kilkenny, in the circumstances, got off lightly.

Pat Delaney, Michael Slattery and Éamon Grimes at the coin toss.

1973 Keeping the Dream Alive

A time when both teams interleaved for the presentation!

1973 Keeping the Dream Alive

Marching to their destiny behind the Artane Boys' Band.

1973 Keeping the Dream Alive

Marching away from the old Canal End and up along the Cusack Stand side.

1973 Keeping the Dream Alive

Turning towards the old Hogan Stand from the Cusack Stand.

1973 Keeping the Dream Alive

Turning towards the old Hogan Stand from the Cusack Stand.

1973 Keeping the Dream Alive

Some of Limerick's play was brilliant. More of it was splendid. Thrown in, too, was a degree of mediocrity as if to prove that this super display was, in fact, being given by men who had also to prove that it was human to err!

Taken over the eighty minutes it was brilliant stuff when one considers the atrocious conditions. Those who thought the occasion would prove too much for Limerick must have been agreeably surprised at the manner which the team knuckled down from the start. There was only the occasional sign of early nerves, and this was understandable considering the inordinate delay in getting the game under way.

But once in action Limerick sparkled. From the very throw-in the team were into their stride and when Frankie Nolan shot the opening point after little over a minute, the stage was set for the great things that were to follow.

Hurling purists will, no doubt, point to the spells of mis-hitting which afflicted both teams on occasions in their bid to lower the quality of the contest. But when the current wave of excitement dies down all will agree that in all the circumstances this was a game to rate with the very best of finals.

While Limerick won by a decisive seven-point margin in the finish the contest was a thrilling one for most of the time. Many times the sides were level - nine in all - and this all added up to make the occasion such a great one.

Throughout the field, Limerick had their stars. Some were more prominent than others but basically this was a triumph for teamwork - including selectors and trainer Mick Cregan.

Selectors, oft maligned and criticised, this time must take a major share of the credit for this glorious triumph. They were who made it all so possible . . . they gambled in converting Eamonn Rea from a full-back into a superb full-forward . . . they risked criticism, too, for taking Eamonn Cregan from the attack, but the Claughaun man turned in a superb display at centre-back.

Trainer Mick Cregan, too, cannot be over-praised for never can a Limerick team have been so well prepared for a major occasion. It was a fantastic experience to see they were bursting with action and it was this all-out activity throughout the field which eventually beat Kilkenny into submission.

But there were times, too, when it seemed that Limerick had taken a "breather" but while some of the players seemed to be easing off there were others at the very precise time who were having their greatest moments.

Kilkenny, strong favourites, were blitzed by the end. They had striven for all their worth to remain champions, but on Sunday's display there was not a team in the country who would have beaten Limerick.

Some of the play of Limerick must rank with the greatest ever given by any team. Their teamwork was a revelation and it was stunning to watch the manner in which passes were picked up by colleagues. It was vintage stuff from a team who had all too often in the past been losers in unlucky circumstances.

It was the blend of youth and experience that won the day against a Kilkenny side that played very well and would obviously have done better if allowed to do so. But they were snuffed out of it by a truly memorable Limerick display.

By the interval, Limerick had edged into a two points lead. Five minutes after the resumption the advantage was gone, and a minute later Kilkenny were back in front again. There were many who wrote off Limerick's chances then. The early flutter of action . . . the slamming over of some of the finest scores ever seen at Croke Park or anywhere else . . . seemed as if it were all in vain as Kilkenny cut loose.

But their best was not near good enough and while many feared that Limerick would crumble, the side only then began to show their true greatness.

Joe McKenna and Phil 'Fan' Larkin in an aerial duel at the Nally Stand side.

1973 Keeping the Dream Alive

1973 Keeping the Dream Alive

Phil Bennis makes it safe as Jim O'Brien holds off Mick Crotty while Claus Dunne and Richie Bennis look on.

1973 Keeping the Dream Alive

Kilkenny had hardly time to realise they had drawn level when they were rocked utterly by a Limerick goal that Mossie Dowling at least three times attempted to hit before finally working it over the line with the considerable help of Eamonn Rea who hustled and bustled and generally spread-eagled the panicking Kilkenny defence. Those were a few great seconds as that goal became a score. It seemed like an eternity before the flag went up and even then there was the fear that somebody might have imagined the effort was illegal. It was not, of course, but it was the type of score that gave rise for doubt . . . such great pulling, pushing and enthusiasm went on.

Jim O'Brien on defensive duty against Kilkenny duo Claus Dunne (left) and Mick Crotty (right).

That was a scene that typified the game. Full-blooded wholehearted manly stuff and the type of stuff that hurling is all about.

But there was the pure, wholesome, and brilliant stuff, too. Who will forget those superb points by Eamonn Rea? Who could not have marvelled at the individual moments of brilliance of certain players? But when all is said and done who is likely to forget the all-round brilliance of red-haired Richie Bennis. This truly was his day . . . the match in which he stamped his claim as being what I described him some few short years ago . . . "The Mackey of the Seventies."

Some of his scores were incredible. In such atrocious conditions it was amazing and breathtaking how he managed all those scores.

His display was truly superb . . . the points, the solo runs and his obvious . . . "anything you can do I can do better" reaction to Pat Delaney and Liam O'Brien's similar efforts for Kilkenny were the gems that delighted the thousands.

Take, too, the utter and positive brilliance of my man of the match, Seán Foley. His crisp striking, his speed in winning the races for possession, his catching and his supreme lengthy clearances stamped his display as one to rate with the finest ever given by a Limerick half-back . . . and that is some praise when one remembers the brilliant half-backs down the years.

Eamonn Rea in a battle for possession with Kilkenny full back Nicky Orr.

1973 Keeping the Dream Alive

With the aid of his defence, Noel Skehan comes to collect the ball under the shadow of the Cusack Stand, leaving Eamonn Rea, Bernie Hartigan and Frankie Nolan in his wake.

1973 Keeping the Dream Alive

"They shall not pass" Mick Crotty's shot is blocked by Eamonn Cregan and Pat Hartigan while Jim Lynch looks on.

Éamon Grimes plays a captain's part in front of the Cusack Stand.

Goalkeeper, Séamus Horgan, made two super-saves when deflecting two almost sure goals over for points. These must have spurred on his colleagues, many of whom must, deep down, have been apprehensive about the occasion being a bit too much for him. But those nerves shown against Clare were well and truly gone out of his system. Now, Limerick have again the greatest goalie in the land . . . following on the famous ones of Jim Hogan, Paddy Scanlan and the others. For thousands, the display of corner back, Jim O'Brien, will be the highlight. He was rampant and completely the master of Mick Crotty, one of the game's greatest corner attackers of the present time. His clearances were powerful, his close marking a feature, and his overall steadiness and skill was a major contribution in the win.

A highlight of the game was the stirring duel between two of the greatest hurlers of modern time, Eamonn Cregan and Pat Delaney. Both were stars, whose deeds will long remain a joyful memory. Cregan lashed out some tremendous clearances. He also found time to cover up momentary gaps when his colleagues had done their work in other areas and his performance was that of the Cregan we all know but had not seen for a long time. He was a centre-back supreme and his clashes with Delaney were such to make one wonder and marvel at. How two men could have torn into each other and given and taken such hard knocks without an untoward or unsporting moment is amazing.

Supporters using umbrellas, hats and makeshift headgear to fend off the rain at Croke Park.

Delaney showed that he is a forward supreme. His cheeky solo runs when the tide was running against him were wonderful and it was no fault of Delaney's that Kilkenny parted with their title.

The other Kilkenny forwards had individual happy moments but generally their attack was well mastered. Pat Hartigan was outstanding at full-back and completely dominated his area. His lengthy clearances frequently turned threatening danger into menacing attacks at the other end of the field where Kilkenny were over-worked throughout.

Limerick's Goal...despite the pile up in the Kilkenny goal-mouth, Limerick's Mossie Dowling, on the ground, manages to poke the ball over the line for a goal.

Sunday was a day apart for Limerick in another sense, too. All too often in the past big games have been lost through failure to make an essential switch. This time towering Joe McKenna was faring brilliantly against Fran Larkin but inside Pat Henderson was having a stormer at centre-back for the champions. But whereas in the past Limerick would have allowed things run their course they took positive and decisive action this time. They moved McKenna in on top of Henderson and this considerably reduced the effectiveness of the centre-back. Now he had to cope with McKenna instead of bursting out of defence and making light of the Limerick attack.

Granted, the switch also, in one way deprived McKenna of achieving more wonders in the corner but the fact that he subdued Henderson and still managed to be quite a force as an attacker put McKenna high on the list of Limerick heroes.

Phil Bennis got through a great amount of work in the Limerick defence. He found Paddy Broderick and others quite a force but generally he emerged on the credit side.

It would be remiss of me were I not to compliment Willie Moore, also, on what was a solid overall display. Occasionally, he was rounded by Mick Brennan and a few of the others, and fear gripped every Limerick supporter as Kilkennymen, as a result, raced towards goal. But most times a colleague was present to cut off or blunt the danger, and on occasion points were conceded when goals looked sure for Kilkenny.

Richie Bennis had his greatest day. But Éamon Grimes, too, hurled himself into history with some great striking. He must have covered miles of ground by his roaming tactics. His fast striking ground play was often a feature, and while there were occasions on which he messed too much, generally his overall performance was in keeping with the high standard which he has set himself.

Kilkenny midfielders, Liam O'Brien and Frank Cummins, could hardly have bargained for the strength of the Limerick pair, and while the two Kilkenny men also shone, the Limerick two achieved most to a far more obvious degree. It was the ability of Bennis and Grimes to always be in the thick of things that eventually wore Kilkenny down.

It was truly astonishing how Kilkenny had so little to offer in the closing stages. At that stage, Limerick did just as they pleased and they picked off a succession of delightful scores.

Hero of the attack was without question the sturdy Eamonn Rea. His full-forward display was again a revelation and was easily on a par with the brilliance shown against Tipperary in the Munster final. In retrospect one can only wonder at how a player of forward talent was allowed to wallow and struggle in defence for so long.

His two points were absolute beauties. Each time his hand went up to catch, a quick turn, and then a flashy shot over the bar. Truly a sight to watch but so was his entire performance and he caused havoc for Nicky Orr and the other Kilkenny backs.

He put in a tremendous eighty minutes of solid, spectacular play. Only a fraction behind him in my mind was Frankie Nolan who reached such heights as he brushed and otherwise harassed Kilkenny men aside as he had one of his finest games.

Another who got through an amount of work was Liam O'Donoghue whose clever running into position for passes from his colleagues was wonderful. He achieved a great amount of work and while he wasn't scoring too great an amount he created the opportunities for a number of the others.

Those who doubted the ability of Joe McKenna were answered in no uncertain terms. The former Offaly man was outstanding.

★ The contrasting feelings of Kilkenny full-back, Nicky Orr, and Limerick full-forward, Ned Rea, can be seen in their faces as the umpire prepares to raise the green flag for one of Limerick's goals.

From the 1974 Our Games Annual.

1973 Keeping the Dream Alive

Excited supporters spill out from Hill 16 anticipating the final whistle and a moment of history.

1973 Keeping the Dream Alive

"It's Ours!" Ecstatic Limerick supporters pour onto the pitch from the Cusack Stand at the final whistle, The time is 4:58PM.

1973 Keeping the Dream Alive

1973 Keeping the Dream Alive

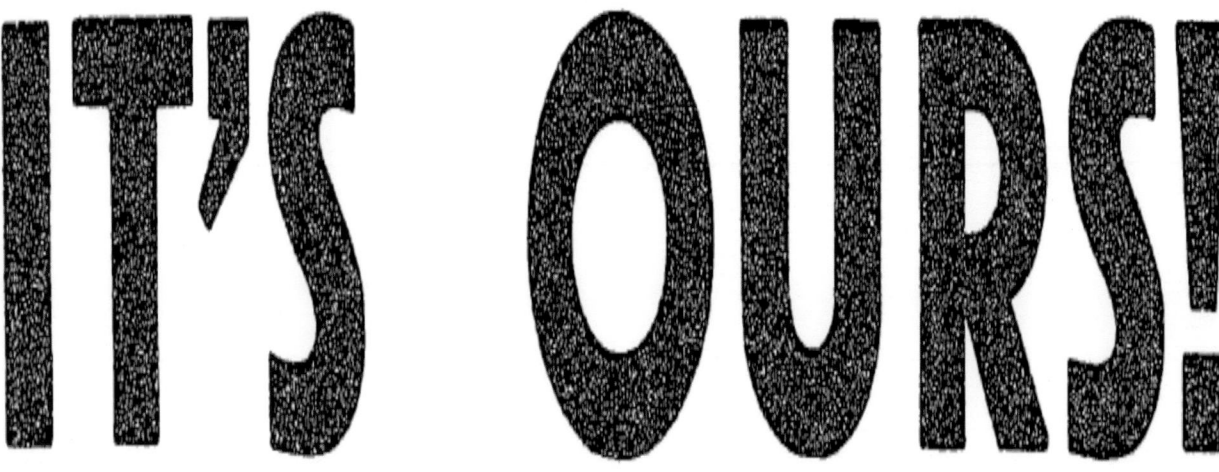

The other members of the Limerick side, Mossie Dowling and Bernie Hartigan, tried extremely hard. While some might be tempted to criticise, the two of them worked very hard, and while both often achieved more, their effectiveness this time also played a part in the win. Hartigan was replaced late in the game by Ryan, but by then victory was almost secured.

Those who had been advocating ground hurling as a formula for Limerick success must have been even more delighted than others. This time the team played more of the typical Limerick brand of hurling, and that the county are the champions now can in a big way be attributed to this tactic.

Kilkenny also had their stars. Two of them stood out more than the others; goal-keeper. Noel Skehan, and centre-back, Pat Henderson, until he himself was curbed by the appearance of McKenna. Skehan made a couple of fantastic saves . . . one from Mossie Dowling and another from Rea immediately spring to mind. Frequently he raced out of his goal in possession, and this was a stirring achievement when one considers the close attention he was getting from Rea and company.

Brian Cody, Liam O'Brien, Claus Dunne and Mick Crotty all did well.

But it was Limerick's day of glory, and rightly, we will be talking and reading about it for many a day . . . we waited long enough for the opportunity to do so.

Scorers

Limerick - R. Bennis 0-10 (0-8 frees); E. Grimes 0-4, M. Dowling 1-1; F. Nolan and E. Rea 0-2; J. McKenna and B. Hartigan 0-1.

Kilkenny - C. Dunne 0-7 frees; P. Delaney 1-2; M. Crotty and L. O'Brien 0-2; M. Brennan 0-1.

Teams

Limerick - S. Horgan; W. Moore, P. Hartigan, J. O'Brien; P. Bennis, E. Cregan, S. Foley; R. Bennis, E. Grimes (Capt); L. O'Donoghue, M. Dowling, B. Hartigan; F. Nolan, E. Rea, J. McKenna. Subs: T. Ryan for B. Hartigan.

Kilkenny - N. Skehan; P. Larkin, N. Orr, P. Cullen; P. Lalor, P. Henderson, B. Cody; F. Cummins, L. O'Brien; C. Dunne, P. Delaney (C), P. Broderick; M. Crotty, J. Lynch, M. Brennan. Subs. K. Purcell for Broderick, W. Harte for Cummins, J. Kinsella for Lynch.

Referee - Michael Slattery (Clare).

Séamus Horgan being chaired off the pitch after the final whistle.

1973 Keeping the Dream Alive

A section of the crowd looking at the presentation in the Hogan Stand.

1973 Keeping the Dream Alive

"We did it!" A jubilant Pat Hartigan celebrates a famous victory.

1973 Keeping the Dream Alive

1973 Keeping the Dream Alive

Victorious Captain Éamon Grimes leads the famous climb up the steps of the Hogan stand.

1973 Keeping the Dream Alive

Mossie Dowling, Frankie Nolan and Bernie Hartigan follow Éamon Grimes up the steps.

1973 Keeping the Dream Alive

1973 Keeping the Dream Alive

Andy Dunworth follows Jim Hogan (in tracksuit), Mossie Dowling, Frankie Nolan and Bernie Hartigan.

1973 All Ireland Winning Speech

Micheál O'Hehir: Twenty four points to seventeen; one goal and twenty one points to Limerick, one fourteen… and Limerick are the champions, and just look…just look at it.

Well, after a wait since nineteen hundred and forty, we have Limerick the All Ireland champions, the worthy All Ireland champions, after a truly memorable game. The day was atrocious, it's pouring rain still, but just look here in the centre of the field where everyone seems to have gathered, every Limerick player being carried shoulder high and I think if Limerick men had an extra pair of shoulders they'd put Richie Bennis up there on top and just in under him they'd put Eamonn Cregan, and not far away they'd put Eamonn Rea and, ah look, you could go through the whole lot of them. Seán Foley, Éamon Grimes, the whole lot of them.

Shades of old decency you might say, shades of the past have come to Croke Park today, as Limerick after so long have won this title. Nineteen forty, well it's thirty three years ago, and there we are, the team that two years ago almost beat Tipperary in Killarney, and everybody said that when they were beaten the following year that that was the end of Limerick. But back they've come and what a brilliant performance they have put up today. And let nobody take away from this victory. True, Kilkenny were short some of their stars, but the way Limerick played, stars or no stars, Limerick are the worthy champions of this day, this September Sunday in 1973.

Here comes the hush…who cares about president's speeches when you have won the All Ireland after 33 years of waiting? Wait 'till you hear the silence when Éamon Grimes comes up on the podium.

GAA President: …*ba mhaith liomsa an corn seo a bhronnadh ar chaptaen Luimnigh*, Éamon Grimes.

Micheál O'Hehir: And now Éamon Grimes at the microphone. You don't have to be a president, just a captain to get silence.

Legendary RTÉ sports commentator Micheál O'Hehir.

Éamon Grimes: A Uachtaráin, a chathaoirligh, a dhaoine uaisle, Is mór an onóir domsa a bheith anseo inniu, mar chaptaen an fhoireann iontach seo. Ba mhaith liom buíochas a ghabháil do gach duine a chabhraigh linn chun an corn seo a rugadh thar n-ais got dtí Contae Luimnigh. Ba mhaith liom freisin bualadh bos a ghabháil do Chontae Chill Chainnigh a d'imríodar go h-an mhaith ar fad.

Mr President, Reverend fathers, ladies and gentlemen, it's a great privilege for me as captain of this great Limerick team to bring the MacCarthy Cup back to Limerick for the first time in 33 years. In doing so I'd like to thank each and every one that helped to bring it back, and I'd like to pay a special tribute to Kilkenny for a very sporting game.

Rita and Erskine Childers (President of Ireland), as well as Tom O'Donnell (Fine Gael TD), look on as Éamon Grimes makes his acceptance speech.

Now three cheers for Kilkenny: Hip, Hip Hurray; Hip, Hip Hurray; Hip, Hip Hurray.

And, also, three cheers for yourselves: Hip, Hip Hurray; Hip, Hip Hurray; Hip, Hip Hurray.

Micheál O'Hehir: There you have it, one of the most exciting scenes that has ever been my privilege or anyone else's privilege to see in Croke Park or anywhere else. The whole county of Limerick seemed to erupt in glorious victory for a glorious hurling team.

And as somebody wrote somewhere during the week, gone will be the talk of the Mackeys, not that they weren't and aren't great, now the children will talk of the Bennises, they'll talk of the Hartigans, they'll talk of the Cregans, with the same reverence with which they have spoken of the Mackeys, the Ryans, and all the others of the great glorious hurling past of Limerick.

Well, the Limerick crowd, I don't think they'll let the Limerick team go down into the crowd or maybe they will. The crowd are going back down, ah heaven help the steps, and in a matter of seconds they are going to go up in the air again, and they'll be up in the air for the next month I'd say after this.

The exuberant Limerick crowd on Hill 16 look on at the presentation in the Hogan Stand.

1973 Keeping the Dream Alive

The Limerick players relax before the presentation.

1973 Keeping the Dream Alive

The Limerick players in the forefront with GAA president Donal Keenan and Taoiseach Liam Cosgrave in the background.

1973 Keeping the Dream Alive

1973 Keeping the Dream Alive

Teammates and dignitaries look on with interest as Limerick captain Éamon Grimes makes his acceptance speech.

1973 Keeping the Dream Alive

1973 Keeping the Dream Alive

"*And, also, three cheers for yourselves: Hip, Hip Hurray; Hip, Hip Hurray; Hip, Hip Hurray.*"

1973 Keeping the Dream Alive

351

1973 Keeping the Dream Alive

We are the champions!

The Check Suits of 1973

By Joe Carrig

Growing up in our house in the sixties and early seventies, we would have been influenced a lot by Kerry football, with our father being a Kerry man. My earliest memory of Croke Park was going up to watch Kerry and Offaly in the 1972 replayed final which Offaly won, driven on by the iron man from Rhode, Paddy McCormack.

At this time my brother Tommy was playing for the Limerick footballers. My father always spoke about Paddy Scanlan, Jackie Power, the Mackeys and that started me following Limerick hurling. In the late sixties, Shannon Airport Free Zone was starting up and factories were offering houses to anyone who would relocate to work and live there. My brothers, John and Paddy, came back from Ellesmere Port in Liverpool to work in the Lana Knit clothing factory, with both being founding members of the Wolfe Tones GAA club in Shannon too.

John later became Vice Chairman of the Limerick County Board and Chairman of the West board. When Limerick won the All Ireland in 1973, we followed them to all the matches. The Munster semi-final win over Clare first. We will never forget Richie Bennis winning Munster with the last puck of the game! Then onto Ennis for the All Ireland semi-final against London a week later. And so we were in the All Ireland final against that great Kilkenny team. Tickets were sourced from the usual people after a lot of asking and begging, and with tickets in hand, we planned our weekend.

At this time, I was playing under age with Askeaton and two friends of mine on the team - Davey Barrett who is an older brother of eighties Limerick footballer Paddy, and my neighbour Michael Ryan - and I decided to go up for the weekend. We booked a BandB off O'Connell Street and the train to Heuston Station. The excitement was unreal. A few days before the game my brother John made three green and white check suits for us, with material donated by Lana Knit. So with these, and crepe paper hats in hand, we set out for Dublin.

After booking in to the BandB we decided to stroll along O'Connell Street dressed in our green and white suits, where we were set upon by a gang of Dublin "youths" who were intent on relieving us of our prized possession.

Thankfully, a decent Dublin man intervened and advised us to take off the suits until match day when there would be thousands of our fellow county men around, which we did.

Sunday, of course, was milling down rain but we didn't care. Michael Ryan thought better of donning the suit so it was left to Davey and myself to wear the colours. Our tickets were for Hill 16, so after eyeing a good vantage spot we got lifted up on the roof of a concrete building, and what with the dye from the paper hats running down our faces, and getting soaked from the rain, we had a ball.

When the final whistle blew we got onto the hallowed Field of Dreams, to watch our heroes lift the Liam MacCarthy cup. Something that I always remember to this day is Noel Skehan going ballistic when a Limerick supporter said something to him about Mossie Dowling and that famous goal.

The train journey back to Limerick will live long in the memory: many songs were sung and stories told about past glories, and we were so proud when a brother of Richie and Phil Bennis shook our hands and thanked us for wearing those now famous green and white suits.

P.S. The 'winning' suits survived at home for a goodly number of years after 1973 but were eventually thrown out without anyone first telling me. A piece of sporting history that would otherwise have been forgotten totally if it weren't for that seminal photograph after the final whistle. Ireland in the old days wasn't always just black and white!

The men in the check suits are (L-R) Michael Ryan (no suit), Joe Carrig (suit) and Davey Barrett (suit).

Limerick At Long Last
(Irish Press, 3 September 1973)
Brilliant Bennis Breaks Kilkenny

By Pádraig Puirséal

Limerick 1-21
Kilkenny 1-14

Amidst scenes of enthusiasm that far surpass anything I have seen in a hurling final in recent years, the All Ireland title and the Liam MacCarthy Cup were won back by Limerick at rain soaked Croke Park yesterday for the first time since 1940, and seldom can the honours and the trophy have been so magnificently and so deservedly earned.

Producing sustained and sometimes inspiring spells of swift, stylish and betimes brilliant hurling, under what were the worst possible conditions of constant rain, slippery sod, and greasy ball, the dashing Munstermen rocked Kilkenny's champions back on their heels from the opening whistle, twice came from behind to peg back the Noresiders, when the holders seemed to be regaining their poise, and they had really taken command midway through the second half, confidently romped to victory in the closing stages.

Fast, fiery and resolute, this was a Limerick team playing Limerick hurling at its effective best, and no wonder their faithful supporters, starved of victory for three and thirty years, had spilled over from the stands and were swarming along the touchlines minutes before the final whistle.

No wonder, too, that, in their delirium of joy those happy Limerick followers swamped television cameras and Garda cordons alike, as they massed in front of the Hogan Stand rostrum to see the Cup presented, and inflicted on their heroes in thumps of congratulations, more punishment than many of these players had sustained in their 80 hard-fought minutes on the way to hurling glory.

Great Contest

But, fair play to Kilkenny, it takes two teams to give us hurling of the calibre we witnessed in the many superlative passages of play yesterday, and, considering the handicaps under which they entered the fray, these Noremen put up a tremendous battle in defence of their title, before the speed and power of the more virile Limerick lads finally wore them down. If Kilkenny went down, they went down like true champions with colours flying, but, from the early stages they were manifestly struggling in all too many sectors.

Just the same, with Claus Dunne taking over Eddie Keher's customary free-taking duties with considerable success, the holder's mentors must have felt reasonably content when they saw their men had contained, even if precariously enough, the fire and fury of Limerick's opening onslaught.

There were times early on when the Shannonsiders, sweeping down on the Railway Goal, seemed certain to swamp Kilkenny in a tidal wave of green jerseys. But, in their eagerness, the Munster champions at this stage tended to concede unnecessary frees both back and forward.

Early Goal

Dunne's pointed frees kept Kilkenny in touch and then, just at the end of the first quarter, when the Mooncoinman show low from an award on the 21, the sliothar rebounded to Mick Crotty, whose drive rebounded again to his captain Pat Delaney who slammed home a goal to leave Kilkenny ahead 1-3 to 0-5 at the end of the very first quarter. That was the period their advisers had worried most about in their pre-match calculations.

But though Dunne promptly pointed another Noreside free it was Limerick who, steadying up as the game progressed, now began to play with greater precision and purpose. A switch which sent tall Joe McKenna to centre-forward and Mossie Dowling to the left-corner nullified some of the dominance that Pat Henderson had been exercising at centre-back for Kilkenny.

Under pressure, the Kilkenny defenders began to concede frees, all of which Richie Bennis gratefully pointed to put Limerick back in the lead, and though Crotty, now on the wing, brought the holders level again twice in succession, Limerick were getting on top at midfield where Bernie Hartigan had now moved in a switch with his captain Éamon Grimes and the challengers deservedly led at the interval by 0-12 to 1-7.

A thunderous roar greeted the appearance of Kieran Purcell at left full forward for Kilkenny on the restart, with Mick Brennan now on the right wing, Dunne on the left and Crotty returned to the right corner.

Eamonn Cregan fends off Kilkenny's Mick Brennan while Phil Bennis looks on.

The men in black and amber went swarming to the attack and after Dunne shot low from a close free, he promptly pointed another and (Liam) 'Chunky' O'Brien, on a sparkling run from midfield, balanced scores at 0-12 to 1-9 with five second-half minutes gone.

Then in a three-minute spell, the All Ireland Senior Hurling title of 1973 was won and lost.

More Cohesion

Kilkenny, playing with far more cohesion at this stage, came back on the attack. Frank Cummins came rampaging through from midfield and placed Crotty, who cut through the defence for a seemingly certain goal. But the James Stephens man chose to palm the ball to the gaping Limerick net. In some miraculous fashion goalkeeper Séamus Horgan managed to turn the leather over the bar. Thus, Kilkenny were ahead, but only by a point instead of by a goal, and, inside 90 seconds, Richie Bennis had levelled scores once more for a free awarded when he was fouled on a solo run.

For the first and only time in the game goal man Noel Skehan's puck-out fell short, to Limerick half-forward Liam O'Donoghue, who lobbed in a high shot. Skehan saved almost on his goal-line but was promptly submerged in a forward rush in which Mossie Dowling had the major part, though Eamonn Rea may also have got a touch to the ball in the goal-line melee.

At once, Bernie Hartigan belted over a point, Limerick were four points clear inside a minute, took fire in every sector of the field, and though there were 31 minutes still to go never again looked in any danger of defeat.

True, there was a kick left in Kilkenny yet. Dunne, with two points from frees, cut the margin back to the half-time deficit of two points, but Limerick were soon back in full cry, and sailing points from far out by Bennis and Grimes really ended Kilkenny's bid at the end of the third quarter.

Lead Stretched

From there on with Grimes and Bennis rampant in a midfield area from which Frank Cummins had retired, the only question still to be answered was the extent of Limerick's winning margin. Kilkenny still had a fair share of the play, but Dunne, by necessity, was now shooting for goals from his frees, and, hard though he tried, could not get them through the packed Limerick goalmouth.

Though the dogged black and amber defence never capitulated, Limerick stretched the lead point by point, and the honours had been well won before O'Brien closed the scoring with a Kilkenny point off the second-last puck of the game.

So Limerick are All Ireland champions again, and, no matter from what aspect you look at it, that must give a tremendous fillip to the game not alone by Shannonside but all over Ireland. It is a long overdue and richly merited reward for these hurlers who have been promising so much ever since they first started to come to the fore around 1966 and who had thus far achieved comparatively little.

But yesterday's victory compensated players, officials and supporters alike and this seventh All Ireland title will be possibly brighter than any of the previous ones in Limerick's hurling crown because its arrival was so eagerly awaited and so long delayed.

Over the 80 minutes, every Limerick player was at some stage or other a hero yesterday. Séamus Horgan, though never unduly troubled, can be thanked for that fantastic save from Crotty. Pat Hartigan enhanced his claims to being the best full-back in the game, while his flankers Willie Moore and Jim O'Brien gave nothing at all away.

Vital Foundation

Eamonn Cregan, after being slipped by Paddy Delaney several times early on, fully justified his switch to centre-back with some brilliant work back later while Seán Foley and Phil Bennis gave no freedom to a variety of Kilkenny wingers. The foundations of this victory were, however, laid at midfield where the tireless Grimes gave his side the captain's lead I had expected of him, and the deadly accurate Richie Bennis has rarely if ever played better than he did in the second half.

Though all the Limerick forwards had their moments, the most constant threat was provided by converted defender Eamonn Rea, who shot two good points, had a hand in the goal, and earned several close frees which Bennis duly converted. The rest all played their part and some of their passing was admirable.

As for Kilkenny, they were well and truly beaten in the end, but one imagines that this set-back is unlikely to affect them unduly. It was not their day, and even at full strength one wonders if they would have held Limerick yesterday. Noel Skehan in goal, without a doubt, saved them from a heavier defeat.

Many Gaps

Pat Henderson and Pat Lawlor performed heroically in the half-back line, but there were too many gaps elsewhere for them to stop them all. The strength of Eamonn Rea made life difficult for Nicky Orr, and Brian Cody lacked the experience as yet for such an ordeal. Phil Cullen and (Phil) 'Fan' Larkin, however, battled manfully in the corner-back positions.

Greatest disappointment for Kilkenny supporters must have been at midfield, where Liam O'Brien and Frank Cummins were rarely in the picture and never with any consistency. O'Brien, however, may well have been upset by a nose injury sustained right at the opening throw-in, while Cummins, never the force he can be, had to retire mid-way through the second half.

Up front, Pat Delaney threatened more than he managed to achieve, Dunne was accurate from the frees, Crotty and Brennan had their moments but Lynch was unable to make any impact on Pat Hartigan, and the sending in of the great-hearted Kieran Purcell only served to emphasise the old sporting adage that a mediocre player fully fit is far more effective than an unfit star.

Finally, it was a great day for Limerick, a great day for the hurling game, and considering the fight the seniors put up, and the victory, however lucky, of the minors, not all that bad a day for Kilkenny either.

Scorers

Limerick - R Bennis 0-10; M. Dowling 1-1 and E. Grimes 0-4; F. Nolan and E. Rea 0-2; J. McKenna and B. Hartigan 0-1.

Kilkenny - C. Dunne 0-7 (all frees); P. Delaney 1-1; M. Crotty 0-3; L. O'Brien 0-2; M. Brennan 0-1.

Teams

Limerick - S. Horgan; W. Moore, P. Hartigan, J. O'Brien; P. Bennis, E. Cregan, S. Foley; R. Bennis, E. Grimes (Capt); L. O'Donoghue, M. Dowling, B. Hartigan; F. Nolan, E. Rea, J. McKenna. Subs: T. Ryan for B. Hartigan.

Kilkenny - N. Skehan; P. Larkin, N. Orr, P. Cullen; P. Lawlor, P. Henderson, B. Cody; F. Cummins, L. O'Brien; C. Dunne, P. Delaney (C), P. Broderick; M, Crotty, J. Lynch, M. Brennan. Subs: K. Purcell for Broderick, W. Harte for Cummins and J. Kinsella for Lynch.

Referee - Michael Slattery (Clare).

1973 Keeping the Dream Alive

LIMERICK

	G	P	'70	Free	Wide
First Half	0	12	0	12	6
Second Half	1	9	1	6	6

KILKENNY

	G	P	'70	Free	Wide
First Half	1	7	1	13	5
Second Half	0	7	3	13	2

Weather to Blame

The two disappointing features of yesterday's hurling final were the weather and the attendance, both, of course, directly related. The crowd of 58,009 was the smallest to witness a senior hurling All Ireland since Tipperary defeated Galway in the final of 1958, and compares very badly indeed with the 66,137 attendance at last year's Kilkenny v Cork decider.

But then the weather must shoulder a great deal of the blame. The rain started to fall in Dublin just before noon and had been falling earlier in the South and West. The result was that while the covered stands were full the uncovered terraces were relatively thinly populated, people obviously preferring to watch the game on television to standing unprotected in the rain.

Incidentally the score, Limerick 1-21 to Kilkenny's 1-14 is by far the lowest ever in an 80-minute final and produced the fewest goals since Wexford lost to Tipperary 2-16 to 0-10 in the final of 1965.

The players attempt to go back across the field after the presentation.

All-Ireland Hurling Championships
FINALS

SUNDAY, 2nd SEPTEMBER 1973

Minor
GALWAY v KILKENNY

Referee:- S. O'CONNOR (Limerick)   1.30 p.m.

Limerick v Kilkenny

Referee:- M. SLATTERY (Clare)   3.15 p.m.

Captains

← Eamon Grimes
Limerick

PAT DELANEY
Kilkenny →

← RICHIE BENNIS
Limerick

FRANK CUMMINS
Kilkenny. →

Official Price   5p

Front cover of the pirate programme of the 1973 All Ireland Hurling Final.

Never Worried Says Winning Captain
(Cork Examiner, 3 September 1973)

Interviews by Michael Ellard

Bedlam reigned in the Limerick dressingroom when I visited it after the match. Next door all was quiet in the Kilkenny camp; but though downhearted in defeat they acknowledged that they had met their master on this occasion.

Éamon Grimes (Limerick) - "Sheer guts, determination and stamina won it for us. I was never worried during the game. The worst part was getting across to the dressing room with the cup."

Richie Bennis (Limerick) - "It was a fantastic win. We had no nerves going out to play and this meant a lot to us. It was a team effort that won it for us."

Seán Foley (Limerick) - "Our fitness was the deciding factor. We were that little bit faster and it meant the difference between victory and defeat. I was a bit worried that we might collapse when we went through a lean period after half time. Happily we got back into our stride and nothing could stop us."

Pat Hartigan (Limerick) - "Team spirit won it for us. Every man played for the man around him. I was a bit worried when Kilkenny hit back at us after the break,"

Eamonn Rea (Limerick) - "What a wonderful day for me. I thought my career was over after the National League final. Now I end up with an All Ireland medal. Fitness and spirit won it for us."

Eamonn Cregan (Limerick) - "We played as if our lives depended on it. Séamus Horgan's save from the palmed ball by Mick Crotty after half time turned the game our way. But I was only certain we would win when we were seven points up with a minute of play left."

Pat Delaney (Kilkenny) - "We were beaten by a better team. They were fitter than us and we could not contain them after Horgan saved Mick Crotty's attempt for a goal."

Noel Skehan (Kilkenny) - "It was a very good game considering the conditions. I knew a win was coming to Limerick when our lads were not scoring in the last ten minutes. Their goal was a lucky scrambled effort."

Eddie Keher (Kilkenny) - "I thought we had it won. But our bad luck was carried on in the game and the injury sustained by Frank Cummins was a major blow to our hopes."

Liam O'Brien (Kilkenny) - "Their great determination won it for them. Horgan's save from Crotty was the turning point."

Phil 'Fan' Larkin (Kilkenny) - "Make no mistake about it the better team won on the day. They were a tremendously fit and spirited side."

Paddy Grace (Kilkenny Secretary) - "Frank Cummins going off changed the match. But we have no excuses. We all knew it would be an uphill battle. It was a wonderful game and we are delighted that at last Limerick have won the All Ireland."

As The Scores Came

By Charlie Mulqueen

First Half

1 minute: Frankie Nolan weaves his way in from the right wing to flash over a glorious left-handed point. The best possible start for Limerick.

Frankie Nolan scores the first point of the All Ireland Hurling Final.

3 minutes: Kilkenny on terms; close-range free by Claus Dunne.
6 minutes: Kilkenny in front; another free by Dunne.
7 minutes: Richie Bennis makes his first impact, pointing a placed ball.
9 minutes: Limerick's class apparent as Richie Bennis places his captain, and Grimes raises Limerick cheers and hopes with a beautiful shot from a tight angle.
12 minutes: There is little the Limerick defence can do as Kilkenny corner-forward, Mick Brennan, clutches a high ball, swivels quickly and sends over the bar.
13 minutes: Big Eamonn Rea shows surprising agility for one of his size as he gets in front of the defence, grabs the ball and sends it flashing left-handed over the crossbar.

Eamonn Rea salutes the crowd after scoring a first half point.

1973 Keeping the Dream Alive

15 minutes: Joe McKenna, having a "blinder" on Fan Larkin, stretches Limerick's lead to two with a fine point.

20 minutes: A five minute gap, now, without a score and then Kilkenny grab a vital goal. Dunne's 21 yard free is blocked, but the rebound comes to Pat Delaney via Mick Crotty and the Johnstown star pulls first time to the net.

21 minutes: Kilkenny, looking good, take their point from a close-in free through Claus Dunne.

25 minutes: Bennis restores Limerick heart with a close-in free.

27 minutes: Calm and cool, Bennis sends over a free from a good fifty yards.

28 minutes: Limerick have recovered from the shock of the goal; they force another free and again Bennis taps it over.

30 minutes: Mick Crotty places Delaney, and over the bar it goes.

31 minutes: The admirable Bennis sends an 85-yard free all the way between the posts.

33 minutes: But Kilkenny are quickly on terms; Crotty this time popping over a point from a good pass by Frank Cummins.

34 minutes: It's dead-eye Richie Bennis again; his sixth point from placed balls.

35 minutes: Limerick are swinging now, and Rea shows his style in sending over a fine point.

37 minutes: Dunne points a short free.

40 minutes: Noel Skehan saves superbly from Eamonn Cregan, but Éamon Grimes bangs over the rebound to give Limerick a two point interval lead: 0-12 to 1-7.

The Half Time scoreline.

Second Half

3 minutes: Limerick are dreadfully slow to settle down and Dunne cuts the deficit with a free.

5 minutes: Midfielder Liam O'Brien levels it with a great point from the right.

6 minutes: Oh, Limerick, where are you? Why is Séamus Horgan left so uncovered as Crotty homed in on him; but the Tournafulla man arguably swings the entire issue by brilliantly turning Crotty's palmed effort over the bar.

7 minutes: Limerick are settled now, and Bennis restores equality with a point from a free.

8 minutes: A vital moment - the goal we wanted so much arrives. Skehan saves superbly from Mossie Dowling but the forwards are on him like a flash. The three full-forwards were all there but Dowling gets the credit.

The Goal!

9 minutes: The Limerick crowd are singing now, and Bernie Hartigan stretches it to four with a fine point.
11 minutes: Dunne free for Kilkenny.
17 minutes: A six minute lapse without a score, before Dunne closes it to two point with another free.
18 minutes: But Limerick aren't going to loosen their grip; Bennis again on the mark with another free.

Richie on the mark again.

20 minutes: A magnificent point by Bennis from the right wing, under pressure, and about 60 yards out.
21 minutes: Grimes with a glorious point for Limerick after a good pass from Bennis. Limerick 1-17; Kilkenny 1-12.
27 minutes: Delaney a point for Kilkenny, for whom time is now running out.
32 minutes: Limerick now enter their glory period as Grimes points.
34 minutes: Bennis, gathering infield, crashes home an absolutely superb point.
35 minutes: Limerick are now rampant and Dowling puts a point over the bar.

Mossie Dowling scores a point with a sweet ground stroke as Limerick pile on the pressure.

36 minutes: Frankie Nolan gets in on the act, pointing smartly to make the score 1-21 to 1-13, and Limerick are home and dried.
40 minutes: A final gesture from exhausted Kilkenny; a point from Liam O'Brien.
40 minutes: The final whistle blows and the Croke Park sward is engulfed in a sea of green and white. The 33 year gap was bridged. Limerick 1-21; Kilkenny 1-14.

The Full Time scoreline.

The All Ireland Final Medal (Celtic Cross)

The medals of the GAA are a mostly overlooked aspect of our Gaelic games. Competitions are won and sets of medals are given to the winners, often to the losing finalists too. Stories abound about these small but incredibly important trinkets. Who was awarded these medals? How were they passed down through the generations? Did they survive in the family of the people who originally won them? How did they avoid, or not, the melting pot? What are they worth nowadays?

Most people know a Celtic cross medal when they see one: there is no better-known or more emblematic medal in Ireland. This unique design was first observed in the mid-1890s, with the Limerick Commercials players of the winning 1896 All Ireland Football championship campaign receiving such a medal, albeit with the central harp slightly enamelled.

These early medals have "Éire" and "Gaelic Athletic Association" on their obverse (front), to be replaced in later times by "Cumann Lúth/Chleas Gael", while retaining "Éire" all through. Similar medals, although without the enamelling, were presented to the victorious hurlers of Kilfinane Emmets the following year, 1897. The engraving on their reverse (back) is almost as important, although it has been redesigned many times over the years.

In the old days this engraving was done by hand and was very skilled work. It was greatly dependent upon the expertise of the engraver and his knowledge of the language he was using. Nowadays, unfortunately, this engraving is done by machine and is not nearly as attractive as it was in earlier times. There are very few people left who can hand engrave such precious metal, especially the old Irish font seen below in the 1973 medal, Cló Gaelach.

All Ireland medals have been produced by John Miller, sometimes Lee Brothers, sometimes Hopkins and Hopkins, to the same general specification for many decades. The classic design has remained in use almost without change since the late nineteenth century. Yes, there have been minor modifications to a more sleek and corporate version in the last 35 years but it is still a distinctive and immediately recognisable medal, though the centre part of the medal has had the harp replaced with the corporate GAA logo during that time.

A smaller version of this medal is given out for U18/17 and U21/20 All Ireland competitions - some other national competitions use the same Celtic cross design, though not the club All Ireland series. All are 9 carat gold hallmarked medals, less substantial as the competition declines in relative importance. Losing All Ireland finalists in earlier times received silver hallmarked medals for a period of time, to be replaced with lesser plaques through the 1970s and later, now discontinued as far as can be ascertained.

In many ways, these medals are priceless to the people who won them but have substantial monetary value too. Keep them safe for future generations. They were hard won and must be preserved as mementos of those long-ago victories.

Front and back of 1973 All Ireland hurling championship winner's medal.

1973 Keeping the Dream Alive

Michael Martin - The Man Behind The Camera

By Michelle Martin

Michael Martin photography was established in 1954 by his father Michael Snr; Michael joined his father's business in the seventies. Prior to this, he worked as Limerick photographer with the *Irish Independent*. During that time he covered such historic occasions as the JFK, Nixon, Mohammad Ali, the President Reagan visits, and many more dignitaries and movie stars. Fondly known as Mick, he had a deep passion for sports. As a young man, he enthusiastically participated in cycling and even competed in the *Rás Tailteann*. His love for cycling persisted throughout his life. Mick also had a keen interest in GAA and was a devoted follower of Limerick hurling. In 1973, he attended the wonderful final in Croke Park between Limerick and Kilkenny. Armed with his press pass and camera, he captured as many pictures as possible that day.

Immediately after the match, he rushed back to Limerick and went straight to his darkroom. With the assistance of his late wife Toni, and his sister-in-law Elsie, Mick promptly began printing the photographs. They wasted no time and headed directly to Patrickswell, where the celebrations were in full swing. They visited Murphy's Pub (Cú Chulainn) and offered the team's print for sale. Mick printed around 70 pictures sized 20 x 16 (inches) for various pubs in Limerick and the surrounding counties, thinking it would be enough for the evening.

However, the barman at Murphy's Pub bought all 70 prints from him. Mick then called his father from a nearby phone booth, urging him to start printing more copies. Over the next two days, he sold dozens of prints to pubs, clubs, and businesses. Even after 50 years, we continue to sell these 1973 pictures to GAA enthusiasts worldwide, every time a Limerick man opens a pub, from New York to Australia.

Whether it was a portrait, a wedding, a communion or confirmation sitting, a graduation ceremony, or a group photograph, Michael's professionalism, patience, and attention to detail were always evident. He took great pride in delivering a spirit of quality and perfection. In 2014, Michael experienced the loss of his beloved Toni, his wife of 46 years. She was his main inspiration in life and career. Despite the heartache, Michael, in memory of Toni, continued to bring his photographic expertise and knowledge to the business that brought them both so much joy.

However, in 2019, Michael passed away after a brief illness, finally reuniting with his beloved Toni. The business now rests with daughter Michelle and nephew Shane. They carry on the traditions established by Michael and his father over the years at their photographic studio on Upper Gerald Griffin Street in Limerick.

Michael's only granddaughter, Ellen Hyde, is involved in film production, showing that the apple doesn't fall far from the tree. He adored Ellen and engaged in daily conversations with her about the movie business, often remarking that he would have loved to be involved if he were 40 years younger. Under the guidance of his uncle Michael and by himself, Shane has achieved numerous national awards in professional photography throughout his career. When Michael was alive he was overjoyed to witness the expansion and growth of the business under the management of Michelle and Shane, knowing that it was in the capable hands of his family.

We can be certain that he would be immensely proud of what they have accomplished for Michael Martin Photography. Undoubtedly, Michael's legacy will never be forgotten.

Ar dheis Dé go raibh a anam.

O'Connor To Referee First Final
(Irish Press, 3 September 1969)

Seán O'Connor, 34-year-old former Limerick hurler, is the referee for the All Ireland senior hurling final, writes Mick Dunne.

The senior final will be Seán O'Connor's first championship appearance in Croke Park, but he has already refereed the 1967 Oireachtas final there between Kilkenny and Clare. Until his appointment as referee for the All Ireland final, that Oireachtas game was his only major assignment outside Munster.

He has, of course, handled National League games outside his own province and in Munster he has been a regular inter-county referee for the past four years. He is refereeing at club level for nearly ten years, but it was this year that he became recognised as one of the leading referees of the moment. He was in charge of the Cork-Clare replay in the Munster championship this year and refereed the Cork-Tipperary provincial final.

Seán played hurling with Limerick from 1957-59 also represented his county at junior football and was on the Limerick minor hurling and football teams in 1953. He still plays hurling with Claughaun, the club with which he has won three senior hurling and three senior football medals in the Limerick championships.

Umpires for the senior final are Jimmy Duggan (Galway), Jimmy Hatton (Wicklow), Jim Kirk (Armagh) and Noel Dalton (Waterford)!

The first five Limerickmen onto the field in Croke Park 1973 - minor final referee and umpires.
(L-R): Declan Moylan, Mick O'Brien, Seán O'Connor, John McCarthy and Mick Savage.

1973 Keeping the Dream Alive

All Ireland Minor Final Report
(Cork Examiner, 3 September 1973)
Ace Forward Foils Galway

Kilkenny 4-5
Galway 3-7

By Tim O'Brien

LATE GOAL FOILS GALWAY

It may seem an exaggeration to state that one player, and one player only, stood between Galway and their first All Ireland minor hurling title at Croke Park yesterday. But an examination of the facts pinpoints the contribution of Kilkenny full-forward Seán O'Brien, who scored four goals and two points, and this related to the winner's final tally of 4-5 demonstrates how well the remainder of the attack were contained.

Just a point separated the sides at the end of an absorbing duel played in a continuous downpour and in my book the better balanced team ended up on the wrong side of the scoreboard. They overcame a nerve wracking opening ten minutes when fortunately for them, they only conceded a goal and, a point without reply and came back ever so impressively to level the scores early in the second half. They then forged narrowly ahead; were pegged back again in dramatic fashion and held the upper hand until four minutes from time when O'Brien, from the James Stephens club, unleashed a tremendous drive from 25 yards to secure what not only was an all important goal but also the game's final score.

Overplayed

In retrospect Galway can apportion some of the blame for not securing ultimate victory on players far too eager to over play the ball. Particularly guilty in this respect was centre-fielder Gerry Holian who spoiled an otherwise outstanding display by constantly going it alone only to be upended or dispossessed when converging on the goal area. No doubt this carrying the ball gambit rallied the Westerners time and again when heroic efforts were so necessary but the disastrous stamina sapping consequences were that Holian ran out of steam in the crucial last ten minutes and the shrewd Kilkenny selectors capitalised on it when the game was delicately poised.

Captain and corner-back Kevin Robinson was dispatched to centre field, and it was from one of his several dangerous lobs that scorer in chief O'Brien out-witted the Galway defence to tip the scales in his side's favour. The winners led by a goal at half-time (1-4 to 0-4) and the 20 minutes after the break produced some or the game's most memorable moments. After centre-fielder Brian Waldron had stretched Kilkenny's advantage with a point Fred Power, a corner-forward of real class, secured the first of his two great goals for the challengers. He picked up a neat pass from the stylish Jack Dervan and raced through from the right to smack the ball to the net.

Breathtaking

A Hanniffy free levelled it in the 40th minute and soon afterwards the same player put Galway ahead for the first time. Within seconds in the twelfth minute we had two breathtaking goals with, Firstly, O'Brien restoring Kilkenny's lead and then his Galway counterpart pushing one home from the edge of the square, to give the Connacht champions the edge on the scoreboard again. Burke added another point, but Kilkenny were rescued from the jaws of defeat with that spectacular late effort from O'Brien. And so Kilkenny retained the title won in such commanding fashion last year, but full marks to Galway for their contribution to a game so keenly and sportingly contested. For Kilkenny it was their ninth All Ireland triumph in the grade but the unpalatable part for Galway is that they have now failed at the final hurdle on the same number of appearances.

Scorers

Kilkenny - S. O'Brien 4-2; J. Lyng 0-2; B. Waldron 0-1.

Galway - F. Power 2-0; G. Burke 1-1; M. Hanniffy 0-3; B. Kelly 0-2; J. Dervan 0-1.

Teams

Kilkenny - P. Dunphy; R. O'Hara, G. Doheny, K. Robinson; J. Hennessy, J. Marnell, O. Bergin; G. Devane, B. Waldron; P. Lennon, P. Mulhall, J. Lyng; P. Treacy, S. O'Brien, M. Lyng. Subs: - S. Purcell for M. Lyng and M. Lanigan for J. Lyng.

Galway - F. Larkin; H. Silke, G. Maher, G. Murphy; J. Dervan, T. Murphy, G. Lohan; G. Holian, S. Linnane; M. Hanniffy, J. Donoghue, B. Kelly; F. Power, G. Burke, E. Dooley.

Referee - Seán O'Connor (Limerick).

1973 Kilkenny Minor team that beat Wexford in the Leinster Final.
Back Row (L-R): Séan O'Brien, Paudie Lennon, Richard O'Hara, Ger Devane, Ger Doheny, Kieran Carroll, Brian Waldron and John Marnell. Front Row (L-R): Paudie Mulhall, Joe Hennessy, Ollie Bergin, Kevin Robinson (Capt.), John Lyng, Michael Lyng and Pat Treacy.

1973 Galway Minor team that beat Tipperary in the All Ireland Semi-final.
Back Row (L-R): John Donoghue, Liam Creaven, Gerry Maher, Eamonn Dooley, Gerry Murphy, Gerry Lohan, Tom Murphy, Frank Larkin and Gerry Burke. Front Row (L-R): Fred Power, Michael Hanniffy, Jack Dervan (Capt.), Hugh Silke, Gerry Holian, Brian Kelly and Sylvie Linnane.

Manager: JP Cusack (Loughrea). **Selectors:** Noel Treacy (Padraig Pearses), Gerald Corbett (Athenry), Brendan Murphy (Gort), Seán Fahy (Tommy Larkins) and John Furey (Oranmore-Maree). **Trainer:** Cyril Farrell (Tommy Larkins).

Limerick's Hurling Triumph Sends Crowd Wild
(Irish Independent, 3 September 1973)

By Raymond Smith

Not since Down won their first senior football crown in 1960 has Croke Park witnessed such scenes of overflowing enthusiasm as those seen at headquarters yesterday afternoon when Éamon Grimes raised the Liam MacCarthy trophy high in triumph after Limerick had beaten the holders, Kilkenny, by 1-21 (24) to 1-14 (17) to win their first All Ireland Senior Hurling title in 33 years.

The fair-haired Limerick captain had to be rescued by Gardaí and assisted to the dressing room after he had been overcome with the back-slapping and pressure from the excited Limerick supporters, who formed a solid phalanx in front of the Hogan Stand. They seemed oblivious of the pouring rain as they continued to chant "Limerick, Limerick, Limerick" long after the president of the GAA, Dr Donal Keenan, had made the presentation of the cup.

In more than twenty years following the game and writing about it, I have seen few, moments to equal this. "A moment worth waiting for," summed up the feelings of all Limerick men and what made it even more memorable was the fact that this superbly-fit team left no ifs and buts and in the final twenty minutes they were going like the proverbial greyhounds. Put out more flags, then, for this magnificent band of Limerick hurlers, all heroes on the day and the civic reception in the city tonight will surely be the climax of a historic achievement that will ever be acclaimed now by the Shannonside. My personal memory will be of corner-forward Frankie Nolan kissing the cup as he mounted the Hogan Stand with the rest of the victorious team behind the captain, Éamon Grimes.

There was something in the gesture that indicated the wiping away of hours of frustration - like that moment of utter disappointment in Killarney two years ago, when, again in the rain they had been beaten with the last puck of the game by one point by Tipperary. They had cried openly with disappointment after that numbing defeat, but yesterday there were tears of joy - and old Limerick hurlers wept with emotion.

As they sensed the victory that was at hand in the final 10 minutes, the feelings of Limerick followers gave vent to a great surging roar and the players themselves caught the mood and were inspired by it. They rose far above themselves and we saw individual feats from hurlers of talent like Seán Foley, the man of the match, Richie Bennis, machine-like in his accuracy, Pat Hartigan, the full-back, uncanny with his catching ability amidst the ruck of players, and the brilliantly-fast Éamon Grimes at midfield, and the experienced Eamonn Cregan at centre-back that will remain etched in the minds of all present.

Kilkenny, to their lasting credit, battled like true champions to overcome the handicap of having to line out without Eddie Keher, Jim Treacy, Kieran Purcell and Eamonn Morrissey (though Purcell bravely came on at the start of the second half) - but in the end it proved too much for them. Yet, they left men to debate and wonder what the result would have been if they had had their full team. The impressive way Limerick finished, there were shrewd judges who came away convinced that they would have won anyway. My own view is that, even though Limerick would still have edged it, they might have been put to the pins of their collars to take their seventh title.

Crucial Save

Kilkenny turned over only two points behind. They quickly wiped out the arrears and then Mick Brennan raced through and with a goal looking certain, goalie Séamus Horgan turned his palmed effort for the net over the bar. This was the crucial save of the match, recalling a similar dramatic save Horgan made in the Munster final from John Flanagan, of Tipperary. Richie Bennis equalised from a free and then came a Limerick goal in a goalmouth scramble, and from that moment they were on the road to victory.

One will remember one brilliant save by Kilkenny goalie. Noel Skehan, who captained the side to their All Ireland victory last year. He came away with the ball on his stick in a solo run in the second half that brought him to midfield and then he centred to the Limerick goalmouth, but the ball was cleared. All neutrals were with Limerick on this day and everyone agreed that it was "the best thing that ever happened for the game of hurling itself." The Kilkenny hurlers were the first to rush and congratulate Limerick on their win and certainly the supporters of the Black and Amber showed the sportsmanship worthy of a great hurling county on the day. Mick Mackey, who captained Limerick to their last success in 1940, also thought the team was magnificent, while it was a memorable hour, too, for the coach, Jackie Power, another link with the 1940 side.

A special cheer went up from the Limerick supporters before the game when it was announced that former President, Mr Eamon de Valera, had arrived for the game. Mr de Valera, who went to school in Bruree, must have been happy that a Bruree player, Jim O'Brien, played an outstanding game in defence. President Childers was witnessing his first All Ireland since he took office - and so was the Taoiseach, Mr Cosgrave. Present, too, were Cardinal Conway, Primate of All Ireland, and the Archbishop of Cashel, Most Rev. Dr Morris, Patron of the GAA

Dublin Dinner

The roar of a jet plane passing overhead was drowned by the thunderous reception given to the victorious Limerick team members when they arrived at the Crofton Airport Hotel last night for the reception given in their honour by the Limerick Association in Dublin. The 450 guests were enjoying their meal unaware of the rush of well-wishers outside, many of whom had tickets for the dinner but were unable to gain admittance. The Liam MacCarthy trophy, gaily decorated in green ribbons, that was last won by the Shannonsiders in 1940, had a place of honour on the top table where it was surrounded by members of the Limerick County Board, team captain, Éamon Grimes and two stars of the '30s, Jackie Power and Mick Mackey.

There, too, to savour the victory was the Minister for the Gaeltacht, Mr Tom O'Donnell, Ald. Steve Coughlan, and the Mayor of Limerick, Mr Mick Lipper, who "piloted" the train with the team to Dublin on Saturday.

Present at the reception also were the President of the GAA Dr Donal Keenan; Mr Rory Kiely, Chairman of the Limerick County Board, and Mr Tom Boland, the Secretary.

Eileen Dowling, wife of Limerick player Mossie Dowling, at the Limerick reception, in the Crofton Airport Hotel.

Silver Presented

A presentation of a silver salver was made to Éamon Grimes by Mrs Maureen Walsh on behalf of the Limerick Association. Even as the dinner concluded, well-wishers still crowded around the entrance to the hotel for autographs from the victorious players, who were kept busy during the meal signing everything from table serviettes to menus for young supporters. Among the team members attending the victory dinner was one of the stars of the Limerick side, Richie Bennis, of Patrickswell, whose seven-weeks-old son - suffering from meningitis was recovering at the Limerick Regional Hospital last night.

Although anxious about the baby's health, his brother, Phil, who was a star of the Limerick team also, said that before joining his team-mates Richie had checked with the family and had been assured that the baby was improving.

Ann Cregan, Castletroy, at the Limerick reception.

Ex-Limerick Hurler Puts Our All Ireland Triumph on Record
(Limerick Leader, 31 May 1975)

By John O'Shaughnessy

Limerick's historic 1973 All Ireland hurling triumph has been put on disc. It is entitled "Limerick '73" and, appropriately enough, it is sung by former camán wielder, Dermot Kelly, who also penned the words. The record was launched this week at a press conference at the Beamish and Crawford depot in Galvone, Limerick. On the flip-side is another Dermot Kelly composition, "John Riley."

Late Late

What prompted him to make a recording almost two years after the event? "Two things really: number one, I was encouraged by the response which "Limerick '73" met after I sang on the *Late Late Show* and, number two, I felt that something needed to be done to act as a reminder." Dermot added that he felt sad that Limerick's great win was so quickly forgotten, especially after over 100,000 people turned out on the streets to welcome them on their return from Dublin. "More important still, I think it will inspire this year's hurlers to another memorable victory at Croke Park," added the Roxboro Shopping Centre bank official.

Indeed Limerick '73 is an all-Limerick combination: It was recorded at the Crescent Recording Studio (CRS), Munster's only professional recording studio. Principally responsible for the disc with Dermot were Eamonn O'Connor, Brendan Frawley and Denis Allen, directors of the CRS.

Dermot, who admitted that he had a passionate love for the game of hurling, is confident that his record will be a success. "It is not a commercial venture . . . I would prefer to look upon it as a collector's item," he said. Four hundred copies were pressed and such is the demand, that further copies are to be made. Orders have come from London and New York for "Limerick '73" which was played on RTÉ radio last Sunday morning. When questioned about Limerick's prospects of All Ireland glory this year Dermot replied, "The honeymoon is now over, and if the players can only get more fire into their play, they have the ability to take the championship."

Winner of four county championships with Claughaun - two in hurling and two in football - the current president of the CBS Past Pupils' Union was the hero of Limerick's 1955 Munster hurling championship win over Clare at the Gaelic Grounds. He set up a personal record for a Munster final that day, when he scored 1-12 over 60 minutes, three points more than the combined Clare total of 2-6. Dermot also won four Railway Cups with Munster, and in all, gave 30 years service to the game.

Co-operation

He remarked that "Limerick '73" would not have been possible but for the wonderful co-operation which he received from Messrs. O'Connor, Frawley and Allen. Replying on behalf of Crescent Recording Studios, Mr Eamonn O'Connor said they were delighted to have the opportunity of releasing the record.

"As well as being a fine hurler in his day, Dermot is also a gifted singer and composer and his latest record is a must for all GAA fans," said Eamonn. He referred to the many facilities at the CRS. "Despite what people might think, it is not too expensive to have a record cut, and anyone interested should contact us."

Eamonn remarked that there were many knockers in Limerick, and they were always very slow to recognise their fellow citizens' achievements. "Limerick '73" is an example of what a group of locals can do," concluded the RTÉ cameraman.

Dermot will make another recording shortly - this time about the legendary Christy Ring.

1973 Keeping the Dream Alive

Dermot Kelly

Dermot in action during the 1955 All Ireland Hurling Semi-final at Croke Park.

Limerick '73

Come all you loyal Irish men and listen to me now
I'll tell you of the hurlers that come from Limerick town
Thirty years or more, me boys, no All Ireland crown
But '73, believe you me, they really won renown

Chorus:
Shout, boys, hooray, this is Limerick's day
Richie Bennis, Hartigan, Foley too, will play
Blondy Cregan, Éamon Grimes, they never will give up
Until we have by Shannon-side the Liam MacCarthy Cup!

Tipp said they would bate us, in Thurles '73
With Keating in the forwards, we could not disagree
'Twas fast and fierce and furious, the hurling of the day
But Limerick had the bonfire set alight by Neddy Rea

Chorus

September, we were in Croke Park, it really was the test
The black and amber from the Nore, put terror in the breast
They hit as hard as marble but shure they should have known
That marble from Kilkenny couldn't shift the Treaty Stone

Chorus

Soon, we'll be back again, All Ireland day once more
The lovely green of Shannon, the amber of the Nore
We'll fight 'em fair and honest, fight hard for every ball
And Limerick will be champions, the finest of them all

Chorus

Chorus

Dermot Kelly

I Never Thought I'd Be Picked

(Sunday Press, 2 September 1973)
Says Limerick's shock selection Joe McKenna

By Eugene McGee

Joe McKenna, a shock selection for Limerick at left corner forward for today's All Ireland final talks to Eugene McGee. I played nearly all my hurling in Offaly and there our big ambition was to win a Leinster championship. It was three years ago that I came to work here in Limerick and it was only last year that I started to play hurling in the county when I helped South Liberties win the county championship. I declared for Limerick this year but I never thought I would be playing in the All Ireland final in my very first year in the green jersey.

It is even more surprising because after I played against Clare in the first round of the championship I was not picked for the Munster final and I was unavailable for the All Ireland semi-final against London. Limerick were having a bit of a problem with the centre half-back position and it was no surprise to the players when they decided to move Eamonn Cregan back to No. 6. This left the way open for me to regain my place. No doubt the fact that I am six foot three, as opposed to my opponent's (Phil 'Fan' Larkin) five foot six, was a big factor in today's game. Extra height doesn't make very much difference in the corner-forward position and although I have never played on Larkin before, I know well that he is a very tight-marking corner back whom it is very hard to get by.

The people in Offaly have been very reasonable about my leaving to play in Limerick, and they have all wished me well for today's game. Actually, I also have a very strong Tipperary background as my father's family were from Borrisokane and my first cousin, Mackey McKenna, won All Irelands with Tipperary. Apart from the thrill of playing in my first All Ireland final, I also expect to win my first All Ireland medal today. Limerick are very fit and have picked up enough experience in the past few years - having played in four League and two Munster finals.

Cormac Liddy with Limerick Leader editor, Brendan Halligan, both holding the Liam MacCarthy cup in late 1973.

Front cover of a souvenir programme produced in New York for the 1973 All Ireland Hurling Final.

G.A.A. Honor Roll

ALL-IRELAND FOOTBALL CHAMPIONSHIPS
1887-1972

Kerry (22): 1903, 1904, 1909, 1913, 1914, 1924, 1926, 1929, 1930, 1931, 1932, 1937, 1939, 1940, 1941, 1946, 1953, 1955, 1959, 1962, 1969, 1970.
Dublin (17): 1891, 1892, 1894, 1897, 1898, 1899, 1901, 1902, 1906, 1907, 1908, 1921, 1922, 1923, 1942, 1958, 1963.
Galway (7): 1925, 1934, 1938, 1956, 1964, 1965, 1966.
Wexford (5): 1893, 1915, 1916, 1917, 1918.
Cavan (5): 1933, 1935, 1947, 1948, 1952.
Tipperary (4): 1889, 1895, 1900, 1920.
Kildare (4): 1905, 1919, 1927, 1928.
Cork (3): 1890, 1911, 1945.
Mayo (3): 1936, 1950, 1951.
Louth (3): 1910, 1912, 1957.
Meath (3): 1949, 1954, 1967.
Down (3): 1960, 1961, 1968.
Limerick (2): 1887, 1896.
Roscommon (2): 1943, 1944.
Offaly (2): 1971, 1972.

ALL-IRELAND HURLING CHAMPIONSHIPS
1887-1972

Tipperary (22): 1887, 1895, 1896, 1898, 1899, 1900, 1906, 1908, 1916, 1925, 1930, 1937, 1945, 1949, 1950, 1951, 1958, 1961, 1962, 1964, 1965, 1971.
Cork (20): 1890, 1893, 1894, 1902, 1903, 1919, 1926, 1928, 1929, 1931, 1941, 1942, 1943, 1944, 1946, 1952, 1953, 1954, 1966, 1970.
Kilkenny (18): 1904, 1905, 1907, 1909, 1911, 1912, 1913, 1922, 1932, 1933, 1935, 1939, 1947, 1957, 1963, 1967, 1969, 1972.
Dublin (6): 1899, 1917, 1920, 1924, 1927, 1938.
Limerick (6): 1897, 1918, 1921, 1934, 1936, 1940.
Wexford (5): 1910, 1955, 1956, 1960, 1968.
Waterford (2): 1948, 1959.
Clare (1): 1914.
Galway (1): 1923.
Kerry (1): 1891.
Laois (1): 1915.
London (1): 1901.

"We Are Geared For Any Weather" - Pat Hartigan
(Limerick Leader, 8 September 1973)

"Leader" hurling columnist, Seán Murphy, joins in the tributes to the Limerick heroes in this article.

"We are geared for anything" remarked full-back Pat Hartigan when I asked him if the rain would affect their chances, prior to the start of last Sunday's historic All Ireland Hurling Final.

This confident reply was a morale booster for my life-long dream of watching Limerick winning the blue riband of the hurling scene and the coveted Liam MacCarthy Cup. On the train journey, and as I queued patiently for the grub at the Castle Hotel, there wasn't a single Doubting Thomas in the huge mass of Limerick supporters. All seemed very confident of breaking the 33 year hoodoo.

"The weather forecast is good," well-known Gaelic Grounds steward, Mick "Dasher" O'Dwyer from Ballysimon said, as Paddy Wade (South Liberties) recalled memories of the 1940 success. The time was coming up to 12 noon when the sad news broke. "It's raining mad," exclaimed a young Shannonside supporter as he peered through the window at the milling fans trudging towards Jones Road.

My heart sank

Had not the experts voted Limerick a dry day team?

Visions of that defeat by Tipperary at Killarney in July 1971 loomed clearly. But I suddenly recalled that fiery comeback in a downpour in the National League semi-final replay at Birr against Tipperary and this renewed my confidence in the Limerick team no matter what the conditions. Under the protection of a popular Sunday national newspaper I made the trek to Croke Park, where at the entrance a vigilant member of the Garda Siochana got suspicious of my carrier bag, but on being assured that it did not contain a bomb, allowed me to continue with a message of goodwill for a Limerick win.

Limerick Hordes

The grounds were filling steadily as Galway and Kilkenny battled out the destiny of the minor crown and it appeared as if Limerick supporters outnumbered their opposite numbers by as many as 5 to 1. Despite the now almost incessant rain, the uncovered terraces were getting thickly populated and the green and white was everywhere to be seen. Ned Grimes, father of team captain, Eamon, and a great old warrior in the Gaelic cause, gave me a firm handshake as he took his seat. "At long last we'll do it," he said in a confident tone of voice.

Paddy Keane, the Murroe press correspondent and a popular musician and step-dancer, was slightly worried by the rain and prevailing underfoot conditions, but consoled us all by saying: "It will upset Kilkenny too - it's as good for the goose as the gander." The tension was rising now as we awaited the arrival of the teams. Then a mighty roar and the green-clad heroes thundered out on to the pitch from under the Cusack Stand.

The players looked resplendent in their new gear, but one noticed the four Patrickswell members of the panel wore their old boots, no doubt in the interest of comfort.

"They are as fit as fiddles," "McKenna is very tall," "Bennis looks nervous," "Do you see the size of Horgan's hurley," are some of the remarks overheard during the pre-match ceremonies which lasted twenty minutes but felt like eternity. Referee Michael Slattery in his now familiar black and white strip made his appearance early on, in the company of what appeared four astronauts but no - they were in fact his umpires, clad in most impressive white track suits. Many dignitaries were welcomed, but one felt this is being overdone.

The boy from Bruree - ex-President, Eamonn de Valera, got a tremendous welcome as he arrived, no doubt to cheer on his fellow parishioners Jim O'Brien. Yes, indeed, even in hurling the savage loves his native shore.

The Artane Boys Band made a fast job of the parade and at long last the game was in motion.

Limerick got off a dream start. In the opening minute Frankie Nolan weaved his way in from the right wing to flash over a glorious point. Although Kilkenny forged ahead in the 6th minute with a Claus Dunne pointed free, Limerick began to show their class. Playing swift, stylish hurling, they matched Kilkenny in every facet of the game and although rocked in the. 20th minute by a Pat Delaney goal, they pegged back the deficit and led 0-12 to 1-7 at the interval.

Myth Explodes

The myth about the dry-day team was beginning to explode as during that opening 40 minutes Limerick overcame the constant rain, greasy ball and slippery sod in the mould of champions. Our hopes are rising again. But, hold it. Limerick went through a dreadful period of uncertainty on resuming. Claus Dunne pointed a free after 3 minutes and Chunky O'Brien lands a great shot from the right wing between the uprights to level matters after 5 minutes. Sixty seconds later came the turning point of the game. Mick Crotty is allowed the freedom of the park and tears goalwards in possession. He tries to palm a shot out of Séamus Horgan's reach, but the agile Tournafulla 'keeper foiled by turning his effort over the bar.

Kilkenny are in front, but only by one point and Limerick are soon on equal terms as ace marksman Richie Bennis raises a white flag from a free.

"Limerick, Limerick. Limerick - we need a goal," chanted the rabid Limerick followers.

And the green flag was duly raised in the 48th minute. Liam O'Donoghue cut in from the right, passed to Frankie Nolan who placed Mossie Dowling for a ground shot. Noel Skehan went down on his knees to save but Eamonn Rea and Mossie Dowling scrambled in and the latter was credited with the score. Bernie Hartigan lashes over a great point at once, and the Limerick fans are in delirious mood. It is becoming obvious that new champions were on the way as Kilkenny succumbed to the power-packed hurling of Limerick. What a magnificent display from a team upon who doubts had been cast on from all angles.

In the last ten minutes, there was only one team in this rip-roaring contest as the superbly fit (fair play to trainer Mick Cregan) Shannonsiders swept aside the Kilkenny challenge as if the Noresiders had left for home. And so, time ticked away and the only question unanswered was Limerick's winning margin. The scoreboard reads: Limerick 1-21 Kilkenny 1-14. The time is 4:58PM and it's all over.

Waited So Long

This is the moment all Limerick have waited so long for. There to lead "the charge of the light brigade" on to the pitch to congratulate our heroes was County Board Secretary, Tom Boland, who was already in full flight as referee Michael Slattery gave his whistle the final blast.

The after-match scenes were incredible as legions of fans gave vent to their feelings. Even the torrential rain failed to dampen their spirit.

Amid a fantastic din of jubilation, Éamon Grimes received the Liam MacCarthy Cup from the President of the GAA, Dr Donal Keenan, and proudly held it aloft to the tremendous cheers of the Limerick fans.

Yes, Limerick are hurling kings again. A new era has begun!

Croke Park Advertisers in September 1973

How many of these businesses still exist in one form or another 50 years on?

Nally Stand and Hill 16

Clubman Shirts
Jockey Menswear
New Ireland Assurance
Allied Irish Banks
Esso Extra
PMPA Insurance
Go B+I To Britain
Guinness Extra
Carrolls GAA All-Stars (scoreboard)
ACC The Farmer's Bank
National Investment Savings 15%
Irish Independent

Canal End

Aer Lingus (scoreboard)
Pepsi (clock)
Carrolls GAA All-Stars
First National Building Society
Condor tobacco
B+I Passenger and Car Ferry Services
Coca Cola
Tayto
Allied Irish Banks
Erin Foods
Dunlop
Philips
GAA Development Scheme

Cusack Stand Sideline

Paddy Whisky
Go Chrysler
Esso Extra
The Irish Press
Henry Winterman - Dutch Cigars
Silvermints
Coca-Cola
Ford
Irish Permanent
Esso Extra
The Irish Press
Smithwicks great!
Go Greyhound Racing

Cusack Stand Upper

Allied Irish Banks
Go B+I To Britain
Wavin
Peace of Mind - Hibernian Insurance
Kerrygold
Avis
Gouldings
Wavin
McInerney
Allied Irish Banks

Hogan Stand

Allied Irish Banks
Go B+I to Britain

 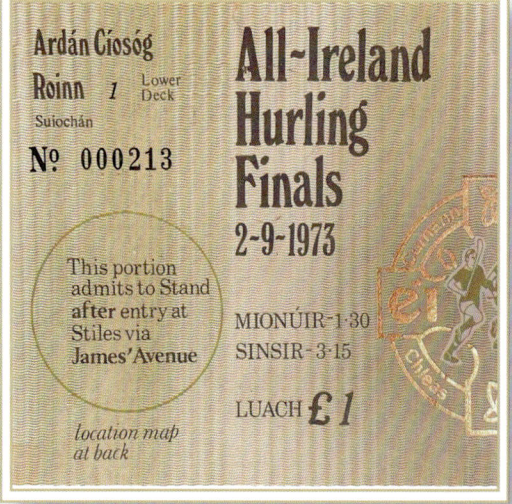

Hogan Stand and Cusack Stand ticket stubs for the 1973 All Ireland Hurling Final.

The 1973 All Ireland Hurling Final on Tape

The first time the 1973 All Ireland Hurling Final was replayed on RTÉ was in late June 1987, on something called RTÉ Mid-West, an early experiment in regional television broadcasting. It was shown on the Monday afternoon after the losing replay against Cork in that year's Munster Hurling Championship, 29 June.

It is reputed that VHS bootlegs of this broadcast reached into the far recesses of Limerick and beyond in the months and years subsequent. The original broadcast is still recalled very clearly some 36 years later by many now middle-aged supporters! Fast forward 10 years, and the advent of TnaG's seminal *All Ireland Gold* series in early March 1997. This was the first time that most people were properly exposed to old All Ireland hurling and football finals, outside of rare highlights programmes or short excerpts shown in other programming.

It was also the first time that RTÉ raided their sporting vaults in a concerted and methodical manner, starting on Tuesday, 4 March with the first half of the 1974 All Ireland Hurling Final and then returning after a short commercial break with the second half of the 1973 All Ireland Hurling Final. Full video of both games exist and no clear explanation has even been found as to why these finals were spliced together that first evening. On Thursday evening of the same week, *All Ireland Gold* showed the 1974 All Ireland football final in full.

All Ireland Gold did not show the presentation, cutting away to the now well-known theme tune of the series, as the Limerick players were being engulfed by their excited supporters. The next time the 1973 All Ireland Hurling Final was shown in full was in mid-December 2002, again on TG4 (renamed from TnaG in 1999) after Eamonn Cregan's *Laochra Gael* was first broadcast on Saturday, 14 December. By this stage, it was possible to order clean and complete copies of the 1973 All Ireland Final from RTÉ Archives, a commercial offshoot. These copies were not cheap but were worth every penny to the committed souls who ordered them.

People have to remember that this was a time before YouTube, and other social media; a time when there was no video on demand and most people could only record programmes via a trusty VHS tape. DVDs had gained a foothold but were still very difficult to produce in non-commercial settings. It was the first time this author saw footage from this wonderful game and a few tears were shed that late evening at the final whistle, the pitch invasion and some of Micheál O'Hehir's parting words, reprinted elsewhere.

29 June 1987 programme listing for RTÉ TV "Mid-West", a short-lived experiment in regional programming.

4 March 1997 programme listing for TnaG, with the first ever All Ireland Gold Hurling programme.

CHAPTER 11

1973

ALL IRELAND HURLING FINAL (iii)

POST-MATCH

Limerick were All Ireland champions again after a 33 year gap. The national newspapers the next morning had a field day with much reportage of the game and the post-match reception in the Crofton Airport Hotel (now the Bonnington Hotel). The team had stayed there on Saturday night, being very convenient to Croke Park, less than a mile away, on the road out to the airport.

A legendary story that the reception had to be discontinued due to the volume of well-wishers who turned up to greet the new champions is not true. There was a very large number of supporters at the reception alright, but it continued nonetheless, even if it was reported that some people with tickets were not able to gain admittance to the actual banquet. The crowd that turned up was dangerously large and some were worried that there could be injuries as a result of crushing and general exuberance. Such receptions in more recent times have been much more muted in comparison, both at City West Hotel in Saggart (2018) and the Clayton Hotel (formally the Burlington) in Ballsbridge (2022). There was no such reception in 2023, a portent of things to come? Another break with past traditions!

Before returning to Limerick on Monday, an unusual post-match reception took place, which would be unthinkable these days. Micheál O'Hehir was the full-time manager of the Leopardstown Racecourse at the time and only worked occasionally with RTÉ. He was instrumental in organising a Monday morning get-together there, for both winning and losing senior and minor teams. It was the scene of a wonderful photo of Éamon Grimes and Pat Delaney holding the MacCarthy Cup, with Mick Mackey smiling benignly between them. Éamon Grimes had a firm hold of the cup while Pat Delaney only had a finger and a half on it. These receptions continued until the late 1980s.

The then current Mayor of Limerick, Mick Lipper, drove the team train up to Dublin on Saturday evening and back down again on Monday afternoon. The train stopped in Castleconnell and the team continued on an open-top lorry from there to Charlotte's Quay for the official homecoming.

There were at least two official receptions for the team over subsequent weeks. One was hosted by Limerick City Council on 21 September in the Parkway Motel. There was another event, hosted by Murphy's Brewery, in the Deerpark Hotel, Charleville, on 12 October, in conjunction with the Cork footballers who won their first All Ireland gaelic football title since 1945. Brochures produced for both these events are reproduced in this chapter, along with a picture of Éamon Grimes and Billy Morgan together with the two cups, *Liam MacCarthy* and *Sam Maguire*.

Éamon Grimes got married to Helen O'Flynn on Monday, 10 September, just over a week after Croke Park. They were married in St. Patrick's Church and it made the front page of a number of the newspapers afterwards. The wedding was originally arranged for the day after the All Ireland final but was postponed for a week due to the unavailability of the officiating priest.

The Liam MacCarthy Cup made its way around the county over the following months and some images and video exist of its visits to the county's towns and villages. It was an era when colour photography was beginning to take over from black and white. It was the original Liam MacCarthy Cup and was first received by Bob McConkey in 1923 (for the 1921 championship). It finally retired in 1991 after a lifetime of use and can now be seen in the GAA Museum.

It was reported afterwards that over 360 events had seen *Liam MacCarthy* attend in the aftermath of the 1973 success. Articles about Limerick's success were published in all the GAA periodicals and magazines of the time, including *Gaelic Sport, Solo, Cúl, Our Games* and *GAA yearbooks* in both Limerick and Kilkenny, some are reproduced here.

A Final View from Kilkenny
(1974 Limerick GAA Yearbook)

By Peter Holohan, Kilkenny People

While Limerick will be celebrating their All Ireland final triumph for many a day Kilkenny followers will be pondering on what might have happened if any of several different approaches were adopted. But only one answer emerges. On the run of the play, Limerick deserved to win and they have the goodwill of every Kilkenny follower in their hour of glory. There are some aspects of the game, however, that can be seen more clearly in retrospect. It is a distinct disadvantage to Kilkenny when they take the field firm favourites, as they were in this year's final. Kilkenny need an incentive in order to produce that determined spirit which has worked wonders in the past. Last year's final is a classical example.

Cork were strongly fancied to win the 1972 final and this was the way Kilkenny wanted it. That is not a complete answer. I discussed the final some days before 2 September with a very shrewd Kilkenny follower and he expressed the view that Kilkenny did not have the beating of Limerick. Kilkenny, for one thing, had to find too many subs for injured players too soon. The hasty analysis which invariably follows every final put the blame on the Kilkenny full back line and did so quite unfairly. Only five of Limerick's twenty one points were scored by the full forward line, and their only goal came from centre half forward Mossie Dowling.

A good many Kilkenny people regarded it as rather doubtful as they held Noel Skehan had been fouled. But if that goal had been disallowed no Kilkenny follower would quibble if the referee had allowed a goal when Mossie Dowling shouldered Noel Skehan over the goal line. Of all the imponderables that arose one that, for Kilkenny people caused the most surprise, was that Kilkenny failed where they usually succeed in the last quarter.

It was at this stage that the absence of Eddie Keher really pinched. Eddie has often appeared rather inactive in games but he is seldom held scoreless. He has that rare quality of being able to get a vital score when the need is greatest. His presence alone is an inspiration and it would, undoubtedly, have been a worry to the Limerick side. And if Mick Crotty's palmed point had not been 'miraculously' tapped over the bar when it seemed certain to be a goal things might have been different.

Limerick's hurling in the last quarter was, no doubt, brilliant. They looked a great team but it was touch and go up to this stage and it was only after the departure of Frank Cummins that Kilkenny's position was rendered hopelessly beyond redemption.

And brilliant as Limerick's midfield and half back line was, it was their goalie, Séamus Horgan, and full back line of Willie Moore, Pat Hartigan and Jim O'Brien that did the greatest damage. They held the fort under some very strong pressure - pressure that wore down the Wexford defence in the Leinster final and the Cork defence in last year's All Ireland final and of the full back trio, Pat Hartigan can claim to have done most to stop Kilkenny.

Few Kilkenny followers will deny that Limerick won on merit. They played some very good ground hurling, they were fitter and faster than Kilkenny and they had a powerful incentive. They had waited 33 years since they last beat Kilkenny in an All Ireland final and were appearing in a final again fully bent on emulating what the men of Mick Mackey's day did.

And they must surely have been pleased that the victory was at Kilkenny's expense. Kilkenny and Limerick have produced some great All Ireland finals and for older followers this final was a throwback to the 1930s when two of the greatest combinations in hurling history from the Shannonside and the Nore provided hurling followers with classical exhibitions. Now that the game is over and the pangs of disappointment have more or less vanished, Kilkenny people wish Limerick well and offer them best wishes in their success in the knowledge that a victory such as this, so long delayed, cannot but be good for the game.

Thirty-three years after...Mick Mackey (centre), who led Limerick to victory in 1940, pictured with victorious captain, Éamon Grimes (left) and Pat Delaney, Kilkenny's captain at the GAA reception for the senior and minor finalists of 1973.

The Mayor of Limerick
(Limerick All Ireland Hurling Champions)
Souvenir of Limerick's Day of Glory

Alderman Michael Lipper

We have been a long time waiting to bring home the All Ireland Senior Hurling Championship title… in fact we have been waiting 33 years but, let me hasten to add, our hurlers never lost hope, They kept on trying. This glorious year of 1973 has gained a special place in the colourful and dramatic history of the Gaelic Athletic Association and it has gained a place of permanence in the memory of every Limerick man and woman, boy and girl here at home and across the world.

For, it was on that memorable day Sunday of 2 September, 1973 that Limerick senior hurlers brought back the All Ireland crown for the first time since 1940 when they defeated Kilkenny in a final that must rank among the greatest to be played on the sod of Croke Park.

They defeated the pride of Kilkenny in a contest that was played with speed and skill in the best traditions of the national game of our land, the sport of hurling. For every young man who wore the colours of green and white that memorable day, it was their greatest honour.

It was also the day when new life and new hope were given to the sport and, to the hurlers who play it in so many parts of this country where All Ireland honours remain the dream. Limerick hurlers have made the dream a reality. May they continue to bring honour to their county and their city.

Their glory on the hurling field is ours. We treasure it with pride.

Mayor Mick Lipper manning the train to Dublin. That was no gimmick either, train engineer was the Labour man's day job.

Ronan Cregan (son of Mick) with Mayor of Limerick, Mick Lipper, soon after the All Ireland Hurling Final.

| King George IV Scotch Whisky say **K.G. 4** | SPEEDI-CABS **4-88-44** ANYTIME! ANYWHERE! | *Limerick* Vol 84. No. 15600. | Price 1p |

WELCOME HER

THERE WILL BE a heroes welcome for the All-Ireland hurling champions when they arrive at Charlotte Quay at approximately 9 o'clock tonight.

The Mayor, Ald. M. Lipper, and City Council members, will receive the team officially in the car park at Charlotte Quay.

Elaborate preparations are being made to welcome the team, which will leave Dublin at 5.45 p.m. by train. They will be taken from the train shortly before it arrives in Limerick and conveyed by a 40-foot CIE suitably bedecked truck to Charlotte Quay.

To ensure a smooth flow of traffic parking on both sides of the Dublin Road will be prohibited from 5 p.m. to 9 p.m. as far as the Parkway Motel.

The public are urged not to go out and meet the train as there will be ample room in Charlotte Quay.

Welcome

It is expected that the welcome to be accorded the team will surpass anything seen in the city for years.

Bonfires are being prepared all over the county and city.

It is estimated that some 15,000 people travelled by road and rail to Croke Park over the weekend. The green and white favours were about six to one in the grounds.

A damper

A damper on the celebrations was the death of Mr. P. A. 'Weeshie' Murphy, Chairman of the Munster Council, who collapsed after the match.

The Chairman of the Limerick Co. Board, Mr. Rory Kiely, paid a tribute to Mr. Murphy's outstanding contribution to the G.A.A.

Congratulations

To-day's meeting of the County Health Committee, in Limerick, was less about health than it was about the All-Ireland Final victory.

But on the subject of health, it was agreed all round that the glorious win was the most healthy boost to morale in Limerick for over 30 years.

The committee's chairman, Councillor Ned Dwyer, started the congratulations rolling with an address full of praise for the Limerick team, their trainers, selectors and advisers.

Great

Formally proposing the vote of congratulations

Leader

MONDAY, SEPTEMBER 3, 1973

BEE MOYNIHAN & Co.
2 O'CONNELL St
Limerick
JEWELLERS
Tel. 45385
Watches Repaired

METRO 4-hour Cleaning now at 61 William St.

E HOME OES

ALL-IRELAND PULL-OUT SUPPLEMENT

A special souvenir supplement —containing pages of pictures and reports of Limerick's dramatic hurling triumph—will be issued free of charge with this week's editions of the Limerick Leader.

FREE THIS WEEK

1973 Keeping the Dream Alive

On the victory lorry coming into Charlotte's Quay from Castleconnell.

1973 Keeping the Dream Alive

A wonderful shot of the homecoming crowd at Charlotte's Quay.

Grimes's Boys Stand Up To Any Scrutiny
(Gaelic Sport, November 1973)

By Owen McCann

Now that the first flush of heady excitement that was provided by Limerick's win over Kilkenny in the All Ireland senior hurling final has melted away, it is possible to sit back and take a more rational look at the team and its achievements, and as well, spotlight some other pleasing features of the great occasion.

It would be presumptuous of me to try and measure this Limerick outfit against the county's great All Ireland championship winning combinations of the past. Like so many more, I was watching Limerick in action in an All Ireland senior final for the first time.

But I am prepared to argue that Éamon Grimes and his talented company of hurlers measure up superbly to the great Liam MacCarthy Cup winning squads of modern times.

Granted, Kilkenny were short men of the calibre of Jim Treacy, Eddie Keher, Eamonn Morrissey and Kieran Purcell, although the latter did go into the game after the interval as a substitute. It is no reflection on their deputies to say that the loss of the combined skills and experience of such outstanding hurlers was a big handicap to the defending champions.

Nevertheless, while I am not unmindful of the quality and the power of the Kilkenny performance against Wexford in the Leinster final, a showing that there and then put the Noresiders in a warm favourite's role for another All Ireland crown, I am still not convinced that had the Eastern county been at full strength they would have foiled Limerick.

This must now remain in the realms of conjecture, but at the same time, there was a poise and authority about Limerick's general work that leads me to the belief that they would have triumphed on the day against any opposition.

Cast your mind back to the showpiece game, and you will appreciate all the more what I mean.

Limerick were a side infused with the will to win, and backed by confident skill, determination and teamwork. In defence, Seán Foley, Eamonn Cregan, a brilliant success in his new and demanding role as pivot, and Jim O'Brien marshalled matters superbly. As they also received the maximum support possible from the other members of the rearguard, it is reasonable to assume that, even with Keher and a fully fit Purcell in action, the Leinster attack would have found it difficult to would have found it difficult to break through often enough for a winning balance.

The Limerick scoring division was also a very efficient force. Eamonn Rea was always a big threat, Frankie Nolan showed many fine touches, and Mossie Dowling put in much valuable work. But they were only three of the stars in a division that overall combined well as a unit, and moved with purpose and ideas.

Doubtless, against Kilkenny's usual defence the southern forwards would have found the going much tougher, but I still maintain that they would have been good enough to outshoot their opposite number - especially with the promptings and inspiration that came from non-stop Éamon Grimes and the sweet-striking Richie Bennis.

So, whether or not Éamon Grimes and his crew are entitled to rank as the master Limerick outfit of all time, one thing at least must be beyond dispute - the men of 1973 are worthy heirs to a great tradition, hurlers who have fused their skills and who have fused their skills and individual talents into a combination that bristled with enthusiasm, industry and inspiration, and one that ranks as the worthiest of champions.

Tribute, too, must be paid to trainer Mick Cregan, who turned out one of the fittest teams ever to win the Liam MacCarthy Cup. Other pleasing features of the great occasion? Well, away altogether from the scene of play, was the excellent service provided by CIÉ to cater for the thousands of Limerick supporters. Many have commented in glowing terms of the excellence of the arrangements.

It is well known, nationally, of course, that the driver of the train on which the team travelled to the final was Alderman Michael Lipper, Mayor of Limerick. What may not be so well known outside of the county, however, is that CIÉ re-opened the small, disused station at Castleconnell especially as an arrival point for the team on the way home. From there, the champion hurlers transferred from the train to a CIÉ float decorated in the Limerick colours to complete the journey.

This wholehearted co-operation and effort gave an added dimension to the great occasion for Limerick people. So, too, did an enjoyable function in the city early in October.

At that, Limerick County Council presented special medals to every team member and substitute, as well as to the trainer.

The silver medals incorporated the county crest on a plaque and were financed by voluntary contribution from the members of the council and the senior administrative staff as the money could not be allocated from public funds.

A splendid gesture this, as also was a decision by Allied Irish Banks to sponsor the reception.

•••

The Long Road to Glory
(Gaelic Sport, November 1973)

By Séamus Ó Ceallaigh

The Limerick hurling renaissance might be said to have started a decade ago (1963) with the winning of the Munster Minor Hurling Championship, in which Limerick beat Tipperary, 4-12 to 5-4.

Although they subsequently lost to Wexford in the All Ireland Final, five players came out of that minor success - Éamon Grimes, Jim O'Brien, Eamonn Cregan, Michael Graham and Andy Dunworth; to join Tony O'Brien of the 1958 All Ireland minor triumph, and form the nucleus of the side that was to make history in 1966, when beating All Ireland champions, Tipperary, 4-12 to 2-9, at Cork Athletic Grounds, in the opening round of the Munster Senior Hurling championship; only to subsequently lose rather unluckily to Cork at Killarney - the Rebel County boys going on to win All Ireland honours.

In this 1966 Limerick team, another very worthwhile quartet were brought to the notice of the hurling fans - Jim Hogan, Eamonn Rea, Phil Bennis and Bernie Hartigan.

In the meantime, Limerick CBS were making history in the Dr Harty Cup tie ranks, and this great campaign brought to the surface in addition to the two blondes Eamon(n)s - Grimes and Cregan, players of the calibre of Pat Hartigan, Seán Foley, Seán Burke and Christy Campbell.

Progress was depressingly slow following the defeat at Killarney by Cork. In the three following years Limerick went out in the opening round of the Munster championship - to Clare in 1967, 3-9 to 2-7, to Cork, the following year, 3-11 to 2-9; and to Tipperary in 1969, 0-14 to 2-5.

Limerick hurling was back in its hum-drum mood, until another simple incident shook it out of its complacency. The Shannonsiders were due to play a then rampant Wexford in a National Hurling League tie in Enniscorthy. Some of the established players failed to make the journey and it was with considerable difficulty the selectors fielded what they considered a very makeshift side. But, wonder of wonders, they beat the Slaneysiders - and Limerick were back in the hurling business in real earnest.

Places were no longer automatically guaranteed on the side to any player - and a healthy rivalry was established. For the first time in many years the county won its way to a National League Final, and although they were well beaten by Cork, a new spirit was in evidence.

Eleven of the recent All Ireland Hurling Final panel were with Limerick in that final. They were Jim Hogan, Jim O'Brien, Eamonn Cregan, Pat and Bernie Hartigan, Jim O'Donnell, Phil and Richie Bennis, Éamon Grimes, Andy Dunworth and Tom Ryan.

They beat Clare, in a replay, in the opening round of the 1970 Munster Championship, but lost to Cork in the semi-final.

Seán Foley and Limerick All Ireland team trainer, Mick Cregan, joined the group for the 1971 League final in which Limerick, with a point from a last-minute free, beat Tipperary 3-12 3-11, in a real thriller at Cork Athletic Grounds - regaining the league crown last held by the Shannonsiders in 1947.

Limerick opened their 1971 Munster Championship campaign with a win over Waterford, 3-10 to 2-8. Later, they beat Cork in the championship for the first time in over thirty years, 2-16 to 2-14, at Thurles, and hopes were extremely high when Tipperary were encountered in the provincial final at Killarney. With rain falling incessantly during that game the Premier County boys adapted themselves better to the conditions and a rather lucky point in the closing minute gave them the Munster Crown, 4-16 to 3-18 - and Tipperary went on to secure All Ireland honours.

This reverse could have shattered Limerick, but they recovered to win the Oireachtas Cup, defeating Kilkenny in a most spectacular game at Limerick, and Wexford in the final at Croke Park.

In the course of the 1972 National Hurling League campaign Frankie Nolan, Willie Moore and Jim Allis were introduced onto the panel and they figured in the final against Cork, which the Leesiders won, 3-14 to 2-14, at Thurles.

Limerick's most disappointing day was probably when Clare beat them in the first round of the 1972 Munster championship.

Meanwhile, fundamental changes had been made in the home championships by Shannonside. For very many years previously, the senior title fights had been played on an all county basis with an open draw. Some of the old strongholds of hurling had dropped out, and the position had been reached where the junior championships were providing greater competition and attracting a lot of the interest that rightly belonged to the senior scene.

A special Commission was set up to study the situation - the senior championships were restored to divisional control, with a stipulation that a minimum of six teams should participate in each Divisional senior championship - this to be achieved in the initial year by enforced promotion from junior ranks where necessary - and thereafter on a system of promotion and relegation.

This arrangement proved an immediate success, and some fine displays in this new championship gained Séamus Horgan his goal-minding job, for the 1973 League.

Then the retirement of stalwarts like Tony O'Brien and Donie Flynn made way for the recall of Eamonn Rea and Mossie Dowling; with the youthful Liam O'Donoghue also gaining the notice of the selectors, and a place on the team that won its way to Limerick's fourth successive National Hurling League final.

This, in itself, must be hailed as an achievement, in view of the wide ramifications of the League, and the sustained effort required to qualify for the final - usually calling for a minimum of ten games, and a meeting with all the leading hurling counties. That fourth League final looked a disaster for Limerick when Wexford beat them, 4-13 to 3-7, at Croke Park last May. It, however, had the reverse effect, in making Limerick more determined than ever to go all out for the championship crown.

They had a right tough struggle with Clare in the opening round of the Munster championship at Thurles, and many considered them rather fortunate to register a very narrow win. Tipperary, having earlier disposed of a stout Waterford challenge, beat Cork with a late flourish of goals - and the stage was set for another great Limerick-Tipperary Munster decider.

The pair tossed for the venue - Limerick lost, so the game was played at Thurles - and an unforgettable one it proved - the lead alternating with bewildering frequency in a thrill-packed finish and Limerick's emergence as champions, with a score from the very last stroke of the game. The excitement of that occasion is indescribable.

Limerick had a tough enough battle with London at Ennis before qualifying for their first All Ireland senior hurling final appearance since 1940, when they won the county's sixth All Ireland title. Into the panel by this (time) had come Joe McKenna and Paudie Fitzmaurice, and with Kilkenny as opponents all the ingredients were there for a power-packed final.

Hurling fever rose to previously inexperienced heights by Shannonside, crowds attended the training sessions, and everywhere one went throughout the county a new found confidence was evident, and hurleys were in profusion everywhere the youth were gathered. All Limerick were involved in the final - huge crowds travelled for the game - and the remainder were glued to the television sets. They were thrilled to the core as the green and white colours emerged triumphant - displaying great craft, speed, skill and staying power, to drive all Shannonside wild with delight, and rebaptise a new generation of hurling folk in the hurling faith.

Nothing like the scenes of wild enthusiasm that greeted the victorious team on their return to Limerick with the MacCarthy Cup has ever previously been witnessed in Sarsfield's City, and green and white flags flying proudly on public buildings, business premises, churches and every known vantage point, proclaimed for weeks after the intense satisfaction derived from the success achieved. The City Dinner given by the Mayor and Corporation in honour of the team was a glittering affair, fully representative of every facet of Limerick life, with the President of the GAA and the Chairman of the Munster Council also there.

And what made it a very special occasion was the presence of the surviving members of the teams that won All Ireland honours in 1918, 1921, 1934, 1936 and 1940 for Limerick. Four All Ireland captains - Willie Hough (1918), Timmy Ryan (1934), Mick Mackey (1936 and 1940) and Éamon Grimes (1973) linked the years in a historic get together, that was highlighted when four County Chairmen - Very Rev. E. Dean Punch, doyen of the Limerick GAA, Rev. Dermot McCarthy, Jackie O'Connell and Rory Kiely also stepped on the rostrum to the plaudits of the big attendance.

Limerick County Council also paid their tribute at a special dinner, at which each member of the panel, and team trainer, Mick Cregan, were presented with a beautiful souvenir of the occasion in the form of the county arms mounted in silver on a plaque. Limerick has truly feted its heroes - and hurling everywhere has got a shot in the arm because of the Shannonside breakthrough.

VIPs Stop Play
(Sunday World, 9 September 1973)

An All Ireland medalist is strongly critical of what he calls the "messing" that went on before last Sunday's senior hurling final. He is Jack Mahon, Galway's centre half-back in the 1956 football final, who says, "Like everybody else I thoroughly enjoyed the sporting spectacle in Croke Park, but why oh why are the senior players subjected to so much pressure before the game?"

Mahon's letter to this column continues, "The authorities have allowed the preliminaries to go mad. This business of lining-up the central figures of the stage - the players to pay homage to Cardinal, Taoiseach, President and ex-President is all wrong. Then after all this the Artane Boys' Band, for want of an order, forgot to get going for a march-round that has now become a joke with the players and public. The GAA authorities would need to cut out a whole lot of this messing and get on with the show.

"The public by their slow handclap last Sunday have made their gesture. New thinking is required. With this new thinking will come, hopefully, more thought for the players, who are the most important people in Croke Park on All Ireland day."

Need it be said that Tadhg O'Sullivan agrees wholeheartedly. Here is a man who knows what it's like in the half hour before the All Ireland final begins. He is now an ex-player doing so much good work for Gaelic games in his native county. So, let's listen to Jack Mahon: cut out the messing.

This was the one sour note of Final Day - apart from the drenching you got if you hadn't a stand ticket - the ordeal the senior teams and the terrace patrons were subjected to because of the misconceived desire to pay tribute to celebrities.

Take the teams. They had to stand to attention before the Hogan Stand while clergy and politicians were shown to their seats in the "Top Peoples' Section". On All Ireland Day the finalists should not be secondary to anybody - clergy or politicians. Limerick and Kilkenny were too important to send into a final "cold" and without any warm-up. Textbooks on every game emphasise the need for a warm-up period prior to the commencement of play. On Sunday it was inconsiderate, at the very least, to have them standing around in the rain.

Celebrities must be told they take their seats in the stand by three o'clock at the latest or not at all. If they don't like it, lump them.

As for the uncovered patrons - and they include a great many at the front of the bottom decks of the two stands - it was a downright discourtesy to have the senior final starting eight minutes late. Because of all the nonsense that went on beforehand the parade didn't start until 3:16PM - one minute after the match should have been under way. There's absolutely no excuse for it.

The lads and lasses on the Hill and the Canal end - and those in the unprotected stand seats - pay in to a match that's billed for 3:15PM. And at 3:15PM it should start. Especially in these days when we are gone mad talking about streamlining the Association. So, let's start on time ... introductions, anthems, parades and New York's Finest notwithstanding.

The Central Council officials must take note of the slow handclap from the impatient spectators last Sunday. If they continue their indifference to the paying public they will have less of the paying public than they had at last Sunday's final. It was from the terraces those absent 8,000 were missing.

Given a choice between being kept standing in the rain and watching the match on television I know which one they will choose. So, the day might come when we will have a pouring wet All Ireland Day and the attendance will consist of 32,000 ticket holders and empty terraces at each end.

1973 Keeping the Dream Alive

City Dinner

In Honour of

THE CAPTAIN AND MEMBERS OF
THE LIMERICK HURLING TEAM

Winners of the 1973 All-Ireland Hurling
Final

at the

Parkway Motel, Limerick

ON FRIDAY, 21st SEPTEMBER, 1973

at 8 p.m.

MENU

Melon Supreme

•

Cream of Asparagus Soup
Consomme Celestine

•

Roast Stuffed Loin of Lamb—Mint Sauce
Fresh Garden Peas—Cauliflower Au Gratin
Parisienne—Biarritz Potatoes

•

Fresh Apple Flan
or
Charlotte Carmen

•

Tea or Coffee

WHITBREAD
Trophy

Victory Reception

by

James J. Murphy & Co. Ltd.

Lady's Well Brewery
CORK

in honour of

LIMERICK ALL-IRELAND HURLING CHAMPIONS

and

CORK ALL-IRELAND FOOTBALL CHAMPIONS

Deerpark Hotel, Charleville

Friday, 12th October 1973

Captain weds
(Irish Press, 11 September 1973)

The wedding took place in Limerick yesterday of Éamon Grimes, captain of the All Ireland winning Limerick hurling team, and Miss Helen O'Flynn, St. Jude's, St. Patrick's Road, Limerick.

There was an overflowing attendance in St. Patrick's Church for the ceremony, which was performed by Rev. David Rea, PP, St. Patrick's, assisted by Rev. David Crowley, PP, Donoughmore.

The best man was Mr Larry Grimes and the groomsman was Mr Joe Grimes, brothers of the groom. The bridesmaids were Miss Nora Grimes and Mrs Noreen Hennessy, sister of the bride.

A guard of honour was formed outside the church by members of the Limerick and South Liberties hurling teams.

Over 130 guests attended the reception in the Shannon Arms Hotel. The couple are spending their honeymoon in Majorca.

Mr and Mrs Éamon Grimes receive a hurler's salute after their wedding at St. Patrick's Church.

A green and white wedding
(Limerick Leader, 15 September 1973)

Limerick hurling Captain, Éamon Grimes, laid aside the MacCarthy Cup this week for a treasure of a different sort - red-haired Miss Helen O'Flynn of St. Patrick's Road, Limerick, whom he married on Monday. St. Patrick's Church, Limerick, was packed for the ceremony and many tried to catch glimpses of the couple from vantage points outside. Very Rev. David Rea PP, St. Patrick's, officiated and as the newly weds left the church they were greeted by a guard of honour. Among those who held hurleys aloft, to form the archway were the Hartigan brothers, Jim Hogan, Joe McKenna and Declan Moylan.

Helen and Eamon make a very fine couple in the midst of their friends from the hurling world.
Back Row (L-R): Laurence Grimes, Walter Shanahan, Jim Hogan and Vincent Byrnes.
Middle Row (L-R): Joe Grimes, John Grimes, Bernie Hartigan, Joe McKenna and Pat Hartigan.
Front Row (L-R): Michael Grimes, Joe McGrath, JP McManus, John McDonagh and Pat Wade.

Handshakes

The bride and groom received many congratulatory handshakes from the well-wishing crowds before they set off in their green and white bedecked car for the Shannon Arms Hotel where they entertained over 130 guests. Miss Nora Grimes, sister of the groom, was bridesmaid and Miss Maureen Hennessy was matron of honour. Best man was Mr Larry Grimes, and Mr Joe Grimes was groomsman - they are brothers of Éamon. Emer Hennessy and Donal Ryan were child attendants.

The couple are currently honeymooning in Spain.

The bride is daughter of Mr Martin O'Flynn and the late Mrs O'Flynn and the groom is son of Mr and Mrs Ned Grimes, Rutagh, Ballysheedy.

1973 Keeping the Dream Alive

Grand old lady of Limerick hurling toasts the champions
(Limerick Leader 15 September 1973)

By Richard Naughton

Kilmallock's grand old lady, 93-year-old Mrs Margaret McCarthy of Bresheen, is a living link between Limerick's first All Ireland hurling championship victory in 1897 and the sensational triumph of 1973. Seventy-six years ago her brother, Tom Brazil, scored the winning point for Limerick in the first All Ireland, and a great hurling tradition has been carried on by her family down through the decades to the present day.

"My father, Michael Brazil, was a member of the Kilfinane team and was hurling as far back as I can remember," she told me in the living room of her beautiful rose-clustered home in Bresheen this week.

"He and my brother Tom hurled together in the local team, and it was from him that Tom learned the skills of the game."

They were hard times, and Tom's hurling apprenticeship was no exception.

Mrs McCarthy recalls one memorable occasion when her father got the nickname "Doon" Brazil. Tom was a member of the Kilfinane team that was playing in Doon that day and he made one or two mistakes that looked like costing the visitors the game. His father, watching from the sideline, bounded over the fence, seized the stick from his son's hand, and showed how fields were won. They called him "Doon" after that. Tom took the lesson to heart, and went on to make hurling history for his county. The members of that first 1897 All Ireland team were: P. Mulcahy, J. Hynes, M. Downes, Seán Og Hanley, M. Finn, J. Flood, P. O'Brien, J. Cattroll, P. Flynn, J. Reidy, T. Casey, P. Buskin, M. Flynn, T. Brazil, D. Grimes (captain), J. Finn and F. Dunworth.

Mrs McCarthy likes to talk of the great part hurling played in the lives of the local community in those far-off days.

Moonlight

She recalls the moonlit nights when the boys would roam the countryside together in search of suitable ash trees which they would cut down to make their own hurleys. She recalls the long horse drays which would put up at her door to take the boys to some fixture in another part of the county. And how the vehicle and its occupants would be blessed with holy water to protect them from danger on their journey.

Times changed, but the great hurling tradition continued in her family. In 1957 her grandson, Tom O'Donnell, captained the Limerick team that defeated London for the junior title. Tom, who was a member of the Kilmallock team, now fields with St. Mary's in London. Also playing with St. Mary's in London is Cal O'Donnell another grandson, who before he went to England won a County minor medal with Kilmallock in 1955 and several other titles.

Medals

At home in Bresheen, 12-year-old grandson, Tadgh McCarthy, has won two medals in the Kilmallock School League. And over in London the two youngest members of this great hurling family, 7-year-old Patrick O'Donnell and 5-year-old Dave O'Donnell, great-great-grandchildren of Mrs McCarthy, play the game.

"Hurling is in our family's blood," she told me proudly. "I love the game and I said months ago that if Limerick won the All Ireland I would go on a spree." And, true to her promise, she went to Kilmallock and had "a drop or two" to toast the victors.

Mrs McCarthy, who will be 93 on the 29th of this month, is the oldest woman in the parish of Kilmallock. And, let me add, one of the sprightliest and most mentally alert. She was born on Main Street, Kilfinane, and is living In Kilmallock for the past 73 years.

She has 13 children, 41 grandchildren, 72 great-grandchildren and 3 great-great-grandchildren.

Good times

She has firm views on the rich and great times of the 1970s. "I am telling them now and I tell them often, that they don't realise the good times they are having. I often had a very hard day."

She recalls the times when one would earn 2/6d or 3/- a week for milking cows, and when walking to work over the dew-drenched fields in the morning, one would take the precaution of stuffing one's stockings in a pocket to keep them dry.

Mrs McCarthy's garden in Bresheen has won three first prizes and a second prize in Kilmallock Garden Show. If you enquire the whereabouts of her home, people in Kilmallock will tell you: "You can't miss it; it is the house with the beautiful rose garden," And they are right: second Tuesday in the September sun, it looked a little corner of heaven.

Ninety-three year-old Mrs Margaret McCarthy, pictured with members of her family: Patrick O'Donnell (great-great grandson), Cal O'Donnell (grandson), Tadgh McCarthy (grandson), Julia McCarthy (grand-daughter), and Mrs Margaret McCarthy (daughter-in-law), in the garden of her home at Bresheen, Kilmallock.

1973 Keeping the Dream Alive

Some of the Limerick players and supporters celebrate the All Ireland success at the Cuchulainn lounge in Patrickswell. (L-R): Catherine Fenton, Gerry Bennis, Mick Tynan, Seán Foley, Willie Foley Richie Bennis, Éamon Grimes, Noel Morrissey, Phil Bennis, Frankie Nolan and Josephine Piggott.

What It Means To Win an All Ireland
(Clare v Limerick NHL programme, 7 October 1973)

By Séamus Ó Ceallaigh

I have been asked to put together a few thoughts on "What it means to win an All Ireland."

All down the years I have always felt that the winning of the All Ireland was the highlight of any player's career and the greatest honour a county could aspire to in either hurling or football.

On some rare occasions doubts were created when an odd player made the observation that a Tour of America would be the height of their sporting ambition.

They usually, however, belonged to one or other of the counties properly associated with fairly regular championships renown - where familiarity with the fruits of All Ireland success cheapened their value. I must hasten to stress though that this remained a rare experience even in counties where victory marches were fairly frequent occurrences.

I think the first time it was brought home to me in a very big way what an All Ireland win meant to a victory starved county was in 1948 when Waterford collected All Ireland renown for the first lime. The scenes at Croke Park in 1960 when Down won their first All Ireland Senior Football championship will always stick in my memory, and Offaly's initial win a few seasons ago was another occasion of great rejoicing.

However, I had to wait until this year to absolutely experience at first hand the unfounded joy an All Ireland win can create in a county denied such success over a long period.

Easily the wildest scenes of enthusiasm and excitement I have ever witnessed - and I have seen the very big bulk of the leading championship games extending over half a century - was at Thurles on the last Sunday of July, when Limerick, with the very last puck of the game regained the Munster championship crown after a very long wait.

Everyone in Limerick talked hurling after and the one topic of conversation was whether the County could win an All Ireland crown that had evaded them since 1940 - which meant that a whole generation had grown up without experiencing the throbs and thrills of an All Ireland win.

Limerick were rank outsiders going into the final but everyone in the county had an absolute faith in their ability to succeed, and the greatest crowd ever of green and white supporters were at Croke Park for their meeting with All Ireland title holders - Kilkenny.

Limerick hurled as never before - they won a great final - and then the green and white literally took over Croke Park. The scenes before and following the presentation of the cup are indescribable; they overflowed to the hotel when the winners were entertained to dinner that night by the Limerickmen's Association, and reached a crescendo the following night where everybody in Limerick and surrounding districts appeared to be shouting themselves hoarse in their welcome to the conquering heroes. Nobody ever remembered a reception anything even remotely to compare with it. It was unforgettable.

The impact that win had on the youth of Limerick is evident in every back street and playing space in the city, and in every area of the county, where young lads and lassies with hurleys are now commonplace - all with new heroes who they want to emulate.

And the recent dinner given by the Mayor and Corporation to honour the hurlers was something unique - the greatest ever and most representative gathering at a civic function by Shannonside - proof of it were needed that every section of the community rejoiced with the gaels of Limerick in this their finest hour.

Cumann Luthchleas Gael
COISTE CO. AN CHLAIR

CLÁR OIFIGIÚIL
7-10-73

Páirc an Ciosaghaigh Inis

NATIONAL HURLING LEAGUE
DIVISION 1 "A"

An Clár v Luimneach

Réiteoir   J. MOLONEY (Tipperary)   3.30 p.m.

SENIOR FOOTBALL CHALLENGE

AN CLÁR   v   ROS COMMÁIN

4.45 p.m.

LUACH 10p

(Runai)

Proceeds from the sale of this Programme will go to the CUSACK PARK FIELD COMMITTEE

1973 Keeping the Dream Alive

Some original 1973 All Ireland Hurling Final memorabilia.

1972/73 Limerick League and Championship Programmes

Limerick played four games in the senior hurling championship of 1973. An official match programme was produced for each of these games and all are very collectable, although some are quite scarce. The programme for the London game is the scarcest of all. Even though there were 12,000 at the Ennis game, few programmes survive. Many experienced collectors still do not own one. It has sold for over €300 in the recent past, yes three hundred euro! It was produced in at least three different colours too, as seen on pages 234-235: blue, white, and yellow. The Munster Hurling Final programme was printed in four different colours: pink, green, white, and yellow. This programme has a valuation of €50 to €75. It is not very common, being as easy or as difficult to obtain as any Munster Final programme of that era. There is at least one pirate (unofficial) programme known for this game too. The "Tipperary Star" printed most Munster championship programmes at the time, perhaps even the programme for the London game.

Limerick played Clare in the Munster Championship in June 1973. This was played as the second part of a double-header, alongside the replay of that year's All Ireland Club Football Final, another competition that produces collectable programmes. The relatively small crowd in attendance on the day means that only a modest number of programmes survive today. Because the programme is doubly collectable, its value is €100-plus in collector circles.

The 1973 All Ireland Hurling Final programme is not scarce but it can be quite expensive to purchase as, for many, it has a certain sentimental value, being the only All Ireland that Limerick won between 1940 and 2018. If this final had been won by Kilkenny, the programme would be worth as little as one third of its current valuation. Many of the programmes that survive from that final are of lesser value due to water damage. Good quality copies made as much as €150 in the aftermath of Limerick's 2018 success but, generally speaking, it sells for between €50 to €75. There is at least one pirate programme known for the 1973 final too. In some instances, at least two different pirate programmes were produced for big games during the early 1970s.

Limerick played ten games in the National Hurling League campaign of 1972-73. There are no programmes known for the four group games played before Christmas 1972: Clare (H), Kilkenny (A), Galway (H) and Offaly (H). Programmes exist for the three group games played in early 1973: Tipperary (H), Cork (A) and Wexford (A). A good programme was produced for the drawn league semi-final in Kilkenny but there is nothing known to exist for the replay held in Birr a few weeks later. Yes, there is a memory of a programme amongst some people who were in Birr but it may have been that the programme for the drawn game was also sold at the replay venue. This was not an unknown occurrence at the time but such programmes were usually marked accordingly. A collector friend produced his own programme for the game, as it is the only proper National Hurling League semi-final that no programme is known to exist for, stretching back to 1963-64 when the two semi-final format was first introduced.

CHAPTER 12

1973

ALL IRELAND HURLING FINAL (iv)

AFTERMATH

Some Carrolls GAA allstar (All-Star) awards came to Limerick in late 1973 but, surprisingly, fewer than were won by the losing team. Kilkenny got seven, while Limerick were awarded just five. Wexford got two (Colm Doran and Martin Quigley) while Tipperary got one (Francis Loughnane). The problems seen in later years with the old system of selection were already raising their heads by this time.

There was no All-Star hurler of the year award in that era, the first being awarded as recently as 1995. Pat Hartigan won his third All-Star in a row, going on to earn five in a row over the first five years of the awards, 1971-75. Limerick captain Éamon Grimes did win the 1973 Texaco Sports Star of the year award for hurling, one of 10 sports that were honoured with a Sports Star award that year, out of a basket of 20 eligible sports.

Kilmallock won that year's Limerick Senior Hurling Championship final. It was the first of a three-in-a-row of titles won by the south Limerick club, with a comfortable win over Killeedy on Sunday, 1 December. There was an unseemly row in the lead-up to the game between the county board and the leading local referees over who should referee the game, with Frank Murphy (Cork) taking the whistle. Murphy had refereed the NHL final early in the year that saw the significant injury to Michael Graham. John Moloney had refereed the 1972 decider between South Liberties and Patrickswell. There was a strong tradition at the time of outside referees officiating at other counties' hurling finals, with many Limerick referees travelling in the opposite direction too. This happens very rarely nowadays.

At one of the victory celebrations, 13-year-old Anthony Brosnan of Garryowen won the "Greatest Supporter" award. Tony still has his award and is as big a supporter 50 years on as he was back in 1973. He was captured on film during the 1973 Munster Final walking off the field with Seán Foley immediately after the full time whistle. This picture was recreated almost 50 years later, earlier this summer, both men still being hale and hearty.

A number of songs and poems were produced to celebrate this victory, from Bryan "The Master" McMahon, to John "The Man" Frawley. The 1974 Limerick GAA County Board Convention secretary's report is reproduced in this chapter and covers the 1973 season. It makes for fascinating reading, especially the financing of the county teams. The "S.H." team cost a grand total of £6607.87 in 1973. The figure to run the same team nowadays is over €1 million, as it is in many other counties.

Two very scarce publications were produced in the winter of 1973 to celebrate Limerick's success. One is a yearbook entitled Limerick Heroes, edited by Séamus Ó Ceallaigh. It was marketed as a celebration of Limerick's then recent success. The other was called Limerick All Ireland Hurling Champions. A similar little booklet was produced for Cork's football success, both published by Gaelic Publications in Dublin. The Limerick (and Cork) Champions booklets are extremely scarce, while Limerick Heroes does turn up on occasion. Outside of Raymond Smith's Book of Hurling sponsored by Player's No. 6 and these booklets, there are no other publications dedicated to this singular Limerick success.

A small amount of memorabilia was produced on the back of the 1973 success, an era before the ubiquitous and pervasive registration plates, albeit a 1973 version has since been produced in recent times to commemorate that historic success. The nicest pieces of memorabilia produced at the time were the triangular pennants featuring the heads of the winning team, produced by MIKCRO International. Mike Cronin of the Limerick Sports Shop produced them and sold them for years afterwards. They are now very scarce, especially those in complete and good condition. There was even a good-quality tea tray produced with the winning team picture depicted on the base of it. The lead author is the proud owner of two of them, both hardly used.

Michael Graham - One of Our Unsung Heroes
(Limerick v Cork MHC Programme, 31 May 1998)

By Harry Greensmyth

The score was 0-5 to 0-2 in favour of Limerick with the time ticking beyond the 11th minute of the first half. Mike Graham anticipated a nicely placed ball coming across the Wexford goalmouth. He was well placed so would he attempt a kicked effort or tap the ball to the side of Pat Nolan for a crucial goal? A snap decision had to be made and knowing full well what could develop in around the square, he opted to use his hurl. Did it make any difference? No. "All I knew," says Mike, "is I failed to connect with the hurley - the ball was not in the net and I was on the green sward of Croke Park. The Wexford defence thundered back to avert danger and I was caught in the cross fire."

The occasion was the 1973 National Hurling League final - all of 25 years ago. Before half time was reached, Mike was in Jervis St Hospital having sustained a broken leg. The best wishes of those Wexford stalwarts, Mick Jacob and Colm Doran, as he was assisted off the field were much appreciated, although when a very promising inter-county hurling career lay in tatters in Jervis St, it was so easy to forget the concern expressed by both friend and foe. Mike had come on the Limerick team in 1968 to come within a step of a league medal (Limerick lost that day), and importantly still, a Celtic cross would have been his a few months later.

Conor Meehan agreed to operate on the leg in Croom Hospital. On the Monday, Mike with his leg in plaster, was collected by Noel Leonard, a well-known Patrickswell hurler, who was working at the Horseshoe House, Ballsbridge, with his late father Mattie and uncle Mick (father of County Board PRO Sandra Marsh). The latter two conveyed Mike to Limerick by car, but it was not the most pleasant of journeys as the trip had numerous interruptions, including a stop at Naas and at Andy Guillfoyle's of Roscrea.

A broken leg in the confinement of a car is not too enjoyable, making Mike wonder why an ambulance was not available. At Birdhill, Mike got a fleeting view of the Order of Malta ambulance speeding towards Dublin. On arrival at Croom, it was learned that Dr Dick Stokes had arranged the same ambulance to collect Mike in Dublin. Mike made a brief return to inter-county hurling in 1975, but since then he has been recognised as one of the greatest servants his club, Claughaun, has known. At under age and adult levels, he has managed various county championship winners, proving where his loyalties lay at sporting level. Fate cut short his playing career a quarter of a century ago, but in the intervening years, his commitment to his club and to the GAA has had few equals.

(Left) Michael Graham takes the field for the 1971 Munster Final against Tipperary in Killarney.
(Right) In action against the same opposition in Thurles during the 1972 NHL.

Pictured: The Man Who Missed Out...Michael Graham, who suffered a fractured leg against Wexford in the league final, missed the thrill of playing in the All Ireland. He is pictured with his wife Mona on the victory special to Limerick.

Row Rages over Referees

(Limerick Leader, 24 November 1973)
Four Threaten to Boycott Local Games

By Charlie Mulqueen

A major row is brewing in Limerick GAA circles less than 48 hours before the showpiece of the year - the county senior hurling final between Killeedy and Kilmallock at the Gaelic Grounds on Sunday. And it is the big game itself that provides the source of controversy.

Four leading Limerick referees decided to boycott all fixtures within the county because of the appointment of Corkman Frank Murphy to handle the final.

The four referees in question are Seán O'Connor, John O'Grady, Brendan Cross and Willie Hayes.

The "Sporting View" column of almost precisely twelve months ago made reference to the County Board's policy of bringing referees into Limerick to handle major championship games. At the time, we spoke out in favour of the Limerick officials, pointing out that we had within the county some of the finest referees in the land. In our view, that situation hasn't changed, and one has only to look at the list of inter-county matches handled each week by Limerickmen to appreciate the high reputation they hold all over the country.

"We are absolutely raging over the latest insult," John O'Grady told me this morning. "To think that Seán O'Connor was good enough to do the recent All Ireland Minor Hurling final, and I refereed last year's Munster final and yet we are not asked to take charge of the most important match on our own domestic programme."

Letter

Mr O'Grady informed me that a letter from the four referees would be sent to the County Board putting down their grievances.

And he stressed:

"WE WILL NOT REFEREE ANY MORE MATCHES WITHIN THE COUNTY UNTIL A SATISFACTORY SOLUTION IS ARRIVED AT."

John is confident that the vast majority of other referees support them in their stand.

"It is in our own best interests to be united on the matter," be said. "What makes the present situation more infuriating is that Seán O'Connor, Brendan Cross and myself are all City Board referees, and with the finalists drawn from the south and west, it is incomprehensible to us that one of us wasn't appointed."

During our conversation, Mr O'Grady went to pains to stress that Frank Murphy, the nominated referee, who is also secretary of the Cork County Board, was an innocent party in the row.

"He is a very good referee, and I know he will do an expert job. Indeed we wish him the very best of good fortune. He was asked to do a job and like the fine man he is, he accepted readily. It is as simple as that." said John O'Grady.

Board's Point of View

Later this morning I contacted Mr Rory Kiely, Chairman of the County Board, at his home in Feenagh. He was aware of the disappointment of the referees and fully understood their position. "We would be only too delighted to have our referees in charge or important matches like county finals and so on, but the wishes and rights to the clubs have to be considered. We asked both Killeedy and Kilmallock to submit the names of three referees in us. They did so and Frank Murphy's was the only name on both lists. Subsequently, the clubs agreed with Mr Murphy and we were quite happy with the arrangement." said Mr Kiely. The chairman also went on to make the point that Limerick was by no means the only county to "import" referees for big matches.

"This year, for example, the Cork County final was handled by Michael Slattery of Clare, and I'm sure there is no talk of boycotts down there. And Cork had Frank Murphy and many other fine referees available. Our own Gerry Fitzgerald often did Cork finals and I only hope that some of our own present referees will be invited to do other county finals in the years ahead. It would be a great honour for them," was Mr Kiely's comment. Having heard both sides of the story, it is difficult indeed to form an opinion as to who is right and who is wrong.

One undoubtedly sympathises with the referees, who naturally want to handle the biggest match on the domestic calendar. At same time, when the clubs agreed on Frank Murphy, it would hardly have been wise for the County Board to rule otherwise.

Rory Kiely, County Board Chairman, makes a presentation to Dr Tiede Herrema, Managing Director, on the occasion of the Ferenka Limited Open Day on 16 September 1973.
Also in the picture are Dr Dick Stokes, Pat Hartigan, Jim Allis and Jimmy Hartigan Snr.

Competent Kilmallock Clear Winners
(Limerick Leader, 1 December 1973)
£2,300 Gate sees Killeedy Go Down

By Seán Murphy

Kilmallock 2-12
Killeedy 2-4

A Kilmallock team that was competent rather than brilliant, won their third County Limerick senior hurling championship crown at the Gaelic Grounds on Sunday when they defeated giant-killers Killeedy 2-12 to 2-4 in a game that proved somewhat of an anti-climax for the big crowd (gate receipts £2,300). In the end Kilmallock won a tight rein but their tidy total resulted more from their rival's shortcomings than from any particular brilliance on their own behalf.

Killeedy came to this encounter with much in their favour. They had eliminated reigning champions, South Liberties, and had a big hosting of supporters to urge them on, but on reflection, the occasion seems to have unnerved many of their key players. Killeedy had plenty of spirit throughout but hurling heart is not enough when pitted against a combination such as Kilmallock, whose craft and teamwork was the deciding factor. The game opened in a frenzy of excitement with Killeedy forcing the pace, and when Paudie Fitzmaurice shot them into the lead, the terraces erupted to show that the west was awake. But their joy was short-lived as Kilmallock began to settle and gradually got a grip on the situation.

Mossie Dowling equalised in the 4th minute and with points from Paddy Kelly and Dan Connolly, Kilmallock had edged to a 0-3 to 0-1 lead after 9 minutes of exciting hurling. A beautiful centre by Paudie Fitzmaurice was doubled on by Willie Cronin in the 11th minute whose fizzling shot sailed wide of the upright. From this juncture onwards, the bottom fell out of the Killeedy challenge and the standard subsided to a low ebb.

Speed and Skill

Kilmallock ran the Killeedy defence ragged and with speed, skill and aggression chalked up the scores. Paddy Kelly set the pattern with a point from play in the 12th minute and Tony Smith answered with a similar effort one minute later. The real telling blow came in the 18th minute when Tony Smith gathered a loose ball on be left wing and sent a spectacular shot, low along the ground.

Francis O'Connor gets in his clearance as Mossie Finn attempts to block it down.

1973 Keeping the Dream Alive

KIlmallock's Paddy Kelly (no. 10) pressurises the Killeedy defence with Moss Finn (left) and Mossie Dowling (right) in support.

A Limerick SHC winner's medal from 1973.

Conor Magner (Killeedy) clears to safety while Ben Mullane (no 13), who had been brought back into defence, holds off Davy O'Riordan with Mossie Finn in attendance.

Pat Meehan seemed confident as he approached to save, but the Killeedy keeper was harassed by Mossie Dowling and the ball entered the net for a simple goal. Killeedy were in real trouble, but despite their perilous position they never wilted and continued to give as good as they got. However, the difference between the sides was becoming more glaring as the game progressed. Kilmallock were playing first time hurling while Killeedy were picking and poking, and trying to walk the ball into the net and all to no avail. Two points from play in the 19th and 26th minutes by Mossie Dowling closed the first-half scoring, and so at half-time led Kilmallock 1-7 to 0-1.

Storming Fashion

Killeedy opened in storming fashion but Paudie Fitzmaurice failed from a 21 yard free and it certainly looked as if Lady Luck had deserted the boys from the hillside West Limerick village. Tommy Hanly (winning a third county senior medal with Kilmallock) made a spectacular save from Willie Fitzmaurice before full-forward Pat O'Connor pointed from play in the 4th minute for Killeedy.

Two more close-in frees for Killeedy were shot wide by Willie Fitzmaurice, and so, after 6 minutes of constant pressure, Killeedy's only reward was a single point. What a contrast for Kilmallock. In a fantastic three minute spell Kilmallock were awarded three 21 yard frees, and with quick-fire rapidity, Tony Smith notched 1-2 from the resulting shots. The goal was a real fluke as Smith's mis-hit free rolled into the corner of the net as the sun dazzled the Killeedy defenders.

So, after 9 minutes, Kilmallock led 2-9 to 0-2 and a run-away victory seemed imminent. Greater teams than this teak-hard Killeedy fifteen would have thrown in the towel at this stage. Instead, they stuck doggedly to the task of staving off impending defeat and during the next 9 minutes had a most successful Innings.

They scored 2-2 themselves, missed numerous chances, and into the bargain, held a hither-to rampant Kilmallock team scoreless.

Lifeless

Killeedy's revival started when Denis O'Connor, after a life-less first half, began to dominate at centre-back and the entire team started to hurl strongly and purposefully. A goal from a free by tireless Willie Fitzmaurice was the spark that ignited Killeedy in the 12th minute and when Ben Mullane crashed the ball to the net in the 14th minute following a goalmouth melee Killeedy were riding high. Willie Fitzmaurice pointed a free in the 15th minute but his attempted shot for a major score from another free was saved in the 17th minute and almost immediately Denis O'Connor scored a flaming point from play.

That, unfortunately, was the end of Killeedy's challenge. Kilmallock rallied their forces and three late points by Mossie Dowling (free), Paddy Kelly (play), and Tony Smith (free) made victory a reality long before referee Frank Murphy (Cork), called a halt to proceedings. By any standards it was a poor county final, and with the exception of the opening few minutes and that superb comeback bid by Killeedy midway through the second half, the fans got little to enthuse about.

In apportioning shares of the winning bouquet to Kilmallock, Paddy Kelly, Tony Moloney, Bernie Savage and Mike Carroll stand far ahead of their colleagues. Kelly still eligible for minor, was the springboard for many of the Kilmallock attacks and showed amazing speed and deft ball control. Tony Moloney was razor keen at midfield and showed an uncanny sense of position for the loose ball from the break.

Mike Carroll, a towering figure, did tremendous hurling in the half-back line, while will-o'-the-wisp Bernie Savage, the smallest man on the winning side, was their most dangerous forward. Others to contribute much to Kilmallock's latest success were Nicholas Hayes, Dan Connolly, John McCarthy, Mossie Dowling and scorer-in-chief Tony Smith.

Heroic

For Killeedy, Willie Fitzmaurice roamed the field in a heroic bid to rally the side, but failed through lack of support. However, it was no fault of Mick Deely, Denis O'Connor, Jim Mulcahy, Mike Fitzmaurice and Pat O'Connor that Killeedy were helpless to stem the tide that eventually engulfed them.

Scorers

Kilmallock - T. Smith 2-4; M. Dowling 0-4; P. Kelly 0-3; D. Connolly 0-1.

Killeedy - W. Fitzmaurice 1-2; B. Mullane 1-0; P. Fitzmaurice and P. O'Connor, 0-1.

Teams

Kilmallock - T. Hanley; J. Fitzgerald, D. Hayes, N. Hayes; M. Carroll, J. McCarthy, S. O'Donovan: T. Moloney, D. Connolly; P. Kelly, T. Smith, M. Finn; D. O'Riordan, M. Dowling, B. Savage. Sub: B. O'Sullivan for M. Finn.

Killeedy - P. Meehan; F. O'Connor, M. Deely, C. Magner; P.J. Cronin, D. O'Connor, J. Mulcahy; C. Herbert, W. Fitzmaurice; M. Fitzmaurice, P. Fitzmaurice, M. Scanlon; S. Mullane, P. O'Connor, W. Cronin. Subs: J. Magner for W. Cronin, D. Mullane for C. Herbert.

Referee - Frank Murphy (Cork).

At the conclusion of the game, Mr Rory Kiely, chairman of Limerick County Board, presented the Daly Cup to Mossie Dowling, captain of the Kilmallock team. He praised both teams for their sporting displays and expressed the hope that Kilmallock will prove worthy leaders for the Limerick team in their bid to retain the All Ireland title in 1974.

1973 Keeping the Dream Alive

Kilmallock: 1973 county senior hurling champions

Back Row (L-R): Aidan Carroll, Tony Moloney, Seánie Donovan, Tommy Hanley, Dom Hayes, Dan Connolly, Mike Carroll, John Fitzgerald, Mossie Finn, Nicholas Hayes and Willie O'Brien.
Front Row (L-R): Davy O'Riordan, Bernie Savage, Donie Burke, Mossie Dowling, Jackie McCarthy, Eamon Dowling, Tony Smith; (Seated at front), mascot Johnny Brazil, Jimmy O'Keeffe and Paddy Kelly.

Killeedy: 1973 county senior hurling finalists

Back Row (L-R): Ben Mullane, Con Herbert, Con O'Connor, Michael Scanlon, John Magner, Paudie Fitzmaurice, James Mulcahy and Denis O'Connor.
Front Row (L-R): Willie Cronin, Pat Joe Cronin, Pat O'Connor, Conor Magner, Willie Fitzmaurice, Michael Deely, Mick Fitzmaurice and Pat Meehan.
Not in picture: Francis O'Connor and Gerard Moloney.

Taken from the 1972 Limerick GAA Yearbook.

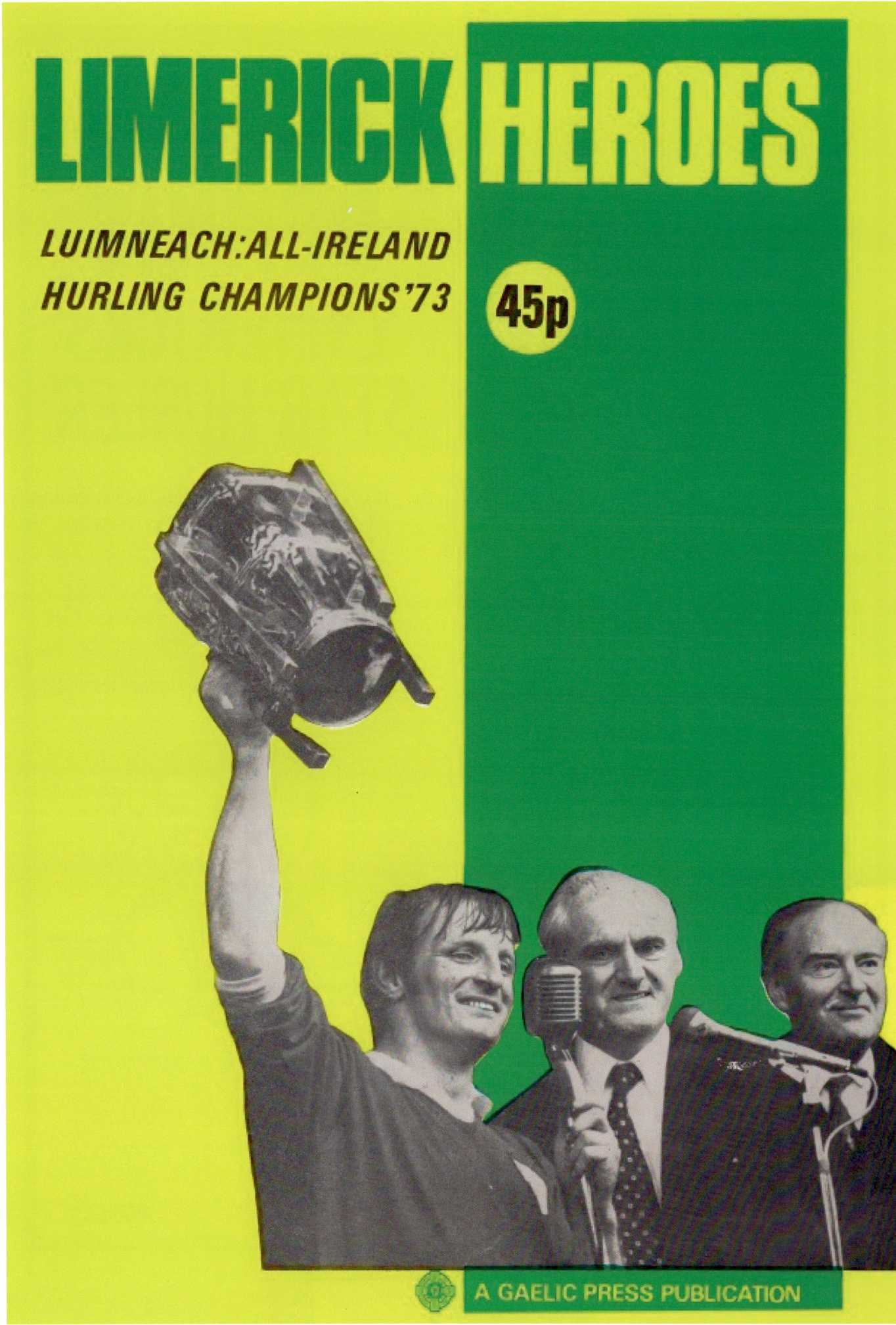

LIMERICK HEROES

RÉAMH RÁ

Anallód bhí cáil ar bháireoirí Luimní theas is thuaidh. Nuair a chlis ar na hiománaithe i gCluiche Ceannais na Mumhan dhá bhliain ó shin ann, shíl cuid dá lucht tacaíochta go mbeadh píosa orthu sula néireodh leo. Ach tharla lá samhraidh eile ann a mhúscail Cathair an Chonartha, an lá ar iompraíodh laochra Luimní go caithréimeach ó pháirc na himeartha i nDúrlas Éile. Ní bheadh coinneáil feasta orthu, agus ní raibh gur scuabadar Corn Mhic Cárthaigh siar go Siona.

The year 1973 will be a year to remember for the people of County Limerick. After the long wait of 33 years, their team succeeded in bringing the All-Ireland Hurling Championship back to their county. They did it in the style of true champions because they overcame a gallant Kilkenny team in one of the best and most sporting finals for many years. The enthusiasm of their supporters in Croke Park after the final and in Limerick when they returned with the McCarthy Cup, shows the great volume of support that the game has in the county, and I have no doubt that this victory will bring a new enthusiasm to the game in Limerick. Over the past few years they have shown that they had the talent and their displays in the National League and Munster Championship was just a foretaste of what was to come in 1973. Their wonderful fitness and dedication to the game was bound to bring success and great credit must be given to their trainer, selectors and County Board officials.

But the real victor this year was the game of hurling. The standard of play and sportsmanship shown by our teams, particularly in the final, cannot but do good for the game. The victory of Limerick after such a long time will give great encouragement to these counties who, like themselves, have been striving for years without ultimate success.

To the team and all connected with them, may I on behalf of the association, offer my sincere thanks and congratulations.

Dónal Ó Ceanáin,
Uachtarán C.L.G.

contents

Press views on Limerick victory	7
Statistics of Limerick honours	11
Surprise team — quotes	12
Interview with Michael O'Hehir	15
1887 Crisis	16
Outside looking in	21
Bord na nOg	22
The man who came to cheer	25
Colour pin-ups	29–32
View from Kilkenny	33
Some reflections	35
Feile na nGael	39
Heyday of Limerick hurling	45
Personalities on parade	47
Leann Luimni	52
Great Limerick clubs	53
An old hurler looks back	55

The Editor: SÉAMUS Ó CEALLAIGH

Published by:
GAELIC PRESS LTD,
21 Great Denmark St, Dublin 1.
Tel. 49557/42709
Printed by Wellbrook Press, Freshford.

Please bring this Report to Convention

CUMANN LUITH CHLEAS GAEL
Coisde Co. Luimni

Limerick Co. Board

CONVENTION

1974

AT PARKWAY MOTEL

SUNDAY, 27th JANUARY, 1974

AT 1.30 O'CLOCK

Preceded by Holy Mass for repose of souls of Departed Members 1 p.m. at Parkway Motel.

SECRETARY'S REPORT
STATEMENT OF ACCOUNTS & BALANCE SHEET
NOMINATIONS, MOTIONS, ETC.

1974 Limerick GAA Convention Secretary's Report
(27 January 1974)

CÚNTAS AN RÚNAÍ

A Chathaoirligh agus a Cháirde Gael

Tionólfar an Chomhdháil Bhliantúil i mbliana san Parkway Motel ar an 27ú Eanáir 1974 ag tosú ar 1.30 i.n. Léifear Aifreann na Marbh ar son na mball atá caillte san halla céanna ar a h-aon a chlog.

Is cúis mhórtais is áthais domsa i mbliana bheith in ann an cuntas bliantúil seo a chur os bhúr gcomhair. Ní mór ná gurb í an bhliain seo caite ceann des na blianta ba mhó clú agus cáil dá raibh riamh againn. Ba í barr céim na bliana éachtaigh seo ná an oíche ghlórmhar úd i mí Mheán Fómhair nuair d'fhill Corn Mhic Chárthaigh chun na cathrach seo 'gainne tar éis dúinn bheith ina éagmais le fada an lá. Is taitneamhach an smaoineamh é freisin bheith ábalta a rá go bhfuil na craobh-chomórtais tagtha chun críche againn i ngach aon ghrád.

To say that the year that is passed was the greatest ever from an inter-county point of view is not in the least to belittle the great years of former times - one has in mind in this respect the stirring time during the thirties and early forties when Limerick county hurling teams set new records in the National League and forged new links in the All Ireland title chain in 1934, 1936 and 1940 as well as a historic visit to America during 1936.

Having in mind however, the heartbreaks and disappointments since 1940 with special painful remembrance of the 1971 Munster Hurling Final at Killarney and the defeat by Wexford in May last year in the National League decider, it is with hearts swelling with pride and joy that we follow the triumphant march of Limerick's hurlers during 1973.

On the 24th June we faced Clare at Thurles in the first round of the championship. To say that the team gave an indifferent display in winning narrowly is not in the least to take from the stout-hearted Banner County men who made us travel all the way to achieve victory and who would have beaten a lesser team than Limerick eventually proved to be. Nevertheless, this match in Thurles showed that we had the material and to use that potential to the full was now our endeavour.

It was a period of relentless preparation by all concerned, players, selectors, trainer and officials to face old rivals Tipperary in their home ground on July 29th. It was a question of now or never for many of the players. Defeat for many might mean the end of the road and for the Association in the county another disappointment. Victory would mean a rejuvenation of the spirit of endeavour that has ever sustained the hurling men of Limerick through all the years of loyalty to our national game.

It was a great moment for us all - that Sunday afternoon in July when our hurlers faced Tipperary in their home ground at Thurles to battle for the Munster Hurling Championship. And what a glorious occasion it proved to be. The ever-faithful followers of Limerick were there in their thousands and gathered from all quarters - a story is told of one excited Limerick man who came all the way from Egypt to see Limerick play. It was indeed a great tussle and a stirring bout to watch.

The changing fortunes of the teams as the battle raged for supremacy had the spectators in a welter of excitement all through the game culminating in a draw as the final seconds were reached when Limerick forced a seventy yards puck. It is not often that it falls to the lot of one player to win or lose a game of so much importance but a Limerick player on that day had to face this responsibility.

It is a well-known fact that many a spectator looked away while Richie Bennis took that seventy yards puck but what Limerick man watching the white flag being raised and heard the final whistle go immediately will ever forget the scenes at Thurles on that historic afternoon? We were Munster Champions again after 18 years and it was only natural that all should show it, players and spectators, on that great day in Thurles.

The following Sunday we faced London at Ennis in the All Ireland semi-final. It was to be expected that the game would not reach the standard of the previous Sunday but we were nevertheless, glad when our team won comfortably.

We now stood to face Kilkenny in the All Ireland Final 2 September, and our hurlers set themselves the onerous task of intensive preparation. No team ever prepared with more vigorous enthusiasm and no team ever exceeded the gruelling thoroughness with which they set about the training.

2 September, 1973 will always be remembered by Limerick people as the great day that our hurling men swept the slate clean of all the sad occasions of the past years when defeat was ours. The team gave a machine-like display of superb hurling. Fit and eager as they were they mastered in no uncertain fashion those great All Ireland hurling specialists - Kilkenny in a glorious show of masterly hurling to be seven points ahead at the final whistle.

And what of the stupendous scenes at the end? Who will ever forget how Croke Park was stormed by the thousands of wild and joyously happy Limerick followers who, after 33 long years, were hailing Limerick as All Ireland Champions. It is true to say that men (and women too) wept with joy and one of the greatest scenes of enthusiasm ever to be seen at the National Stadium took place on that day and the news of Limerick's victory rang around the world to where Limerick men and women were gathered in waiting.

The Homecoming on the following night was contributed to by many thousands of grateful citizens with the Mayor and Corporation members playing a prominent part and the many functions to fete the champions since had paid tribute to the wonderful prowess of Limerick's hurling men.

It is indeed a wonderful tribute to the team to record that in spite of the rejoicing and festivities that always follow such a great victory our National League reputation is still intact.

My wish for the year ahead "let the bonfires keep on burning..."

What can one say of Football? Once again, displays have been indifferent and disappointing. There were some promising displays but it must be admitted that a lot of hard work lies ahead before we can be regarded as a force in this code.

Our Under 21 sides made their exit at the hands of Kerry in football and Cork in the hurling decider which we reached without a game.

In the minor grade we were defeated in the first rounds of both the Special Minor Football competition and the Championship while in hurling were victorious over Kerry and Clare to qualify for the final. In that game at Thurles we did not live up to the promise of the earlier rounds and challenge games.

After the All Ireland victory, the completion of our championships together with the carry-over from the previous year was an outstanding achievement and all concerned must be congratulated. We may have been lucky in that, unlike other years, we did not have any one club involved in the concluding stages of both hurling and football. I mention this fact to emphasise that early completion of Divisional Championships is vital if we are to repeat the performance in the years ahead.

HONOURS LIST

Senior Hurling:	Cill Moicheallog	Runners-Up:	Cill Ide
Junior Hurling:	Bothar	Runners-Up:	Na Fianna
Under 21 Hurling:	Dromin-Athlacca	Runners-Up:	Tuar Na Fola
Minor Hurling:	Cill Moicheallog	Runners-Up:	Athain
Senior Football:	Connradh Sairsealaigh	Runners-Up:	Naomh Ciarain
Junior Football:	Naomh Seánain	Runners-Up:	Na Piarsaigh
Under 21 Football:	Na Piarsaigh	Runners-Up:	Ubhla
Minor Football:	Clochan	Runners-Up:	An tAthair Cathasaigh
Under 21 Hurling 1971:	Tobar Phadraig	Runners-Up:	Garrdha Ui Spolain
Senior Football 1972:	Eas Geitine	Runners-Up:	Caislean Nua Thiar
Junior Football 1972:	Clochan	Runners-Up:	Fiaddamair
Under 21 Football 1972:	An tAthair Cathasaigh	Runners-Up:	Galbaile
Under 21 Hurling 1972:	Fiodhnach-Cilimide	Runners-Up:	Garrdha Ui Spolain

The completion of the carry-over from 1972 resulted in championship honours for Askeaton (SF), Claughaun (JF), Fr Caseys (U21F), Feenagh-Kilmeedy (U21H'72) and Patrickswell (U21H'71).

In the 1973 senior championships the standard of the previous year was well maintained in all divisions. Both title-holders lost their crowns, South Liberties in the quarter final and Askeaton in the semi-final. Killeedy, young in senior ranks, were the surprise of the hurling scene. After their defeat of champions Liberties they qualified for the final following a drawn game with Pallasgreen.

Kilmallock who defeated Ballybrown and Patrickswell on their way to the final proved too strong for the Westerners in a game which attracted a record attendance (gate receipts £2305). Treaty Sarsfields having taken the City title from Claughaun had good wins over Galbally and Croom to qualify for the Football decider. St. Kierans who had earlier ended Oola's hopes reversed the West final result when putting out champions Askeaton and went on to meet the City champions in the decider. After a good and sporting game the honours went to the Thomondgate side.

While not detracting from the teams taking part it is only fair to say that Junior Hurling has lost a lot of its glamour since the upgradings to senior ranks of 1972. Boher and Na Fianna qualified for the final at the expense of Monagea and Treaty Sarsfield. In a well-contested decider the East champions were narrow winners. In Junior football St. Senans, having accounted for Oola in the semi-final were victors over Na Piarsaigh, conquerers of Bruree in a very well contested final.

The Under 21 grade produced some fine games. In hurling Dromin-Athlacca are champions after defeating Tournafulla at the second attempt. Ballybrown and Doon were the beaten semi-finalists. Na Piarsaigh and Oola qualified for the football decider, defeating Ballylanders and Fr Caseys. The City side captured their first title when proving too strong for the East champions.

In Minor ranks Kilmallock retained their hurling crown when defeating Ahane, and Claughaun were victors over Fr Caseys when taking the football honours.

County and Divisional Bord na nÓg report a successful year completing championships in Under 14 and Under 16 Hurling and Football. Unfortunately, the finals were not played until late in the season and all concerned must accept that it is most unfair to the boys in these age groups when games are allowed to drag on until late in the year.

Champions for 1973 are:

Under 14 Hurling: An Ceapach Mhór   Under 16 Hurling: Ath Dara
Under 14 Football: Scoil Na mBraithre   Under 16 Football: Eas Geitine

Once again we had a very high standard in the Talent Competition "Scór 73". Ahane, our representatives in Question Time repeated their Munster championship win of the previous year. In the Juvenile "Scór 73" Galtee Gaels were Munster champions in Question Time and Michael Ryan of Pallasgreen captured Munster and All Ireland honours in Solo Ballad Singing.

The staging and success of Féile na nGael deserves heartiest congratulations to all concerned. The Féile week-end will long be remembered and to Br Guthrie, Pádraig Ó Maoldomhnaigh, Seán O'Connor and their many Committees – go raibh míle maith agaibh. The Feile will again be staged in Limerick in July and it is our sincere wish that it will surpass that of 1973 if such is possible. Congratulations to Br Perkins and the Mini-Olympic Committee on the success of the Games and to Dromcollogher on their All Ireland Hurling success. A word of praise also to the various Bord na nÓg, Schools, camogie and Handball Boards on their great work. A report from the Handball Secretary is attached. Congratulations to Ballybrown and Monaleen on winning out their respective divisions.

Many thanks to our Referees who were always on hand when required. The appointment of a referee from outside the county for the Hurling final led to a number of our leading referees intimating that they were not prepared to officiate for the Board. Discussions have taken place between Representatives of the Referees and the Board Officials. It is with regret we note the retirement of South Board Chairman, Pádraig S. Ó Riain. First elected in 1951 he held the respect of all with his firm but fair handling of the affairs of the Association in South Limerick. Even though Pádraig has retired we know that he will never be far removed from our activities.

Called to their reward during the year were our beloved Bishop, Dr Murphy, Mick Neville, Kilfinny, Mick Minihan, Ahane and Tommie Hehir, Bruff. To their relatives, the Clergy of the Diocese and to all who suffered bereavement our deepest sympathy. Ar dheis Dé go raibh a n-anamacha go léir.

Buíochas do gach duine a chabhraigh liom - an tArd-Stiúrthóir, Rúnaí Chomhairle na Mumhan, mo Chó-oifigigh, Rúnaithe Bhoird is Chumann, lucht na bpáipéar nuachta agus na daoine cúntacha uile.

Rath Dé oraibh go léir.

Mise,

TOMÁS Ó BEOLÁIN

County Board

Chairperson: Rory Kiely
Vice Chairperson: John Whelan

Secretary: Tom Boland
Assistant Secretary: Michael Tynan

Treasurer: Declan Moylan

Munster Council Delegate: Mick Mackey
Central Council Delegate: Jackie O'Connell

County teams' expenses for the years of 1972 and 1973

COUNTY TEAMS' EXPENSES

	£ p
S. H.	2376.03
S. F.	931.26
I. H.	134.15
J. F.	145.10
U-21 H.	386.58
U-21 F.	84.47
M. H.	505.19
M. F.	197.39
Hurling Balls	147.00
Hurleys	148.05
Football	9.50
Laundry	45.75
First Aid	1.50

COUNTY TEAMS' EXPENSES

	£ p
S.H.	6606.87
S.F.	1014.19
U.21H.	313.65
U.21F.	107.82
M.H.	861.59
M.F.	144.40
Hurleys	185.40
Hurling Balls	307.77
Footballs	31.70
Laundry	50.00
First Aid	12.16

1973 Keeping the Dream Alive

Texaco Sportstar of the Year (Hurling) in 1973 was awarded to Éamon Grimes.

The Texaco Sports Stars for 1973 will be chosen from ten of a list of twenty sports decided on by the panel of (newspaper) Sports Editors.

The ten sports categories will be decided at the next meeting, as well as the category from which the Hall of Fame will be awarded. The twenty sports left for further considerations are:

Athletics
Horse Racing
Boxing
Cricket
Hurling

Cycling
Motor Sports
Equestrian Sports
Rowing
Gaelic Football

Rugby
Soccer
Golf
Squash
Greyhound Racing

Swimming
Tennis
Handball
Yachting
Hockey

RUGBY . . . IN! BOXING . . . OUT! That was the decision of the panel of judges for the annual Texaco Sports Stars awards who picked the ten sports yesterday from which the awards will be made.

The chosen sports are Athletics, Cricket, Gaelic Football, Golf, Greyhound Racing, Horse Racing, Hurling, Rowing, Rugby, Soccer.

This is the first time that boxing has been omitted from the list and the first time that rugby has been included. The respective decisions will cause an amount of "heartburn" in both headquarters, but for entirely different reasons.

The following are the ten Texaco Sports Stars of 1973:

Athletics - Mary Tracey
Cricket - Dermot Monteith
Gaelic Football - Billy Morgan
Golf - Maisie Mooney
Greyhound Racing - Ger McKenna
Horse Racing - Ron Barry
Hurling - Éamon Grimes
Rowing - Seán Drea
Rugby - Mike Gibson
Soccer - Pat Jennings

When you think of the great days of Irish showjumping, the Army teams of the past immediately spring to mind. With the Texaco Hall of Fame award to go to equestrian sport this year, it was natural that the winner should be one of the legendary foundation members of the Army Equestrian School, Dan Corry.

What a career Corry had. He rode in Army teams for 1926 to 1958 and during that time set up a fantastic sequence of successes all over the world. His appearance in 1958 must have set some kind of record as he had not ridden in international competition for five years when he partnered Ballynonty in the Nations Cup at Rotterdam. Lt. R. Molony had been injured, so Corry, the non-riding team captain, substituted and contributed a clear round and 8 faults as Ireland finished third.

The 1973 Texaco GAA Stars
(Gaelic Sport, February 1974)

By Neil McCavana

Limerick and Cork have produced some great captains down the years and in Éamon Grimes and Billy Morgan, who have just added the Texaco trophies to their impressive collections of top awards, they have men well qualified to command prominent places among the outstanding team leaders in hurling and football. Their strong, purposeful leadership did much to create the mood for those long-awaited All Ireland senior triumphs by Limerick and Cork.

Grimes, whether at midfield or in attack, set a bright standard all through the Shannonsiders' glory march with his darting, skilled hurling and inexhaustible energy. Morgan matched the headline consistently on the football front with his coolness and dependability in goal, and deft and intelligent clearances that so often sent Cork sweeping out from defence into attack. Truly, captains who were shining examples to their team-mates.

Éamon Grimes, now 25, and Billy Morgan, who will be 29 this month, have more in common than their great qualities as inspiring captains of All Ireland senior title winning outfits. Both are former Colleges' players, although the Limerick native enjoyed the greater success nationally as a schoolboy. He won All Ireland senior hurling medals with Limerick CBS in 1964 and 1966.

This pair also put their budding skills on parade on the inter-county minor front. In those days, however, as in the Colleges' matches, the man, who has now carved out such a proud reputation for himself as a master of the goalkeeper's art, was chasing scores as a forward.

Morgan moved into goal around the mid-'sixties, and quickly won honours with Cork in the position in both the junior and Under-21 grades. In addition, he collected Sigerson Cup medals with UCC in 1965 and 1966.

This now celebrated duo continued virtually in step during 1966. Billy was called up to the senior inter-county grade for a challenge game on Easter Sunday, and a few months later Eamon made his debut with the premier Limerick squad in a Munster Championship encounter with Tipperary.

Since then they have been consistently to the forefront in the top rank, perfecting the matchless skills that helped them to earn such acclaim during the past year.

As is so often the case, however, the early days in inter-county senior competitions did not prove especially fruitful for Grimes or Morgan as regards the top national honours. The 'seventies have brought a dramatic change in fortune, however.

COMPETITIVE SPIRIT

Eamon, with his great competitive spirit and skill, proved a vital link in the side that completed a rare double for Limerick in 1971 by winning the National League title and the Oireachtas Cup. Some months later Morgan, who has been Munster's first choice in goal since 1967, was putting up the type of barrier that was invaluable in helping the South to power in 1972 to a first Railway Cup title win in 23 years.

The vigilant and brave goal-keeper figured in another celebrated win later that year when his club, Nemo Rangers, took the Cork senior football championship for the first time. And yet again the Limerick hurler, a native of Donoughmore, kept firmly in step.

He pulled his weight in impressive style in a victory over Patrickswell that earned for South Liberties a first county senior hurling final triumph since 1890.

In their reigns as county captains this gifted pair marshalled their many telling skills to a degree that made each the type of rallying force that means so much to a team. They grew in stature with leadership that was brimful of intelligence and inspiration.

Small wonder, then, that Éamon Grimes and Billy Morgan continued firmly in step by taking their places for the first time in the ranks of the Carrolls All-Stars awards winners in December, and then went on to emerge as the Texaco Gaelic players of 1973.

They well deserve these latest distinctions, for they have served not only their counties, but the games really well. There can be little doubt, either, that they will continue in the seasons ahead to adorn the games with their power-packed play and sportsmanship.

As long as hurling and football keeps producing men of the dedication and high qualities of Éamon Grimes and Billy Morgan, then there is no need to be fearful for the future of the national games.

Jersey, ball, hurley: £140
(Limerick Leader, 17 November 1973)

A showcase containing the jersey worn by Limerick captain, Éamon Grimes, in the All Ireland Hurling Final, and a sliothar and hurley autographed by the members of the team, were auctioned at the Parkway Motor Inn in aid of the Irish Wheelchair Association.

The items were knocked down for £140 to Mr J.P. McManus, chairman of the South Liberties club for which Grimes plays.

Carrolls GAA All-Stars poster (smaller format) for 1973.
They were hung in many pubs through the halcyon days of these awards during the 1970s and 1980s.

1973 Keeping the Dream Alive

Jim O'Brien (Limerick)
Left full back. Club: Bruree.
Carrolls GAA All-Stars Award 1973
"For his rare bravery and mobility: for the all-round splender of his contribution to Limerick's much delayed return to championship honours."

Seán Foley (Limerick)
Left half back. Club: Patrickswell.
Carrolls GAA All-Stars Award 1973
"For his fervour he brings to all facets of hurling, and particularly for his dedicated half-back play which contributed so much to Limerick's 1973 success."

Richie Bennis (Limerick)
Centrefield. Club: Patrickswell.
Carrolls GAA All-Stars Award 1973
"For his level-headedness he has so frequently shown in the tightest of situations and his exceptionally high rate of scoring."

Éamon Grimes (Limerick)
Left half forward. Club: South Liberties.
Carrolls GAA All-Stars Award 1973
"For his seemingly limitless energy and his desire to work all over the field: qualities which have made him a natural leader and a high scorer."

Éamon Grimes' 1973 Carrolls GAA All-Stars hurling award.

The third Carrolls GAA All-Stars hurling team was announced at a Press Reception in Dublin on Monday, 29 October. The team for 1973 was selected from 49 nominations and as in previous years the two principal requirements were sportsmanship and playing ability. The Selection Committee was made up of leading GAA writers representing the Belfast, Cork, and Dublin newspapers, as well as Raidió Teilifís Éireann. Both Dr Donal Keenan and Mr Seán Ó Siocháin, President and Director General of the GAA, sat on the Committee as observers and Pat Heneghan Public Relations Manager of P.J. Carroll and Company Limited acted as non-voting Chairman.

Pat Hartigan (Limerick) who was unanimously chosen for the full back position on this year's team is joined by Francis Loughnane (Tipperary) and Eddie Keher (Kilkenny) as the only three hurlers who have received three consecutive Carrolls GAA All-Stars awards. At Monday night's reception Dr Donal Keenan, President of the GAA, said, "This evening we are assembled again to announce the Carrolls GAA All-Stars hurling team. This is the third occasion on which this team has been selected and it is safe to say that interest in the selection of the team is increasing as it gives an opportunity of honouring the players, particularly those individuals who do not figure in the role of All Ireland medal winners.

"It is a signal honour to be selected, because not alone is the player selected for his skill but also for his sportsmanship on the field of play. These men are a credit to the game of hurling and are fine examples to the youth of our country.

"P.J. Carroll and Company who present the All-Stars Awards have shown a great interest in our Irish games and I would like to thank them for their willingness to establish this Awards Scheme and for the great co-operation that exists between them and the GAA. My thanks and congratulations to the Gaelic sports writers who were the originators of the All-Stars Awards. Their sense of dedication has been shown by this great effort which honours our best players." The Carrolls GAA All-Stars football award winners for 1973 will be announced on Monday, 12 November and the trophies will be presented at a banquet in Dublin on Wednesday, 12 December.

PAT HARTIGAN (Limerick)
Full back. Club: South Liberties.
Carrolls GAA All-Stars Award 1971, '72, '73
"For his undiminished skill and dependability in a very demanding position where quite often brawn is substituted for hurling artistry."

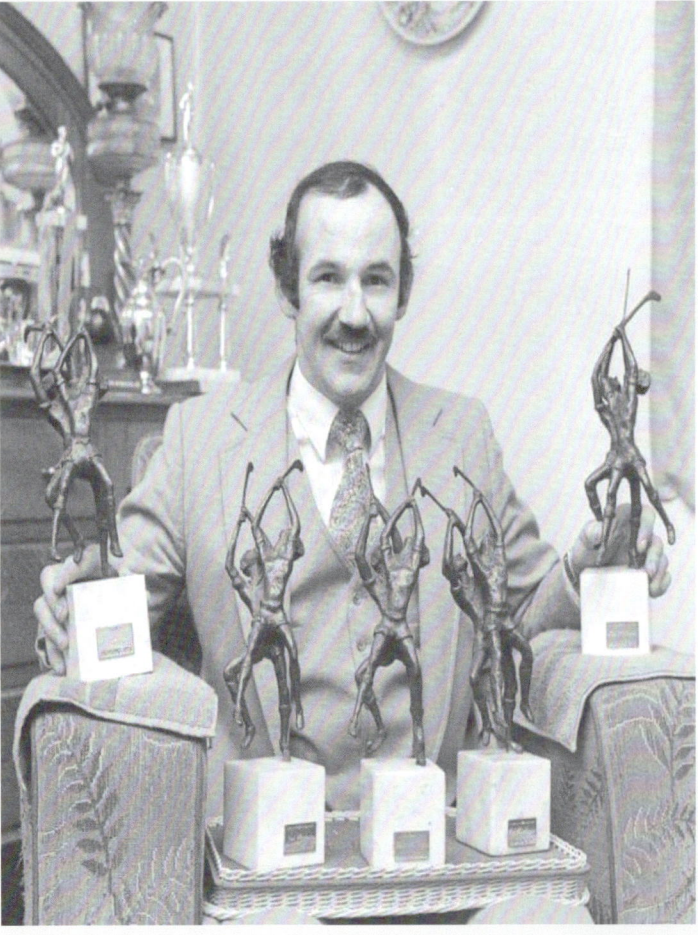

— THE TOP FIFTEEN —
The All Stars Selection.

This is the Carrolls All Star Selection for 1973:—

Noel Skehan
(Kilkenny)

Fan Larkin   Pat Hartigan   Jim O'Brien
(Kilkenny)   (Limerick)   (Limerick)

Colm Doran   Pat Henderson   Sean Foley
(Wexford)   (Kilkenny)   (Limerick)

Liam O'Brien   Richie Bennis
(Kilkenny)   (Limerick)

Francis Loughnane   Pat Delaney   Eamonn Grimes
(Tipperary)   (Kilkenny)   (Limerick)

Martin Quigley   Kieran Purcell   Eddie Keher
(Wexford)   (Kilkenny)   (Kilkenny)

Carrolls 1973 All-Star hurling team.
Back Row (L-R): Pat Henderson, Pat Delaney, Eddie Keher, Kieran Purcell, Richie Bennis and Pat Hartigan.
Front Row (L-R): Colm Doran, Phil 'Fan' Larkin, Noel Skehan, Liam O'Brien, Francis Loughnane and Éamon Grimes.
Insets (L-R): Seán Foley, Martin Quigley and Jim O'Brien.

Limerick's Green and White
Air: 'The Felons of Our Land'

The month it was September and Seventy-three the year
When Limerick and Kilkenny met, to make the verdict clear
Croke Park's green sward was wet but hard, it shone like Velveteen
Kilkenny wore the Black and Gold, and Limerick, White and Green

In days gone by the cup of joy, we raised on many a day
But oft alas, it came to pass, 'twas dashed unto the clay
For thirty years midst bitter tears, our fondest hopes had been
That Mackey's skill and hurling thrill would rest on White and Green

The ball is thrown between the host and swift as lightning
Frankie Nolan opens the score with a merry flick of ash
Kilkenny's back in quick attack, they move like oiled machines
But brave and high against the sky stands Limerick's White and Green

Kilkenny strove with all their force our heroes to subdue
RememberingNore's most pleasant shores and the hills beside Slieverue
Then from the crowd in accents loud emerged in vibrant tone
A rebel yell from Patrickswell and Limerick's Treaty Stone.

The games waxed furious and fast as the sliotar rose and fell
And no man flinched a single inch in the game he loved so well
And when at last the whistle blast, pealed out upon the scene
What flag was raised to pride of place but Limerick's White and Green

In future times we'll boast of Grimes, a captain tried and true
Those mighty men the Hartigans and Liam O'Donoghue
With Séamus Horgan in the gap, McKenna, Moore between
And Foley sweet, whom none could beat, in Limerick's White and Green

I praise Ned Cregan to the skies, of Claughaun and Monagea
And peerless Bennis Brothers too with Dowling and Eamonn Rea
And Jim O'Brien that fearless lion and Nolan too the cream
And the hurling stick of trainer Mick who schooled the White and Green

Mick Lipper in his Mayor's robes stood up and proudly spoke
The very sky o'er Lisnagry was filled with flame and smoke
And thirty thousand cheering fans did in the streets convene
As shouldering high, they raised the cry, 'Hurrah for White and Green

Old Limerick's gates in former days have seen some wondrous sights
But none so fair as could compare with that famous night of nights
For strong men cried with joy and pride in Tour and Ballysteen
As silver shone above the throng and Limerick's White and Green

So Limerick's sons, I pray each one be loyal fast and true
And be your aim to play the game, your hurling fathers knew
On Final Day with hearts so gay may you with prideful men
Restore its own to the Treaty Stone and Limerick's White and Green

Bryan "The Master" MacMahon

Limerick 1973

Air: The Juice of The Barley

In the year of the Lord 1973
All the experts were saying it would be Kilkenny
But their faces were red when they saw the last score
Twenty four to the Shannon, seventeen to the Nore
and Limerick are All Ireland champions
Hats off to that gallant fifteen.

At the back there was Philly and bold Willie Moore
Glorious Pat Hartigan, Séamus from Tour
Jim O'Brien, Seán Foley, all joys to behold
Held the foemen at bay just like Sarsfield of old
And Limerick are All Ireland champions
Hats off to that gallant fifteen.

Now they say Pat Delaney is a wonderful man
Sure how will they stop him, Kilkenny men sang
But their song was stopped almost before it began
By a green shirted hero named Eamonn Cregan
And Limerick are All Ireland champion
Hats off to that gallant fifteen.

You could search the whole country from Derry to Ennis
But where would you find a sweet striker than Bennis
Not a free or a seventy for five miles around
But straight as a die o'er the bar would be bound
And Limerick are All Ireland champions
Hats off to that gallant fifteen.

There had to be one to be captain that day
To lead on his men by example and play
He was here, there and everywhere until at times
You would think there were ten of the bold Éamon Grimes
And Limerick are All Ireland champions
Hats off to that gallant fifteen.

Well they all played their hearts out that wonderful day
Frankie Nolan, Mossie Dowling and the burly Eamonn Rea
Liam O'Donoghue, Bernie and Joe from Shinrone
Put the Treaty Stone up on the All Ireland throne
And Limerick are All Ireland champions
Hats off to that gallant fifteen.

Now that all's said and done and Kilkenny are beat
Everyone will admit they were grand in defeat
With the cup proudly resting on Shannon's green shore
We look forward to seeing them in seventy four
And Limerick are All Ireland champions
Hats off to that gallant fifteen.

John "The Man" Frawley

1973 Keeping the Dream Alive

A presentation of trays marking Limerick's historic All Ireland win. (L-R): Seán Foley, Jimmy Carroll (President of Patrickswell GAA), Phil Bennis, Frankie Nolan, Richie Bennis and Gerry Bennis (Chairperson of Patrickswell GAA).

1973 Keeping the Dream Alive

All-Stars tour programmes from March 1974.

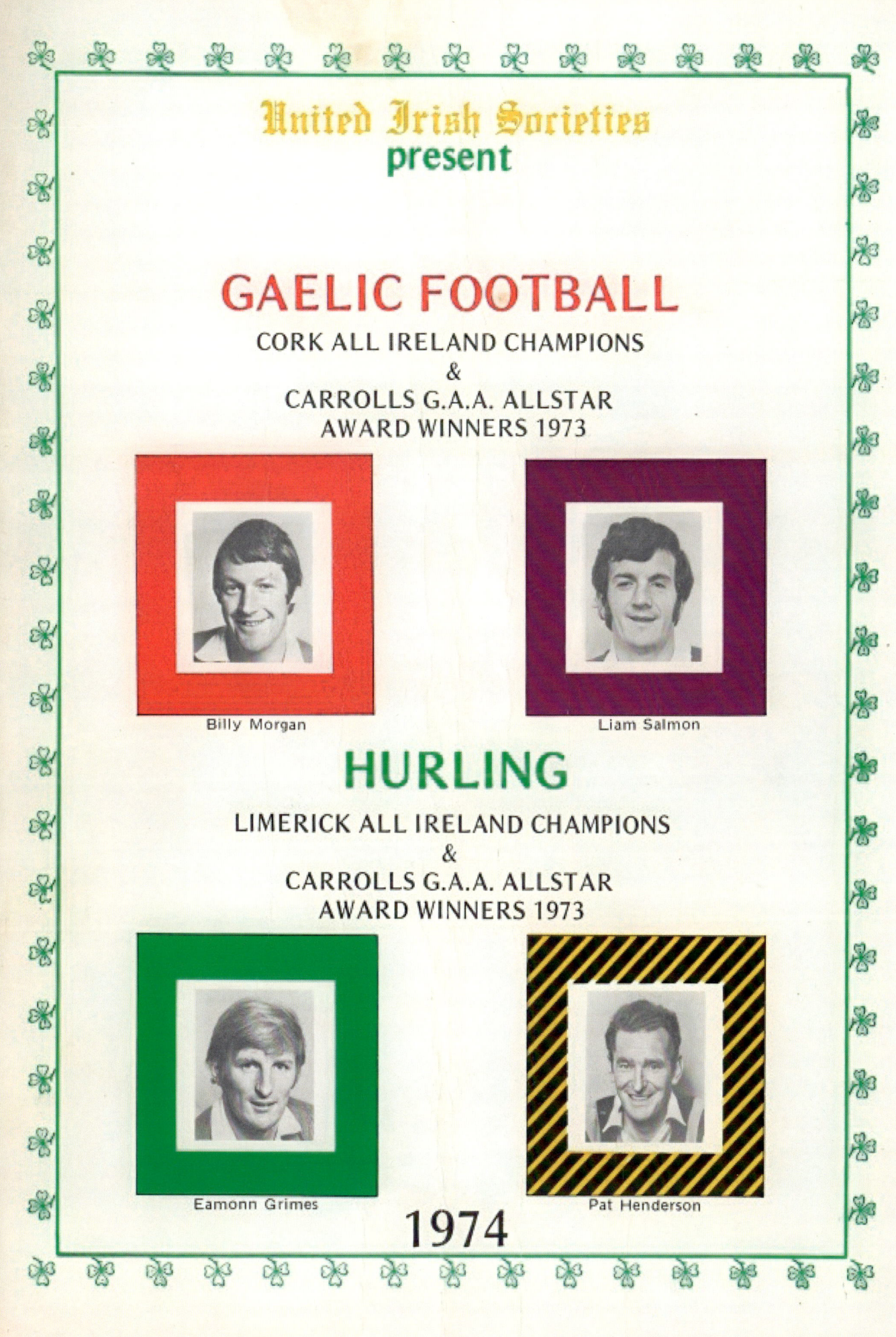

Special Ovation
(Limerick Leader, 22 December 1973)

A standing ovation was given at Tuesday night's Limerick victory to 13-years-old Tony Brosnan of Garryowen, who was described by team captain, Éamon Grimes, as having been the team's greatest supporter.

A special trophy was presented by the players to Tony, who was stated to have hitched lifts to all parts of Ireland to see Limerick play. The trophy Tony received from the players was identical to that presented to the County Board officials. A student at St. John's CBS, Tony was given a hero's welcome by the huge crowd present. Indeed he was accorded the only standing ovation of the night when thunderous applause greeted each of the players as they went forward to receive their trophies.

Another huge ovation was given to Mr Tommy Casey, who was also presented with a special trophy as Limerick's most loyal taximan for about 40 years.

Anthony Brosnan and Seán Foley coming off the field after the final whistle of the 1973 Munster Hurling Final and re-united almost 50 years later at The Strand Hotel in May 2023.

Anthony Brosnan still cherishes the plaque he received in December 1973 for being the team's greatest supporter.

Playing Rule Changes Approved by GAA Congress
(Cork Examiner, 15 April 1974)
Delegates in Experimental Mood

Changes in the playing rules, originally recommended by the Rules Revision Committee, and sponsored in the form of motions from Roscommon, Tyrone and Tipperary, were, with a few exceptions, approved for a 12 month trial period at the annual Congress of the GAA in Sligo yesterday. The most revolutionary of the rule changes involved the introduction of the enlarged parallelogram in both hurling and football, and the imposition of bigger penalties for infringements inside these areas.

Delegates were in an experimental mood when the much-debated motions came up for discussion after the luncheon break. Several rules which were not expected to be supported were passed surprisingly, as in the case of the limiting of defending players in a goalmouth to three when a 21 yard free in hurling is being taken.

Main Changes

The main changes are: larger parallelogram and (in football) awarding of a penalty for a foul within that area; same in hurling with a free puck being awarded from a centre spot on 21 yard line for any foul in the enlarged area, and limiting of defending players to three: goalkeeper (in football), not to be charged within the smaller rectangle; an offence for attacking players to be inside the smaller rectangle before the ball (hurling and football); outlawing of third man tackle - an offence to charge a player unless he has possession, or is about to play the ball (hurling and football); players to be put off for persistent fouling after having been warned by the referee (hurling and football); return of the hand-pass - in addition to present fisted pass. The larger parallelogram means that there will be two rectangles - one 15 yards by 5 yards, and the other 21 yards by 14 yards.

Rule 133, Paragraph 1 to be amended to read: "Four lines shall be marked two five yards long and four yards from each goalpost and two 14 yards long and seven yards from each goalpost. The ends to form two rectangles, one 15 yards by 5 yards and the other 21 yards by 14 yards".

Rule 149 to be amended to additionally read: "In hurling when a foul is committed by the defence within the larger rectangle the referee shall place the ball on the centre spot of the 21 yard line and only three players may stand on the goal line, all other players must be outside the 21 yard line. When a foul is committed by the defence within the 21 yard line a free shall be given on the 21 yard line opposite where the foul is committed".

Connacht Tribune - 10 May 1974

This weekend sees the introduction in County Galway of the rule changes approved by Congress in Sligo. All games played in the county over the week end will be affected, including the Jack Whelan memorial games in Killimor between Galway and Limerick hurlers and the Galway and Longford footballers.

Irish Independent - 14 May 1974

Following is the Committee's direction on Rule 149 - a foul within the larger rectangle in hurling:

"This rule could be best described as the introduction of a Penalty Rule to hurling. A free is given from the centre spot of 21 yard line for all fouls within the larger rectangle with only three defenders allowed on goal line. All other players must be outside the 21 yard line and 21 yards from ball.

"For all other fouls committed by defence within the 21 yard line, and outside the larger rectangle, a free puck is given on the 21 yard line and opposite the point where the foul was committed. All other players to be a minimum of 21 yards from the ball, even though they may be inside the 21 yard line."

It was learned at the meeting that the Rules Revision Committee has not been disbanded. It will continue to function up to the 1975 Congress to note the good or ill-effects of the new rules.

Major Changes in Playing Rules Adopted (Irish Examiner, 31 March 1975)

The major changes in the playing rules, introduced on a trial basis last year, were formally adopted at Bundoran, County Donegal, yesterday. Approval was given for the enlarged parallelogram: goalkeepers in both hurling and football are to be afforded the same protection inside the small square, and the third man tackle will continue to be outlawed. Several new rules were passed, the most significant being the decision to replace the 80-minute game, which pertained to provincial finals, All Ireland semi-finals and finals since 1970, with 70-minute games in all senior inter-county championships.

Clarification of the rules governing fouls in the larger square came in a Wexford motion which sets down that technical fouls do not warrant the awarding of a penalty. However, in the small square all types of fouls must be penalised with a penalty.

[Author's Note: At some stage since then, technical fouls in the small square in hurling were downgraded to a 21 yard (20 metre) free. There have been other small tweaks of this rule since then.]

Bill O'Connell, Managing Director of Murphy's Brewery, and Dr Donal Keenan, President of the GAA, congratulate Billy Morgan and Éamon Grimes at the All Ireland Victory celebration.

CHAPTER 13
1974
AND BEYOND

EPILOGUE

Limerick qualified for the National Hurling League (NHL) final of 1973-74 but fell to Cork in the Gaelic Grounds in May, 6-15 to 1-12. This was a third loss to Cork at this stage since 1970. Sports science was only in its infancy at the time, and it seemed that the team were overtrained in the week before the game and played accordingly. The league campaign had gone well with only one loss and two draws from the 7 group games, coming second to Cork in Division 1A. Tipperary had been beaten in the semi-final in late April, after losing to them in the group stages two months earlier. It was Limerick's fourth defeat in the final in five seasons, appearing in five finals in a row.

The All-Stars trip to the US took place in March. At least two games were played between Limerick and the All-Stars selection while on the west coast. An invite to participate in the Wembley Games tournament on Whit Sunday, 26 May, in London, was accepted but the result there was no better than 1972 team's, losing to Kilkenny after extra time, 2-15 to 1-13. It was to be the third last year of this venerable tournament, which had been going in one form or another in the city since 1927, and since 1958 at Wembley Stadium. The dimensions of a soccer pitch are usually 105 by 68 metres, while Croke Park is maximally sized at 145 by 90 metres.

The Munster championship of 1974 started with a game against Waterford in Thurles. The Déise led for much of the game but were undone in the final stages by a spirited comeback, including a sensational goal from Éamon Grimes. Clare were later well beaten in the Munster Final, 6-14 to 3-9. Clare had beaten Tipperary while Waterford had earlier beaten Cork. Kilkenny had beaten Wexford in the Leinster Final by the incredible score of 6-13 to 2-24. It would be another Limerick/Kilkenny final in September. Kilkenny beat Galway in the only semi-final that year! The outcome would not be the same as the year before. Limerick were well beaten, even after a very good start, 3-19 to 1-13, in the last 80 minute final.

Limerick qualified for the next two Munster Finals but lost both of them by wide margins. It was then the turn of Clare to challenge for Muster honours, narrowly losing the 1977 and 1978 Munster Finals; Limerick came again in 1979, but lost another Munster Final. All these finals were lost to Cork. However, with the help of no less than six 1973 veterans, the Shannonsiders did gain revenge on the Rebels in an exciting final in Thurles in 1980. The Limerick team of 1973 played a number of exhibition games as a group in the 1980s. They played against Clare's team of 1977/1978 in 1982, the 1973 Tipperary team in 1986 in Newcastle West, and a Kerry all-stars selection in 1989 for the opening of Austin Stacks clubhouse, a compliment to stalwart, Jackie Power.

The team got together again in 1998 for the jubilee team presentation during that year's All Ireland Hurling Final between Offaly and Kilkenny. It was captured by RTE television cameras. The Friends of Limerick '73 organised a series of events for the 40th anniversary in 2013. Their worthy efforts are recalled here, especially the limited-edition signed jersey, of which only four were produced at the time. The opening of the Fr John Ryan Memorial Park in Kilbreedy in May 2013 was the centrepiece of these celebrations, with both 1973 All Ireland Hurling Final teams getting together again. Two of the 1973 Kilkenny panel were ill at the time and were to pass away soon afterwards. Only Liam O'Donoghue and Andy Dunworth were missing from the 21 Limerick players named in the 1973 All Ireland Hurling Final programme. Four have gone to their eternal reward since then, two starters, Jim O'Brien and Eamonn Rea, as well as two substitutes, Jim Hogan and Andy Dunworth.

The 50th anniversary celebrations in May 2023 included a function on the day of the Munster Championship round-robin game with Cork. A formal function took place at The Strand Hotel before the game, with most of the 1973 players, or representatives of same, attending. These players were later presented at half time, where they received the warm and heartfelt applause of the 41,000 people in attendance. This book forms the other major part of these anniversary celebrations.

The Day a County's Pride was Reborn
(1974 Our Games Annual)

By Pádraig Ó Fainín

2 September 1973, will be remembered as Limerick's Day of Resurgence, the day on which a county's pride was re-born, the day on which a team of green-clad young hurlers lived up to the demands of a tradition that, betimes, had threatened to overwhelm them. It will be recalled, too, as a day of glory for all who had worked through the long, lean years, that a tradition might survive and guarantee ultimate triumph.

For this was more than a victory for Éamon Grimes and his men: this was a victory for a hurling county, as it was a victory for hurling men, whatever their allegiance. Here was a glorious display of all that makes hurling an art form, a game of surprising excellence that is so uniquely Ireland's own.

Let us now recall aspects and facets, not so much of the game itself but of the great occasion, the better to understand the significance of Limerick's victory. The praises of the men who achieved fame that day in Croke Park have been well and truly sung. Their achievement has become part of hurling history. The stories of their courage and their dedication and their prowess will be told and told again in the years to come. And these stories will inspire youngsters long after the Hartigans and the Cregans and the rest have faded from the scene. After all, wasn't it the example of the Mackeys and the Clohessys that inspired the Limerick men of '73! That is what tradition is all about.

But, it is not of the players alone that would write in this brief article. The causes of victory go deeper; the effects of victory are diverse and widespread. Limerick had waited long for this day - all of thirty-two years to be exact. Between 1940 and 1973, Limerick hurling languished at inter-county level with only occasional spurts and starts that ended with promise unfulfilled. Frustration at times threatened to give way to despair. The old-timers expressed the view that Limerick was not breeding them anymore. The young fellows, their hopes blighted by nagging fears that the old-timers might be right, could easily have given up the ghost.

But, tradition dies hard. The spark remained, and it was soon to burst into flame. Limerick, in 1973, determined that this must be their year. They were not prepared to wait any longer. They knew they had the hurling. Now they would show that they had the heart, the spirit, the will to win to match the hurling. The rest is history. They had their moment of luck against resurgent Clare. There was courage in the manner in which they snatched victory from Tipperary with the last stroke of a memorable Munster final.

Gallant London could not stay the march of Limerick. But, it was against Kilkenny that Limerick achieved greatness. There was suddenly revealed the surge and sweep and power and enthusiasm that was irresistible. The magic of another generation was a reality again. Limerick were All Ireland champions. They could not have failed that day. They were unbeatable.

Three unrelated incidents marked for me the depth, the significance of the great event. The game over, Éamon Grimes made his way to the stand. It was a scene of indescribable enthusiasm. But, as the hero of Limerick received the cup, I caught a glimpse of Jackie O'Connell, a hurler from the past, and a man who had given a life-time of service that the GAA and its ideal should live on in Limerick. In his eyes were tears, and in his expression I realised what the long years of labour and waiting had meant to the county. I saw in that face a hurling county re-born.

Limerick's chairman, Rory Kiely, was on the stand with Éamon Grimes. Kiely found himself pressing in on Eamon De Valera, himself a Limerick man from Bruree. Suddenly, impulsively, Rory grasped the former President's hand and said excitedly: "The boy from Bruree - Jim O'Brien - played his part for Limerick today." There, for me, was demonstrated the source from which Limerick drew its strength, pride in club and parish.

Finally, a day or so after the final, television carried the visit of the team to the Sexton Street CBS, the alma mater of so many of the champions, and a great hurling nursery. The scene again beggared description, but the obviously impressed RTÉ newsreader fairly caught the mood of it all with the observation: "There's hero worship for you!"

And that simple remark convinced me that Limerick, in celebration of a great victory, were guaranteeing an even greater future for Limerick hurling. There was the significance of 2 September 1973, for Limerick and for the game of hurling.

Carrickmacross Remembers Limerick
(Monaghan GAA Yearbook 1975)

Carrickmacross Juvenile GAA Club, who have competed in Féile na nGael since its inception, were in Limerick last year, and paid tribute to their host club Ballybricken at their annual dinner and social in Carrickmacross recently.

On leaving Limerick for home after last year's Féile, Br Gregory of the Carrickmacross club invited the officials of the Ballybricken club to their annual function and he stated at that time that he hoped that Limerick would win the All Ireland hurling championship and that they would have the MacCarthy Cup to bring with them to the Northern town. The Ballybricken club had great pleasure in accepting the invitation and on January 4th last, a happy group set out for the Northern town.

The party that travelled from Limerick for this outstanding gala occasion at the Nuremore Hotel, Carrickmacross, were Rory Kiely Chairman Limerick County Board, Jim Kirby Féile na nGael executive member, Jack White Vice-Chairman, Brendan Crehan Secretary, and Michael Weekes Treasurer, of the Ballybricken Club respectively. Two members of the All Ireland winning team, All-star Pat Hartigan and Joe McKenna also travelled.

The attendance also included many northern officials: Michael Feeney (Chairman of the Monaghan County Board), Padraig O'Rourke (Treasurer), and former County Chairman Michael Duffy, (who held the chair in Monaghan for a record 21 consecutive years), as well as Rev. G. Ferguson (C.C. Carrickmacross), Br Gregory (Chairman), Tony Lynch (Secretary) Carrickmacross juvenile (club) and many others.

A big Céad Míle Fáilte to the Limerick delegation in Carrickmacross in January 1974.

Br Gregory of the Patrician Brothers who is doing outstanding work in the interest of the youth in Monaghan presided at the dinner and stated during his welcoming address that the occasion was a memorable one for his club, and their supporters, and he could not give enough praise to the Limerick County Board for allowing the Liam MacCarthy Cup and some Limerick team members to travel to the border town in the hope of promoting the game of hurling. His concluding remarks were "Long live Féile na nGael" and counties like Limerick who are making a general effort to foster hurling in the weaker counties.

(L-R): Michael Weekes, Joe McKenna, Pat Hartigan and Br Gregory in Carrickmacross, County Monaghan, with the Liam MacCarthy Cup.

The highlight of the function was when Jim Kirby of Féile na nGael presented the youth of Carrickmacross with a quantity of Juvenile hurleys. The Ballybricken Club also presented Br Gregory with a hurley autographed by the Limerick officials and All Ireland panel. Br Gregory returned this gesture by presenting the Limerick party with beautiful inscribed plaques.

The Ballybricken Club would like to thank the people of Carrickmacross for the wonderful reception accorded to them and hoped that their visit with the MacCarthy Cup which was in Ulster for the first time, will in some small way help to promote hurling in the Northern County. Michael Weekes recalled one elderly Monaghan man who had never missed a Munster or an All Ireland Hurling Final for many years saying, "I feel like an All-star" when he held the MacCarthy Cup over his head.

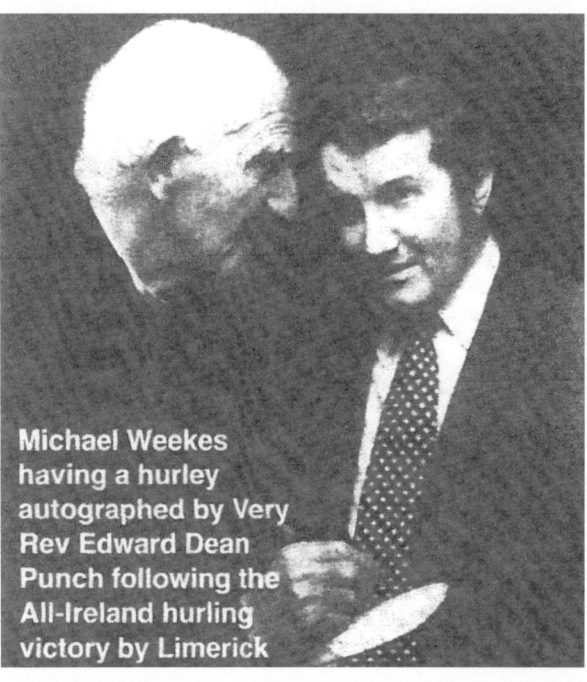

Michael Weekes having a hurley autographed by Very Rev Edward Dean Punch following the All-Ireland hurling victory by Limerick

Railway Cup
(Cork Examiner, 19 March 1974)
Leinster Again The Masters As...Munster Continue Losing Sequence.

By Jim O'Sullivan

Leinster 2-15
Munster 1-11

How does one relate the failure of Munster hurlers in the Railway Cup final for the fourth successive year at Croke Park yesterday to the fact that the province has supplied three of the teams for the League semi-finals? It wasn't Munster's carelessness or lack of effort that enabled Leinster to achieve the four-in-a-row; they were simply the better side and their victory was seldom in doubt. The obvious explanation of course, is that the best team wasn't chosen and this was borne out by the difference in the attack after the introduction of Cork's Gerald McCarthy in particular, and the Waterford captain, Martin Hickey in the last twenty minutes. And apart from the fact that Ray Cummins was not available, several other in-form players were not even on the Selection. Leinster won with a well-balanced team but their overall advantage at midfield from Christy Kehoe and Frank Cummins, and the greater thrust of their forwards, were really the decisive factors. The success of their attack, even allowing for first half inaccuracy, was highlighted by the comparative weakness of the Munster forwards - as evidenced by the contribution of 1-6 of their total score from frees.

Declining Interest

The game again confirmed the declining interest in the Railway Cup. The attendance was even smaller than the previous day, and while the teams compensated for a lifeless first half with a good contest in the second half, they were handicapped considerably by the general lack of atmosphere. Leinster, with wind advantage in the first half, held a slight edge from the beginning. Kehoe and Frank Cummins were on top at midfield against Séamus Hogan and Seán Foley but some wild shooting kept their scoring down a great deal. Munster, who had Liam O'Donoghue in the full-forward line for the absent Michael Keating, failed to win much possession from the half-forward line - where Lawlor and Colm Doran were dominant on the wings. And even though O'Donoghue won quite a lot of the ball from Pat Dunny in the right corner, much of his efforts went to waste because of the strength of the Leinster backs around the goalmouth area. Munster fell behind after Eamonn Rea opened the scoring with a first minute point and did not lead again until the 25th minute when Francis Loughnane goaled from a 21 yards free. However, within thirty seconds Eddie Keher cancelled this with a similar score. And then, a minute later, left winger. Pat Quigley from Dublin had another goal to put them in front 2-6 to 1-4 at half time.

Improvement

There was a noticeable improvement in the Munster team early in the second half. They scored four points to Leinster's two in the first nine minutes and when Gerald McCarthy pointed seconds after his introduction in the left corner, only two points separated the teams, However, this was the nearest that Munster came. Séamus Hogan lost his early sparkle, Éamon Grimes had only occasional success at left half forward and Francis Loughnane made an impression when he moved to centre-forward, only to lose his form gradually. Eamonn Cregan dominated at centre-back against Tony Doran (who had switched earlier in the game with Pat Delaney) and for a while wing backs Tadhg O`Connor and Con Roche looked to have come to grips with the strong challenges from Pat Quigley and Martin Quigley respectively. Munster had a Liam O'Donoghue point disallowed in the 46th minute because substitute Martin Hickey (who had made the pass for the score) had not reported to the referee as he came on the field. But it hardly made any difference, since Leinster maintained their lead in the face of continuing - but in the circumstances, weak - pressure.

Staying Power

In fact, Munster failed to score after Loughnane pointed a free in the 48th minute - at a stage in the game when they were only two points behind, and playing well enough to recover. The selectors introduced a third substitute, Pat McGrath, in the 54th minute and switched Eamonn Cregan to full-forward in a desperate bid to save the game, but to no avail. Leinster had the staying power, and more important, the skill in defence to frustrate the Munster attackers, the game moved to its inevitable conclusion, with the home province adding on five points in the last eleven minutes. Leinster's best were Padraig Horan, Pat Dunny (who was also a member of the winning Leinster football team the previous day becoming only the 4th player to win Railway Cup medals in both hurling and football), Pat Lawlor, Colm Doran, Christy Kehoe, Frank Cummins, Martin Quigley and Tony Doran. Eamonn Cregan was Munster's outstanding performer, with Brian Murphy, Tadhg O'Connor, Seán Foley, Francis Loughnane, Éamon Grimes and Liam O'Donoghue impressing at stages. Gerald McCarthy played so well after his introduction to suggest that he should have been on from the start.

Scorers:

Leinster - E. Keher 1-7 (1-6 frees); K. Purcell 0-4; P. Quigley 1-0; M. Quigley 0-2; C. Kehoe. and T. Doran 0-1.

Munster - F. Loughnane 1-4 all frees; E. Grimes 0-3 (0-1 free); G. McCarthy 0-2; S. Hogan 0-1 free; E. Rea 0-1.

Teams:

Leinster - N. Skehan (Kilkenny); P. Larkin (Kilkenny), P. Horan (Offaly), P. Dunny (Kildare); P Lawlor (Kilkenny), P. Henderson (Kilkenny Capt.), C. Doran (Wexford); C. Keogh (Wexford), F. Cummins (Kilkenny); M. Quigley (Wexford), P. Delaney (Kilkenny), P. Quigley (Dublin); K. Purcell (Kilkenny), T. Doran (Wexford), E. Keher (Kilkenny).

Referee - Tommy Kelly (Galway).

The Munster team that lost to Leinster in the 1974 Railway Cup Hurling Final. It contained 8 Limerick men.

Back Row (L-R): B. Murphy (Cork #2), J. O'Brien (Limerick #4), S. Foley (Limerick #9), A. Heffernan (Waterford #11), S. Hogan (Tipperary #8), E. Cregan (Limerick #6), E. Rea (Limerick #14), C. Roche (Cork #7) and P. Hartigan (Limerick #3).
Front Row (L-R): F. Loughnane (Tipperary #10), T. O'Connor (Tipperary #5), L. O'Donoghue (Limerick #15), E. Grimes (Limerick Capt. #12), S. Durack (Clare #1) and F. Nolan (Limerick #13).
Subs: G. McCarthy (Cork) for Heffernan, M. Hickey (Waterford) for Nolan and P. McGrath (Waterford) for Rea.

Cumann Luthchleas Gael
Coisde Conndae Lonndain

Allied Irish Banks
WEMBLEY GAMES
Wembley Stadium
SUNDAY 26th MAY 1974

Football 1.30 pm
LONDON v A.I.B.

Hurling 3.00 pm
Limerick v Kilkenny

Football 4.30 pm
Cork v Galway

Under 16 Football at 12 noon
LONDON v DUBLIN

Limerick Lose to Kilkenny in Extra Time Thriller
(Limerick Leader, 27 May 1974)
Tragic "O.G." by Seán Foley
Wembley Game of All the Skills

By "Leader" Special from Wembley Stadium

Kilkenny 2-15
Limerick 1-13

Kilkenny avenged their All Ireland defeat by Limerick when they scored a five-point triumph, 2-15 to 1-13, over the Shannonsiders in a tremendously entertaining challenge at Wembley Stadium yesterday. But they had to go to extra time to do it, and Limerick, even in defeat, lost no credit or respect as they hurled to such a high level as to suggest, that they will be again a major force by the time their turn in the Munster Championship comes round.

The matches (the football affair that followed was won decisively by Galway, who defeated Cork by 8 points) were sponsored by Allied Irish Banks and the decision to switch them to Sunday proved a major success with the crowd of 20,000, about 8,000 up on 1973.

Even though Kilkenny played very well and in many ways merited their triumph, the sad aspect of it all from Limerick's point of view is that their vital goal, coming in the first seconds of extra time, was an "O.G." by Seán Foley, who throughout the match had shown that he is very nearly back to the brilliant best that saw him the star of last year's All Ireland final.

But that goal gave Kilkenny the leeway in an extra time period that stretched to only five minutes each way, and they went on to win by five points, 2-15 to 1-13.

Once again, Eamonn Cregan was a majestic figure in the Limerick side, with Pat Hartigan, Willie Fitzmaurice, Bernie Hartigan, after coming on as a half time substitute, Liam O'Donoghue and Frankie Nolan in fine fettle.

Limerick were kept in touch by the magnificent Cregan in the first half, at the end of which they led 1-6 to 1-5 because Kilkenny had most of the play, but threw away numerous chances. Limerick took theirs, despite the dominance of Frank Cummins around the middle of the field.

In that opening 30 minutes, scores were level three times and Kilkenny had more than enough chances to win the match, but their full forward line was not getting the supply from outfield and only Mick Brennan and Eddie Keher looked dangerous.

The Hartigan-Foley move was cancelled by Kilkenny's fine defensive display in the second half, and it was left to Keher to keep Kilkenny in touch in those last hectic moments.

It was Keher who scored his side's equalising point in the 59th minute, which made Wembley history for, sixty seconds earlier, Cregan had pointed a superb seventy to put his side into the lead.

Little Right

The extra time was tragic for Limerick. Hit by the first minute goal, they could do little right from there to the finish. At the end of the first five minute spell, they were 2-14 to 1-13 behind, but there was simply no way through that Kilkenny defence in the last five minutes. It is amazing how Wembley seems to bring out the best in many of these hurlers. Although Cregan was the outstanding figure in the game, Keher, cool as you like, did everything with a touch of class.

Had Kilkenny a few more forwards like him or Mick Brennan, the match might never have had to go to extra time. Goalkeeper Noel Skehan, Fan Larkin, Jim Treacy, and Pat Henderson in the defence, were first class. Frank Cummins faded after a bright start, and Keher and Brennan impressed in the attack.

Scorers

Kilkenny - E. Keher 0-10; M. Brennan 1-2; L. O'Brien 1-1; P. Broderick and P. Delaney 0-1.

Limerick - P. Fitzmaurice 0-5; L. O'Donoghue 1-2; F. Nolan and E. Cregan 0-2; E. Rea and E. Grimes 0-1.

Teams

Kilkenny - N. Skehan; F. Larkin, N. Orr, J. Treacy; P. Lawlor, P. Henderson, P. Cullen; F. Cummins, B. Harte; J. Kinsella, P. Delaney, L. O'Brien; M. Brennan, M. Crotty, E. Keher. Sub: P. Broderick for Kinsella.

Limerick - S. Horgan; P. Bennis, P. Hartigan, J. O'Brien; T. Ryan, E. Cregan, P. Herbert; W. Fitzmaurice, S. Foley; P. Fitzmaurice, J. McKenna, E. Grimes; L. O'Donoghue, E. Rea, F. Nolan. Subs: B. Hartigan for Herbert and M. Dowling for Rea.

Referee - E. Murray (Wicklow/London).

Photographed at O'Dea's Pub on Mulgrave St.
Back (L-R); Declan Moylan, Jim Hogan, Andy Dunworth, Michael Graham, Christy Murphy, John Doran, Patsy Flannery and Gerry Bennis.
Front (L-R): Anne Finnan, John Joe O'Dea, Éamon Grimes, Rory Kiely and Mrs Margaret O'Dea.

1973 Keeping the Dream Alive

AS DESCRIBED BY THE AMERICAN SCRIBES

Taken from the Limerick GAA Yearbook.

Limerick All The Way
(Limerick Leader, 29 July 1974)
Clare Outclassed in Munster Final
No dispute this time as champions coast to a great win

Limerick 6-13
Clare 3-9

By Seán Murphy

Limerick's reign as undisputed kings of Munster hurling continues. At Semple Stadium, Thurles, on Sunday before a crowd of 36,446 they crushed the aspirations of a youthful Clare team with a display of exciting hurling, full of purpose and drive and were well and truly worth even more than their fourteen point winning margin, 6-14 to 3-9 at the final whistle.The Munster Final is regarded as a magical day in the hurling scene, but Sunday's encounter lacked the atmosphere and hurling class one usually associates with the southern decider. Clare were just simply out of class. Even Biddy Early, the famous East Clare witch from Feakle, who was said to have uncanny accuracy in forecasting future events was wrong, for once. She forecast that Clare would win the All Ireland after a lapse of 60 years. It will be recalled that Clare won their only All Ireland crown in 1914. Limerick, although weak spots were apparent at times, were magnificent in victory. Always aggressively confident, they played power-packed hurling with flawless finesse and had the Banner side reeling from the word go. The expected early onslaught from Clare never materialised, and for a change it was Limerick who forced the issue from the throw-in. Liam O'Donoghue raced on to a centre after two minutes to flash home a point, who was whistled back, and Richie Bennis pointed the resultant free to open the scoring.

With the wind in their favour, Limerick continued to dazzle Clare with speed and craft reminiscent of 1955. In fact, four explosive minutes saw the death-knell of Clare sealed. In a beautiful synchronised move Seán Foley and Liam O'Donoghue carved open the defence, and Frankie Nolan was through for a great goal in the 7th minute. Two minutes later a high lobbing centre from Joe McKenna was deflected past Séamus Durack by Clare's Seán Stack when harassed by Eamonn Rea.

Richie Bennis taking a free with his left hand on top though he is naturally right handed.

Shock Waves

Limerick really sent shock waves reverberating through the Clare ranks after a further lapse of a mere two minutes, when Bernie Hartigan, who was simply toying with the opposition at mid-field, set up Eamonn Rea for goal number three. Stunned to the core, Clare struggled manfully to come to grips with their game, but it was only the accuracy of Clonlara's Colm Honan that maintained any hope of a Clare revival.

However, Limerick continued to move with lethal efficiency, and points from play per Joe McKenna, Richie Bennis and a beauty from Bernie Hartigan after a great inter-passing movement left them ahead 3-5 to 0-4 after 25 minutes.

The old scoreboard in Semple Stadium still in operation and a vantage point for many supporters.

Suddenly Clare regained their composure somewhat, and after Séamus Horgan saved a lively shot, Gus Lohan availed of a defensive slip-up to lash home a Clare goal. Two magnificent points from play by Liam O'Donoghue and an exchange of white flags from frees by Richie Bennis and Colm Honan brought proceedings to the 30th minute of the first half

Hammer Blow

Then came a real hammer blow for Clare. Eamonn Rea gained possession away out on the left wing and soloed unimpeded right through the defence before firing home a spectacular goal.

Although Limerick had the advantage of the elements in the first half, the die looked cast for Clare when they retired at the interval, 4-8 to 1-5 in arrears.

However, the resumption saw Clare move on the offensive. For a fleeting period Limerick appeared to relax their approach and the Banner forwards were allowed more scope. Séamus Horgan had to save a pile driver in the opening 30 seconds, while in a fierce onslaught Pat Hartigan was forced to concede a '70 which Colm Honan pointed.

Back stormed Clare and Timmy Ryan pierced the Limerick rearguard for a goal and when Colm Honan pointed a free after four minutes to reduce the deficit to seven points, a Clare comeback seemed on the cards.

Perilous

But Limerick realising their perilous position quickly regained the initiative when Richie Bennis pointed a free in the 7th minute.

The ace marksman from Patrickswell had his most prolific hour for many moons on Sunday. In the 12th he blasted a "penalty" to the Clare netting after Frankie Nolan was upended in the square.

But his next goal was a real gem. Now operating in the unaccustomed position of wing forward, he received a pass from young Paddy Kelly, who had replaced Frankie Nolan and soloed his way through a rake of Clare defenders to blaze home a great goal. That was the final nail in Clare's coffin of doom, and further points from Bennis (three), including two from play, and Liam O'Donoghue, left Limerick strolling to victory as time pounded on.

Clare put in a grandstand finish and in the 33rd minute Michael O'Connor crashed through a goalmouth melee for a goal. Tragedy struck for Limerick here as their gladiator of the hour - staunch full-back Pat Hartigan - was forced to retire with a suspected fracture of the collar bone and was replaced by Jim O'Donnell.

Fizzled Out

Willie Moore went full-back with Jim O'Donnell operating at right-corner back. The game fizzled out to a very tame ending and even the presentation of the cup to team captain Seán Foley failed to generate any real excitement amongst the huge Limerick following. They felt it had come just that bit too easy. The main topic of discussion at this stage was the condition of the injured Pat Hartigan.

What a pity Hartigan was injured after giving his greatest performance ever in the Limerick jersey. His display reminded the adults of Bobby Rackard in the 1954 All Ireland final. Hartigan literally threw defiance at Lohan and his aides with timely anticipation and quicksilver reflexes.

Those who doubted his high rating as full-back certainly got their answer as Hartigan turned in a real stormer. His courageous tackling, grabbing of balls in the air and his lengthy clearances provided the highlights of the game. Next in line for the plaudits must, in my book, be Richie Bennis who proved himself to be fast and elusive and a cunning score-getter into the bargain. In a series of positions, Richie was in unconquerable mood and proved a real menace to the Clare defence.

Limerick held the sway at mid-field for most of the game where Éamon Grimes and Bernie Hartigan provided the forwards with a luxury service of the ball. The splendid cohesion between mid-field and the half-forwards was a vital factor in Limerick tactics.

Mature

Bernie Hartigan celebrated his come-back on the team with a mature display. His alertness off the mark and his fierce weight instilled panic into opposition, which they failed to cope with. Grimes, after a slow start, came out of his shell in the second half to play a major role in his side's triumph. The indomitable half-back partnership of Tom Ryan, improving with every outing; Eamonn Cregan, soundness personified, and Seán Foley, who improved immensely as the game progressed, offered granite-like resistance right through and was the rock on which many Clare attacks perished.

Behind this trio Willie Moore and Jim O'Brien seldom budged an inch and in goal Séamus Horgan came to the rescue with several scintillating saves.

Liam O'Donoghue and Frankie Nolan are lethal weapons in any attack and on Sunday their speed and skill caused much anxiety in the Clare defence. Eamonn Rea was a big success at full-forward. Rea moved to every ball with tigerish enthusiasm and took his first-half goals with deadly enthusiasm.

Joe McKenna moved with lightning acceleration in another progressive performance. He distributed some clever balls and created many openings for his colleagues.

Paudie Fitzmaurice won much possession in the first-half, although pitted against the best defender in the Clare outfit, Ger Loughnane.

He was replaced in the second half by his brother, Willie.

Paddy Kelly made a big impression when he came on for Frankie Nolan. He seems to have the attributes to command a place on the side.

Scorers

Limerick - R. Bennis 2-8 (1-6 frees); E. Rea 2-0; L. O'Donoghue 0-4; S. Stack [O.G.] and F. Nolan 1-0; B. Hartigan and J. McKenna 0-1.

Clare - C. Honan 0-8 (0-7 frees); E. O'Connor, G. Lohan and T. Ryan 1-0; C. Woods 0-1;

Teams

Limerick - S. Horgan; W. Moore, P. Hartigan, J. O'Brien; T. Ryan, E. Cregan, S. Foley (capt.); B. Hartigan, E. Grimes; J. McKenna, R. Bennis, P. Fitzmaurice; L. O'Donoghue, E. Rea, F. Nolan. Subs: P. Kelly for Nolan, (54 minutes), W. Fitzmaurice for P. Fitzmaurice (65 minutes) and J. O'Donnell for P. Hartigan (75 minutes).

Clare - S. Durack; S. Stack, V. Loftus, J. Power; G. Loughnane, S. Hehir, J. O'Gorman; C. Woods, M. Moroney; J. Cullinan, N. Casey, C. Honan; E. O'Connor, G. Lohan (capt.), T. Ryan. Sub: P. O'Connor for Moroney (76 minutes).

Referee - John Moloney (Tipperary).

Figures of the Game

Limerick	Wides	Frees	70s
First Half	12	9	1
Second Half	6	11	1

Clare	Wides	Frees	70s
First Half	5	11	0
Second Half	14	7	4

Attendance: 36,446 (1973: 41,723),

1973 Keeping the Dream Alive

The Limerick team that [...]
Back Row (L-R): Bernie Hartigan, Richie Bennis, Eamonn Crega[n...]
Front Row (L-R): Frankie Nolan, Paudie Fitzmaurice, Liam O'L[...]

... the 1974 Munster Final.
...na, Pat Hartigan, Eamonn Rea, Jim O'Brien and Éamon Grimes.
...eán Foley (Capt.), Tom Ryan, Séamus Horgan and Willie Moore.

73 Munster Final recalled
(Tipperary Star, 12 July 1986)

Memories of the epic Munster Senior Hurling Final between Limerick and Tipperary in 1973 which Limerick won by virtue of a last minute point by Richie Bennis will be recalled at Newcastle West on Friday, 18 July at 7:30PM when the Tipperary and Limerick teams of that day will meet in a senior hurling tournament in aid of charity.

The charity involved is the Brothers of Charity Workshops for the handicapped, which like many other aspects of the health services, are suffering from financial cutbacks. The Brothers cater for some 300 handicapped people in the Mid West, and the organisers are hoping for a generous response to this venture.

Tipperary will field the bulk of those who were involved in the panel in the game and already Séamus Shinnors, Jim Fogarty, Tadgh O'Connor, Len Gaynor, Séamus Hogan, Jimmy Doyle, Francis Loughnane, Roger Ryan, Dinny Ryan, Martin Esmonde, Paddy Williams, Jim Keogh, John Kelly, Noel O'Dwyer, P.J. Ryan and Jack Ryan have indicated their intention of turning out.

The Limerick response has also been most gratifying, according to a spokesman for the organisers, who are also very appreciative of the assistance given by Tommy Barrett, Tipp. County Secretary in getting the team together.

Among the Tipperary absentees will be Babs Keating and John Gleeson who will be on holidays; Tadhg Murphy, who is out of the country; Jimmy Crompton, injured; and Paul Byrne who will be teaching in the Gaeltacht.

It promises to be a great occasion and an event worthy of support.

Brothers Of Charity Services

MID-WESTERN REGION

Bawnmore, Limerick.

CHARGE 10P

TIPPERARY SENIOR TEAM

1. T. Murphy
2. J. Fogarty
3. J. Kelly
4. J. Gleeson
5. J. Crampton
6. T. O'Connor
7. L. Gaynor
8. S. Hogan
9. P. J. Ryan
10. F. Loughnane
11. M. Roche
12. N. O'Dwyer
13. J. Flanagan
14. R. Ryan
15. M. Keating.

Subs:
16. P. Byrne
17. D. Ryan
18. J. Ryan
19. S. Shinnors
20. J. Doyle
21. M. Esmonde
22. J. Keogh
23. P. Williams

LIMERICK SENIOR TEAM

1. S. Horgan
2. W. Moore
3. P. Hartigan
4. J. O'Brien
5. P. Bennis
6. J. O'Donnell
7. S. Foley
8. R. Bennis
9. E. Grimes
10. L. O'Donoghue
11. M. Dowling
12. B. Hartigan
13. F. Nolan
14. E. Rea
15. E. Cregan

Subs:
16. J. Allis
17. J. McKenna
18. P. Fitzmaurice
19. A. Dunworth
20. T. Ryan
21. J. Hogan

Stacks' Clubhouse Opened in Style
(The Kerryman, 9 June 1989)

The chairman of the Austin Stacks Club, Brendan Dowling, thanked the Limerick and Dublin teams for the great support which they had given for the club's opening celebrations.

Alan Larkin spoke on behalf of the visiting Dublin team. He thanked the Stacks Club for the invitation and said it spoke well for Kerry and the people of Kerry that they considered inviting their foes of bygone days. He tendered an apology for Kevin Moran who was unavoidably absent because of the fact that he was playing soccer for Ireland.

The Dublin man's remarks were endorsed by Éamon Grimes on behalf of the 1973 Limerick hurling team. They were very happy to be given the honour of attending and playing for the opening of the new clubhouse.

Mr Grimes said that not alone were they honouring Austin Stacks Club but it was also a measure of the esteem in which Jackie Power was held. He thanked all the players who had made such an effort to come here for the opening.

Anthony O'Keeffe, chairman of the organising committee, thanked the Mount Brandon Hotel for the excellent meal which had been served up at the banquet. Éamon Grimes made a special presentation on behalf of the Limerick 1973 team to Jackie Power who was coach/selector to the team.

It was a particularly nostalgic week-end for the great Ahane man. For not alone did he have such a close link with the '73 Limerick hurling team but Jackie also trained the Stacks team which regained the county football championship after a lapse of 37 years in '73.

After Limerick had defeated Kerry on Saturday evening Jackie was in ebullient mood.

"I could not believe that our lads were as fit as they were," said the man who is regarded as one of the all-time hurling great.

"This is a wonderful occasion. It is a great personal delight for me to see the Limerick '73 team turning up.

"This is an unbelievable development by Austin Stacks. This pitch is as good as you would find anywhere."

The Limerick hurlers led at half time by 3-6 to 0-8 and in a highly entertaining second half they maintained their advantage, even though Kerry turned in a fine display in this half, and grabbed two goals by Pat Moriarty in the process.

The teams lined out as follows:

Limerick - S. Horgan; W. Moore, J. O'Brien, P. Fitzmaurice; P. Bennis, E. Cregan, S. Foley; R. Bennis E. Grimes; P. Kelly, M. Dowling, B. Hartigan; F. Nolan, E. Rea, J. McKenna.

Kerry - T. ("Bracker") Regan; J. Barry, W. Maguire, S. McCarthy; B. Reidy, W. Power, P. McCarthy; M. Brick, B. Neenan; S. Flaherty, J. Bunyan, J. Sullivan; T. Nolan, P. Moriarty, J. Gannon.

1973 Keeping the Dream Alive

Back Row: LtoR, Jim Allis, Richie Bennis, Liam
Willie Moore, Eamonn Rea
Front Row: LtoR, Seán Foley, Mossie Dowling
Eamon Grimes (Capt), Mick Cregan (Representin
Not present when photo was taken: Bernie Hartigan, Phil Be

1973 Keeping the Dream Alive

...ck panel
...n 1998

...oghue, Jim O'Brien, Pat Hartigan, Joe McKenna,
...ogan & Paudie Fitzmaurice.
...us Hartigan (Representing his brother Bernie),
...other Eamonn), Frankie Nolan & Séamus Horgan.
...n O'Donnell, Andy Dunworth, Tom Ryan & Eamonn Cregan.

'73 Hurlers to Lift County Spirits Again
(Limerick Leader, 8 February 2013)
Replica Jerseys Signed by Triumphant Limerick All Ireland Winning Team to be Auctioned and Raffled for Charity

By Donal O'Regan

The late Páidí Ó Sé has inspired a group of Limerick hurling fanatics to celebrate the great 1973 panel who are all still alive. John Franklin, Knockane travelled to Ventry on December 30 with his son Jack and friends Danny Beary, Pallasgreen and Tom O'Dwyer, Doon.

"We paid our respects at Páidí Ó Sé's grave and on the way home we were saying how sad it was that he had passed away at such a young age.

"I said it would be much better to meet fellows while they are alive," said Mr Franklin.

The massive hurling fan, who goes to all Limerick's matches, was looking at a picture of the 1973 All Ireland champions in Danny Beary's GAA museum (located in Barna, Pallasgreen).

"We were talking about them, what a fantastic team they were and we remarked that of a panel of 21 that they were all still alive," said Mr Franklin.

A couple of days later he came up with the plan to start Friends of Limerick '73.

"I got three replica 1973 jerseys from Retro GAA and we set about making contact with all the players.

"We are going to meet them all and get them signed. All the players I've written to came back to me and they think it is a great idea," said Mr Franklin, who has even written a poem (see below).

They will get the three jerseys, hurleys donated by current hurler Niall Maher and Sliotars signed by the legendary 1973 team. One jersey will be auctioned in June and the other items will be prizes in a monster charity raffle. The only obstacle they haven't overcome thus far is they can't track down one of the players.

"There is 21 on the panel in the match programme from the day.

"One man we can't find is Andy Dunworth who is in America. He is the only one we haven't got an address for.

"He was originally from Banogue but he played for Claughaun - he was a sub forward in 1973, a fine hurler. If anyone has contact information for Andy in America please let me know," said Mr Franklin, who is joined on the committee by Danny Beary, Knockane; Paddy Coleman, Doon; Ger O'Connell, Pallasgreen; Eibhear O'Dea, Kilteely; James O'Connor, Knockane and Tom O'Dwyer, Doon. They plan a number of fundraising events beginning with the launch in Moore's Bar in Doon on February 23. Proprietor, Anna Moore, is a sister of corner-back in 1973, Willie. All the proceeds will go to the Daughters of Charity in Lisnagry, MS Limerick and Milford Hospice.

"All the money will be divided equally between them. They are three very worthwhile charities," said Mr Franklin. Raffle lines start from just €2 and will be sold at matches and at the launch in February 23.

They well also be on sale at a quiz in the Idler Bar in Knockane on March 2; a cake sale in the old library in Doon on March 3; a "brain of Limerick" quiz in the Woodlands Hotel on April 4; quiz in Ahern's Bar, Kilteely on April 13; 5km run/walk in Knockane on April 27, culminating with the auction and raffle in Kilteely on June 7.

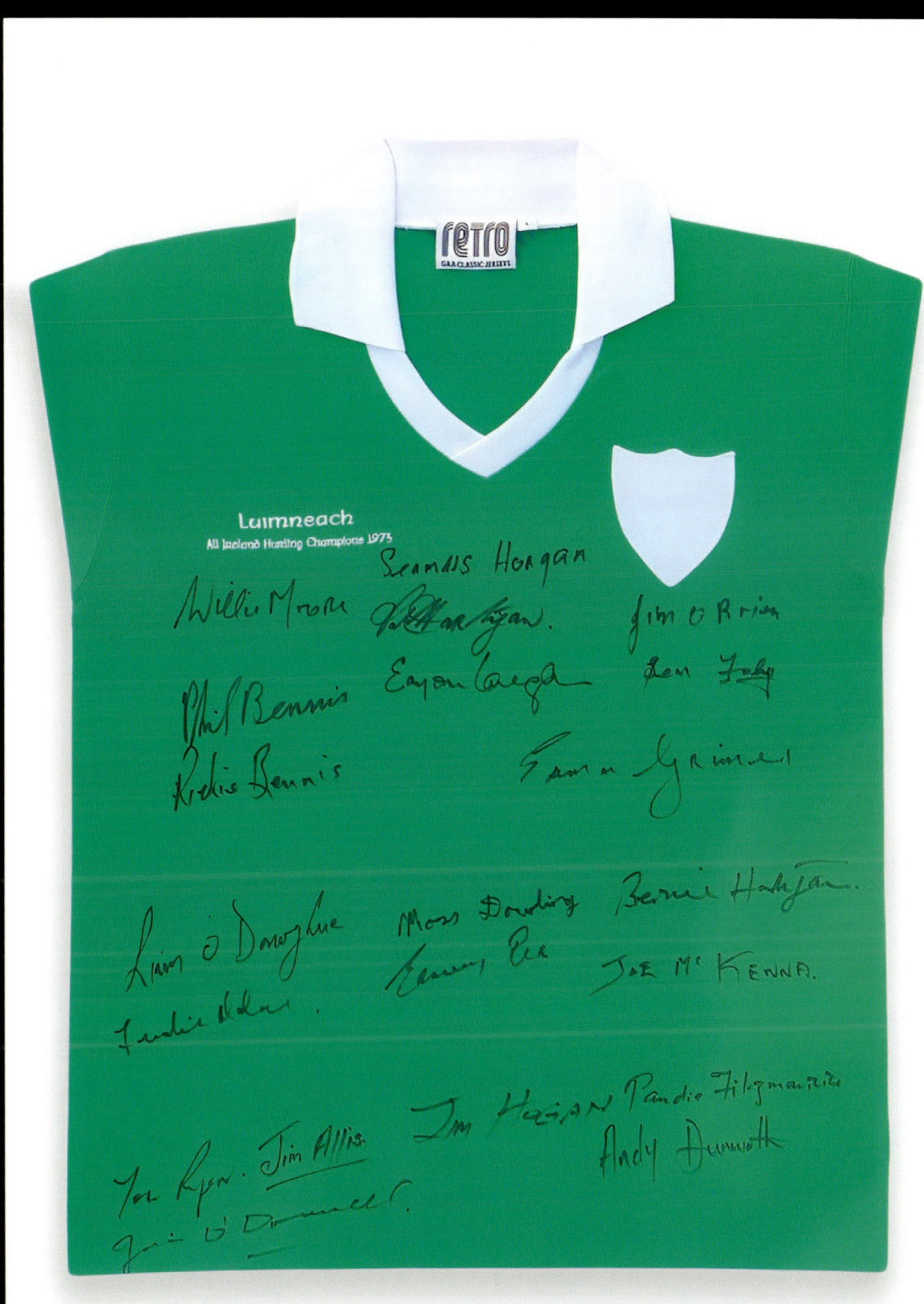

Signed retro jersey raffled by Friends of Limerick '73 in 2013.

Mr Franklin and his fellow committee members started doing their rounds to meet the players and get their jerseys signed on Monday night.

Mr Franklin admitted this is an added bonus to raising money for charity.

"That's the highlight for me, to meet all the lads and hear all the old stories," said Mr Franklin.

They started in defence with Tournafulla's Séamus Horgan. He even showed them his 1973 goalie's jersey. Staying at the back they headed to Bruree to meet corner-back Jim O'Brien, who showed them his well deserved all-star award. His son James was captain in Limerick's last All Ireland appearance in 2007. They rounded off the night with a visit to Mossie Dowling's Kilmallock home. He pulled out his hurley from the day.

While Mr Franklin's Friends of Limerick '73 idea is proving a big hit, he sincerely hopes it won't be replicated in 2023 when it is fifty years.

"Let's hope we have new Limerick legends in the meantime," said Mr Franklin.

Limerick '73 Forty Years On

I was below in Dromkeen cutting a hedge
Thinking of hurling and maybe taking a pledge
Into my head came '73
Grimes, McKenna, the Hartigans Pat and Bernie

Horgan in the goal would give a big shout
Moore and O'Brien were keeping them out
Pat at full-back, a great hurler no doubt
He would slip back and hit every puck out

Cregan at six oh what a display
High balls or low he had a great day
Five and seven they came from the Well
Bennis and Foley were sound as a bell

Lár Na Páirce was Richie the great
Where he donned the number eight
From free or play he did not miss
Only every time the uprights split

Captain that day was Éamon Grimes
Outstanding he was in the number nine
Up into the Hogan he did go
Picked up the cup and to all he did show

Ten was Liam Donoghue the child of the team
And 12 was Bernie fulfilling his dream
Mossie Dowling from Kilmallock in the centre was he
I'd swear he got the goal and he down on one knee

He scored first and last from number 13
Frankie Nolan from the 'Well as good as we've seen
Inside in the square was big Eamonn Rea
Ball after ball he won it that day

Big Joe from the 'Libs was wearing 15
O'Hehir said after, the best he had seen
If you went into Parnell Street he'd sell you a grinder
And of 73 you might get a reminder

Tom Ryan came on and did his bit
Andy Dunworth and Jim Hogan both from Claughaun
Two Jims from Doon O'Donnell and Allis
And from Killeedy was Paudie Fitzmaurice

We're asking these greats a jersey to sign
And hope ye the public will buy a line
To charity then all proceeds will go
If you're lucky enough the jersey you can show

The phone is ringing and the hedge is cut
Who owns that number that coming up?
T'is a lifetime ago says Lar Hayes to me
Since that famous Sunday in '73.

John Franklin

Friends of Limerick '73 Charity Event Culminated This Friday
(Limerick Leader, 7 June 2013)
Chance to own a piece of Limerick hurling history and raise money for three causes

By Donal O'Regan

At the unveiling of the Mick Mackey statue in Castleconnell a few weeks ago Mícheál Ó Muircheartaigh noted that Limerick had won just one All Ireland since 1940.

"Limerick was always a hurling county, a truly hurling county.

"It is something I cannot understand – there must be no fairness in whoever decides who wins," said the GAA legend.

Many weren't born when the men of 1973 triumphed over Kilkenny, but their names roll off the tongue of every Limerick hurling fan. They were recently honoured by JP McManus in Staker Wallace GAA Club and this Friday, June 7, the Friends of Limerick '73 culminates in Ahern's Pub, Kilteely.

The idea of John Franklin, Knockane was to get two jerseys and two hurleys signed by every member of the '73 team. One of each will be auctioned and raffled this Friday night. The idea caught the public's imagination and table quizzes, cake sales and a run were organised.

Seán Foley presented them with his 1973 All-Star jersey for their auction and Ed Shanahan from Clarina gave a hurley with a picture of the Limerick 1973 team on it. Another person to support the project is well known photographer Michael Martin.

He gave organisers a framed collection of photographs from the '73 All Ireland signed by both teams. This will also be auctioned off on Friday. All the funds raised will be divided between Daughters of Charity in Lisnagry, MS Limerick and Milford Hospice. Mr Martin says he has very fond memories of the day.

Limerick photographer Michael Martin with the picture montage of Limerick's win in 1973 All Ireland Hurling Final. (L-R): Shane Larkin, Séamus Horgan, Michael Martin, Joe McKenna, Eamonn Rea, Jim O'Brien and Éamon Grimes. The piece was auctioned with signed jerseys and hurleys by Friends of Limerick '73 in 2013.

"I saw the piece in the Leader a couple of months ago and I have all these photos from the final that were never published," said Mr Martin.

He collated them and the five feet by three feet collection of photos would be treasured by any Limerick hurling fan. Things were a lot easier going in those days. The young photographer arrived up to Croke Park with no accreditation or affiliation but got on to the pitch.

"I just chanced my arm," he jokes.

"It lashed rain all day, but I shot everything that moved," said Mr Martin,

Like many, the young photographer stayed up all night but he was one of the few not to celebrate.

"No, I didn't go drinking. I went straight home to the dark room and printed them all off," said Mr Martin.

To this day Michael Martin Photography still get orders from all over the world. His 1973 pictures adorn pubs in Australia and America and many points in between. John Franklin said the framed photographs will be a popular lot on the night. He expects a bumper crowd and all are welcome to come to Kilteely this Friday night to buy a raffle ticket or bid.

The most enjoyable part of the project for Mr Franklin has been meeting all the players and celebrating the men 40 years on.

Conor Fitzgerald of the Woodlands Hotel (who bought this picture collage) with Ger Mulcair, Danny Beary, James Heffernan, Sr. Phyllis Donnellon (Milford Hospice), James O'Connor, Jack "Donie" Franklin, Paddy Coleman, Joss Lowry RIP (Milford Hospice), John Franklin and John O'Connor (St. Albie's Credit Union).

From the programme of the Official Opening of Fr John Ryan Memorial Park at Kilbreedy
(19 May 2013)

By Matt O'Callaghan (Vale Star)

There is nothing more the Limerick hurling heroes of 1973 would like better than to shed the title of the last Limerick senior hurling team to lift the MacCarthy Cup and claim All Ireland success. They will be honoured, together with their Kilkenny opponents, this evening at the official opening of the Staker Wallace facility at Kilbreedy and their special place in the annals of Limerick hurling deserves to be recognised.

It is now 40 years since the Liam MacCarthy Cup last found repose on Shannonside and there has been much heartbreak and near misses along the way. Final defeats in 1974, 1980, 1994, 1996 and 2007 have been bitter pills to swallow but these disappointments have not in the least dampened the county's enthusiasm for our native game.

The 1960s were a very bleak decade for Limerick in senior hurling; it was the only decade in the last century that Limerick did not win a Munster senior hurling championship. The county suffered some very heavy defeats in the Munster championship, especially in the first half of the decade, when Tipperary were the kingpins of the hurling world. In 1966, a new hope dawned after a young Limerick team travelled to the Athletic Grounds in Cork to face Tipperary in the first round of the Munster championship and shocked the defending Munster and All Ireland champions.

It was a display and a result that rocked the hurling world as Tipperary had been All Ireland champions in four of the previous five years. The dream of glory ended in the Munster semi-final when Cork just got the measure of the luckless Shannonsiders in Killarney before going on to win the All Ireland that year.

As the decade came to a close there were tangible signs that the 1970s would bring a new dawn and better days for the county senior hurlers. The building blocks were slowly and quietly being laid during the 1960s, with All Ireland minor final appearances in 1963 and 1965. Another more significant positive development was the rise and domination of Limerick CBS who won four Dr Harty Cups in a row from 1964 to 1967.

During that period the famed Sexton St. hurling nursery reached four All Ireland finals, winning two in 1964 and 1966. Those four great CBS teams produced Eamonn Cregan, Éamon Grimes, Pat Hartigan and Seán Foley and with Jim O'Brien, Richie Bennis and Andy Dunworth from the 1963 minor team, they were to go on and become central figures in Limerick's re-emergence as a hurling force in the early 1970s.

In 1971 the Limerick resurgence began and in that year Limerick and arch rivals Tipperary crossed sticks on no fewer than four occasions, three times in the league and in the most dramatic of Munster finals in Killarney. The counties first met at the Gaelic Grounds in April in the league with a semi-final place at stake. Limerick won by two points, thereby causing something of a surprise, a result that necessitated the teams meeting a week later in a play off in Croke Park. Limerick again inflicted defeat on the Premier County, this time by a goal.

The counties subsequently progressed to the final and the Limerick v Tipperary saga moved to Cork's Athletic Grounds for the final. In what was a dress rehearsal for what would happen in the 1973 Munster final, Richie Bennis landed a late free in the dying seconds of the game on Leeside to help Limerick squeeze home 3-12 to 3-11 to be crowned, under the captaincy of Tony O'Brien, National League champions for the first time since 1947.

Hopes were high in the championship and Limerick's new found status as a reincarnated hurling force was confirmed when Cork were beaten in the Munster semi-final for the first time in 33 years to set up a fourth meeting with Tipperary in the Munster final.

1973 Keeping the Dream Alive

When the counties failed to agree to a home and away arrangement for the final, the Munster Council settled on Killarney and if the three previous games had been dramatic, they paled in comparison to what unfolded on a wet day in the beautiful Kerry town. All was going well for Limerick. By the end of the first half the Treaty men had established a 2-10 to 1-7 lead. Late in the game, with the result in the balance, Tipperary were awarded a close in free. What has now become remembered as the 'dry ball' incident occurred as Tipperary were reputed to have swapped the soggy sliothar that was in play for a new dry ball before Michael 'Babs' Keating stepped up and rammed the ball to the Limerick net. Tipperary went on to win a memorable final and score a first win from four over Limerick, alas a very important one, 4-16 to 3-18. The momentum of 1971 did not carry over to 1972 as Limerick relinquished their league title and lost out to Clare in the Munster championship.

So 1973 was the year of the next big drive and a few significant developments occurred, Mick Cregan took over from Joe McGrath as team trainer, Eamonn Rea was moved from full back to full forward and an emerging Offaly star Joe McKenna threw in his lot with his adopted county. Limerick were beaten in the league final that year by Wexford at Croke Park 4-13 to 3-7. In the Munster championship Limerick luckily avenged the defeat of the previous year by Clare to qualify for the provincial final. It set up another episode of the ongoing saga with Tipperary in that year's Munster final.

As had been the situation in the previous years, nothing separated the counties and that is how it played out at the end when Richie Bennis, with the last puck of the game, repeated his heroics of two years earlier in the league final in Cork and landed a 70 between the sticks after which Clare referee, Michael Slattery, immediately blew the final whistle. It sparked off unprecedented scenes of jubilation among the Limerick faithful as the county had finally ended an 18 year barren spell without a senior title going all the way back to Mackey's Greyhounds in 1955.

Limerick's next hurdle on the road to a first All Ireland final appearance since 1940 was a meeting with London, who had beaten Galway in the quarter final. Limerick and the Exiles met in the semi-final at Ennis on 5th August. When the teams were announced for the clash, Eamonn Rea was named at full forward for Limerick while his brother Gerry was named at full back for London. The brothers did face each other directly as Limerick progressed 1-15 to 0-7. Kilkenny were the final opponents, the same opposition that Limerick had beaten in the final of 33 years previously in 1940.

The excitement in the build-up to the final was palpable as a whole new generation of Limerick hurling folk prepared for a novel experience. News filtered through from the Kilkenny camp of injury concerns to some key players, Kieran Purcell, Jim Treacy, the legendary Eddie Keher and Eamonn Morrissey. All four were to miss out though Purcell was introduced as a substitute. The debate still rages about what would have happened had the quartet been included in the black and amber and would Kilkenny have carried the day? The answer is almost definitely not as the Limerick performance on the occasion reached new heights as they ran out winners 1-21 to 1-14.

Limerick had reached the Holy Grail under the guidance of selectors Jackie Power, Dick Stokes, Denis Barrett, Seán Cunningham and Jim Quaid, trainer Mick Cregan and physio Vincent O'Connor and it was a very proud Éamon Grimes that went up the steps of the Hogan Stand to finally signify the end of the All Ireland senior famine on Shannonside and accept the Liam MacCarthy Cup from the then President of the Association Dr Donal Keenan. The respective squads on that memorable day for Limerick hurling were:

Limerick: Séamus Horgan (Tournafulla): Willie Moore (Doon), Pat Hartigan (South Liberties), Jim O'Brien (Bruree); Phil Bennis (Patrickswell), Eamonn Cregan (Claughaun), Seán Foley (Patrickswell); Richie Bennis (Patrickswell), Éamon Grimes (South Liberties) Captain; Liam O'Donoghue (Mungret), Mossie Dowling (Kilmallock), Bernie Hartigan (Old Christians); Frankie Nolan (Patrickswell), Eamonn Rea (Faughs) and Joe McKenna (South Liberties).

Subs: Jim O'Donnell (Doon), Tom Ryan (Ballybrown), Jim Allis (Doon), Paudie Fitzmaurice (Killeedy), Andy Dunworth (Claughaun) and Jim Hogan (Claughaun).

Kilkenny: Noel Skehan (Bennettsbridge); Phil Larkin (James Stephens), Nicky Orr (Fenians, Johnstown), Phil Cullen (Bennettsbridge); Pat Lawlor (Bennettsbridge), Pat Henderson (Fenians, Johnstown), Brian Cody (James Stephens); Liam O'Brien (James Stephens), Frank Cummins (Blackrock, Cork); Claus Dunne (Mooncoin), Pat Delaney (Fenians) Captain, Paddy Broderick (Fenians); Mick Crotty (James Stephens), Jim Lynch (Mooncoin) and Mick Brennan (Castlecomer).

Subs: Kieran Purcell (Windgap), Billy Harte (Galmoy), John Kinsella (Bennettsbridge), Michael Moore (James Stephens), Pa Dillon (St. Lachtain's), Martin Coogan (Castlecomer), and Senan Cooke (Kilmacow).

These men of 40 years ago will come face to face again this evening, in less tense surroundings, as guests of JP McManus for the opening of the Staker Wallace's fine new facility. In those four decades, the counties have experienced contrasting levels of success but hope springs eternal in Limerick hearts for a change of hurling fortunes.

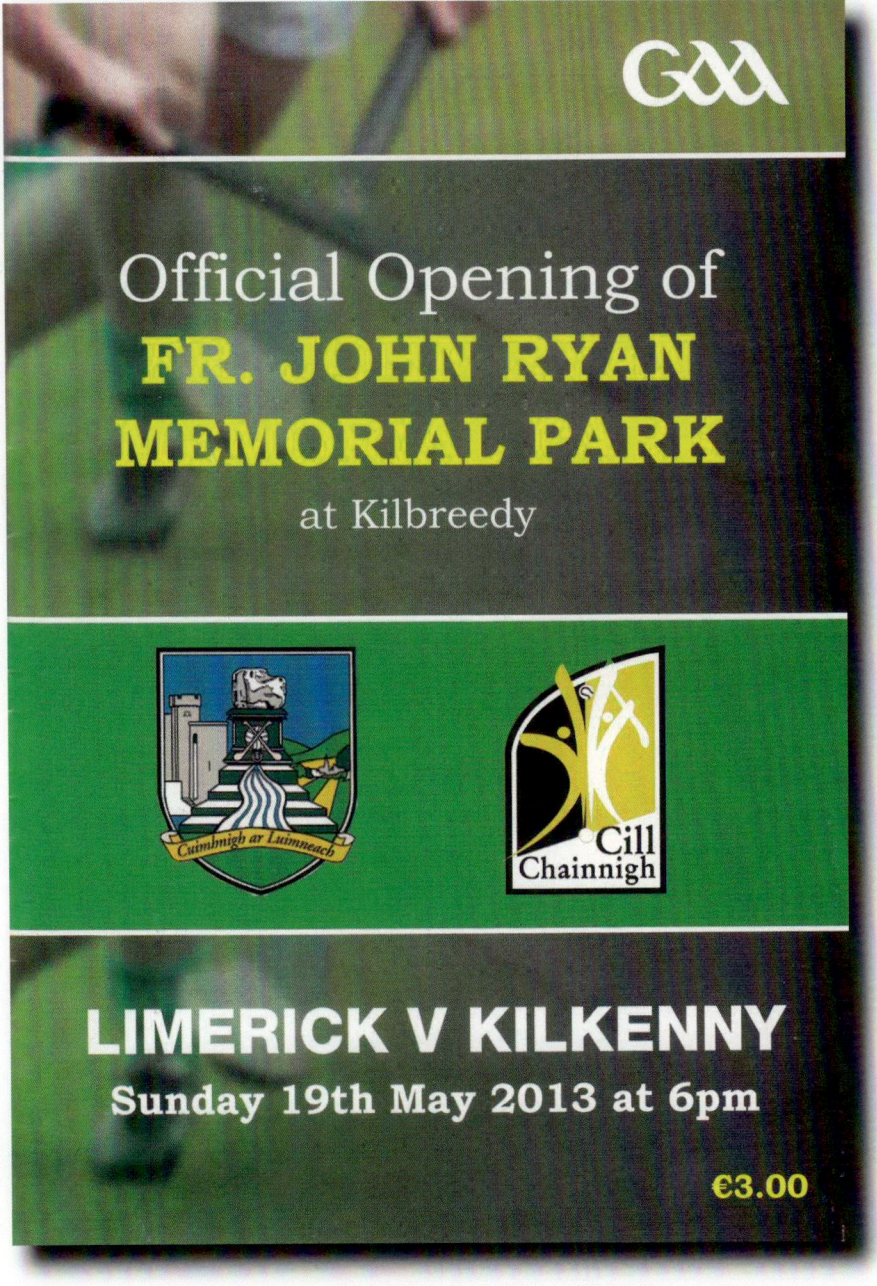

From cover of the programme from Kilbreedy.

Heroes of '73 Back Together for JP's Party

(Limerick Leader, 25 May 2013)

Staker Wallace club pull out all the stops as a who's who of sporting legends gather for opening of new facility

By Aine Fitzgerald

GAA president Liam O'Neill was in a ridiculously fortunate position at the Staker Wallace GAA clubhouse on Sunday night. There he was nestled between JP McManus and Aidan O'Brien. He had, some might say, the luckiest seat in the land. But it was a waste, a terrible waste. He even admitted it himself. "I'm not a great racing man but I've two brothers who are very into racing," the self-confessed 'shy' president remarked in a witty speech which set the tone for an evening of celebration to mark the opening of the Fr John Ryan Memorial Park. "Just for fun, I texted them to tell them that I was sitting between Aidan O'Brien and JP McManus." One of them texted him back immediately. "He said he had tears in his eyes just thinking of the waste."

The GAA figurehead was among an esteemed list of sporting personalities who made their way to Kilbreedy West near Martinstown for the opening ceremony of the state-of-the-art GAA grounds. The occasion also marked the 40th anniversary of Limerick's last All Ireland senior hurling victory in 1973. On the guest list were both the teams of that day - Limerick and Kilkenny - all looking dapper in their crisp new two-piece suits from Connolly Man, paid for out of JP's pocket. Not to be outdone, the present-day teams were also suited and booted for the occasion. In three-piece suits this time, teamed with tan leather shoes.

JP McManus with Henry Shefflin and Aidan O'Brien.

Séamus, Willie, Pat, Jim, Phil and Eamonn looking very dapper in Martinstown.

1973 Keeping the Dream Alive

Rugby legend Keith Wood was also there, as were leading horse trainers Enda Bolger and Aidan O'Brien, and former Tipperary hurler and manager, Nicky English. Following a pre-championship challenge game which saw Limerick come out on top by a five point margin, 340 invited guests were treated to a four course meal inside the clubhouse. On the menu: classical Dublin Bay prawn cocktail, aged fillet of beef with a fondant potato, and, for desert, iced passion fruit parfait with summer berry compote, tapped off with an edible sliotar and a set of hurleys.

As guests settled in at their tables, fond memories of that rainy day in 1973 were reignited as footage of the famous All Ireland win was played on a giant screen. "Looking at the match brought back some great memories," said JP McManus with a smile, as the speeches continued, "The Limerick lads - ye have been my heroes for far too long," he continued, indicating the thirst in Limerick for more All Ireland glory. To the Limerick team of today, he offered these words of encouragement, "We have great hopes and great aspirations for you and we saw tonight, a little bit of what can be done. Ye were great out there tonight."

Months of preparation had gone into this event. JP complimented the Staker Wallace club for their efforts. The parish, he said, was looking its best. The ditches on all approach roads to the club grounds had been trimmed back for the occasion. The entrance was freshly tarmacadamed. Cars were directed to parking spaces by locals, with military precision. "Full marks," said Mr McManus. "I take a lot of pride in the way you had the parish looking and the way we have lifted our game. It is a credit to you all."

The presence of legendary commentator Mícheál Ó Muircheartaigh, who was MC for the night, he said, "brought the occasion to a whole new level." "He is just very, very special, not alone to Staker Wallace but to our national games." Forty years after he had the honourable task a lifting the Liam MacCarthy cup aloft, the ribbon cutting ceremony was left in the capable hands of South Liberties man Éamon Grimes.

Our 1973 heroes line up in front of the appreciative crowd at Martinstown.

"JP, I want to thank you sincerely for everything you did for us as a team in '73," he said. "A lot of people will not realise how much he was involved with us. He was the youngest chairman of our club and when he came on board at that time, we got more than any other county would have got." Chairman of Staker Wallace GAA club, Kenneth Heelan, thanked all the four teams for travelling to Kilbreedy for the occasion. "It really brings a community together. Days like this can transform a parish," he said before making a presentation to JP.

"There had been," he said, "a lot of head scratching to figure out what to present him with - that was until one clubman piped up - I bet he doesn't have a Stakers jersey!" Problem solved. The jersey was ironed, framed and presented. Even Aidan O'Brien felt like an honorary Stakers man on Sunday. "It is unbelievable," said the horseman. "The atmosphere is incredible." The modest, quietly spoken trainer doesn't look like the kind of guy who would "pull hard" on a hurling pitch.

However, he told us, that as a Wexford native living in Tipperary and married to a Kilkenny woman - Anne-Marie - he keeps an eye on the games. "We are always in awe of these players," he smiled. "They are so passionate and skilful." And judging by the group of Limerick hurlers waiting in the wings to shake his hand, the feeling was mutual.

JP McManus receiving a framed Stalker Wallace GAA jersey from club chairman Kenneth Heelan.

Seán T. Ryan holding his signed 1973 newspaper with the legendary Mícheál Ó Muircheartaigh.

1973 Keeping the Dream Alive

Back Row (L-R): Jim Allis, Pat Hartigan, Joe McKenna, Jim O'Brien, Richie
Front Row (L-R): Bernie Hartigan, Mossie Dowling, Éamon Grimes, Phil Ben
Missing: Andy Dunw

Foley, Jim O'Donnell, Willie Moore, Eamonn Rea and Eamonn Cregan.
Horgan, Frankie Nolan, Jim Hogan, Tom Ryan and Paudie Fitzmaurice.
m O'Donoghue.

1973 Keeping the Dream Alive

Back Row (L-R): Phil 'Fan' Larkin, Nicky Orr, Liam 'Chunky' O'Brie
Jim Lynch, Michael Moore, Kieran Purcell
Front Row (L-R): Frank Cummins, Noel Skehan, Pat Lawlor, Ji
Pat Kavanagh, John Kinsell
Missing: Phil Cullen, Martin Co

1973 Keeping the Dream Alive

...e, PJ Delaney (son of Pat Delaney), Pat Henderson, Mick Crotty,
..., Martin Fitzpatrick and Eddie Keher.
...ian Dillon (daughter of Pa Dillon), Mick 'Cloney' Brennan,
...erick and Senan Cooke.
...ody and Eamonn Morrissey.

Bennis Recalls the Heroes of '73
(Irish Examiner, 20 May 2013)

In 1973, ending a famine that had lasted 33 years, Limerick won the All Ireland hurling title with victory over Kilkenny. Forty years on and still waiting on their next triumph, midfielder and top scorer on that day, Richie Bennis, met with Diarmuid O'Flynn to recall the side that brought Liam MacCarthy back to the county.

Séamus Horgan (Club: Tournafulla - Age: 24, Height: 5'11", Weight: 11-7): "Like a lot of goalkeepers Séamus was also a very good outfield player but ended up in goals because he could be a bit wild out there! And yet he was a fierce quiet man, wouldn't say much. We wouldn't have won the All Ireland without him though; he made two fantastic saves during that championship, the first in the Munster final against Tipperary, from Babs Keating just at the start of the second half, the other from Crotty in the All Ireland final, again in the second half Séamus didn't actually play in the All Ireland semi-final against London, replaced by Jim Hogan who had been the goalkeeper for years. No one seems to know why, maybe the county board thought we were going to walk away with the London match, which didn't happen. Séamus was back though for the All Ireland final."

Willie Moore (Doon - 23, 5'10", 12-7): "Another very quiet man, a teacher in the CBS in Limerick. Had been a forward in '71 when he scored the 'goal' that wasn't! Was moved back to the defence and proved an outstanding corner-back. Played in every match, rock solid, no change from him which is exactly what you wanted from your last line of defence. I never came across him on the pitch which is kind of unusual within the one county - in fact I don't know if I ever played against Doon at any level. They always had good players though, and still have."

Pat Hartigan (South Liberties - 23, 6'4", 14-7): "A giant of a man, an inspiring figure at full-back, a real crowd-pleaser the way he'd catch a ball, burst his way out. He wasn't a dirty player; in fact he was the opposite. Against Cork for example, before the throw-in he'd walk up to Ray Cummins and shake his hand, instead of rattling his bones with a good belt of a shoulder! Even if he did play in the last line of defence Pat was an attacking kind of full-back, loved to come out and deliver the long clearance."

Jim O'Brien (Bruree - 28, 6'1", 12-4): "The prince of corner-backs, so tidy - an artist. The late Andy Dunworth was a sub on that team but he often blamed Jim for not being on the starting 15: night after night Andy would be on Jim in training, and that was that, never got a chance to shine. Great man to read a game, great man also to get himself out of a tight corner, through his sheer hurling ability. Played centre-back for his club and could have played there for any county in the country. Very underrated nationally but not in Limerick, I can assure you that."

Phil Bennis (Patrickswell - 31, 5'7 1/2", 11-2): "A pure defender. No forward relished an hour on Phil, not even the best, and Eddie Keher himself would vouch for that, saying he was one of the best defenders he ever came across. A very intelligent hurler and proved it later when he went in to management. A pity he wasn't given more time by the county board - Phil brought the team of the 90s through and if they'd left him alone, he'd have won an All Ireland with them, I'm certain of that. A pity, that would have put an end to all the talk of '73 and of course I wouldn't be writing this today."

Eamonn Cregan (Claughaun - 28, 5'11", 12-1): "A handy enough player! God we had a lot of duels in Limerick so I got to know him well both as teammate and as rival. I would say this, and don't say it lightly - Eamonn Cregan was the best all-round hurler I ever saw. If we had one more Eamonn Cregan, that Limerick team would have won all round us for years. He could play anywhere, and did - even played in goals at minor. I remember that game, against Galway, who were in Munster at the time. Limerick were in trouble and Eamonn was brought out the field and turned the game. I think we ended up drawing it and then won the replay. His shift to centre-back for the All Ireland final was a masterstroke. He was a natural, could walk up to a free and whatever side it was on, take it left or right. A little known fact about Eamonn: he was equally good at football, would have played for any team in the country. A handy golfer as well."

Seán Foley (Patrickswell - 24, 5'11", 12-4): "Born in London but his father had played for Limerick and won a Junior All Ireland title in 1939 when that was a big title to win. Seán was ahead of his time, a modern-day type of wing-back playing in the 70s. He loved to sweep forward, grab a score or set one up, had fantastic energy. I played with him for a long, long time with the club, a lovely hurler, gave great service to both Patrickswell and to Limerick."

Éamon Grimes (South Liberties - 26. 5'8", 12-6): "Talking of energy, Eamon was the blonde bombshell, an absolute dynamo and with loads of hurling ability to back it up. Brilliant captain, led by example on the field but a good motivator off it as well, knew the right few words to say and the right time to say them. A thorough gentleman, always was and still is, off the field and on. Great man to track back a player long before that became the norm for a midfielder, but also got his share of scores. I think it's safe to say he did more running in midfield than I did but we were a good combination - he was the runner, I was the stayer! A sweet hurler."

Richie Bennis (Patrickswell - 28, 6'0", 13-0 - by Eamonn Cregan): "Richie was the coolest man I ever saw, and I played with and against him for many a year - he was Mr Cool, always was. He was made for the big occasion. When I look back on that All Ireland final, a wet miserable day, Richie took off one solo run, waltzed through the Kilkenny defence and scored. Another time he was falling but still, from nearly 80 yards put a wet ball over the bar. His ability to score from midfield, regardless of conditions, from play or from placed balls, set him apart. He had that awkward left-below-right stroke, the awkward stance, and people underestimated his ability because of that. The point he scored in the Munster final, the 65 with the final puck of the game to win it, anyone else would have been trembling in their boots - not Richie, he revelled in it. Babs was roaring at him, he just ignored it, got the point. Irrespective of what anyone might say about moving goalposts, the flag went up, we won."

Liam O'Donoghue (Mungret - 21, 5'7", 10-7): "The youngest man on that team and he was being marked by the youngest man on the Kilkenny team in the All Ireland final, a certain Brian Cody, left halfback for Kilkenny that day. A really good forward, lovely striker, great workrate. Timed his run on to the team very well - that was his first year playing senior with Limerick! Wasn't his last though, Liam later became an outstanding wing back. He was a great man to recover if caught out of position, a real swashbuckling player. Scored two great points in the Munster final, and we didn't score too many that day! Won a few vital frees also, often forgotten about forwards who maybe weren't scoring."

Mossie Dowling (Kilmallock - 27, 5'10", 12-6):"A very important link on the team, bold and aggressive - he'd have been a great flank forward in rugby. An outstanding worker, did a huge amount of spadework for the rest of us, most of which would have gone unnoticed by the crowd. Speaking of rugby, Mossie was centrally involved in that famous first 'pushover try' in Croke Park, the goal against Kilkenny in the All Ireland final!"

Bernie Hartigan (Old Christians - 30, 5'11". 14-8): "Another powerhouse, Bernie was a tremendous athlete who gave massive service to Limerick hurling. If anyone should be singled out for praise for winning the Munster final it was Bernie who really opened his shoulders in the second half. Like his brother Pat, a thorough gentleman, and like Pat, fierce power but finally like Pat, didn't use that power enough. Ah, if they only had Cregan's bit of devil… Bernie was a fine footballer also."

Frankie Nolan (Patrickswell - 23, 5'7", 11-0): "A half-twin to Benny, another fine hurler, almost equally as good as Frankie and could also have been on that team but didn't have the same commitment. Frankie was a real corner-forward, the prototype. Something a lot of people may not know, he scored the first point and the last point in the '73 final. A poacher, a good man to win a ball, take on his man and score. Two of his best games that year were in the two biggest games of the year, the Munster final and the All Ireland final. I think himself and Cregan got five goals between them in the Munster final."

Eamonn Rea (Faughs and Effin - 30, 6'1", 14-3): "Big Ned was converted from corner-back and became the final piece of the jigsaw for 1973. Ned played in the full-back line in the National League final that year, against Wexford, a game we lost. Rory Kiely was a selector on that team, had an accident on his farm, and Ned and Jackie Power - former Limerick great and another selector - went in to see him in hospital. We were playing Waterford that night in a challenge game in the Gaelic Grounds and I think it was there, in that hospital ward, that the decision was made to play Eamonn Rea at full-forward.

The rest, as they say, is history. People have the wrong impression of Ned, they think he was just a bustler - he was far from that! He was a great hurler, won man of the match against us in 1963 as a right half-back for Emmets in a county semi-final. He proved some handful for every full-back he met that year, had the size and the strength but also had the hurling. Mossie Dowling takes the credit for the pushover goal, but his near-neighbour also had a hand, or a foot, in it!"

Joe McKenna (South Liberties - 22, 6'3", 14-2): "Another big man - when I think back on it, that was a big team. Joe didn't play in the Munster final, had come from Shinrone in Offaly but was now playing for South Liberties. He was young, on the fringes of the team all year, but the All Ireland final was when he really broke through, made a major contribution to the win. Won a lot of possession, not all of it converted to scores, but on a wet day possession is vital. Went on to become a great player for Limerick, was more suited to the middle of the road than the edge, an outstanding full-forward."

Subs

Jim Hogan (Claughaun): "Sub keeper, gave sterling service to Limerick, nearly 20 years. That win came at the end of his term and he played against London - fitting reward for all that service. A pure keeper, very agile, very alert and had to be - you got no sympathy from the full-forward that time!"

Tom Ryan (Ballybrown): "Came on in the Munster final and also in the All Ireland final, contributed to that game. A fine hurler, a good mix of physical and ball-player, tough defender. Started the following year, 1974, when Limerick again won the Munster title but Kilkenny got their revenge in the All Ireland final."

Jim O'Donnell (Doon): "Was only coming back in 1973 after breaking his leg in a club match. I'd rate Jim as one of the finest centre-backs I ever saw but he was so unfortunate that year. A fine hurler as anyone who ever played on him would verify. Jim played in the Munster final of 1971 in Killarney when Tipperary robbed us!"

Jim Allis (Doon): "Father of current Limerick player Conor. Came on as a sub in the Munster semi-final against Clare when Pat Hartigan got injured, did very well on no less a hurler than Noel Casey. Jim was strong, handled Noel, did his bit that year."

Andy Dunworth (Claughaun and Banogue): The only member of that panel no longer alive. Andy was a classy hurler, played in the famous win over Tipperary in 1966 when Tipp were classed as the greatest team of all time. He was outstanding in that game and Cork should be forever grateful to him - they would have won no All Ireland in 1966 if it hadn't been for Limerick beating Tipp!"

Paudie Fitzmaurice (Killeedy): "Was only a youngster that year but [almost] came on as a sub in the All Ireland final. Paudie's brother Willie also played for Limerick, both priests; they inspired Killeedy to win a Limerick county senior in 1980 and Paudie captained Limerick in 1981 to win another Munster title, then beaten by Galway in the All Ireland semi-final."

Captain Grimes recall fond memories of that glorious day
(Limerick Leader 7 September 2013)

By Aine Fitzgerald

The eyes of the country were on Éamon Grimes as he lifted the Liam MacCarthy Cup aloft, but only hours earlier the Limerick captain had been on the missing list!

As the team bus pulled out from the Crofton Airport Hotel on 2 September 1973, headed to Croke Part, the star midfielder was asleep in his bed.

"We went to Mass and had our breakfast. As you can imagine, we were up early that morning so we went for a bit of a rest," says the South Liberties man.

"The next thing, the bus was gone and somebody discovered that I wasn't on it so they had to come back. They hadn't gone too far"

Forty years to the week later, Eamon has many fond memories of that sacred day. What first springs to mind is the lead-up to the game - the excitement, the anticipation, the hype.

"We hadn't won it for 33 years prior to that and we hadn't been in a final for 33 years," he recalls.

"The communication cord wasn't as great then as it is now. You had the *Limerick Leader* - that was the only paper really at the time that would be doing anything major. Now, you have the television and radio, you have coverage from all angles. There was nothing like that when we were there. Everything that was spoken about was what was written in the paper. The Leader was the bible."

On the day prior to the game, the first day of September, the players took the train from Limerick to Dublin.

In the cab was none other than the mayor of Limerick at the time, Mick Lipper. "He drove us up and back," Eamon recalls.

On the night before the game, the players headed into town for a walkabout. It was tradition at the time that the All Ireland final trophies would be displayed in the window of Clerys department store on O'Connell Street, the night before the hurling and football deciders. As Eamon peered through the glass, he could only hope that the Liam MacCarthy cup would be between his palms the following night.

Memories of the big day itself are vivid. The dressing room, Eamon recalls, was fairly basic - "but way ahead of anything we ever had anywhere else."

"There was a swimming pool in between the two dressing rooms at that time." Running out onto the pitch is something he will never forget. It was a wet day and the players had to wait 10 minutes for the president at the time, Erskine Childers, to arrive.

Once the game started, it was all about the hurling. Hype, build-up and speculation counted for nothing.

"Once you get a ball and hit that ball, that's all gone. You would nearly have commissioned your mind to concentrate."

When the final whistle was blown, a 33-year weight was lifted.

"It's the very same as though we had been walking through smoke and all of a sudden a wind blew, took it away and there was clear day light again," Eamon recalls.

He remembers too the faces of the supporters, smudged and lined with green and white dye from their dripping-wet paper hats.

The lifting of the cup was, he says, "monumental". "The people were waiting, they were starved hungry for success. My dad, [Edward] God rest his soul was quite near."

He can remember the walk from the Hogan Stand across to the Cusack Stand where the dressing rooms were located. "That was a back slapping situation," he smiles.

Inside the dressing room, the players reflected on what had just happened. JP McManus joined them for the celebrations. We got JP into the dressing room, through the window."

The return home to Limerick was "beautiful." The team's first stop was Castleconnell where Eamon had the privilege of meeting the one and only Mick Mackey. He presented me with a lovely trophy," he recalls. The team travelled by bus into Charlotte Quay and were presented to the Corporation officials.

Then, the party started. We went out to my local, Spellacy's pub in Ballysheedy. It was supervised, you might say, by Cormac Hurley, who monitored all the traffic.

"We had a great time. People passed us going to work the following morning."

Hurling stars of '73 relive the magic of Croke Park 40 years after famous win
(Limerick Leader, 7 September 2013)

Hartigan and Cregan share special memories of Limerick's cherished victory

By Aine Fitzgerald

Forty years after Limerick claimed their last senior All Ireland Hurling Final title, Pat Hartigan can still distinctly remember the pair of socks he wore on that famous day in 1973. At the last training session before the big day, the Limerick team were presented with a set of socks - white with two green hoops on the top.

Speaking only hours after millions of euro exchanged hands as transfer deadline day came to a close for European soccer clubs, Pat recalled this week how big a deal it was back then for he and his hurling teammates to be presented with a simple pair of socks.

"These socks were very unique," he enthuses. "We got them on the last night of training so we could try them on."

Limerick team photographs taken on the day show all the players with the socks pulled up to their knees. "They were so nice you didn't want to have them down around your ankles. I generally wore them around my ankles but these socks looked so modern we said we might as well maximise them"

At that time, the players had only one jersey each. The All Ireland final on 2 September 1973 was a very wet day but Pat doesn't recall the players changing their jerseys at half-time. "We went out in the same wet jerseys in the second half, from my recollections." The South Liberties man was quite young at the time, just turned 23. It was his first time in Croke Park for an All Ireland final.

"Once you left the hotel you said to yourself, 'When I get back again, there is going to be widespread changes'."

He remembers travelling down Jones Road, pulling into Croke Park and seeing the huge crowd gathered over on the Cusack Stand.

"The mass of people there was something extraordinary," he recalls. "We had witnessed big crowds in Munster but the stadiums in Munster in those days were very open. It was a claustrophobic feel you got when you looked into Croke Park."

Running out onto the pitch with the roar of the crowd, "you felt everybody was in on top of you."

For teammate Eamonn Cregan, the experience was a little different. "I had gone to the bathroom and the team had gone out. The roar was over. I missed it. I missed the famous roar," he smiles.

"The whole Croke Park setting," Pat says, "was very different to what the players were used to. We were used to balls coming through the blue sky but in Croke Park you were seeing them coming out from the faces in the crowd, the stands were so high."

He remembers their opponents, Kilkenny, as being a "very strong, powerful team". "I cannot let this opportunity go without paying tribute to Pat Delaney who captained Kilkenny that day. He died in recent weeks. He was a real warrior." he adds.

Once the final whistle went, people were coming from all sides of the pitch to shoulder the players. Pat was trying to get up into the stand to meet the players for the presentation and he remembers looking down at a very loyal Limerick supporter by the name of Jim Keogh.

"Jim Keogh hurled with Limerick and had a garage in Lower Gerald Griffin Street. You are talking about a powerfully strong man with tears rolling down his face. To this day, Jim Keogh's face crying in front of the stand is very much in my mind."

For Eamonn Cregan, his abiding memory is of Éamon Grimes receiving the cup. "It was something we had all been dreaming about for years, going back to secondary school. There was nothing like it."

While the dressing room was strictly for players and management in those days, the South Liberties boys managed to sneak in one of their own. We spotted JP [McManus] and we got him in the window and rightly so," says Pat. "He was chairman of South Liberties and he was the man who single-handedly, in my opinion, put South Liberties in the right direction. He was ahead of his time when it came to South Liberties and Limerick."

Alter the game, Pat was asked by RTÉ to do an interview for Sunday Sport which would air after the evening news. "Mick Dunne was chairing it," Pat recalls. "At that time, RTÉ didn't make arrangements for you to be collected from the hotel. At about 8PM that night I said, 'I have to go to RTÉ' but I couldn't get out at the hotel because they couldn't open the doors to let me out - the crowd outside was so big and trying to get in. I had to go out through a fire exit, got a bus into the city and then a taxi outside to Montrose."

When he returned to the hotel there were thousands gathered outside. The team were unwinding inside.

"Everyone was sitting down because of the exhaustion of the day. Tom Boland was a good pianist. We went into a room where there was a piano and we sang 'til the early hours."

The homecoming on Monday night was "phenomenal." Pat recalls the scene coming in the Dublin Road. "Once you got to the top of the hill you could see a mass of people all the way into Limerick."

1973 Keeping the Dream Alive

"Jed O'Dwyer's father [John] of the Hurlers Pub was out on the road with a bonfire, and my God it was fairly blazing."

From Castleconnell into Limerick city, the bus, Eamonn Cregan recalls, travelled at a snail's pace. "We passed our house on the way in on the Dublin Road. My father [Ned] had just died the year before but my mother was there, Hannie. It was significant," he says.

While each player has their own cherished Individual memories of '73, there is also the shared pride, and sense of achievement.

"There is always a bond there," says Eamonn. "It will always be there, no matter what happens."

Pat Hartigan, Eamonn Cregan and Éamon Grimes admiring a newspaper from the All Ireland Hurling Final weekend of 1973.

"I wouldn't be a strategist but I like the way they're playing"
(Irish Examiner, 28 July 2018)

By John Fogarty

The Halfway House in Walkinstown is as Dublin as you can get. The blue and navy festoons the ceiling but there's one corner of the premises sporting the green and white. It is owner Gerry O'Malley's nod to the presence of Eamonn Rea behind the bar.

After over 20 years manning the pumps in Parkgate Street, this is where the Limerick hurling legend can be found most weekdays.

Names like Charlie Chawke and Tom Moran are synonymous with Limerick's pub presence in the capital but for years the pre-Croke Park custom for Limerick crowds stepping off the trains in Heuston Station was to make the short walk across the Liffey and in to see Ned.

Now 74, it's not for the need of work that he occupies himself but activity. Or to cure, as he says, "boredom".

"When you come from a farm, your father would always have had a job for you no matter what age you were. whether it be picking stones, cutting weeds, or thinning turnips.

"There was always something."

It's very hard to drop things all of a sudden. Dave Allen always told a great one about working nine to five, getting home at 6:30PM and bed at 9:30PM. You do that all your life then you retire and what do they give you but a clock or a watch."

Eamonn Rea's is now P. Duggans, named after Paul, the late brother of Ger Duggan who took over 25 Parkgate Street after Rea.

Not that he would ever regret Limerick making those big days in Croke Park but they were difficult for them. There were the nerves for a start but then the responsibilities attached too.

"When your name is over the door... say this weekend now, you'd go in Friday and you wouldn't get out until Tuesday. Crazy stuff! It was just too small for the crowds. I've no doubt there'll be fellas on Saturday night looking for me. If he's (Paul) smart enough he'll say, 'Oh, he's gone on his break' or 'he'll be back tomorrow.

"1994 was unreal, I mean, the road. It was physically impossible. We took all the furniture out. It was standing room only. The local pubs after it came looking for all their glasses because we had them. "Fellas were buying pints in them but coming back to ours to be with the crowd.

There were a couple of hundred glasses that weren't ours after it. "There was no real enjoyment and I couldn't be part of it. After Croke Park, I was coming straight back. If your name was there, fellas expected to see you there.

"The biggest mistake was going behind the bar because they all wanted to buy off you. They wanted you to know they were there. There could be another barman there twiddling his thumbs."

He was there too for those last big days for Limerick like 2007 when they saw off a fancied Waterford to reach the All Ireland semi-final.

"JP (McManus) called in that evening."

There was 2014 too but the quieter build-up is much more to his liking. It's on weeks like these that he doesn't feel he's missing out but then he's heavily involved with Club Limerick. It's 50 years last March that Rea has been living in the capital, "I came up here for a week," he smiles.

Before the pub trade, there was Galtee Food Products for 24 years in Ringsend but Effin has never left him. He is up to date on most current affairs there, like Nickie Quaid becoming a co-owner of Davy's Bar in the parish.

"A lot of people wouldn't have a clue who I am there now. That's the nature of the game. I'd be asking my brother Tom about who is this and who is that.

"All the same, I don't think I missed a match when Effin were going well. The most satisfying day for me was winning the Munster (intermediate) championship (in 2011)."

There is a precondition to this interview. Rea is an engaging man but it tires him to talk about 1973. He knows it tires others too and he doesn't want to "haunt" this current group, he says. "In our time, we were hearing about Mick Mackey and the Clohessys and all that and it would be sort of annoying you. That's why you would be awful conscious now to leave '73 where it is."

What he has no problem discussing is his duel with brother Gerry in the All Ireland semi-final that year. Gerry had captained London to a famous quarter-final win over Galway before they squared off against Limerick in Ennis. Speaking to the *Irish Examiner* last year, Gerry mentioned that Micheal O'Hehir had mentioned in commentary that the siblings were "having a bit of a word with each other, but I don't think they are talking about saving hay!"

"I don't know if O'Hehir was even there," Rea smiles. "Maybe he was.

"People exaggerate things. In the Munster final, Tadhg Murphy was in goals for Tipperary. A ball went wide, we were a couple of points down and they were going to kill time. I actually handed the ball back to Tadhg. A number of people made things up that I said to him that would be libellous. The same stuff was said about Babs (Keating) making a bet with Richie Bennis when he stood over that 65. People like fairytales.

"We hurled each other for Effin and were good mates as brothers go.

"Why would we go out to do damage to each other? It wasn't like that.

"The *Limerick Leader* got hold of it and they spoke to my father (Matt). He was saying he was going to shout for London and my mother for Limerick. He was only having the banter. He was asked about us going up against each other but his reply was 'when you have two sons playing in an All Ireland semi-final you come back to me. It was a great remark."

He senses a moment of inspiration could be the difference tomorrow.

The reappearance of Clare in Croke Park today reminds him of Domhnall O'Donovan's equaliser against Cork and his grandfather who was the postmaster in Kilmallock.

"I often think about individual things that happen in matches and what he did that year stuck out for me. There was a guy who was corner-back, the match was virtually over, who had the presence of mind to move up the field and you never know what might happen. It was the incident of that year, more so for his frame of mind that he was thinking positively.

"That's not to say he is optimistic, though Graeme Mulcahy's rebirth fills him with hope. "This is the first year we've been seeing it and it's because he's finally getting decent ball."

That directness appeals to him. "I believe that the short passing should only be used when a fella is in trouble or a better position and that's what they have been doing."

And their points totals are grounds for optimism. "Look at the last Cork game, they picked off 27 points. Against Kilkenny, it was 24 points and (Aaron) Gillane only scored two points from frees."

He knows how Limerick finished out the game against Kilkenny will stand to them. He knows Anthony Nash might have to emulate the outstanding shot-stopping of Eoin Murphy. But he also knows how excitement has got the better of Limerick in the past. "I wouldn't be a strategist but I just like the way they're playing.

"There's consistency there this year. The Clare game was funny this year because you'd usually have one or two guys standing up when a team is going bad but nobody did, and yet with 10 minutes to go they were only four or five points behind. Then Ennis was always a difficulty for Limerick.

"I think it's 50-50. You have to give Cork credit for winning another Munster and they're all well able to hurl and the wide open spaces of Croke Park will be to their liking. Your plus and minus points are all exposed there. I wouldn't be getting carried away about Limerick. We have in the past and it didn't amount to anything."

In a way, Rea is glad Murphy was so good in Thurles. A trouncing of Kilkenny and Limerick would have gone silly. "You couldn't ask for a better way to win it. If they won it by 12 points, you would have heard 'Kilkenny are a spent team' and that type of thing but anybody who says that now are not in the real world of analysing hurling because Kilkenny are never gone. They're judged by the fact they haven't won an All Ireland whereas for other counties getting to an All Ireland semi-final is massive progress."

For Rea, it means home comes to his adopted home. Another visit next month wouldn't go amiss.

Eamonn Rea at the The Halfway House in Walkinstown.

1973 Golden Jubilee Celebrations

Limerick GAA County Board celebrated our 1973 All Ireland hurling championship success with a wonderful set of events on Sunday, 28 May 2023. Limerick played Cork that afternoon in the last round-robin Munster Championship game in the Gaelic Grounds, with a victory required to ensure Limerick's continued progression in the championship. As it turned out, a victory guaranteed our qualification for the 2023 Munster Hurling Final against Clare, as Tipperary lost to Waterford in the other game played that day.

The Strand Hotel was the venue which included a lunch organised for the men who represented Limerick in the All Ireland final of 2 September 1973. Of the 21 players in the programme that Sunday afternoon, 16 attended. Four of the 21 have passed on since 1973: starters Jim O'Brien and Eamonn Rea, as well as substitutes Jim Hogan and Andy Dunworth. All these fine men had close family at the event. Liam O'Donoghue was represented by his brother. Family of the 1973 selectors, trainer as well as county board executive were all represented. Mick Cregan was away that day too. The event was compered by *Sunday Game* legend, Michael Lyster.

It was also attended by Mayor of Limerick, Francis Foley. A three-course lunch was taken. Short speeches were made by present County Board chairperson, Séamus McNamara, as well as JP McManus, and Francis Foley. This book was unveiled at this event and a few words were spoken by the lead author.

Authors Niall Deegan, Liam O'Brien and James Lundon.

James Lundon (left) and Mayor Francis Foley (right) make their speeches as MC Michael Lyster looks on.

1973 Keeping the Dream Alive

Players who attended on the day : Jim Allis, Phil Bennis, Richie Bennis, Eamonn Cregan, Mossie Dowling, Paudie Fitzmaurice, Seán Foley, Michael Graham, Éamon Grimes, Bernie Hartigan, Pat Hartigan, Séamus Horgan, Joe McKenna. Willie Moore, Frankie Nolan, Jim O'Donnell and Tom Ryan.

Each player was presented with a current jersey as well as a framed picture of the 1973 All Ireland winning team and substitutes by Séamus and JP. This framed picture was Michael Martin's from the day.

Seán Foley, Richie Bennis and Eamonn Cregan receive their awards from JP McManus and Séamus McNamara.

LIMERICK ALL IRELAND SENIOR HURLING CHAMPIONS 1973

Back (L-R): Richie Bennis, Liam O'Donoghue, Jim O'Brien, Pat Hartigan, Joe McKenna, Eamonn Cregan, Willie Moore and Eamonn Rea.
Front (L-R): Seán Foley, Mossie Dowling, Bernie Hartigan, Éamon Grimes, Phil Bennis, Frankie Nolan and Séamus Horgan.

1973 Keeping the Dream Alive

At The Strand Hotel in May 2023 on the afternoon of the rou...
Back Row (L-R): Seán Rea (son of Eamonn Rea), Pat Ha...
Seán Foley, Joe O'Donoghue (brother of Liam O'Don...
Front Row (L-R): Michael Graham, Séamus Horgan, Paudie Fitzmaurice, Mossie D...
David O'Brien (son of Jim O'Brien) and Séa...

...ne against Cork that qualified Limerick for the Munster Final.
... Dunworth, Dan Hogan, Eamonn Cregan, Joe McKenna,
... Allis, Richie Bennis, Willie Moore and Jim O'Donnell.
...l Bennis, Éamon Grimes, JP McManus, Bernie Hartigan, Frankie Nolan, Tom Ryan,
...mara (Chairman of Limerick County Board).

1973 Keeping the Dream Alive

The players and representative were presented to the crow[d]
Back Row (L-R): Jim Allis, John Dunworth, Jim O'Donnell, Seán Rea, Joe McKenna, Pat Hartigan, S[...]
Front Row (L-R): Dan Hogan, Paudie Fitzmaurice, Tom Ryan, Mossie Dowli[ng]

...ld at half time in the Gaelic Grounds, to general acclaim.
...e O'Donoghue, David O'Brien, Séamus Horgan, Willie Moore, Eamonn Cregan and Richie Bennis.
...Nolan, Éamon Grimes, Bernie Hartigan, Phil Bennis and Michael Graham.

Some Reminiscences of 1973

By Cormac Liddy

During my 60 odd years as a journalist there were many highlights and, of course, some disappointing occasions. As these are glory days for Limerick hurling it brought to mind many of my happiest moments. Top of the list has always been the All Ireland hurling win in 1973, closely followed by travelling on the plane with Pope John Paul on his visit to this country. As he sat beside me and blessed me, he noticed my accreditation and gave me the shortest 'interview' of my career when he said, "I will see you on Monday." He went on to become a saint but our lives subsequently went in opposite directions.

I was blessed in many other ways though, not least of which was being the GAA writer for the *Limerick Leader* in the early 1970s. No All Ireland had been won since 1940 and the county had the initial breakthrough with the National Hurling League win in 1971. That was a significant success but instead of building on that came a massive controversy as the services of the man credited with playing a major role in the win, Joe McGrath, was replaced in the summer of 1972. I recall the resulting fractious meetings of the county board and at one such meeting Jackie O'Connell begged the feuding parties to stop the disharmony. It petered out, eventually, and heading into 1973, Mick Cregan, an army officer, was appointed trainer. He had played in the 1971 league win and was, therefore, very familiar with the various players.

But those days were vastly different to modern times and I sometimes wonder if the old days, and methods, produced a different type of hurling. Ground hurling was very much more part of the game then than it is now. In my time I had the 'distinction' of being assured by many that I knew nothing about hurling, Gaelic football, greyhound racing and coursing, soccer, and rugby, plus any other sport I wrote about. Times, and preparation of teams also changed. We hear stories of players being sent climbing mountains, going to foreign climes for warm weather training, only to end up playing in torrential rain but, of course, the warm weather spells away helps to create better team spirit. Imagine if Michael Cregan asked his players to run up a mountain. I know well what the answer would be and it would end with the words, "take a hike."

While it all seemed happiness and joy to the general public, 1973 was not without its controversies apart from the team and those close to it. For instance there was some form of industrial action by the National Union of journalists round the time of the semi-final against London which was played in Ennis. The game was to be boycotted by those working in provincial papers. That sure was a dilemma for me and I arranged for Séamus O Ceallaigh, a non journalist but a huge writer of a weekly GAA column under the name of 'Camán' to 'cover' the game. I remember getting torrents of abuse after it emerged that I did a report of that game.

The year was not without its on-field drama too. The end of the Munster final was one of the most remarkable for many years. The wonderful Richie Bennis stood over a '70 with the last puck of the game to make Limerick Munster champions. A well-known Tipperary player did his best to distract Bennis but to no avail. I was seated in between Raymond Smith and Paddy Downey and we each had a role to play as the '70 was being taken. My 'job' was to watch the officials, which was not easy as one of the umpires was turned upside down by a defender, as Richie put over the point. I saw clearly who was responsible but it was not my duty to confirm what I had seen when the Munster Council later met at Halla Íde in Thomas Street to discuss the issue.

There followed the win over London and it was all systems go in preparation for the 80 minute final against Kilkenny. Green and white flags were flown on the front of the train which was driven by former Limerick soccer player and a member of the city council and then current mayor, Mick Lipper. I was very close to those involved and frequently would be with players and officials at the Shannon Arms Hotel in Henry Street for post-training food. As the excitement grew in late August I was tipped off that a super switch was to be made on the team for the final. It transpired that Eamonn Cregan was to play at centre-back!

I travelled with the team on the train on the eve of final and enjoyed card games involving, amongst others, the late Seán Cunningham, a selector, and the late Jim Hogan who played in goal in the semi-final, though it was another outstanding goalie Séamus Horgan who played in the final. It was always great fun to be so close to those mighty men, many of whom I am proud to consider as friends to this day. Indeed, when those players were being honoured at Croke Park 25 years later, the captain Éamon Grimes insisted that I be included, with the players and management, in getting the outfits to be worn.

On All Ireland Sunday morning, the players attended Mass and then many of them did a walkabout. On, then, to Croke Park and the awful rain. It was so wet that President Erskine Childers was late arriving to greet the drenched players. Limerick went on to win by seven points. I still cannot get it out of system my continued annoyance at the moaning from Kilkenny that they were without, Eddie Keher and a few others. I have no doubt that Limerick on that occasion would have beaten a full strength opposition. In those days CIÉ operated an all-in train with full wine and food facilities. I opted to miss the celebrations in the Dublin hotel but many of the players still talk about the huge crowd. Goal scorer, Mossie Dowling from Kilmallock, once told me that he saw many climbing in through a hotel window! The same Dowling has the distinction of being the only player to have scored a goal in a winning Limerick All Ireland side over almost 80 years (1940-2018).

I had my match report written by the time the highlights were shown on RTÉ and was determined not to start changing it from what I saw on the television. During the All Ireland final, a journalist colleague left out a huge roar of delight in support of Limerick, which would be tut-tut. An American seated in front, remarked that he believed journalists should be impartial. My colleague's reply was a gem, "we have waited 33 years for this." I was amongst the thousands who gathered outside the Railway Station as the team arrived home the evening after. I was invited to get on the bus with the team and the procession down O'Connell Street was memorable. To me, it will always be top of my highlights list, which also includes the win by Limerick United in what was their first FAI Cup win in 1971, the success by Young Munster in the All Ireland League, wins galore for my favourite rugby club, Shannon, a trip to South Africa for the 1995 Rugby World Cup. Ireland's Call was given its first airing there and an Ulster player also insisted that the Ulster flag be shown at all the Irish games. It was a glorious era to be covering sport and I thank the many GAA people who allowed me to share their journey. It was occasionally a rocky road but peace and friendship always won out.

P.S. There was no Limerick anthem in those days but within a few years Denis Allen brought out a record called "Limerick You're A Lady" which I contend should still be the 'official' anthem, with all due respects to the wonderful singing by the late Dolores O'Riordan of "Dreams".

THE PASSING OF THE TORCH...

Our hurling heroes of 1973 line up in front of the Mackey Stand, ahead of their heartwarming celebratory half-time appearance at the Gaelic Grounds on 28 May 2023. It must gladden the hearts of these Limerick greats to know that their legacy and spirit still burns brightly in the current generation of young men in green and white jerseys who they see on the pitch before them.

CHAPTER 14
1972-73

FACTS AND FIGURES

Limerick played ten games in the 1972-73 National Hurling League (NHL) season. On only one occasion, in 1979-80, did Limerick ever play more games in a single league season. Limerick qualified second to Kilkenny in Division 1A and won a semi-final replay with Tipperary before losing the final to Wexford. Twenty five different players played some part in that NHL campaign, with all of them starting at least one of the ten games. Six men started all ten games: Richie Bennis, Seán Foley, Willie Moore, Frankie Nolan, Jim O'Brien and Jim O'Donnell. Another four made nine starting appearances: Eamonn Cregan, Éamon Grimes, Pat Hartigan and Séamus Horgan. Two more started eight of these ten games: Michael Graham and Eamonn Rea. Only 14 substitutes' appearances were recorded across the ten games, a facet of the game that has changed radically in the modern era. It was a time when tactical changes were only grudgingly made, as was the case in other team sports. The concept of experimental teams was an almost alien one!

Richie Bennis was top league scorer with 8-45, failing to score only once, against Kilkenny. Frankie Nolan was next with 5-8, while Éamon Grimes was only a point further behind on 3-13. Willie Moore started the campaign in the forwards and registered 2-3 before being pushed much further back the field. Twelve different men contributed to the 32-95 scored during that NHL season.

There are records of five challenge games being played. Full lineouts and scorers are available for four of them. Only the Offaly challenge in January lacks a full lineout, though the newspapers did name 11 starters and all the scorers. This includes one player who is not recorded as having otherwise played in 1973, Dan Connolly of Kilmallock.

Limerick played four games in the 1973 championship season. A backdoor championship in any form was not instituted for another 24 years, in 1997, when the Munster and Leinster provincial finalists got a second chance in the All Ireland series. A full backdoor was not put in place until 2002, when all top teams played at least two games each. Clare (24 June), Tipperary (29 July), London (5 August), and Kilkenny (2 September) were played, with the full set of results from the 1973 championship listed in this chapter.

There was no Ulster championship of any form. Galway entered at the quarter-final stage, not at the semi-final stage, as was the case since they left Munster after the 1969 championship. London had played semi-finals since 1969, as they won the 1968 All Ireland Intermediate championship. London played Galway and the winner played Limerick, with Kilkenny getting a bye to the final. In 1974, the winners of Galway (having beaten Kildare in a pre-quarter final) and London played Kilkenny, while Limerick got a bye into the final. London were never as strong again after the 1968-1974 era.

Twelve men started all four of Limerick's championship games in 1973, with only Séamus Horgan, Eamonn Rea and Joe McKenna, of the All Ireland final starting 15, beginning fewer than four games. Only five substitutions were made across the four games, with Tom Ryan the only man to make two appearances from the bench, in both major finals. Jack O'Dwyer started against Clare, having not played a competitive game for Limerick before that. It was his only league or championship appearance for the county. Jim O'Donnell started two games and appeared in one more, while Jim Hogan started, instead of Séamus Horgan, against London. Both Jim Allis and Andy Dunworth made one substitute appearance each during the 1973 championship.

Richie Bennis scored a whopping 2-25 of Limerick's championship total of 11-54, with Eamonn Cregan next on 4-3, while Frankie Nolan got 2-5. Nine different scorers contributed to the 11-54 scored that championship season. Twenty-one different players played championship for Limerick in 1973. This title was hard earned in the old knock-out system, playing two of the top three counties along the way. To quote an old-timer, "No All Ireland hurling title, past or present, is easily won."

National Hurling League

8 October 1972 - NHL Div. 1A (Round 1)
Limerick 3-8 - 4-5 Clare @ Limerick
Jim Hogan; Phil Bennis, Pat Hartigan, Jim O'Brien; Christy Campbell, Jim O'Donnell, Willie Conway; Leonard Enright, Seán Foley; Frankie Nolan, Richie Bennis (2-4), Éamon Grimes (0-1); Michael Graham (0-1), Willie Moore (1-0), Eamonn Cregan (0-2). Subs: Andy Dunworth for Michael Graham.

22 October 1972 - NHL Div. 1A (Round 2)
Limerick 4-2 - 1-16 Kilkenny @ Kilkenny
Séamus Horgan; Phil Bennis, Pat Hartigan, Jim O'Brien; Christy Campbell, Jim O'Donnell, Michael Graham (1-0); Leonard Enright, Seán Foley; Frankie Nolan (1-1), Richie Bennis, Éamon Grimes (1-0); Matt Grace, Willie Moore (1-1), Eamonn Cregan. Subs: Mossie Dowling for Matt Grace, Eamonn Rea for Mossie Dowling.

5 November 1972 - NHL Div. 1A (Round 3)
Limerick 2-18 - 1-1 Galway @ Limerick
Séamus Horgan; Pat Hartigan, Eamonn Rea, Jim O'Brien; Tom Ryan, Jim O'Donnell, Seán Foley (0-1); Richie Bennis (0-7), Leonard Enright; Frankie Nolan (0-2), Michael Graham, Éamon Grimes (0-5); Andy Dunworth (2-2), Willie Moore, Eamonn Cregan (0-1). Sub: None.

3 December 1972 - NHL Div. 1A (Round 5)
Limerick 3-8 - 3-4 Offaly @ Limerick
Séamus Horgan; Pat Hartigan, Eamonn Rea, Jim O'Brien; Tom Ryan, Jim O'Donnell, Seán Foley; Richie Bennis (2-2), Leonard Enright; Frankie Nolan, Michael Graham, Éamon Grimes (1-2); Andy Dunworth (0-2), Willie Moore (0-1), Eamonn Cregan (0-1). Sub: None.

11 February 1973 - NHL Div. 1A (Round 6)
Limerick 3-7 - 2-10 Tipperary @ Limerick
Séamus Horgan; Willie Moore, Eamonn Rea, Jim O'Brien; Tom Ryan, Jim O'Donnell, Seán Foley; Richie Bennis (1-2), John Quinlan; Liam O'Donoghue (0-2), Eamonn Cregan (0-3), Pat Fogarty (1-0); Andy Dunworth, Mossie Dowling (1-0), Frankie Nolan. Subs: Michael Graham for Andy Dunworth, Andy Dunworth for Dowling.

4 March 1973 - NHL Div. 1A (Round 7)
Limerick 3-13 - 1-7 Cork @ Cork, Athletic Grounds
Séamus Horgan; Willie Moore, Eamonn Rea, Jim O'Brien; Jim O'Donnell, Pat Hartigan, Seán Foley; Bernie Hartigan, Éamon Grimes (0-1); Richie Bennis (1-5), Eamonn Cregan (1-0), Michael Graham (1-1); Liam O'Donoghue (0-1), Mossie Dowling (0-2), Frankie Nolan (0-3). Subs: Tom Ryan for Jim O'Donnell.

11 March 1973 - NHL Div. 1A (Round 4)
Limerick 4-11 - 2-12 Wexford @ Enniscorthy
Séamus Horgan; Willie Moore, Eamonn Rea, Jim O'Brien; Jim O'Donnell, Pat Hartigan (0-2), Seán Foley; Bernie Hartigan, Éamon Grimes (1-2); Richie Bennis (1-5), Pat Fogarty (0-1), Michael Graham; Liam O'Donoghue, Mossie Dowling (1-0), Frankie Nolan (1-0). Subs: Andy Dunworth (0-1) for Pat Fogarty.

15 April 1973 - NHL Semi-Final
Limerick 2-11 - 2-11 Tipperary @ Kilkenny

Séamus Horgan; Willie Moore, Eamonn Rea, Jim O'Brien; Pat Hartigan, Jim O'Donnell, Seán Foley; Bernie Hartigan, Éamon Grimes; Richie Bennis (0-8), Eamonn Cregan (0-1), Liam O'Donoghue (2-1); Andy Dunworth, Mossie Dowling, Frankie Nolan (0-1). Subs: Pat Fogarty for Andy Dunworth, Andy Dunworth for Frankie Nolan.

29 April 1973 - NHL Semi-Final (replay-AET)
Limerick 5-10 - 3-14 Tipperary @ Birr

Séamus Horgan; Pat Hartigan, Eamonn Rea, Jim O'Brien; Mossie Dowling, Jim O'Donnell, Seán Foley; Bernie Hartigan, Éamon Grimes; Richie Bennis (0-8), Eamonn Cregan (1-0), Michael Graham; Liam O'Donoghue (1-0), Willie Moore (0-1), Frankie Nolan (3-1). Subs: Andy Dunworth for Liam O'Donoghue, Phil Bennis for Mossie Dowling, Leonard Enright for Michael Graham, Pat Fogarty for Leonard Enright, Michael Graham for Seán Foley.

13 May 1973 - NHL Final
Limerick 3-7 - 4-13 Wexford @ Croke Park

Séamus Horgan; Pat Hartigan, Eamonn Rea, Jim O'Brien; Mossie Dowling (1-1), Jim O'Donnell, Seán Foley; Bernie Hartigan, Éamon Grimes (0-2); Richie Bennis (1-4), Eamonn Cregan (1-0), Michael Graham; Liam O'Donoghue, Willie Moore, Frankie Nolan. Subs: Andy Dunworth for Michael Graham, Phil Bennis for Andy Dunworth, Leonard Enright for Jim O'Donnell.

Munster and All Ireland Hurling Championship

24 June 1973 - Munster Semi-Final
Limerick 3-11 - 3-9 Clare @ Thurles

Séamus Horgan; Willie Moore, Pat Hartigan, Jim O'Brien; Phil Bennis, Seán Foley, Jack O'Dwyer; Richie Bennis (0-3), Éamon Grimes (0-2); Bernie Hartigan (1-1), Eamonn Cregan (2-1), Liam O'Donoghue (0-1); Joe McKenna, Mossie Dowling (0-2), Frankie Nolan (0-1). Subs: Jim O'Donnell for Jack O'Dwyer, Jim Allis for Pat Hartigan.

29 July 1973 – Munster Final
Limerick 6-7 - 2-18 Tipperary @ Thurles

Séamus Horgan; Willie Moore, Pat Hartigan, Jim O'Brien; Phil Bennis, Jim O'Donnell, Seán Foley; Richie Bennis (1-5), Éamon Grimes; Liam O'Donoghue (0-1), Mossie Dowling (1-0), Bernie Hartigan; Frankie Nolan (2-1), Eamonn Rea, Eamonn Cregan (2-0). Sub: Tom Ryan for Jim O'Donnell.

5 August 1973 - All Ireland Semi-Final
Limerick 1-15 - 0-7 London @ Ennis

Jim Hogan; Willie Moore, Pat Hartigan, Jim O'Brien; Phil Bennis, Jim O'Donnell, Seán Foley; Richie Bennis (1-7), Éamon Grimes; Liam O'Donoghue (0-4), Mossie Dowling, Bernie Hartigan (0-1); Frankie Nolan (0-1), Eamonn Rea, Eamonn Cregan (0-2). Sub: Andy Dunworth for Eamonn Cregan.

2 September 1973 - All Ireland Final
Limerick 1-21 - 1-14 Kilkenny @ Croke Park

Séamus Horgan; Willie Moore, Pat Hartigan, Jim O'Brien; Phil Bennis, Eamonn Cregan, Seán Foley; Richie Bennis (0-10), Éamon Grimes (0-4); Liam O'Donoghue, Mossie Dowling (1-1), Bernie Hartigan (0-1); Frankie Nolan (0-2), Eamonn Rea (0-2), Joe McKenna (0-1). Sub: Tom Ryan for Bernie Hartigan.

1972/73 NHL Division 1A Results

Round	Date	Home	Score	Away	Venue
1	8 October 1972	Limerick	3-8 - 4-5	Clare	Limerick
1	8 October 1972	Offaly	1-8 - 0-14	Galway	Birr
1	4 February 1973	Tipperary	3-14 - 2-9	Kilkenny	Thurles
1	4 February 1973	Cork	1-7 - 1-9	Wexford	Cork
2	22 October 1972	Kilkenny	1-16 - 4-2	Limerick	Kilkenny
2	22 October 1972	Galway	0-12 - 5-11	Cork	Ballinasloe
2	22 October 1972	Clare	3-7 - 1-10	Offaly	Ennis
2	22 October 1972	Wexford	4-15 - 2-9	Tipperary	New Ross
3	5 November 1972	Limerick	2-18 - 1-1	Galway	Limerick
3	5 November 1972	Tipperary	1-11 - 1-11	Clare	Tipperary Town
3	5 November 1972	Cork	1-7 - 1-11	Kilkenny	Cork
3	5 November 1972	Offaly	2-9 - 2-11	Wexford	Birr
4	11 March 1973	Wexford	2-12 - 4-11	Limerick	Enniscorthy
4	19 November 1972	Clare	3-4 - 1-9	Cork	Ennis
4	19 November 1972	Galway	2-6 - 3-12	Tipperary	Portumna
4	19 November 1972	Kilkenny	1-11 - 2-6	Offaly	Kilkenny
5	3 December 1972	Limerick	3-8 - 3-4	Offaly	Limerick
5	3 December 1972	Tipperary	2-7 - 1-4	Cork	Thurles
5	3 December 1972	Wexford	3-6 - 3-16	Kilkenny	Wexford
5	3 December 1972	Galway	0-7 - 4-4	Clare	Galway
6	11 February 1973	Limerick	3-7 - 2-10	Tipperary	Limerick
6	11 February 1973	Clare	2-3 - 1-9	Wexford	Ennis
6	11 February 1973	Cork	3-8 - 1-10	Offaly	Cork
6	11 February 1973	Kilkenny	1-14 - 1-12	Galway	Ballyraggett
7	4 March 1973	Cork	1-7 - 3-13	Limerick	Cork
7	4 March 1973	Kilkenny	0-17 - 0-6	Clare	Kilkenny
7	4 March 1973	Wexford	4-14 - 2-1	Galway	Gorey
7	4 March 1973	Offaly	0-3 - 0-15	Tipperary	Birr

1972/73 NHL Division 1A Table

Team	P	W	D	L	For	Aga	Pts	+/-
Kilkenny	7	6	0	1	9-94	14-53	12	27
Limerick	7	4	2	1	22-67	14-55	10	36
Tipperary	7	4	2	1	13-78	13-55	10	23
Wexford	7	5	0	2	17-76	16-56	10	23
Clare	7	3	2	2	17-40	7-71	8	-1
Cork	7	2	0	5	13-53	11-66	4	-7
Galway	7	1	0	6	6-53	20-81	2	-70
Offaly	7	0	0	7	10-50	12-74	0	-30

1972/73 NHL Division 1B Table

Team	P	W	D	L	For	Aga	Pts	+/-
Waterford	7	6	1	0	138	84	13	54
Kildare	7	4	1	2	133	112	9	21
Dublin	7	4	1	2	124	114	9	10
Antrim	7	4	0	3	119	121	8	-2
Laois	7	3	1	3	140	97	7	43
Wicklow	7	2	0	5	89	120	4	-31
Westmeath	7	2	0	5	96	147	4	-51
Kerry	7	1	0	6	92	136	2	-44

1972/73 NHL Knockout Results

Stage	Date	Winner	Score	Loser	Venue
QF	8 April 1973	Wexford	1-9 - 1-9	Waterford	Kilkenny
QFr	15 April 1973	Wexford	2-16 - 4-7	Waterford	Kilkenny
QF	8 April 1973	Tipperary	5-18 - 2-9	Kildare	Newbridge
SF	15 April 1973	Limerick	2-11 - 2-11	Tipperary	Kilkenny
SFr	29 April 1973	Limerick	5-10 - 3-14	Tipperary	Birr
SF	29 April 1973	Wexford	2-10 - 2-9	Kilkenny	Waterford
Final	13 May 1973	Wexford	4-13 - 3-7	Limerick	Croke Park

1972/73 NHL Appearances

Player (Club)	Full (Sub)	Score
Richie Bennis (Patrickswell)	10 (0)	8-45
Seán Foley (Patrickswell)	10 (0)	0-1
Willie Moore (Doon)	10 (0)	2-3
Frankie Nolan (Patrickswell)	10 (0)	5-8
Jim O'Brien (Bruree)	10 (0)	0-0
Jim O'Donnell (Doon)	10 (0)	0-0
Eamonn Cregan (Claughaun)	9 (0)	3-8
Eamon Grimes (South Liberties)	9 (0)	3-13
Pat Hartigan (South Liberties)	9 (0)	0-2
Séamus Horgan (Tournafulla)	9 (0)	0-0
Michael Graham (Claughaun)	8 (1)	2-2
Ned Rea (Faughs)	8 (1)	0-0
Mossie Dowling (Kilmallock)	6 (1)	3-3
Liam O'Donoghue (Mungret)	6 (0)	3-4
Bernie Hartigan (Old Christians)	5 (0)	0-0
Andy Dunworth (Claughaun)	4 (4)	2-5
Leonard Enright (Patrickswell)	4 (2)	0-0
Tom Ryan (Ballybrown)	3 (1)	0-0
Phil Bennis (Patrickswell)	2 (2)	0-0
Pat Fogarty (Ballybrown)	2 (2)	1-1
Christy Campbell (Old Christians)	2 (0)	0-0
Willie Conway (Bruff)	1 (0)	0-0
Matt Grace (Claughaun)	1 (0)	0-0
Jim Hogan (Claughaun)	1 (0)	0-0
John Quinlan (Doon)	1 (0)	0-0

1973 Championship Appearances

Player (Club)	Full (Sub)	Score
Richie Bennis (Patrickswell)	4 (0)	2-25
Phil Bennis (Patrickswell)	4 (0)	0-0
Eamonn Cregan (Claughaun)	4 (0)	4-3
Mossie Dowling (Kilmallock)	4 (0)	2-3
Seán Foley (Patrickswell)	4 (0)	0-0
Eamon Grimes (South Liberties)	4 (0)	0-6
Pat Hartigan (South Liberties)	4 (0)	0-0
Bernie Hartigan (Old Christians)	4 (0)	1-3
Willie Moore (Doon)	4 (0)	0-0
Frankie Nolan (Patrickswell)	4 (0)	2-5
Jim O'Brien (Bruree)	4 (0)	0-0
Liam O'Donoghue (Mungret)	4 (0)	0-6
Séamus Horgan (Tournafulla)	3 (0)	0-0
Ned Rea (Faughs)	3 (0)	0-2
Jim O'Donnell (Doon)	2 (1)	0-0
Joe McKenna (South Liberties)	2 (0)	0-1
Jim Hogan (Claughaun)	1 (0)	0-0
Jack O'Dwyer (Pallasgreen)	1 (0)	0-0
Tom Ryan (Ballybrown)	0 (2)	0-0
Jim Allis (Doon)	0 (1)	0-0
Andy Dunworth (Claughaun)	0 (1)	0-0

Limerick's 1972/73 NHL, 197

Type	Date	Limerick	Full Time	Opposition
NHL Group	8 October 1972	Limerick	3-8 - 4-5	Clare
NHL Group	22 October 1972	Limerick	4-2 - 1-16	Kilkenny
NHL Group	5 November 1972	Limerick	2-18 - 1-1	Galway
NHL Group	3 December 1972	Limerick	3-8 - 3-4	Offaly
Challenge	21 January 1973	Limerick	4-9 - 3-5	Offaly
NHL Group	11 February 1973	Limerick	3-7 - 2-10	Tipperary
NHL Group	4 March 1973	Limerick	3-13 - 1-7	Cork
NHL Group	11 March 1973	Limerick	4-11 - 2-12	Wexford
NHL SF	15 April 1973	Limerick	2-11 - 2-11	Tipperary
NHL SFr	29 April 1973	Limerick	5-10 - 3-14	Tipperary
NHL Final	13 May 1973	Limerick	3-7 - 4-13	Wexford
Challenge	25 May 1973	Limerick	3-16 - 4-9	Cork
Challenge	31 May 1973	Limerick	3-14 - 4-5	Kilkenny
Challenge	10 June 1973	Limerick	1-12 - 2-9	Cork
MHC	24 June 1973	Limerick	3-11 - 3-9	Clare
Challenge	9 July 1973	Limerick	4-18 - 4-11	Waterford
MH Final	29 July 1973	Limerick	6-7 - 2-18	Tipperary
AIHSF	5 August 1973	Limerick	1-15 - 0-7	London
AIH Final	2 September 1973	Limerick	1-21 - 1-14	Kilkenny

llenge & Championship Games

Venue	Referee	Half Time	Crowd
Gaelic Grounds	Frank Murphy (Cork)	1-5 - 3-3	
Kilkenny	John O'Regan (Waterford)	1-1 - 1-7	
Gaelic Grounds	Paddy Cronin (Cork)	1-10 - 0-1	
Gaelic Grounds	Michael Slattery (Clare)	1-5 - 1-2	
Birr	Gerry Kirwan (Offaly)	4-3 - 1-4	
Gaelic Grounds	Michael Slattery (Clare)	3-4 - 1-2	
hletic Grounds, Cork	Noel Dalton (Waterford)	3-7 - 0-4	
Enniscorthy	Jim Dunphy (Waterford)	0-7 - 1-7	
Kilkenny	Noel Dalton (Waterford)	0-9 - 1-5	15,000
Birr	Mick Spain (Offaly)	1-4 - 1-4	14,000
Croke Park	Frank Murphy (Cork)	0-5 - 3-6	20,814
Gaelic Grounds	John Moloney (Tipperary)	2-8 - 1-6	
Gaelic Grounds	Jack Quaid (Limerick)	2-7 - 2-5	
astlelyons, Co. Cork	Derry O'Brien (Cork)	1-6 - 2-4	
Thurles	John Moloney (Tipperary)	2-7 - 2-5	12,981
Gaelic Grounds	Michael Slattery (Clare)	3-14 - 0-5	
Thurles	Michael Slattery (Clare)	3-2 - 2-9	41,723
Ennis	Mick Spain (Offaly)	0-10 - 0-5	12,000
Croke Park	Michael Slattery (Clare)	0-12 - 1-7	58,009

Limerick 1972/73 NHL, 1973 Challenge & Championship Games Appearance Data

Name (Club)	8/10/72 CE NHL	22/10/72 KK NHL	5/11/72 GY NHL	3/12/72 OY NHL	21/1/73 OY Cha	11/2/73 TY NHL	4/3/73 CK NHL	11/3/73 WX NHL	15/4/73 TY NHL	29/4/73 TY NHL	13/5/73 WX NHL	24/5/73 CK Cha	31/5/73 KK Cha	10/6/73 CK Cha	24/6/73 CE MHC	09/7/73 WD Cha	29/7/73 TY MHF	5/8/73 LN AIHSF	2/9/73 KK AIHF
Séamus Horgan (Tournafulla)	s	1	1	1		1	1	1	1	1	1	1	1	1	1	1	1	1	1
Willie Moore (Doon)	14	14	14	14	p	2	2	2	2	14	13	2	2	2	2	2	2	2	2
Pat Hartigan (South Liberties)	3	3	2	2			6	5	5	2	2	3			3		3	3	3
Jim O'Brien (Bruree)	4	4	4	4	p	4	4	4	4	4	4	4	4		4	4	4	4	4
Phil Bennis (Patrickswell)	2	2	s			s	s	s	s	17	17	5	5	4	5	5	5	5	5
Eamonn Cregan (Claughaun)	15	15	15	15	p	11	11		11	11	10	6		5	11	13	15	15	6
Seán Foley (Patrickswell)	9	9	7	7		7	7	7	7	7	6			6	6	6	7	7	7
Richie Bennis (Patrickswell)	11	11	8	8		8	10	10	10	10	9	11	8	8	8	9	8	8	8
Eamon Grimes (South Liberties)	12	12	12	12	p		9	9	8	9	8	9		9	9	18	9	9	9
Liam O'Donoghue (Mungret)						10	13	13	12	13	12	13	13	13	12	12	10	10	10
Mossie Dowling (Kilmallock)		16			p	14	14	14	14	5	14	14	14	14	14	14	11	11	11
Bernie Hartigan (Old Christians)					p		8	8	9	8	7	8	9			10	10	12	12	12
Frankie Nolan (Patrickswell)	10	10	10	10	p	15	15	15	15	15	15	15	15	15	15	15	13	13	13
Ned Rea (Faughs)	s	17	3	3		3	3	3	3	3	3				14	14	14	14
Joe McKenna (South Liberties)												10		11	13		s	s	15
Tom Ryan (Ballybrown)	s	5	5		p	5	16	s									16	s	16
Jim Hogan (Claughaun)	1						s	s	s	s	s	s			s			1	s
Jim O'Donnell (Doon)	6	6	6	6		6	5	5	6	6	5				16	6	6	6	s
Andy Dunworth (Claughaun)	16		13	13		13		16	13	16	16					s	16	s	
Jim Allis (Doon)	s					s	s	s	s	s	s	s	3	3	17	3	s	s	s
Jack O'Dwyer (Pallasgreen)												7	7	7	7	17			
Michael Graham (Claughaun)	13	7	11	11		16	12	12		12	11								
Leonard Enright (Patrickswell)	9	8	9	9						18	18								
Pat Fogarty (Ballybrown)					p	12	s	11	16	19	s	12							
John Quinlan (Doon)					p	9	s	s	s	s									
Christy Campbell (Old Christians)	5	5	s									16	6	17		16			
Matt Grace (Claughaun)	s	13	s																
Willie Conway (Bruff)	7																		
Matt Ruth (Old Christians)													17	12	12				
Murty Ahearne (Ahane)													18						
Paudie Fitzmaurice (Killeedy)													10	10	s	8		s	s
Tony Smith (Kilmallock)													11	16					
John Ryan (Pallasgreen)													16						
Joe Grimes (South Liberties)							s	s	s	s		s			s				
Dan Connolly (Kilmallock)					p		s	s		s	s								
Tom Hehir (Bruff)						s	s	s	s	s									

p = played

s = unused sub

Limerick 1972/73 League & Championship Player - Lifetime Statistics

Name (Club)	Debut	Swansong	League Apps	League Score	Championship Apps	Championship Score
Séamus Horgan (Tournafulla)	22 October 1972	27 July 1975	20 (0)	0-0	9 (0)	0-0
Willie Moore (Doon)	6 December 1970	1 September 1974	28 (0)	12-14	8 (1)	0-2
Pat Hartigan (South Liberties)	27 October 1968	10 June 1979	79 (0)	3-10	25 (0)	0-1
Jim O'Brien (Bruree)	3 October 1965	8 July 1979	74 (0)	0-0	24 (0)	0-0
Phil Bennis (Patrickswell)	28 November 1965	1 September 1974	42 (3)	0-1	13 (1)	0-2
Eamonn Cregan (Claughaun)	29 September 1963	26 June 1983	110 (3)	61-221	39 (1)	27-97
Seán Foley (Patrickswell)	23 March 1969	26 June 1983	87 (6)	2-19	31 (1)	0-11
Richie Bennis (Patrickswell)	28 November 1965	13 March 1977	55 (6)	21-244	18 (1)	9-105
Eamon Grimes (South Liberties)	5 June 1966	8 March 1981	73 (8)	17-93	26 (4)	3-29
Liam O'Donoghue (Mungret)	11 February 1973	5 June 1988	114 (5)	15-47	35 (2)	2-22
Mossie Dowling (Kilmallock)	5 November 1967	1 August 1976	27 (3)	12-10	9 (2)	2-8
Bernie Hartigan (Old Christians)	14 October 1962	1 September 1974	58 (1)	6-40	22 (1)	1-24
Frankie Nolan (Patrickswell)	7 March 1971	26 June 1983	34 (9)	11-31	13 (5)	3-17
Ned Rea (Faughs)	29 September 1963	13 March 1977	37 (1)	6-7	15 (0)	3-8
Joe McKenna (South Liberties)	24 June 1973	16 June 1985	76 (2)	51-83	30 (0)	18-39
Tom Ryan (Ballybrown)	28 November 1965	1 August 1976	34 (5)	0-2	10 (3)	0-1
Jim Hogan (Claughaun)	1 June 1958	5 August 1973	64 (0)	0-0	24 (0)	0-0
Jim O'Donnell (Doon)	11 October 1964	28 July 1974	34 (1)	1-1	12 (2)	0-2
Andy Dunworth (Claughaun)	5 June 1966	4 November 1973	22 (10)	12-28	5 (4)	0-6
Jim Allis (Doon)	5 November 1967	4 November 1973	25 (0)	0-0	2 (1)	0-0
Jack O'Dwyer (Pallasgreen)	24 June 1973	24 June 1973	n/a	n/a	1 (0)	0-0
Michael Graham (Claughaun)	27 October 1968	6 July 1975	28 (2)	10-11	5 (1)	2-5
Leonard Enright (Patrickswell)	7 March 1971	6 November 1988	66 (5)	1-5	20 (1)	0-2
Pat Fogarty (Ballybrown)	11 February 1973	29 April 1973	2 (2)	1-1	n/a	n/a
John Quinlan (Doon)	11 February 1973	24 November 1974	3 (0)	0-0	n/a	n/a
Christy Campbell (Old Christians)	6 December 1970	19 October 1975	7 (2)	0-0	2 (0)	0-0
Matt Grace (Claughaun)	3 March 1968	22 October 1972	1 (1)	0-1	n/a	n/a
Willie Conway (Bruff)	8 October 1972	29 September 1974	4 (0)	0-0	1 (0)	0-0
Matt Ruth (Old Christians)	4 November 1973	1 September 1974	7 (0)	4-15	2 (0)	0-2
Paudie Fitzmaurice (Killeedy)	7 October 1973	1 June 1986	79 (6)	0-11	26 (3)	0-2
Joe Grimes (South Liberties)	31 October 1976	8 July 1979	2 (1)	0-1	0 (1)	0-0

1973 All Ireland Hurling Championship Results

Round	Date	Winner	Score	Loser	Venue
\multicolumn{6}{c}{Leinster Championship}
1st	13 May 1973	Offaly	4-12 - 3-6	Kildare	Portlaoise
QF	27 May 1973	Dublin	0-17 - 1-6	Westmeath	Navan
QF	27 May 1973	Offaly	3-10 - 3-10	Laois	Birr
QFr	10 June 1973	Offaly	5-6 - 3-10	Laois	Portlaoise
SF	10 June 1973	Kilkenny	2-19 - 2-11	Dublin	Wexford
SF	24 June 1973	Wexford	2-14 - 2-9	Offaly	Kilkenny
Final	8 July 1973	Kilkenny	4-22 - 3-15	Wexford	Croke Park
\multicolumn{6}{c}{Munster Championship}
QF	20 May 1973	Tipperary	1-16 - 2-8	Waterford	Thurles
SF	24 June 1973	Limerick	3-11 - 3-9	Clare	Thurles
SF	1 July 1973	Tipperary	5-4 - 1-10	Cork	Gaelic Grounds
Final	29 July 1973	Limerick	6-7 - 2-18	Tipperary	Thurles
\multicolumn{6}{c}{All Ireland Championship Series}
QF	29 July 1973	London	4-7 - 3-5	Galway	Ballinasloe
SF	5 August 1973	Limerick	1-15 - 0-7	London	Ennis
Final	2 September 1973	Limerick	1-21 - 1-14	Kilkenny	Croke Park

1971-75 All Ireland Hurling Finals

Year	Winner	Score	Loser	Winning Captain
1971	Tipperary	5-17 - 5-14	Kilkenny	Tadhg O'Connor
1972	Kilkenny	3-24 - 5-11	Cork	Noel Skehan
1973	Limerick	1-21 - 1-14	Kilkenny	Eamon Grimes
1974	Kilkenny	3-19 - 1-13	Limerick	Nicky Orr
1975	Kilkenny	2-22 - 2-10	Galway	Billy Fitzpatrick

Bibliography

Newspapers

Limerick Leader
The Irish Independent
The Clare Champion
Connacht Tribune
The Sunday Independent
The Sunday World
The (Evening) Herald

Irish (Cork) Examiner
The Irish Press
Kilkenny People
The Irish Times
The Sunday Press
Nenagh Guardian
The Evening Press

Magazines

Gaelic Sport
Our Games

Cúl
Limerick GAA Yearbooks

Books

Player's No. 6 Book of Hurling
Limerick Heroes
Limerick, All Ireland Hurling Champions
South Liberties, 1972 Limerick Senior Hurling Champions
GAA Family Silver, The People and Stories behind 101 Cups and Trophies
Limerick GAA County Convention booklets (1973 and 1974)
One Hundred Years of Glory: A History of Limerick GAA
Munster GAA Story, Vol II 1986-2001
GAA Treoraí Oifigiúil (1973)
Over 50 Years of Clare Hurling Teams 1949-2001
The Life and Times of Jackie Power "The Prince of Hurlers"
Richie Bennis, A Game That Smiles
Mick Mackey, Hurling Legend in a Troubled County
Unlimited Heartbreak, The Inside Story of Limerick Hurling
CBS 200, 1816-2016 CBS Sexton Street
From the Great Depression to NAMA: Limerick Senior Inter-county Hurling Championship Records, 1929-2009

Web

IrishNewsArchive.com
TippStudiesDigital.ie (Fr Kennedy)
YouTube.com

FromLimerickWithLove.limerick.ie
HoganStand.com

Programmes and Memorabilia (except medals)

Main author's collection

Acknowledgements

Firstly, we would like to thank our three wives, Clare Lundon, Carol O'Brien and Denise Deegan for their infinite patience and support at all times during the production of this book.

Much gratitude to our proof readers, all of whom read parts, or all, of the book in draft form:
Paul Anglim, Gerry Carty, Finbarr Connolly, Ciarán Crowe, Enda Dooley, Patrick Donegan, Niall Flynn, Henry J Martin, Donal McAnallen, Caroline McLoughlin, Gerry McNamara, Enda Mongan, Eddie O'Dea, PM O'Sullivan, John Page, Bosco Ryan, Cathal Ryan and Seamus Walsh.

We would like to thank the following people for their specific help in the production of this book:
Joan Aherne, Tom Aherne, Eddie Barrett, Dan Beary, Mary and Richie Bennis, Anthony Brosnan, Liam Bourke, Joe Carrig, Gerald Corbett, Eamonn Coffey, Ann and Eamonn Cregan, James Cregan, Dermot Crowe, Sean Curtin, Cathal Doherty, Ed Donnelly, Eileen and Mossie Dowling, Kevin Downes, Paul English, Aideen Fitzpatrick, Aine Fitzgerald, Conor Fitzgerald, Mike Fitzgerald (K), Mike Fitzpatrick (SL), Pat Fogarty, Paul Foley, John Franklin, Gerry Glynn, Mona and Michael Graham, Helen and Éamon Grimes, Mike Halpin, Pat Hartigan, Florrie and Bernie Hartigan, Mary Hassett, Phil Healy and Caroline Murphy, Roger Healy, Liz Howard, Dermot Kavanagh, John Keogh, Seamus King, Seoirse Laffan, Cliodhna and Cormac Liddy, Luke Liddy, Joe Lonergan, Joe Lyons, Mike Maguire, Michelle Martin, Ryan McNamara, Brendan McWilliams, Mayor Gerald Mitchell, Tom Morrison, Jack Neville, Matt O'Callaghan, Pierce O'Callaghan, John O'Carroll, Peter O'Carroll, Willie O'Dea TD, Gerard O'Donnell, Jim O'Donnell, Ivan O'Donnell, Liam O'Donoghue, Ray O'Dowd, Jack O'Dwyer, Donal O'Regan, Dr Matthew Potter, Gerry Rea, John Ryan (Hunt Café), Larry Ryan, Sean T. Ryan, TJ Ryan, Cllr Catherine Slattery, Michael Slattery, Thomond Archaeological and Historical Society, Michael Weekes and Jim Whelan.

Particular thanks to Seamus McNamara and Limerick GAA County Board.

Each of you has contributed in your own way to our celebration of this wonderful year in Limerick GAA. If we have forgotten anyone, our sincerest apologies!

IrishNewspaperArchive.com (INA) is a wonderful website. It contains an almost complete archive of most local newspapers of record, particularly: Limerick Leader, The Irish Independent, The Irish Press and Irish (Cork) Examiner. Many other newspapers were consulted at various junctures, some on INA, some not. See the attached Bibliography. There is an equivalent BritishNewspaperArchive.co.uk website that also contains some hidden gems. The GAA magazines, *Gaelic Sport, Cúl* and *Our Games* were very popular at the time and we have used articles and pictures from each.

The authors would like to pay particular tribute to local journalists, Cormac Liddy, Charlie Mulqueen and Sean Murphy ('S.M.') for producing evocative articles, through late 1972 to All Ireland Final day 1973 and beyond. Much of them are reprinted in this book. Likewise, Raymond Smith's Player's Nº 6 Book of Hurling brilliantly captures the times we write about.

The private Facebook group *Cuimhnigh Ar Luimneach* was set up in March 2020 and has proven to be a wonderful resource, as well as a virtual meeting place, for all good Limerick GAA supporters. This is the second book produced by people who got together only because of this group. Get someone to invite you into it.

The use in this book of footnotes and endnotes has been eschewed. We have made it very clear where we sourced our reportage and photos, where it was possible to do so. Please make contact if you would like to know more about our sources and research methods.

Finally, we thank CUBE for printing the book.

Photo Credits

Michael Martin - 290, 291, 292, 293, 294, 295, 299, 300, 301, 304, 305, 306, 307, 308, 309, 316, 317, 330, 331, 336, 337, 338, 339, 344, 345, 346, 347, 348, 349, 352, 353, 360, 368, 476, 477.

Limerick Leader - 110, 111, 112, 114, 115, 116, 117, 118, 150, 162, 163, 164, 165, 166, 167, 168, 170, 171, 173, 174, 175, 176, 181, 208, 210, 211, 212, 213, 218, 230, 248, 249, 250, 390, 391.

Tipperary Studies Digital Archive (Fr Kennedy) - 188, 189, 193, 196, 197, 204, 205, 209, 215, 216, 217, 218.

Seán Curtin (A Stroll Down Memory Lane) - 260, 324, 325, 329, 360, 392, 393.

Sportsfile (Connolly Collection) - 302, 303, 334, 345, 350, 351.

Seán T. Ryan - 487, 488, 489, 490, 491, 492, 493.

Brendan Gleeson - 505, 506, 507, 508, 509.

The Irish Independent - 315, 316, 332, 333.

Evening Herald - 238, 239, 240, 241.

Helen and Éamon Grimes - 404, 405.

Irish (Cork) Examiner - 194, 195.

Seán Walsh / Irish Photo Archive - 22, 23.

Aideen Fitzpatrick - 504, 511.

We would also like to thank Jim Whelan, Caroline Murphy, The Sunday World and The Irish Press.

Published 2023 by James Lundon, Athenry, County Galway
© James Lundon 2023

All rights reserved. No part of this publication may be reproduced, stored in or introduced into a retrieval system, or transmitted in any form or by any means
(electronic, mechanical, photocopying, recording or otherwise)
without the prior written permission of the authors.

A catalogue record for this book is available from the British Library.

ISBN 978-1-3999-6014-4

Cover design: Niall Deegan and Liam O'Brien.
Design and layout: Niall Deegan and Liam O'Brien.
Printed in Ireland by: CUBE, Limerick City V94 AX99.

Captain Eamonn Grimes holds the cup aloft as he addresses jubilant s...

Ritchie Bennis and Tadgh O'Connor in a battle for possession.

Ned Rea and Seamus Horgan see thi...

...rotty is not allowing him the use...

Willie Moore takes on a Wexford man at Croke Park.

...down, Joe McKenna and Frankie Nolan lay siege on the Kil-

...away in possession (left) and...